BAKING WITH JULIA

BASED ON THE PBS SERIES HOSTED BY
Julia Child

WRITTEN BY
Dorie Greenspan

PHOTOGRAPHS BY
Gentl & Hyers

William Morrow and Company, Inc.
NEW YORK

FOOD PHOTOGRAPHS copyright © 1996 by Gentl & Hyers
ILLUSTRATIONS BY Ward Schumaker
PHOTOGRAPHY COORDINATOR: David Nussbaum
FOOD STYLISTS: Peggy Cullen, Roscoe Betsill, Michael Pederson
WEDDING CAKE STYLISTS: Susan Spungen, Wendy Kromer, Kim Jurado
PROP STYLISTS: Edward Kemper Design
Additional credits appear on page 468.

It is the policy of William Morrow and Company, Inc., and its imprints and affiliates, recognizing the importance of preserving what has been written, to print the books we publish on acid-free paper, and we exert our best efforts to that end.

LIBRARY OF CONGRESS CATALOGING-IN-PUBLICATION DATA

Greenspan, Dorie.
Baking with Julia : based on the PBS series hosted by Julia Child / written by Dorie Greenspan.
p.   cm.
Includes bibliographical references and index.
ISBN 0-688-14657-0
1. Baking.   I. Title. II. Child, Julia.
TX763.G654 1996
641.8'15—dc20
96-23061
CIP

PRINTED IN THE UNITED STATES OF AMERICA

First Edition

1 2 3 4 5 6 7 8 9 10

ORIGINAL DESIGN BY DON MORRIS DESIGN
ADDITIONAL DESIGN BY VERTIGO DESIGN, NYC

BAKING WITH JULIA

FOREWORD

BAKING WITH JULIA is the third book based on our Master Chefs television series and is a book written in everyday language for home cooks using family proportions and baking in home ovens. As with our previous series, it all does actually take place in my kitchen in a period of seven midsummer weeks. The kitchen becomes the studio set, with two long stainless steel rods running across the ceiling where the TV lights are strung, and the kitchen table replaced by an island containing a work space and stove top—just enough room between island and sink for the baker and me to stand, and just enough room in front for our three cameras to squeeze in. With three of them, we get action from many levels and long shots as well as close-ups. It is the same kitchen that you've seen, but there is one exception: I have a new wall oven that opens and closes with nary a word—but we all miss the old one's squeaking door.

The cellar is the prep space, where all the advance cookery and bakery work is done. On yeasty days, there'll be tubs and pans of dough at all stages of the rise, plus bread pans, rolling pins, and the like. On dessert days, there'll be half-dressed cakes, naked ladyfingers waiting on a tray, fragrant bowls of melting chocolate, and the sweet aroma of baking pies. You should have seen it one morning when we had seventeen (17!) bread machines all throbbing together on the floor.

Although most of our staff and crew—our family from the previous series—are with us again, it's the actors who change. People invariably ask us how we pick our chefs and bakers. We naturally want the best of the best, and because in the established professional culinary community almost everyone knows everyone else, we ask around. Our choice rests on several factors, including who is available during our span of seven weeks. We can't start, stop for a week or two, and start and stop again, or we would lose our valuable crew. Another consideration is a balance of male versus female, as well as a regional balance, and a diversity of talents. We hope for talented people who are reasonably comfortable at teaching and at working in front of a camera, who are lively and can communicate, and, above all, who thoroughly know the subject. It's a plus, too, when they're easy to work with. If you present yourself with all those qualities, you're hired!

My role once again was to be with the bakers on the set, in order to move things along if necessary, but principally to assume the function of pupil as well as member of the audience. We also wanted to make sure that all ingredients, times, temperatures, and measurements were clearly mentioned so that the viewer could rush out to the market, scoop up the necessaries, and start in on the recipe immediately. (Some enthusiasts are like that!) We also wanted to review and redo with the chef occasional tricky techniques as they were happening, such as special kneading methods, or odd formings or twistings, so that all of us could understand them—"Play it again, Sam!" in other words. I thoroughly enjoyed being a part of the action and, as always, learned so much every time.

JULIA CHILD

ACKNOWLEDGMENTS

ALL BOOKS ARE COLLABORATIONS, but some books have more collaborators than others. This one had three dozen or so, all of whom deserve more thanks than I can give them here.

It was Geoffrey Drummond who knew a baking series with Julia would be a smash, and Geof who told me that this was the book I was meant to write—even while I was telling him I had other plans. I am grateful to him for his prescience and persistence, and thankful for his unswerving support throughout the months of writing and editing.

Julia Child's grace, warmth, intelligence, and boundless interest in everything around her and all that I was doing made the year that we worked together one that I'll treasure always. When she said I could call her anytime I needed a little encouragement, she meant it, and I did.

The recipes in this book come from twenty-seven bakers of enormous talent and generosity. Each shared recipes eagerly and answered testers' questions quickly—again, and again, and again—proving that patience is not just a virtue, but a basic part of a baker's personality. Thank goodness and thanks to them.

All of the recipes were tested for the home kitchen by a team of meticulous bakers. Many thanks to our testers, Rena and Gary Coyle, Stephanie Hersh, Rick Katz, David Nussbaum, and Martha Stafford. And special thanks to Katja Shaye, who got the recipes and the writer ready for the taping sessions in Cambridge.

I am especially grateful to David Nussbaum, who, throughout the project, provided astute editorial advice, bread-baking wisdom, and the best critical reading possible—at some point I think he knew the manuscript better than I did.

Finally, thanks and toques off to the exceptional team at William Morrow for producing such a handsome book.

DORIE GREENSPAN

SINCERE THANKS

To the Cast of Characters Our cast of characters on the televison side was and is headed, as well as shouldered, by our favorite father figure, Executive Producer Geoffrey Drummond, who is also president of our production company, A La Carte Communications.

Bruce Franchini, well known to PBS audiences, has directed such beautiful series as *Gardens of the World* and *Lorenza de'Medici's Kitchen*. He delights in shooting beautiful food arrangements and telling close-ups, and we were fortunate indeed that he was free to direct this baking series as well as the two previous Master Chefs.

Herb Sevush has been our video editor, responsible for certainly one of the most difficult as well as crucial arts in the business. He also edited the previous Master Chefs, and is said to have become a fine cook during the process. Will he now take on *pâtisserie*?

Herb was ably assisted in the final editing by Deb Barcelo, who was also intently focused on her monitor screen at Bruce's side during all the taping.

Dorie Greenspan, our author and former editor of the James Beard Foundation *News from the Beard House*, also author of *Sweet Times*, *Waffles: From Morning to Midnight*, and the forthcoming *Pancakes: From Morning to Midnight*, was on hand for every aspect, interviewing the bakers before they arrived, interviewing them again during their preparations, and then staying glued to the TV monitor and her laptop computer while the shows were being taped. I don't think she missed a word, and you are getting the whole story in this book.

Nancy Verde Barr, author of her own book on Italian cooking, *They Called It Macaroni*, and coauthor with me of the last Master Chefs book, was culinary producer this time. Her role was to block out the shows with each baker and to see that every item of food and equipment was in its place as each show went on— not an easy task.

Kimberly Nolan, line producer, was responsible for providing all the pots, pans, knives, vegetable peelers, stoves, ovens, pretty plates, and napkins—in fact, for everything on the set, including the set itself. She was seemingly always calm, she was always smiling, and her sneakers were always immaculately white. How did she achieve that and do a very good job as well?

Rick Katz and Rena Coyle were our head bakers, living down in the cellar, working with our star bakers, and providing the endless duplicate doughs, cakes, and fillings always needed at once when the director yells, "Cut! Retake, starting with the risen dough!" Woe if they didn't bring it up on the double.

Other stalwarts in the kitchen were Mary Donlan, our charming attorney, who made a career change from law to our kitchen dish washer and then graduated to kitchen expediter. Liz Jackson, who has been with us before, proved herself again to be a most versatile prep cook and baker, as well as all-purpose kitchen expert.

Of course there would have been nothing to see and hear without Dean Gaskill, director of photography, sound, and lighting—and everything else to do with the television recording. Dean has filled the same role before. He is used to the kitchen, and to us, and we would be lost without him and his remarkably able crew.

Peter Dingle and Mark Rast completed the culinary camera trio with Dean, and they were so close to the action that they also served as convenient tasters from time to time. Gilles Moran was, as before, our sound expert, always starting off the morning with his joyful "*Bonjour!*" as he adjusted the microphones. Our "technogeek," as he styled himself, Eliat Goldman, was in charge of the perfect working order of all video equipment, and it seemed to me there was nothing he couldn't fix.

Stephanie Hersh, able pastry chef, caterer, and office manager, has been my longtime executive assistant and permanent resident ogre. She is unusually capable at providing interference and polite refusals, as well as expert computer and baking assistance. She does recipe testing, makes travel arrangements, and is also good company. Joi Ann Loewy, Stephanie's invaluable assistant, was always ready to help all of us with endless office affairs, telephoning, and copy machine work. When things heat up, we've gratefully turned for help to Annie Copps, who is fast, well organized, and capable both in the office and at the stove.

Makeup artist Louise Miller, of Pisces Unlimited, did faces for all our bakers, and has done her best with mine for more than twenty-five years. Kurt Sarver worked his wonders to turn every day into a good hair day, in spite of summer humidity. We thank them both on bended knee.

To Our Publisher We love our publisher, William Morrow and Company, Inc. They have been good people to deal with, they have put much time, effort, and creativity into our book, and we are proud to be with them under the leadership of our kind and imaginative book-mother figure, our editor, Ann Bramson.

To Our Sponsors Deepest thanks to our sponsors, whose very generous support made this series possible. Farberware Millennium no-stick cookware has sponsored all our Master Chefs series, and we are grateful indeed for their dozens of big, medium, and small frying pans, sauté pans, saucepans, baking pans, covered and uncovered pans—in fact, if we needed anything, they were quick and generous to respond.

Arm & Hammer Baking Soda is a new sponsor, providing us with endless boxes of baking soda to freshen our refrigerators and leaven our biscuits, spray cans for sweet-smelling plumbing, products for easy laundering—we never knew there were so many modern uses for that humble and ancient resource.

Land O Lakes Butter seems a natural for a baking series. *La cuisine au beurre est toujours meilleur*—it's always better with butter! We couldn't agree more, and we actually used 573 pounds of the best and freshest unsalted butter in seven weeks. Loved every spoonful! But don't forget that that modest figure includes all those retakes too.

An essential ingredient was flour, flour, and more flour. Can we even begin to count the pounds of King Arthur that Frank and Brina Sands posted, expressed, and personally brought to us? They have always enthusiastically supported home bakers with help and advice, and we are proud to number King Arthur Flour among our very special sponsors.

Just as some of our bakers have almost single-handedly raised the level of good bread across the country, so has Starbucks made it possible to get a great cup of coffee all over America—by land, by sea, and in the air. Thank you, Starbucks, for sustaining us royally during our taping sessions, and for helping to make this series possible through your sponsorship.

For Generous Loans and Gifts The following companies loaned or gave us so many essentials that we would have been hard-pressed without them. We deeply appreciate their generosity and give them our most sincere thanks:

The Charles Hotel in Cambridge housed our bakers, loaned us the use of their prep kitchen, and threw us a bang-up final party in their inner courtyard with wine and food and all the fixings.

Shreve, Crump & Low generously loaned us our handsome dinnerware and silver service.

Williams-Sonoma was generous indeed—always prompt and always willing to offer us all sorts of props and supplies.

Wilton Industries/Rowoco provided a host of kitchen tools, lovely gadgets, and baking supplies.

New Hearth Family of Products provided our Viking stove top and the double ovens for our prep kitchen.

Thermador supplied our new oven with a nonsqueaking door.

KitchenAid/Whirlpool provided our handsome new refrigerator, silent dishwasher, ice machine, hand-held electric blender, and heavy-duty mixers.

Olgo Russo of A. Russo and Sons, Inc., as for our previous series, personally chose and delivered to us his beautiful and impeccably fresh fruits, vegetables, and herbs.

The following local sources also provided us with generous production support: Dutch Flower Garden in Cambridge; Por-Shun, Inc., in Wilmington; Kitchen Arts in Boston; Kitchen Etc. in Dedham; and Be Our Guest in Boston, Massachusetts.

JULIA CHILD

CONTENTS

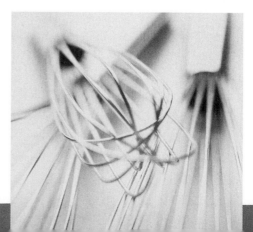

INTRODUCTION

THIS IS AN ALL-PURPOSE HOW-TO BAKING BOOK illustrated not only by hundreds of photographs but also, if you wish, by a series of thirty-nine half-hour television shows. It aims to teach you the basics of how to bake a plain loaf of bread as well as the more complicated secrets of sourdoughs, brioches and croissants, flatbreads, pizzas, focaccias, and bagels. Tart doughs and puff pastry are also an essential part of baking, and you'll find a great roster of cakes, including full directions for assembling a three-tiered beauty as well as one of the most fancy of fancy chocolate cakes. This book, in other words, is a remarkably full course in the art of baking.

The idea for doing a baking book came through our two previous Master Chefs series, from which recipes for bread and pastries continue to be unusually popular. PBS stations get floods of requests every time there is a rerun of our program on yeast starters and rustic breads, or on a magnificent chocolate cake, or on bread sticks and country breads. Then why not have a television series based entirely on baking and a big basic book to go with it? So here we are, with thirty-nine television shows and this big beautiful baking book you have in your hands.

Although written with one voice, that of our experienced baker-author Dorie Greenspan, each special recipe in this baking course is by one of our twenty-seven baker-professors. Most are professionals working in bakery kitchens with professional proportions and equipment, but here they have tailored their methods and techniques to the home cook. We approached Steve Sullivan, for instance, of the famous Acme Bakery in Berkley, California. "Oh no," he said. "You can't make my type of bread at home!" But the idea intrigued him, he began experimenting in his own home, and soon he produced the unique mixed-starter dough for baguettes, couronnes, and other French-style breads starting on page 113. Thus, when you see any of the TV programs, you will note that our bakers are assembling their breads, desserts, or pastries right here in my home and baking them in my own home oven. In other words, everything in this book is designed for you to make in your own kitchen.

As an example of how to use this book, let's say you were given a bread machine for your birthday and you've used it a couple of times but you haven't liked the look of the machine-baked loaf. Then one day you happen to turn on the TV and see one of our bakers, Lora Brody, who is a bread-machine specialist. She has made her dough and let it rise in the machine but, rather than allowing the machine to finish up, she removes the risen dough, forms it in a bread pan, and bakes it in the oven. To verify details, you look up the recipe in this book. You try it, you like it, and then you try out Lora's easy machine dough for rolls and bread sticks. Next you might be daring enough to make your own dough, and you succeed royally with Lauren Groveman's handmade bagels on page 87. When you really need a great sandwich bread, you try Craig Kominiak's white bread, on page 81, and have such success with it that you decide (and bless the day you did!) that you really need a heavy-duty mixer with dough hook—and not for your next birthday. Now! Then as you browse through the book, you dream of yeast starters and baguettes, brioches and rum babas—and you are fast becoming a passionate baker. It's a scenario that can easily happen!

Professional bakers usually specialize either in *boulangerie*—yeast doughs like breads and rolls—or in *pâtisserie*—cakes, cookies, and desserts. Chefs de cuisine, on the other hand, and we all-purpose home cooks, must do a little of both, including pie doughs, puff pastry, and choux paste if we want to produce well-rounded menus. Anyone who claims to be a cook must, for example, be able to produce a tender, gently crisp, and nicely flaky pie dough. You turn to page 31 and find Leslie Mackie's exemplary example here, carefully explained. You decide you will learn pie dough as you would learn your backhand in tennis, or the hows of tossing an omelette: You make omelette after omelette after omelette, and pie after pie after pie. Finally, and at last, you are at ease with pie dough forevermore. You can make it, and roll it out, and form it, and bake it with utter confidence—and with pride and pleasure too.

Just the work you have done with that pie dough has given you familiarity with the feel of dough, with the handling of the pin, and with rolling in general. You can go on to puff pastry on page 46 with that talented Frenchman Michel Richard. Then you move to page 52 and that master French *croissantière*, Esther McManus (if there is no such title as *croissantière*, there should be in this case). These examples can naturally lead you to the rich delights of Beatrice Ojakangas and her ways with Danish pastry on pages 200 to 206. It's a progression, since if you can make yeast dough, pie dough, and puff pastry, it's a small step to those cousins, croissants and Danish. One skill leads to a host of others.

Certainly one of the unique qualities of this book is that the recipes are tied to the PBS television series. Although you don't need the television to use the book, and, in fact, the recipes may not be done here exactly as they were on television, it is helpful to see the recipe in action, to hear the baker's explanations, and to know how the baker intended it to look. Consider, for example, that elegant wrapping of the chocolate sheet around Alice Medrich's stunning ruffle cake on page 263, and the making of the ruffles themselves. You have seen it done. Now you can read all about it in this book—the hows, the whys, the ifs and buts, and the intimate details that a television show rarely has time to include. The book gives you the whole story, plus the fast-and-easy reference that a well-indexed book provides.

When you turn your attention to cakes, another basic deserves an important place in your learning experience—it is the génoise on pages 39 to 42. Whether or not you have seen Flo Braker make it on TV, the directions are so clearly outlined here that you can't fail to bake a beauty on your first try. As our genial author assures us, the génoise is actually "a very well behaved cake," and the one to bake when you want moist liqueur-soaked layer cakes and petits four.

Once you have started in on the génoise, as an example, bake it again several times soon, making notes as needed, so that you feel quite at home with it. Then pick another type, such as Mary Bergin's chiffon roll on page 277, or Johanne Killeen's butter cakes on pages 247 to 250, and don't miss Charlotte Akota's splendid directions for mastering the meringue on page 37. When you are comfortable with these standard brands, you will begin to realize that cake making is really an assembly job—you have certain fillings and toppings in your repertoire, and it is the way you combine them that defines the cake as yours.

If you have followed the television series, you will note that not only does the book give all of the series recipes from our twenty-seven bakers, but also that each of them has contributed several additional ones. It's a big book, and it contains many imaginative treatments and ideas from bakers all over the country. I should not have to assure you that all of the recipes, whether done on television or not, have received the same detailed treatment and that our team has carefully tested them all in home kitchens.

The marvel of this gathering of more than two dozen bakers means that we have a wealth of personalities, styles, and specialties. Among the many original treatments in the bread chapters is an oversize pumpernickel, a semolina loaf with a tender nutty taste, French breads made with mixed starters, and decorated country breads, as well as muffins, extra-sticky sticky buns, popovers, and Danish pockets. Gingerbread Baby Cakes are baked in individual pans, and there's an unusual Poppy Seed Torte, a Chocolate Mocha Brownie Cake, and a White Chocolate Patty Cake. Jeffrey Alford and Naomi Duguid, thanks to their worldwide travels, have given us an intriguing international group of mostly quick-to-bake flatbreads, while others have given us matzos, pizzas, and even hardtack. To serve with these, for lunch or as hors d'oeuvres, try our fine lentil salad, or the Smoked Trout Spread, or a large helping of the best-ever chopped chicken livers.

Wandering through the chapters, you will agree that something is here for everyone, from the simple Gingersnaps to the Inside-out Upside-down Tirami Sù. I'm only skimming a few of the high points in this generous and most original collection of recipes from some of America's best bakers. Have a wonderful time with this book in your own home bakery, and *bon appétit!*

JULIA CHILD

THE BAKERS

MARION CUNNINGHAM

ALICE MEDRICH

GALE GAND

NANCY SILVERTON

BEATRICE OJAKANGAS

CHARLOTTE AKOTO

JOE ORTIZ AND JULIA CHILD

MARY BERGIN

NICK MALGIERI

JULIA CHILD, JEFFREY ALFORD, AND NAOMI DUGUID

ESTHER McMANUS

DAVID BLOM

DAVID OGONOWSKI AND JULIA CHILD

JOHANNE KILLEEN

MARCEL DESAULNIERS

LORA BRODY

JULIA CHILD AND MARTHA STEWART

LAUREN GROVEMAN

MARKUS FARBINGER

STEVE SULLIVAN

CRAIG KOMINIAK

DANIELLE FORESTIER

FLO BRAKER AND DORIE GREENSPAN

LESLIE MACKIE

MICHEL RICHARD AND JULIA CHILD

NORMAN LOVE

BAKING WITH JULIA

Baking Basics
TERMS, TECHNIQUES, AND EQUIPMENT

THINK OF THIS as a quick course in baking, an alphabetical run-through of all the terms, equipment, ingredients, and techniques you'll encounter as you work your way through *Baking with Julia.* Here's where you'll find everything you need to know about dozens of matters as important as how to measure liquid and dry ingredients; measure and soften butter; buy, keep, and melt chocolate; make pie dough in the food processor; and store eggs properly. You'll turn to this chapter when you want to know what "proofing" means, how to use a docker, what to look for when beating eggs and sugar to a ribbon, how to "fold the egg whites in gently," and which sizes and shapes are standard for baking pans.

And here's where you'll learn the rules by which the contributing bakers played when creating these recipes. Page through to discover that they use only Grade A large eggs, unsalted butter, and pure vanilla extract, that they call a jelly-roll pan a "sheet pan," and that pastry flour can be made at home by blending cake and all-purpose flours. Having this chapter at hand is like having a teacher at your side—reassurance at the ready.

ALMOND PASTE Almond paste is marzipan's firmer, ever-so-slightly less malleable, cousin. For most decorating tasks, you can substitute one for the other. However, in baking, if your recipe calls for almond paste, as it will for amaretti, you're meant to use the paste, which is a blend of ground almonds, confectioner's sugar, and corn syrup or glucose. Almond paste is available in supermarkets and specialty stores; many bakers prefer canned paste to that found in tubes. Because almond paste dries out quickly, once opened, it should be wrapped tightly in plastic wrap and stored in the refrigerator. Wrapped properly, it can be kept for about six months.

BAKING POWDER Baking powder is a leavening agent that comes in two varieties: double- and single-acting. Single-acting baking powder releases its rising power when it comes in contact with liquid; double-acting baking powder, the "supermarket" type and the kind used in the recipes in this book, releases its first puff of power (in the form of carbon dioxide bubbles) in combination with liquid and its second when the oven's heat hits it. Quick breads, like biscuits, muffins, and scones, and some cakes, particularly butter cakes, rely on baking powder for their rise. Baking powder should be kept tightly covered in a cool, dry cupboard and replaced every six months.

BAKING SHEETS When professional bakers refer to sheet pans, they mean the type of pan home bakers call a jelly-roll pan, a shallow rimmed rectangular pan. Baking sheets, to home bakers, and in this book, are cookie sheets: large flat sheets, one or both ends of which are slightly raised for grippability. The rimless sides make it easy to lift cookies off the sheet with a wide spatula. Since you'll use baking sheets primarily for cookies, you should buy the heaviest sheets you can find, as heavy sheets will not warp at high temperatures and will hold the heat longer and more evenly. (Although they are advertised as perfect for cookies, think twice before purchasing cushioned baking sheets—they keep the bottoms of baked goods from browning too quickly, but often do not allow the bottoms to brown enough.) A baker's kitchen should have at least two baking sheets; four would be ideal—while two sheets are in the oven, you can use the other two to get the next batch of cookies ready. In a pinch, a baking sheet will serve as a baker's peel. Dusted with cornmeal, it can be used to transfer free-form breads and pizzas to the oven.

BAKING SODA Baking soda, or bicarbonate of soda, is both a component of baking powder and a leavener in its own right, albeit one that gets its leavening power in conjunction with acids such as yogurt, sour cream, crème fraîche, buttermilk, or molasses. Because baking soda's single action occurs in the mixing bowl, it's best to work quickly after the soda has been activated to get the batter into the oven as soon as possible.

BAKING STONES Lining an oven rack with baking stones, unglazed quarry tiles, or fire bricks is the best way to recreate the conditions found in hearth-style bread ovens. Fire bricks and quarry tiles are found in building supply outlets, and baking stones, sometimes called pizza stones, are available in house-wares departments and gourmet/specialty stores. While they are easy to find, they are often too small to accommodate the results of an active day of dough making. If you can, buy two stones and have one cut (by a tile cutter), as will probably be necessary, so that the pair will line your oven rack to within an inch of the oven walls: You must leave at least an inch of space around the stones so that the heat can circulate. If you're using quarry tiles or fire bricks, line the oven rack in the same way. When you preheat the oven, preheat the stones or tiles as well. Many bakers keep their baking stones in the oven at all times, claiming that the stones, because they retain heat so well, make their ovens more efficient, eliminating the need for the oven's heating unit to cycle on and off as frequently. Experiment for yourself.

BANNETON The word *banneton* comes from a French word for basket, *banne*, and has passed into the American baker's lexicon as well as his kitchen. Bannetons are linen-lined baskets, available in long, thin shapes similar to baguettes and in rounds, ovals, and rounds with open centers, used to hold the dough in shape during the last rise before it's turned out onto a peel and slid onto the oven's hearth or baking stone. Bannetons are expensive but sturdy—buy one and you'll have it forever. You can achieve similar results, if not the perfect shape, by lining a wicker or other open-weave basket with a linen towel that has been well rubbed with flour. You can even use a flour-lined colander as a makeshift banneton.

BATTER The term for the unbaked or, sometimes, uncooked mixture that forms the base of cakes, muffins, pancakes, and other similar baked goods. Unlike doughs, batters are usually pourable.

BENCH OR DOUGH SCRAPERS When you're working with wet, sticky bread doughs, the types of doughs that produce most of the artisanal breads in this book, you'll think of a bench or dough scraper as an invaluable extension of your hand. The scraper is a square piece of slightly flexible metal attached to a grip, somewhat like a pancake turner without the long handle. Reach for it when you're kneading—it will lift the dough off the work surface cleanly so you can grab it and give it a push and turn—or use it when you're working with any of the laminated doughs, like puff, croissant, or Danish, that need to be lifted off the counter before you fold them. And when you've finished the sticky work, use the scraper to clean your work surface; it will help you get up the flour and fat that have a way of crusting on the counter.

BLOWTORCH Next to the baking supply house, the hardware store is a baker's best resource for equipment, and a small blowtorch, the purchase of choice. An inexpensive propane torch is the only thing that will give you professional-quality crème brûlée (page 280) in your home kitchen, and an even browning on meringue.

BUTTER Nothing tastes like butter, nothing bakes like butter. Use "the other spread," and all the work you put into a recipe will be for naught—it just won't have the taste, texture, or look you want. That said, there's the question of salted or unsalted butter. Across the country there are regional preferences among home bakers—the Midwest is salted butter territory, the East Coast unsalted. However, professional bakers rarely use salted butter, preferring to be able to control the amount of salt they use in a recipe and realizing that salted butter often contains more moisture than unsalted. All the recipes in this book call for unsalted butter.

Measuring Butter Butter measurements are given in tablespoons, sticks or parts of sticks, and in ounces or pounds. It's handy to know that 1 stick of butter weighs 4 ounces and equals 8 tablespoons.

Softening Butter In most cases, butter that will be mixed with other ingredients—for example, butter to be creamed or blended with sugar—should be softened. Softened butter should never be gooey or oily, but rather still slightly cool and just pliable. Butter can be softened by leaving it at room temperature or by bashing or smearing it. To bash butter, place the sticks of butter between two sheets of waxed paper and beat the butter with the end of a rolling pin. Gentler souls can achieve the same results by placing the butter on a work surface and smearing tablespoon-sized pieces across the surface with the heels of their hands. You can also soften butter in a microwave oven, but it's a bit trickier—a second or two too long, and you've got goo to deal with.

Clarifying Butter The easiest way to clarify butter is the professional way: Cut the butter into small chunks, place the chunks in a saucepan, and slowly bring the butter to a boil. When the popping and crackling have almost stopped, the butter is clarified. Keep close watch, though, because it's at this point that you risk overdoing it and browning the butter. Pour the clear yellow clarified butter into a heatproof jar through a tea strainer, which will catch the residue of milk solids. Store the clarified butter in a tightly sealed jar in the refrigerator or freeze it; it will keep refrigerated or frozen for several months.

Buttering Pans Professional bakers who generally have lots of pans to butter keep a big bowl of softened butter and a pastry brush close at hand; it's a good idea for home bakers to do the same. Using a pastry brush to apply the butter means you get an even coating and can work the brush into corners and crannies. If the recipe calls for buttering and flouring a pan, butter the pan evenly, then add a few spoonfuls of flour to the pan. Shake the flour around in the pan, tapping the sides of the pan to distribute a light dusting of flour all over the pan, and then turn the pan upside down over a trash bin and tap it to knock out the excess flour.

Vegetable oil spray is an alternative to buttering pans, one particularly well suited to muffin tins and small tartlet pans.

The amount of butter and flour needed to prepare pans is always separate from the amount of butter and flour in a recipe's ingredients list.

BUTTERMILK While few people seem to belly up to the soda fountain and order buttermilk anymore, bakers use it often in butter cakes, muffins, and quick breads to give them tang and a tender crumb. If you can't find buttermilk, substitute ⅔ cup plain, low-, or nonfat yogurt mixed with ⅓ cup milk (whole or low-fat) for each cup of buttermilk. Powdered buttermilk is available in many supermarkets and can be used in any recipe calling for buttermilk; follow the directions on the package to reconstitute it.

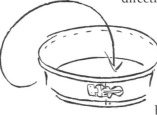

CAKE AND PIE PANS If you're just starting to build your collection of pans for baking, you will want to start, naturally, with the basics (and then when you, like all bakers, become obsessed, you can move on to the fanciful molds and beautifully shaped pans that always capture the baker's imagination).

A BEGINNER'S *BATTERIE DE CUISINE*:

   two 8-inch round cake pans (1½ to 2 inches tall)

   two 9-inch round cake pans (1½ to 2 inches tall)

   two 8-inch square cake pans (1½ to 2 inches tall)

   two 9-inch square cake pans (1½ to 2 inches tall)

   two 8½- by 4½- by 2½-inch loaf pans

   two 9- by 5- by 3-inch loaf pans

   Bundt pan and/or tube pan (at least 10-cup capacity)

   one or two 9- and 10-inch springform pans (if you buy only one, buy the 9-inch pan)

   one or two 12-cup muffin tins (2½ inches across is standard)

   9-inch pie plate

   9-inch tart pan with removable bottom

   10-inch tart pan with removable bottom

You will find other pans used in some of the recipes in this book, but you'll get by nicely with this basic *batterie*. As with all kitchen equipment, it's wise to buy the best you can afford; buy highest-quality, heavy-gauge pans, and you'll have them for a lifetime.

CARDBOARD CAKE ROUNDS Corrugated cardboard rounds come in many sizes and are useful for turning out cakes, holding cakes on a base when you're frosting them, and transporting cakes in and out of the refrigerator or from your kitchen to someone else's. Available from bakers' supply houses, they're a convenience. However, if you do not wish to purchase a supply (they're often sold only in large quantities), you can cut your own from heavy cardboard and wrap them in foil.

CHOCOLATE As you bake your way through the recipes in this book, you'll find you'll be using the entire gamut of chocolates: unsweetened, bittersweet, semisweet, milk, and white—the not-really chocolate that must be considered in any discussion of chocolate.

What makes chocolate chocolate is the presence of chocolate liquor, made from roasted, blended, and ground cocoa bean nibs. Unsweetened chocolate is pure chocolate liquor; bittersweet chocolate is a blend of chocolate liquor, cocoa butter, sugar, and vanilla; semisweet chocolate is bittersweet chocolate with a greater quantity of sugar added to the mixture; and milk chocolate is a blend similar to that used for bitter- or semisweet with the addition of milk solids. White chocolate derives its taste from cocoa butter, milk solids, sugar, and vanilla. When buying it, look for a brand that contains cocoa butter—that's what will give you the flavor you want. By law, white chocolate that does not contain cocoa butter cannot be called chocolate; without cocoa butter, the product is called summer coating or confectionery coating.

Use the best-quality chocolate you can and choose a chocolate you'd like to eat out of hand, because what you start with is what you end with when you're working with chocolate—baking doesn't change chocolate's flavor enough to mask deficits.

Chocolate should be stored in a cool, dry cupboard, not in the refrigerator or freezer, where it can attract unwanted moisture. Once opened, chocolate should be wrapped in foil. Stored properly, unsweetened, bittersweet, and semisweet chocolates can be kept for years; milk and white chocolates have shorter shelf lives, but still can be kept for about a year. If your chocolate clouds or develops a grayish look, called bloom, it still can be used. The look is unpleasant—a sign that the cocoa butter has separated—but everything will be fine when the chocolate is melted.

Melting Chocolate Unsweetened, bittersweet, and semisweet chocolates are finicky, milk and white chocolates finickier still when it comes to melting. The simplest, surest way to melt chocolate is to break or cut it into even pieces and place the pieces in the top of a double boiler (you can use a heatproof bowl fitted into a saucepan) over, but never touching, about an inch of simmering, not boiling, water. Keep the double boiler over very low heat and stir the chocolate frequently. Remove from the heat as soon as the chocolate is melted, and stir until smooth.

Alternatively, you can melt unsweetened, bittersweet, or semisweet chocolates in a microwave oven, a method rarely used by professionals but one that home bakers with small amounts of chocolate to melt find convenient. (Because milk and white chocolates melt and then burn rapidly, it's best to work with them in a double boiler—you'll have greater control.) Place the cut or broken chocolate in a microwave-safe container, cover with plastic wrap, and microwave on medium power for 1 minute; stir, re-cover, and continue to microwave, checking at 30-second intervals, until melted. Beware—chocolate melted in the microwave oven often retains its shape even though it is fully melted. To avoid burning the chocolate, press it with your finger to check, and stop cooking when it is just melted. Stir to smooth.

Whichever method you use, just keep in mind that water is chocolate's worst enemy. If you get even a droplet of water into the chocolate while it's melting, the chocolate will seize and you'll have a rough, dull, unusable mass. (Chocolate can be "unseized" with the addition of oil, but then you won't have the quality of chocolate you want.) If a recipe calls for melting chocolate with liquid, however, fear not—if you start with the liquid you'll be fine, it's only mid-melt moisture that seizes chocolate.

CLARIFIED BUTTER Clarified butter is butter from which the milk solids have been removed. Without milk solids, butter can be brought to a higher temperature without burning, a boon when you're sautéing. Clarified butter is the classic addition to génoise and the form of butter bakers prefer when they're swathing phyllo layers. See page 5 for directions on how to clarify butter, a simple procedure.

COCOA POWDER Cocoa powder can be either "Dutched" or not. Dutch-processed cocoa powder has been treated with alkali, a process that darkens its color and reduces its acidity. Recipes in this book usually specify which type of cocoa powder is recommended; if no preference is listed, you can use either type.

COOLING RACKS Cooling racks, which can be round, square, or rectangular, large or small, are footed racks made of closely spaced metal wires or mesh. The best are sturdy and have feet that are at least ½ inch high, allowing air to circulate freely around the cooling baked goods.

CORNMEAL Ground from dried corn, cornmeal can be either steel-cut, in which case the bran and germ are removed, or stone-ground, a process that retains the bran and germ. In general, supermarket-brand cornmeals are steel-cut, health food store cornmeals stone-ground. You can store steel-cut cornmeal in a cool, dry cupboard, but stone-ground meal must be stored in a covered container in the refrigerator. Cornmeal can be either yellow, as it is most often, or white, the kind of cornmeal preferred by Rhode Islanders and referred to by them as johnnymeal.

CREAM Recipes calling for heavy cream can take either whipping cream, which contains between 30 and 36 percent butterfat, or heavy cream, which weighs in with between 36 and 40 percent butterfat. Both types of cream can be whipped.

To Whip Cream Cream whips best when it is chilled, even better when the bowl and whisk or beater are chilled as well. Start beating cream slowly, then increase the speed as the cream thickens slightly. If you are going to use the cream as an accompaniment rather than a decoration, you might want to whip the cream just to a soft peak. If you plan to pipe the cream through a pastry bag and tip, you'll need to whip it until it holds its shape firmly. To avoid overbeating cream, it's best to whip it slightly less than is needed and then to whisk it by hand to the just-right point. When you want sweetened whipped cream, use confectioner's rather than granulated sugar and add it when the cream just starts to thicken. (It's always best to sift the confectioner's sugar into the cream so you're sure it's lump-free.) Wait to add liquids, such as extracts or liqueurs, until the cream is beaten to the desired consistency; add the liquid and then whisk by hand to blend it in and bring back the cream's volume. Cream should be whipped right before it's needed; if you must keep it, cover it well and refrigerate it. (You can also whip cream, spoon it into a strainer, place the strainer over a bowl, cover the setup with plastic wrap, and keep the cream refrigerated for up to 24 hours, during which time it will drain off excess moisture and become slightly denser. This is a good method for keeping cream that you will use either as a cake filling or as an accompaniment to a dessert.)

CRÈME FRAÎCHE Tangy crème fraîche is similar in taste and texture to sour cream, but it has the added benefits of being able to be heated without separating and to be whipped when chilled. A common ingredient in France but an expensive one here, crème fraîche can be made easily at home. Add 1 tablespoon of buttermilk to 1 cup of heavy cream, stir well, cover, and allow the mixture to remain at room temperature until it thickens slightly, 12 to 24 hours, depending on the temperature of the room. Chill it thoroughly before using. Crème fraîche can be kept refrigerated for about 2 weeks, during which time it will become tangier.

CRUMB The inside of a bread or cake is referred to as its crumb.

DOCKER Also known as a pastry pricker, a docker looks like a medieval instrument of torture or, less dramatically, a paint roller with spikes. It is a long-handled roller, about 6 inches long, studded with either plastic or metal spikes (the older dockers had nails protruding from them), and it is used most frequently with sheets of puff pastry that are meant to bake without puffing. It is the most efficient and effective way to prick or dock pastry, but you can get similar results from the tines of a fork and some energy.

DOUGH The term for the uncooked or unbaked mixture used to make breads, cookies, or pastry crusts. Unlike a batter, a dough is usually thick and meant to be rolled or otherwise molded.

DRIED FRUITS Before adding dried fruits to a mixture, check them for plumpness. Fruits should be moist and plump at the start, because they're not going to get any moister or plumper during baking. If your fruits are shriveled and hard, simmer them in, or steam them over, boiling water for a minute or two and then pat them dry in a kitchen towel. If you're working with small dried fruits like currants or raisins, you may be able to restore them to deliciousness by placing them in a strainer and simply running hot tap water over them for a minute; drain and dry.

EGGS All of these recipes were tested with U.S. Grade A large eggs.

Eggs, nature's most perfect food and a baker's basic building block, need special care and handling because there is evidence that some eggs contain salmonella, a bacteria that can cause unpleasant, flulike illness. (Actually, only a very small percentage of salmonella cases reported in the United States can be traced to contaminated eggs; raw and undercooked meat and poultry are more often the culprits.) Although salmonella is rarely fatal for healthy people, some people are more susceptible to salmonella than others. Those at risk include the very young, the very old, ill people, pregnant women, and anyone with a weakened immune system.

If you take proper care of eggs from purchase to pastry, you should never encounter a problem. Here are some tips to heed:

- Buy your eggs from a store where they are kept refrigerated at all times.

- Always keep eggs refrigerated at home; if a recipe calls for eggs at room temperature, as many do, remove the eggs from the refrigerator about 20 minutes before you plan to bake; never leave eggs at room temperature for more than 2 hours.

- Never use an egg with a cracked shell.

- Wash your hands before and after handling eggs; make certain to scrub your utensils and work surfaces after working with raw eggs.

- Although egg yolks are more likely to carry bacteria than are whites, both should be handled carefully.

- In order to kill salmonella bacteria, eggs must be either brought to a temperature of 160°F or held at a temperature of 140°F for at least 3½ minutes.

Separating Eggs Many recipes call for separated eggs, most often because you'll need to whip the whites. When this is the case, it is mandatory that the eggs be separated cleanly, since even a speck of yolk in the whites is enough to keep the whites from whipping to their full capacity. Whether you're separating two eggs or twenty, here's the safest way to perform this task (it can be the most economical too, especially when you're cracking a quantity—follow this method and even if you have a mishap with the last egg, the rest of your batch will be fine): Have three clean bowls on your counter and start with cold eggs (they separate most easily). Working over one bowl, pour the egg white from one half-shell into the bowl, taking care to catch the yolk with the other half-shell. Continue passing the egg back and forth between the half-shells until all of the white is in the bowl and only the yolk remains in the shell. Dump the yolk into the second bowl and the white into the third; continue until all the eggs are separated. If any yolk falls into a white, try to scoop it out. If you can't, add the whole yolk to the white and save the egg, tightly covered in the refrigerator, for another purpose.

Whipping Egg Whites For information on whipping egg whites, see Meringue, page 37.

Working with Yolks and Sugar When a recipe calls for mixing yolks with sugar, blend them as soon as you've added the sugar. Leaving sugar sitting on the yolks will thicken and lumpen them, a condition bakers refer to as "burning." After mixing the sugar and yolks, it is best to continue with the recipe immediately.

EXTRACTS Extracts are an easy way to give your baked goods a concentrated flavor boost, but choose your extracts carefully: Artificially flavored extracts will throw off the taste of your recipe. Pure extracts are more expensive than imitations, but they're always worth the extra expense. Like herbs and spices, extracts can lose their oomph and should be replaced when their fragrance is no longer deep and full. If you don't get the aroma you want, you won't get the flavor either. Store extracts in a cool, dark cupboard.

FLOUR Flour is the most basic baking ingredient and potentially the most confusing, since there are so many flours available and so much talk about which should be used for what. Leaving aside flours milled from grains other than wheat (such as barley, rice, corn, or rye), the question of which flour for what purpose often comes down to numbers: What percentage of gluten-forming protein does the flour contain? Gluten is the protein that forms webs in flour; it's what makes yeast baking so satisfying, since it's the gluten network developed in dough that gives it the strength to rise. Great in bread, gluten is a disaster when you're after a tender pie crust or a delicately crumbed cake.

Although each recipe in this book calls for the flour the baker prescribed, it's good to know how one flour differs from another. Here's a listing, from the most glutenous to the least.

- *Bread flour* With a protein content of about 14 grams per cup, bread flour is the flour of choice for yeast doughs. High-gluten flour, with a slightly higher proportion of protein than that found in bread flour, is usually only available to professionals. (It's probably what your local pizza maker uses.) In most cases, if a recipe calls for high-gluten flour, you can obtain good results with bread flour.

- *All-purpose flour* Flours labeled "all-purpose" are usually a blend of high-gluten hard wheat and low-gluten soft wheat. Unbleached all-purpose flours milled in the northern United States, such as Hecker's and King Arthur, have protein counts almost as high as those of bread flour; they weigh in at between 12 and 13 grams per cup. National "supermarket" brands, bleached all-purpose flours such as Gold Medal and Pillsbury, contain 10 to 12 grams of protein per cup. Southern brands, like White Lily, are very low in protein, containing about 9 grams per cup, making them more like cake flour than the usual all-purpose flour.

    When a recipe calls for all-purpose flour, you can use either bleached or unbleached all-purpose flour.

- *Cake and pastry flours* These flours are very low in protein (having about 8 grams per cup) and are used when a tender crumb is the desired outcome. Cake flour is chlorinated, making it a little acidic; pastry flour is not. Cake flour is a supermarket staple; pastry flour is not. While some health food stores carry pastry flour, it is often whole wheat pastry flour, which is not what most recipes call for. If you cannot find pastry flour, you can substitute all-purpose flour for the full amount or make your own pastry flour using 3 parts all-purpose flour to 1 part cake flour.

There are, of course, flours milled from grains other than wheat, flours such as semolina (milled from durum wheat), rye, rice, or whole wheat. These flours are often milled from the entire grain.

Bleached Versus Unbleached Flour By the time flour reaches your kitchen, it's usually bleached to some extent, whether chemically or naturally. Untreated, but exposed to air for a while, flour will oxidize, or bleach, to a creamy, ivory color. The addition of oxidants or bleaches, indicated by the word "bleached" on the packages, speeds the process. If the sack says "bromated," this means the oxidant used was potassium bromate. As a rule of thumb, unbleached flour is usually higher in protein than bleached.

Storing Flour White flour, bleached or not, should be kept in an airtight container in a cool, dry cupboard. Under good conditions, white flours (all-purpose, bread, cake, and pastry) can be kept for about six months. Whole wheat and other flours that contain the oily germ can go rancid quickly and should be stored in airtight containers in the refrigerator or freezer.

Measuring Flour Professional bakers weigh all their ingredients and, indeed, weighing is the most accurate method of measuring anything, particularly flour. However, most home bakers work without a scale—not a problem if you're careful and consistent.

"Scoop" and "level" are the bywords for measuring flour by volume (as opposed to weight). Start with a set of metal measuring cups (glass cups are for liquid measures and plastic cups are for naught—they're unreliable) and flour that's in a bin, sack, or canister with a wide mouth. Using a fork, fluff up the flour, aerating it as best as you can, and then, using your measuring cup, scoop up enough flour to fill the cup to overflowing—don't pack the flour down and don't shake the cup. Sweep a straightedge (the back of a knife, a metal spatula, a bench scraper, or a ruler) across the top of the measuring cup, leveling the top. Measured this way, a cup of flour weighs approximately 5 ounces.

Sifting Flour Sifting is a method of aerating flour; when a recipe calls for sifting the flour with salt, baking powder, baking soda, and/or spices, it's often as much to blend the dry ingredients as to aerate them. Depending on the recipe, you may be asked to sift the ingredients several times, a process that used to be simpler when triple sifters (sifters with three mesh screens) were easily available. These days, professionals use a fine-mesh strainer—a good tool to have on hand—for sifting. (When all you need to do is blend the flour with other dry ingredients, you can use a whisk.)

Most recipes using bread or all-purpose flours do not require sifting, whereas fine-textured, often lumpy cake flour always needs to be sifted before using. When a recipe says "1 cup sifted flour," it means the flour should be sifted before it is measured; "1 cup flour, sifted," means you should measure out 1 cup of flour and then sift it.

The easiest and most accurate way to measure sifted flour is to place the measuring cup on a piece of waxed or parchment paper and to sift flour over and into the cup until it overflows the cup; sweep and level the flour with a straightedge. The excess flour can be returned to its bin and used again.

Professional bakers always sift ingredients onto a piece of parchment and then, when the dry ingredients need to be added to a mixture, lift the parchment and use it as a funnel—a simple process easily and efficiently duplicated at home.

FOLDING A gentle method of mixing ingredients together, folding is usually called for when you need to blend a light, airy ingredient into a heavier one—for example, beaten egg whites or whipped cream into a batter. Folding is most easily accomplished with a sturdy but flexible rubber spatula, in a bowl that's large enough to give you room to maneuver.

In most cases, the lighter ingredient is folded into the heavier. If the batter is particularly heavy, it's a good idea to start by stirring about a quarter of the lighter mixture into it. (If you try to fold an airy mixture into a really stiff mixture, you're bound to knock the airy one flat.) Turn the lighter mixture out on top of the heavier batter and cut through the two mixtures with the spatula, pushing down gently until the tip of the rubber spatula reaches the bottom of the bowl. Now flick your wrist so that you can draw the spatula's flat side up against the side of the bowl; continue this upward movement until the spatula arcs above the bowl. As you pull the spatula up and break the surface, use your free hand to give the bowl a quarter turn so that the ingredients the spatula brings up are folded over and rest gently on top of the mixture. It is the repetition of these motions—cutting down, lifting up, and turning—that constitutes folding. Continue to fold until the blending is complete.

FOOD PROCESSOR There are things the food processor does in a flash that used to take us hours, or used to be too difficult for us to do at home—who ever made fish mousses at the flick of a fin before the food processor? In a professional kitchen, the chefs make more use of the processor than do the bakers and pastry chefs, probably because the capacity is too small for most bakers' tasks. But that doesn't mean you shouldn't take advantage of the machine's speed and power at home.

If you're buying a food processor for the first time, buy one with the largest capacity you can afford; that way, you'll have plenty of room for making pastry and bread doughs in reasonable quantities.

Making Pastry in the Food Processor You'll find complete instructions for preparing pastry and pie doughs in the processor on page 32, but here are some basics.

Pastry should be made with the metal blade. While pastry making always calls for using cold ingredients, with the processor you should be certain the ingredients are cold indeed, since the motor heats up everything. In addition, while some recipes may tell you to work the dough until it forms a ball that rides on the blade, most pastry doughs should be turned out of the work bowl before that point. The ideal time to remove the dough is when it forms small, moist clumps and sticks together when pressed between your fingers.

The general rule for converting a pastry recipe from hand to processor is to put all the dry ingredients into the work bowl and pulse just to mix; add the cut-up butter and/or shortening and pulse and process until the mixture resembles very coarse, moist cornmeal; add the liquid ingredients, about a third at a time, and pulse and/or process after each addition until you reach the stick-together-clump stage.

Making Bread in the Food Processor Many bakers use the processor regularly to make bread dough, preferring it to the mixer for recipes with small yields. But before you embark on food-processor doughs, check the capacity of your machine and, if necessary, divide the ingredients evenly so that you can make your recipe in batches. To convert a basic mixer-made bread recipe to the processor, fit the machine with the plastic or dough blade. If necessary, separate the liquid in the recipes so that only ¼ cup of the liquid is warm (105°F to 115°F), to dissolve the yeast, and the remaining liquid is cool (even cold)—you need the extra chill to counterbalance the heat generated by the machine. Dissolve the yeast in the small quantity of warm liquid. Put the flour and any other dry ingredients into the work bowl of the processor and pulse a couple of times just to mix. With the machine running, add the dissolved yeast, followed rapidly by the remaining liquid, and process just until the dough starts to form a ball. Turn the machine off and allow the dough to rest in the work bowl for 3 to 5 minutes—you're giving the flour a chance to absorb the liquid. Then process the dough for 45 seconds—this is the kneading period—and turn the dough into the rising bowl. Proceed with the recipe in the conventional manner. If you're making the dough in batches, make the remaining batches, knead all the dough together briefly on a lightly floured work surface, and set the dough aside to rise as usual.

FREEZING Whenever applicable, recipes in this book are followed by instructions for storing, which, in many cases, means freezing. To maintain the quality of doughs and baked goods, be sure they are sealed airtight before they are frozen. Pack the doughs, sweets, or breads into a plastic bag and press out as much air from the bag as you can before gathering the opening of the bag to form a "neck." Grasp the neck and draw out the air remaining in the bag either by just sucking the air out with your mouth or by inserting a plastic straw into the bag and sucking the air out through the straw. Either way, as soon as you've pulled out the air, seal the bag with a twist tie, making sure not to let any air back in. For extra protection against freezer burn, place the sealed bag inside another plastic bag and repeat the procedure for removing the air. This is "double wrapping." Label each bag with date and contents. If you have the time, the best way to thaw most sweets or breads is to allow them to rest overnight at room temperature. If the sweets are iced or meant to be served cold, thaw them in the refrigerator. In general, doughs also should be defrosted in the refrigerator (individual recipes will provide additional guidelines). Whether you thaw in the refrigerator or at room temperature, keep the baked good in its bag to prevent drying out.

JELLY-ROLL PANS These are the pans professional bakers refer to as half-sheet pans. The pans are rectangular and, unlike baking sheets, have raised sides, which make them perfect for preparing sheet and jelly-roll cakes (hence their name), toasting nuts, transferring doughs in and out of the refrigerator, and tens of other tasks—and inappropriate for cookies. Jelly-roll pans come in two sizes, 10½- by 15½- by 1-inch and 12½- by 17½- by 1-inch, and can be purchased with nonstick finishes.

KNEADING To knead is to work a dough until it is smooth. Yeast doughs are kneaded until they are elastic in order to develop the gluten (page 11) in the flour. A rythmic push, turn, and fold that can be accomplished either by hand or in an electric mixer is the basic pattern of a knead. For instructions on kneading, see page 67.

MARBLE Buttery doughs like puff pastry, croissant, and Danish, as well as rich doughs for pies and tarts, are most easily rolled out on a smooth, cool surface, and marble is the smoothest and coolest. (Onyx and polished granite counter-tops, popular if very expensive, are also ideal.) While a permanently installed marble pastry counter is a delightful luxury, in many ways a large marble slab that will fit on a shelf in your refrigerator is the most practical. (Marble can be cut to size.) With such a slab, when your pastry becomes warm or soft, or the butter starts to seep out, you've only to pop the pastry, slab and all, into the fridge and wait until the chill repairs the situation.

MARZIPAN Slightly sweeter and softer than almond paste, marzipan is a mixture of almonds, corn syrup, and egg whites. It is available in supermarkets and specialty shops and easily made at home (see page 300). Marzipan is most often used to make decorations for cakes, but it can also be rolled and used to cover a cake, a common practice in Europe. Once wrapped airtight, marzipan has good keeping qualities; it can be stored in the refrigerator or freezer for about six months.

MASCARPONE A soft, ultrarich cow's milk cheese, originally from Italy, mascarpone has become a popular ingredient among American pastry chefs. Because of its very high butterfat content, it should be handled with a light touch—beat it, and you'll have mascarpone butter. It has a subtle flavor that blends nicely with other ingredients and so is often used in fillings or as an accompaniment or garnish.

MEASURING To say that measuring is important in baking is to state the obvious. A bit more of this or a little less of that and there's no telling what you'll end up with. The first step to proper measuring is to equip yourself with a proper set of measuring cups and spoons.

Measuring Cups For dry measuring, metal cups and spoons are preferable to those made of plastic. You should have cups to measure ¼, ⅓, ½, and 1 cup; an ⅛-cup and 2-cup measure are optional but handy. Measuring spoons should be for ¼, ½, and 1 teaspoon as well as for 1 tablespoon.

Leveling The most important concept in measuring dry ingredients is leveling—you always want a measure that is level with the top of the measuring cup or spoon. If a recipe calls for ¼ cup sugar, for example, you dip the ¼-cup measure into the sugar bin, scoop up enough sugar to fill it to overflowing, and level it with a sweep of a straight edge. Never use a larger measuring cup and shake the ingredients level to come to a measure—it will be only a rough approximation.

To Measure Dry Ingredients When you're measuring flour, you want to aerate the flour in the bin by fluffing it up with a fork before scooping and leveling (see measuring flour, page 13) and to be gentle—you never want to pack the flour down. Brown sugar, on the other hand, needs packing; granulated sugar is a self-packer. Confectioner's sugar should be sifted after it's measured because it's invariably lumpy.

Keep the leveling law in mind when you're measuring dry ingredients by spoonfuls as well.

To Measure Liquids Liquid ingredients should be measured in a calibrated glass measuring cup. Place the measuring cup on the counter, crouch down so that the measuring cup is at eye level, and pour in the liquid, keeping an eye on the calibrations so you can stop when the liquid hits the mark. Lifting the measuring cup to eye level, rather than keeping it on a flat surface and bending, won't give you an accurate measure. If you need to measure less than ¼ cup of liquid, it's probably best to use your metal measuring spoons, keeping in mind that 2 tablespoons equal 1 ounce, or ⅛ cup.

MILK Unless otherwise noted, whole milk was used to test these recipes. However, unless the recipe specifies whole milk, you can experiment with lower-fat milk. In general, using 2% instead of full-fat milk in a cake batter is fine; substitutions become more difficult when you're making a cream, frosting, mousse, or custard that depends on a certain amount of fat for its consistency.

MIXERS Many of these recipes, especially the bread recipes, are for serious home bakers and call for serious home equipment, most particularly a heavy-duty mixer, one with a 4½- or 5-quart mixing bowl and paddle, whisk, and dough hook attachments. Machines like these are very expensive (about $250), but they're worth saving up for and will serve you for years. Without a heavy-duty mixer, making brioche, focaccia, and other soft, sticky doughs that require long mixing periods may be difficult, but you'll be able to make more than the lion's share of the recipes in this book using a hand-held mixer with variable speeds.

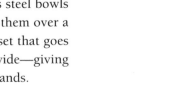

MIXING BOWLS A set of nesting stainless steel mixing bowls is a kitchen must—a double set is not a luxury. Of course you can use glass or plastic mixing bowls (in fact, a very large plastic mixing bowl, one with high, straight sides, makes a nice container for rising bread dough), but stainless steel bowls are durable, heatable (there may be times when you'll want to put them over a burner), inexpensive, and readily available. Equip yourself with a set that goes from small—just right for beating an egg or two—to large and wide—giving you enough room to fold in ingredients or mix dough with both hands.

MOLASSES Molasses is a by-product of refining sugar. Thick, dark, and sweet, it is used to add moisture, flavor, and color to cakes and cookies. Blackstrap molasses is the strongest variety and is often considered an acquired taste; it is "unsulfured" molasses, or mild molasses, that is preferred in baking.

NUTS Nuts, a great source of flavor and texture in baked goods, can also be a source of despair, since they spoil quickly. The key is to taste before you buy (if possible) or bake. Ideally, buy your nuts from a shop that sells them in bulk so you can taste one before you buy in quantity. Similarly, you should pop a nut into your mouth before measuring them out for a recipe. It's the oils in nuts that make them so tasty and so tricky. Satisfied that you've purchased fresh nuts, you'll want to keep them fresh by packing them in airtight containers and storing them in the freezer; use them without thawing.

To Toast Nuts Place nuts in a single layer on a jelly-roll pan and toast in a 350°F oven for about 10 minutes, stirring once or twice during baking. To test that the nuts are fully toasted, break or bite one in half—the center of the nut should have taken on some color.

To Grind Nuts Nuts can be ground in a nut grinder, which will produce a fluffy mass, or in a food processor fitted with the metal blade. If you are using the food processor, add some of the recipe's sugar to the nuts before whirring them—this will keep them from turning to nut butter, a hazard of overprocessing.

PARCHMENT PAPER Available in large sheets and rolls, parchment paper is nonstick, sometimes silicon-treated, and indispensable in a baker's kitchen. Professional bakers, who rarely if ever have waxed paper in their kitchens, use parchment to line baking sheets or jelly-roll pans when they're making cookies or meringues, and cake pans when the bottom of the cake might have a delicate crumb; they form parchment triangles into small piping cones for decorating petits fours, writing messages in icing or chocolate, and adding fine squiggles and flourishes to desserts; and they use a sheet of parchment paper as a transporter, sifting dry ingredients onto the paper and folding the paper into a funnel to slowly slide the dry ingredients into a batter in a mixing bowl.

PASTRY BAGS AND TIPS Sometimes called piping bags, pastry bags are used to shape batters, doughs, and decorations. The cone-shaped bags come in many materials, including plastic-coated canvas, nylon, and plastic, and assorted sizes, and are most generally fitted with a pastry tip, plain or decorative, before using. (Plastic piping bags, made from the same material as storage bags and available at professional supply houses in perforated rolls, are usually disposable.) While most home bakers pull out their pastry bags when they want to decorate a cake, the professional baker will keep a pastry bag at the ready to do small jobs like filling muffin tins or tartlet shells (no need to use the pastry tip, just push the batter or filling out the bottom of the bag), getting an even layer of frosting onto a cake layer (even if you're going to spread it level with a spatula, it's easy to move the frosting from bowl to cake with a pastry bag), or making fast work of filling profiteroles or babas with cream.

If you've got a quick job to do that doesn't require precision, you can turn a zipper-lock plastic bag into an adequate pastry bag. Fill and seal the bag, gather it at the top, and use scissors to snip off a corner to become your piping tip.

Filling a Pastry Bag This is the kind of task that makes you wish you had three hands, but there are several tricks that can make getting a mixture from bowl to bag a sure thing. Experienced pipers find it easy to fold the top of the pastry bag over to form a deep cuff, to slip their left hand (or right, if they are left-handed) under the cuff so that they can hold the bag loosely between their thumb and their fingers, and to transfer the piping mixture from bowl to bag with a large rubber spatula, scraping the spatula clean against the inside of the bag (their thumbs support the spatula's pressure). Those less certain of their dexterity find it easier to place the bag in a tall glass and fold the top of the bag over the rim of the glass to form a cuff, leaving both hands free for filling. And those who are most adept use this method (taught by Markus Farbinger): Pinch the bottom of the bag, just above the pastry tip, between the pinky and ring finger of your left hand (or right, if you're left-handed) and fold the top cuff over your thumb, on one side, and index and middle fingers on the other. This not only opens the bag up for filling, it also assures that the filling won't dribble out the tip end while you're packing it into the wide end. (If you have a liquidy filling and are using one of the other methods, before starting to fill the bag, grab the tip, lightly twist a little of the fabric just above it, and tuck the fabric into the tip. When you've filled the bag and are ready to pipe, undo the twist and push the filling down into the tip area.) It is easiest to pipe if the pastry bag is filled to half-capacity.

Making a Parchment Cone Small decorating jobs, such as piping polka dots or thin lines on miniature pastries, call for small decorating cones. Professionals fold parchment cones in a flash whenever they need to do this kind of decorating or when they're writing with melted chocolate. The easiest way to construct a parchment cone is to start with a parchment rectangle that's 5 inches by 7 inches and to cut it in half diagonally—this will give you the right-size triangle for almost any small job (illustration 1).

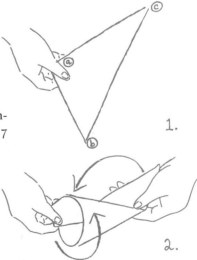

1.

Holding the parchment at the midpoint of its long side (use your right hand if you're right-handed, your left if you're left-handed), grab the point at angle *b* and start rolling it in on itself to form a cone (illustration 2). Secure it with your free hand at the top. Roll the remaining tail of parchment, angle *c*, around the cone. Angle *c* should now be pointing to the top.

2.

With one hand, grasp the point of the piping cone gently; with the other hand, tuck the parchment tail into the top of the cone (illustration 3). The bag will probably have a very tiny hole at its tip. If you need a larger hole, just snip the tip with a scissors. After you've filled the bag, fold the top down to hold in the chocolate or icing.

3.

Piping When the bag is half-filled, twist the top of the pastry bag to close it. Use your right hand (or left, if you are left-handed) to grab the top of the pastry bag, hooking your thumb around the twist and using your other fingers to apply gentle pressure against the piping mixture; use your other hand to guide the pastry tip. Hold the pastry bag a little above and at an angle to the surface on which you are piping and apply gentle and even pressure to force the mixture out of the bag. Individual recipes will give you piping instructions for particular batters, shapes, and decorations.

PASTRY BLENDER Used to cut butter and/or shortening into the dry ingredients in a pastry or biscuit dough, a pastry blender is a set of parallel curved wires attached to a handle. Inexpensive and available in supermarkets and housewares stores, the pastry blender does a good job of working the fat into the flour until the mixture is coarse and crumbly—just what you want for these doughs. (Of course, your fingers do this job well too.)

PASTRY BRUSH Wooden- or plastic-handled with natural bristles, pastry brushes come in varying widths. You'll want a narrow brush, perhaps ½ inch wide, to brush a puffy, risen dough with egg wash, and you'll reach for a wider brush, one with a width of an inch or more, to brush excess flour off pastry doughs. You'll find pastry brushes in cookware shops— or head for the hardware store and stock up on paintbrushes.

PASTRY SCRAPER A pastry scraper, sometimes known by its French name, *corne,* is a curved piece of thin, flexible plastic that is used to scrape down the sides of a bowl (it's very useful with sticky doughs like that for the Rustic Potato Loaves, page 138) or to help get a batter out of a bowl and into a pan. Its flexibility allows you to press it against the curve of a bowl. Scrapers are inexpensive and available in specialty housewares shops.

PASTRY SOCK A mesh or cloth casing or sock that fits over a rolling pin, a pastry sock is sometimes used to roll out doughs that are very delicate (the recipe for Potato Lefse, page 165, calls for one). The sock should be rubbed with flour before use. If you do not have a sock, rub your rolling pin well with flour.

PEEL A peel is a large, thin rectangle of wood with a long handle used to transfer pizzas and free-form breads into and out of the oven. To help the doughs slide from peel to oven, rub the peel with cornmeal or rice flour.

PHYLLO Phyllo, from the Greek word meaning "leaf," is a paper-thin dough made of flour and water. Available in the frozen foods section or refrigerated case of supermarkets, phyllo is a versatile dough that can be used for both sweets and savories. The dough, sometimes referred to as filo or strudel leaves, should be kept frozen until the day before it is to be used and then defrosted, in its packaging, overnight in the refrigerator. Because it is so thin, the dough dries out very quickly. Remove the sheets of dough you need and keep them covered on the counter as you work; wrap the remaining dough and keep it refrigerated.

PROOFING When you mix dry yeast with liquid to activate its leavening powers, you're proofing the yeast. When you set your dough aside to rise, this fermentation period is also called proofing.

PUFF PASTRY Puff is the quintessential laminated dough. A simple dough is wrapped around a block of butter, then rolled, folded, and turned six times, so that when the final dough is baked, it puffs mightily and forms almost one thousand seemingly laminated layers. There is a recipe for exceptionally good (and easy-to-make) puff pastry on page 46, but, if you want to bake the Tourte Milanese (page 423) or Sunny-side-up Apricot Pastries (page 192), for example, and haven't the time to make the dough from scratch, you can use store-bought puff pastry. If you're lucky enough to live near a bakery or specialty market that sells all-butter puff pastry by the pound, by all means buy it. But if you can find puff pastry only in the freezer section of your supermarket, and it's not made with butter, buy it anyway—the things you can make with it are too good to give up because you can't find the perfect pastry.

PUNCHING DOWN This is the expression that is often used to describe the action of deflating a yeast dough after it has risen. Punching, however, is not what you want to do to risen dough—a gentler deflation, performed by folding the dough over on itself a few times to lightly push out the accumulated gases, is a better technique.

RIBBON "Forming a ribbon" refers to beating sugar and eggs (and often butter) together until a bit of the batter dropped from a lifted whisk onto the batter in the bowl holds its shape for a few seconds before dissolving. The ribbon is an important stage in preparing génoise and other whole egg sponge and butter cakes. Usually, by the time the mixture forms the ribbon, it has also tripled in volume.

ROLLING PINS You know you've become a serious baker when your kitchen sports a collection of rolling pins. If you can have just one pin, start with a French pin, a wooden cylinder about 1½ inches in diameter and about 19 inches long that has no handles. The French pin gives you good control over the dough and, because it's handleless, can be used for kitchen chores like butter bashing (a technique for softening butter). When you're ready for a second pin, buy a heavy wooden pin with handles that are set on ball bearings. This type of pin is terrific for rolling heavy doughs, particularly yeast doughs. Optional pins include a marble rolling pin, nice for doughs that need to remain very cold, since the pin can be refrigerated and will hold its chill, and a tapered handleless pin, good for rolling circles of dough.

In addition to the standard *batterie* of rolling pins, you'll come across recipes that call for a hardtack pin (Swedish Oatmeal Hardtack, page 162), a wooden rolling pin with little wooden points, like hobnails, and a grooved lefse pin (Potato Lefse, page 165); both are available at well-equipped specialty shops.

ROOM TEMPERATURE Recipes often call for butter and eggs at room temperature, which means that they have been removed from the refrigerator and have been allowed to sit until they come up to the ambient temperature. Room temperature generally means somewhere between 68°F and 75°F and is also used to describe the temperature at which bread doughs are often set to rise. Variations in room temperature are a fact of life and invariably you can work around them. The cooler the room, the slower the rise (for more on temperatures and timing, see the introduction to the recipe on page 123). When a warmer temperature (75°F to 85°F) is preferable, try to find a warm place in your kitchen and set the dough there, but not on a radiator or other direct source of heat.

ROTATING PANS When you have positioned the racks to divide your oven into thirds and are baking cakes or cookies on both racks, it's a good idea to rotate the pans midway through the baking period. The most effective way to rotate is to turn the pans around, so that the side of the pan or baking sheet that was at the front of the oven is now at the back, and to put the top pan on the bottom rack and the bottom pan on the top. This technique makes up for any hot spots or other inconsistencies in your oven.

SALT Salt is not a major ingredient in baking, but it is an important one. As it does with savories, salt lifts the flavors of sweets; in fact, a pinch of salt is indispensable in anything that includes chocolate. Bakers may not use much salt, but many are fussy about the kind they do use. Some bakers use table salt, the iodized salt most often found in supermarkets, while others claim that the iodine adversely affects the flavor of their baked goods. Kosher salt and sea salt are additive-free and often the salts of choice among bakers. Most recipes in this book specify the baker's choice of salt, but, of course, you're free to experiment as you wish. Just keep in mind that kosher and sea salts are less salty than table salt, so you might have to make adjustments. If you're using salt as a topping for breads and rolls, focaccia, and other flat-breads, you'll want to use coarse salt, because it will bake onto, not into, the crust.

SCALE A serious kitchen should have a scale, one that allows you to weigh something to within, at least, a quarter ounce. While you may not use your scale as often for pastry as you will for bread—bread bakers always weigh their flour and then weigh their dough to make sure their pound loaves are just that—weighing is a good habit to get into. Balance scales are accurate and versatile—one side is usually equipped with a basket or pan that has a handy pour spout, great when you're weighing flour—but electronic scales are more compact and stowable. Either way, you'll want to get a scale that also has metric measurements, because if you are, or do become, a serious baker, you'll want to try a few European recipes, which use grams.

SIFTERS, SIEVES, AND STRAINERS A sifter is a mechanical device that pushes dry ingredients through a mesh. If you do not have a sifter and the recipe directions call for sifting the flour or sifting the dry ingredients together, use a fine-meshed sieve or strainer. Hold the sieve above the measuring cup or a piece of waxed or parchment paper, and use your free hand to tap the side of the sieve to get the dry ingredients moving through the mesh.

SIFTING See Flour (page 13) for information about techniques.

SIMPLE SYRUP A combination of sugar and water, simple syrup is most frequently used to make sorbets and to poach fruits. The standard simple syrup is made by combining equal parts water and sugar: Bring the mixture to a boil, boil for 1 minute, and remove from the heat.

SPATULAS The baker's kitchen needs two kinds of spatulas, rubber and metal. You'll use rubber spatulas for many tasks, including scraping down the sides of a mixing bowl and folding in ingredients. Buy small, medium, and large rubber spatulas (two of each would be ideal), and look for commercial-quality spatulas—they are usually more flexible and always more durable than supermarket equipment.

offset spatula

Metal spatulas are vital for filling and frosting cakes, smoothing batter in a pan, and lifting cakes and cookies from baking sheets and cooling racks. Equip your kitchen with spatulas of varying widths and lengths and make sure to include a couple of offset spatulas in your supply. Offset spatulas are the ones whose blades are set at an angle and a little below their handles, like pancake turners.

SPICES Like extracts, spices should be stored in a cool, dark cupboard and checked periodically. Your nose is the best inspector when it comes to dried spices: If you don't get a powerful fragrance, you won't get a powerful flavor.

SPONGE As a baking term, *sponge* can refer to either a type of cake or a component of a yeast dough. When used for cakes, it refers to cakes that are leavened by beaten eggs, either génoise-type cakes based on whole egg sponges, or chiffon cakes, which get their puff from beaten egg whites.

When the matter at hand is bread dough, *sponge* refers to a starter, or "pre-dough," usually a mini-mix of yeast, liquid, and flour that's set aside to rise for a while before being mixed with the remaining ingredients. Using a sponge, called a *poolish* by French bakers and a *biga* by Italians, gives bread extra flavor and character.

STARTER A starter is a pre-mix for a yeast dough. It might be sourdough, a chef, or a sponge (see above). It is a mixture that contains commercial yeast or, in the case of a sourdough or a chef, wild or naturally fermented yeast, and is developed before the main dough is prepared.

STRAIGHT RISE The term refers to a method of making bread that does not include a starter. In a straight-rise, or direct-rise, bread, the dough is mixed, allowed to rise one or two times, shaped, and baked.

SUGAR When a recipe lists "sugar" as an ingredient, you're meant to use granulated sugar. However, you'll want to have an array of sugars on hand, including: confectioner's sugar, also known as powdered or 10-X sugar; light and dark brown sugars; dazzle or sparkle sugar, a decorative sugar; pearl sugar, another decorative sugar available through bakers' supply houses; and turbinado sugar, a coarse natural sugar that can be purchased in health food markets.

Granulated sugar is measured by the scoop-and-level method, for which you dip your metal measuring cup into the sugar bin, fill the cup to overflowing, and then sweep a straightedge across the top of the cup to level the sugar. Confectioner's sugar, which is usually spooned into the measuring cup and then leveled, needs to be sifted or sieved before you use it, since it tends to form lumps. The lumps you find in confectioner's sugar are soft compared to the rock-hard lumps you may get in brown sugar, lumps that won't disappear during baking. Push brown sugar through a sieve to break up the lumps and discard those that are beyond pushable, then measure out the amount of sugar you need by packing it firmly into a metal measuring cup. When you dump out a packed cup of brown sugar, the sugar should retain the cup's shape—that's what packed means.

The decorative sugars, like dazzle, sparkle, or pearl, maintain their shape during baking. Dazzle and sparkle do just what their names suggest, while granules of pearl sugar are, not surprisingly, small, round, and very white. Although these sugars are particularly attractive on Danish pastries and cookies, they are not a vital ingredient in any recipe—if you can't find them, don't let that stop you from making a recipe.

Like dazzle and pearl sugars, turbinado sugar, a light brown sugar, is most often used as a decorative or finishing sugar. Because it retains its shape during baking, it's a nice addition to the tops of sweet breads and pie crusts.

TEMPERING The term *tempering* refers to the process of melting and cooling chocolate in such a way that the cocoa butter in the chocolate is stabilized. When you purchase a block of chocolate, it has already been tempered: That's why it is shiny and smooth and snaps with a clean crack. Chocolate goes out of temper when it is melted, a condition that's fine if you want to use the chocolate in a cake, filling, or cream. However, if you want to mold the chocolate, use it as a coating, or dip it, as you would if you were making candies, then you need to temper it. There are only a very few recipes in this book that call for tempering; when needed, you'll find the instructions in the body of the recipe.

THERMOMETERS A baker's kitchen needs at least three thermometers: one for the oven, one for doughs, and one for sugar. The best oven thermometers are mercury rather than spring thermometers and can either hang from or rest on an oven rack. It is wise to test your oven periodically by checking with a thermometer, making certain that the reading on the oven's dial matches that on the thermometer. Many cooks keep an oven thermometer in the oven at all times—not a bad idea.

An instant-read thermometer is a handy tool in the kitchen. You can use it to take the temperature of water you're using to proof yeast, to check that bread dough is the right temperature after mixing (something professional bakers do all the time and home bakers might want to get into the habit of doing), and to verify that a loaf is baked through. If an instant-read thermometer plunged into the center of the loaf registers 200°F to 210°F, you can be certain your bread is fully baked.

A sugar or candy thermometer is a mercury thermometer (a metal cage surrounds the best ones), often equipped with a clip that can be used to attach the thermometer to the side of the pan. This is the thermometer you'll use when a recipe calls for boiling sugar to the soft-ball or other stage. (The exact temperature needed for a specific preparation is indicated in the individual recipe.)

VANILLA It is impossible to imagine baking without vanilla, either in bean or extract form. Vanilla lifts the flavor of chocolate, mellows egginess, and rounds out a mélange of ingredients. When using extract, make certain that it is pure vanilla extract; imitation vanilla has a harsh flavor and an unpleasant (unnatural) aroma.

Vanilla beans, or pods, come from many parts of the world, with those from Madagascar and Tahiti being the most prized. (Those from Tahiti are the most expensive and the hardest to find, since their production is limited.) Fresh vanilla beans are plump, pliable, and, of course, wildly aromatic. Both the pod (the outer part of the bean) and the pulpy interior are used, and each recipe tells you what part of the bean you need and how to handle it. Generally, vanilla beans are used to infuse liquids with flavor. Often you'll be instructed to slit the bean lengthwise, to scrape the soft, pulpy little seeds into the liquid, and then to drop in the pod as well. When the liquid has been brought to a boil, it is allowed to steep (to rest covered so that it can be infused with the vanilla flavor) and then, in all likelihood, the pod is removed. Keep that bean: You can rinse the pod, leave it to dry at room temperature, or in a slow oven, and then use it to flavor sugar, either by burying the pods you've saved in the sugar canister or pulverizing the pods and mixing them with granulated sugar.

VEGETABLE OIL SPRAY Vegetable oil sprays, found on supermarket shelves near shortenings and oils, are ideal for greasing the insides of muffin tins or baking pans with nooks and crannies. In addition, if you're measuring a sticky ingredient like honey, molasses, or corn syrup in a measuring cup, it's a good idea to give the inside of the cup a light film of vegetable oil spray—the sticky stuff will slide out of the cup easily and you'll get every little drop of it into your batter.

WHISK A whisk is the tool of choice for aerating dry ingredients that do not need to be sifted, beating eggs, blending liquid ingredients, or giving the finishing touches to whipped cream. A whisk is a set of bulb-shaped metal wires attached to a handle and can come in sizes from small to huge and shapes from flat to balloon. A flat whisk is a blending or folding whisk, a balloon whisk the tool to use for incorporating air into a mixture.

YEAST Yeast, a natural leavening (so natural it's found in the air around us), is the "magic" ingredient in breads. Yeast is activated by the addition of water, and different yeasts, bakers, and breads call for slightly different water temperatures, ranging from cool (75°F to 80°F), to tepid (80°F to 90°F), to lukewarm (95°F to 105°F), to warm (105°F to 115°F), to hot (115°F to 120°F).

The most commonly available types of yeast are fresh (or compressed), active dry, rapid-rise, and instant. Active dry yeast, found in supermarkets, is the yeast used most often in bread recipes, but each recipe in this book indicates the preferred type of yeast.

Fresh yeast is sold in cakes; it is soft, crumbly, a little rubbery, and ivory-colored; it should not be hard and crusty. It can be mixed directly into a dough or stirred into tepid water and allowed to rest for about 5 minutes and proof—that is, to become creamy and perhaps bubble. (Yeast will not always bubble when proofed.) Fresh yeast should be wrapped airtight and kept in the refrigerator or frozen. It has a very short shelf life; pay attention to the date on the package.

Active dry yeast is dormant yeast that is brought to life when proofed in lukewarm and warm water. While active dry yeast can be stored at room temperature, it's best preserved in the refrigerator or freezer. The two most commonly available brands of active dry yeast (Fleischmann's and Red Star) are sold in packets at the supermarket. It is wise to spill the yeast out into a small bowl and then measure it into your recipe.

Rapid-rise or quick-rise yeast is another strain of yeast and one that promises to cut in half the amount of time needed to rise a dough. While the timesaving promise is appealing (and true), most professional bakers want their leavened goods to rise as slowly as possible, since it is during the fermentation period that the dough develops its flavor. Unless you are specifically instructed in a recipe to use rapid-rise, it's best to stick to other types of yeast.

Instant yeast is yet another strain of yeast, and it should not be confused with rapid-rise. It was developed in France in the 1960s and has only recently been made available to home bakers. The brand used by most professional bakers (and available to home bakers) is SAF Instant Yeast. (Fleischmann's markets an instant yeast as well.) Although dried, like active dry yeast, instant yeast is used differently from active dry. Because it contains more "live" yeast cells, you use 25 percent less instant yeast than you would active dry in any recipe. Finally, instant yeast doesn't need to proof in liquid; it can be added directly to a recipe with the dry ingredients (although soaking won't hurt it). In addition, instant yeast has a greater tolerance to temperatures; it can be activated in temperatures ranging from tepid to hot.

You'll notice as you read through bread recipes that salt is often added to a recipe only after the yeast has been proofed and some flour has been incorporated into the dough. This is because salt inhibits yeast's growth. Similarly, you may see that a pinch of sugar is often added to the proofing pot—sugar feeds the yeast. Follow the recipe's directions carefully when working with yeast.

ZEST The outer rind of citrus fruit is referred to as zest. When a recipe calls for grated zest, it's the colored peel, not the white, cottony pith that lies just beneath its surface, that you want. To grate zest, choose the diagonal-hole side of a box grater—it will give you a cleaner zesting than if you use the nail-hole side—and rub lightly to avoid getting the pith, which is bitter. For broader strips of zest, use a swivel-blade peeler or a sharp knife to cut away the peel.

Batters and Doughs
THE BASICS

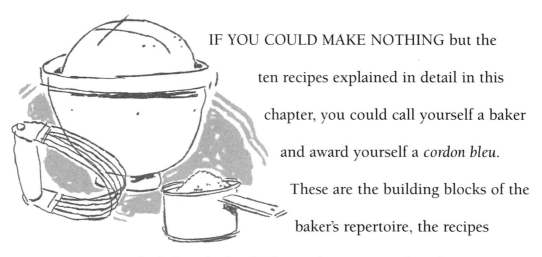

IF YOU COULD MAKE NOTHING but the
ten recipes explained in detail in this
chapter, you could call yourself a baker
and award yourself a *cordon bleu.*
These are the building blocks of the
baker's repertoire, the recipes
upon which hundreds of cakes and pastries are based.

Each of these recipes, whether for pie dough or rich and
shiny choux paste, meringues, or buttery croissants, is a model of
its kind. And each includes a rundown of tips and techniques,
pointers to keep in mind while you're working. Read through
these and you'll find that puff pastry needn't be intimidating, that
the key to making and rolling a great pie crust is keeping everything cold, and that the French classic sponge cake, génoise,

which can be made three ways (and filled, frosted, and decorated three hundred ways), is rather well behaved—no matter if it looks deflated when you fold in the melted butter, it will pick itself up and rise when baked. Here you'll learn that the "laminates"—puff, Danish, and croissant doughs—that are wrapped around a hefty amount of butter and rolled, folded, and turned form almost a thousand layers of dough and butter, just what's needed to make them puff majestically.

This chapter of must-know recipes, coupled with Baking Basics, constitutes a beginner's course in baking. Together, these chapters teach you not just *how* to make the fundamental doughs and batters, but *why* you make them as you do. Once you've mastered these ten basic recipes, you'll not only have enough dough and batter to create dozens of pastries and cakes, you'll have the confidence—and the knowledge—to make any recipe in this book.

Flaky Pie Dough

Makes enough dough for four 9- to 10-inch tarts or open-faced pies or 2 double-crusted pies ■ Bakers like to talk about the "secrets" of making great pie crusts. In truth, there are tips, but no unknowable secrets and nothing daunting enough to explain why cool, calm, collected types turn nervous at the thought of tackling a pie crust.

Like the fillings they cradle, crusts have personalities: crisp, tender, and flaky—or some combination thereof. Which traits are dominant is, in good measure, a result of ingredients: Butter is the great giver of flavor and vegetable shortening the flake maker; together they produce a crust both flaky and tender, sweet and full-flavored, the kind most prized by American pie hands. This mixed crust (the best example of which follows) can be used for pies and tarts, sweet and savory, American- or European-style.

An all-butter dough (like the Chocolate Dough, page 372, and its nonchocolate version) will give you a crisp, sturdy crust with little flakiness (unless the butter is left in largish pieces). When prebaked on its own, a butter crust will stand firm against juicy fillings. Handled properly, a butter crust is strong enough to be rolled out and molded into a free-form shape or a galette (see page 371). For most bakers, an all-shortening crust is usually not an option, because, although it produces lots of flake, it delivers almost no flavor.

If you could have only one pie dough in your repertoire (heaven forbid), it would have to be this one, the classic dough that earns blue ribbons at county fairs and stars at esteemed pastry shops. The mix of butter and shortening guarantees that the dough will be flaky, flavorful, and tender. You can use this dough to make any kind of pie or tart, sweet or savory, plain or fancy. It is easy to roll and crimp and is made quickly by hand, in a mixer, or food processor. The recipe is large and can be cut in half or even quartered, but since the dough can be frozen for up to a month, it's practical to make the full batch. You can freeze the dough in disks, rolled out in circles, or already fitted into pie pans or tart molds, ready to go into the oven—without thawing—when you're in a crunch for a crust.

> 5¼ cups pastry flour or all-purpose flour
> 1 tablespoon kosher salt
> 1½ sticks (6 ounces) cold unsalted butter, cut into small pieces
> 1¾ cups (11 ounces) solid vegetable shortening, chilled
> 1 cup ice water

continued

TO MAKE THE DOUGH BY HAND, mix the flour and salt together in a large bowl. Add the butter and, using a pastry blender (or your fingers, if you prefer), cut it into the flour until the mixture looks like coarse crumbs. Be patient—this takes a while. Break up the shortening and add it in bits to the bowl. Still working with the pastry blender (or your fingers), cut in the shortening until the mixture has small clumps and curds. Switch to a wooden spoon and add the ice water, stirring to incorporate it. Turn the dough out onto a work surface and fold it over on itself a few times—don't get carried away. The dough will be soft, but it will firm sufficiently in the refrigerator.

TO MAKE THE DOUGH IN A MIXER FITTED WITH THE PADDLE ATTACHMENT, put the flour and salt into the bowl and stir to mix. Add the butter and mix on low until it is cut into the dry ingredients and the mixture looks coarse and crumbly. Add the shortening in small bits and continue to mix on low. When the mixture is clumpy and curdy and holds together when a small bit is pressed between your fingers, add the water and mix only until it is incorporated. Turn the dough out onto a work surface and fold it over on itself two or three times, just to finish the mixing and to gather it together.

TO MAKE THE DOUGH IN A FOOD PROCESSOR, start with very cold ingredients and take care not to overwork them. Place the dry ingredients in the food processor fitted with a metal blade and pulse just to mix. Take the top off, scatter the chilled cubed butter and shortening over the flour, cover, and pulse again, working only until the fats are cut in and the mixture resembles slightly moist cornmeal. Add a little of the liquid and pulse a few times, then add more liquid and pulse again. Continue until the mixture has curds and clumps and sticks together when pressed between your fingers. Don't process until the dough forms a ball that rides on the blade—that's overdoing it.

Chilling the Dough Wrap the dough in plastic and refrigerate for at least 2 hours or for as long as 5 days.

When the dough is thoroughly chilled and firm, it is ready to roll out and use in any recipe calling for flaky pie crust.

Storing The dough can be kept in the refrigerator for 5 days or frozen for 1 month. It's a good idea to divide the dough into quarters for freezing since one quarter of the recipe is generally enough for one pie crust or tart shell. Defrost, still wrapped, in the refrigerator.

Contributing Baker **LESLIE MACKIE**

Pie Dough by Hand

1. With a pastry blender, cut chilled butter into the flour and salt until the mixture looks like coarse crumbs. Cut in the chilled shortening until it forms curds.

2. Add the ice water gradually and toss to blend.

3. When the dough is sufficiently moist, pinch it—it will stick together.

4. Lightly gather the dough into a round and chill before rolling.

Tips on Perfect Pie Dough

There are a few general rules that obtain no matter what kind of crust or filling you choose; follow these and you and your crust will be golden. (In fact, these same tips will help you make lovely biscuits and scones too.)

- Work in a bowl that's large enough for you to dig into with both hands.
- Always use unsalted butter and make sure it is extremely cold. Cut the butter into ½-inch cubes before adding it to the flour.
- Use a pastry blender or your fingertips to cut the butter into the flour. Work as quickly as you comfortably can and stop when the mixture resembles coarse crumbs.
- When you use solid vegetable shortening, chill it and cut it into chunks a bit bigger than the butter cubes. Work the shortening into the dough until

the mixture forms moist clumps and curds—when you add the liquid, you'll get even larger clumps.

- Keep the liquid icy-cold. Add it a spoonful at a time, using a fork to toss the mixture and incorporate the liquid into the dough. When the dough has curds and clumps that stick together when pressed lightly between your fingers, it's just right. If you have any doubts, keep in mind that it's better to add too much liquid than too little; too little, and the crust will be dry and difficult to roll.

- Gently gather the dough into a round and then flatten it into a rough approximation of the shape you'll be rolling it into.

- Chill it. Even if the dough feels cool to the touch, give it at least 30 minutes, preferably an hour, in the refrigerator. This rest gives the gluten (the protein that forms webs in flour) a chance to calm down so that when you start to roll the dough, it won't spring back.

- Roll the dough on a flour-dusted smooth, cool surface—marble is great, chilled marble is ideal.

- Roll the dough from the center out, rolling on one side and making certain to roll across the entire surface of the dough evenly. Lift the dough frequently to make sure it doesn't stick. As you roll, turn the dough—an eighth of a turn each time will keep it round.

- Transfer the dough to your pie or tart pan either by folding the dough in quarters, centering it in the pan, and unfolding it, or by rolling it up around your rolling pin and unrolling it over the pan.

- Don't pull or stretch the dough—what you stretch now will shrink back later. Gently work the dough into the pan, lifting it to get a smooth fit against the bottom and up the sides. Follow the recipe's directions for forming and crimping the edge of the pie or tart.

- Chill the crust. Whether you are going to bake the crust blind (that is, bake it without filling, lined with foil or parchment and filled with pie weights or beans) or with a filling, give it a rest in the refrigerator. It's had a tough workout during the rolling and the gluten needs another chance to relax.

Choux Paste

Makes enough dough for about 60 small puffs or éclairs ■ Like soufflés, popovers, and pita breads, choux paste is one of the miracles of the kitchen. You spoon an ordinary-looking batter onto a baking sheet and minutes later you've got a puffed pastry that appears to be threatening flight. This is the stuff of cream puffs, éclairs, profiteroles, and dreams.

Choux paste (*choux* sounds like "shoe" and means "cabbage" in French) has been around since the sixteenth century and is a must-know dough and a classic among pâtissiers of note. It is a wonderful dough, which would be used more often today if caterers hadn't made pâte à choux swans a cliché.

The dough is unusual in that it is twice-cooked: The mixture is mixed and heated on the stove top and then baked. And it is versatile, as much at home nestling savory mixtures as sweet ones. The ideal choux paste pastry has a light, very tender crust and an almost completely hollow interior, made for filling with anything from ice cream to a rich seafood stew. Once you've mastered the technique, get fanciful and try the savory puffs (page 432), the chocolate beignets (page 407), or the profiteroles (page 411)—and variations of your own.

Pointers for Puffs

- The liquid must be heated to a full boil, meaning there are bubbles all over the pot, not just skirting the edges.

- Add the flour all at once and stir madly until every last speck of flour is incorporated, then keep cooking and stirring some more—it's this last bit of cooking that will take the raw taste out of the flour; you'll know you're ready to quit when the dough forms a ball around your wooden spoon and the bottom of the pan is covered with a light crust.

- Don't hesitate—add the eggs to the dough as soon as it comes off the stove and is still very hot.

- Beat the eggs in thoroughly with a wooden spoon, spatula, or the paddle attachment of a mixer; don't use a whisk—it will beat in unwanted air.

- Stop mixing when you still have one egg left to add and inspect the dough. Depending on the condition of the flour, the room, or the moods of the pastry gods, the dough may or may not need the last egg. The dough is finished when you lift the paddle or spoon and it pulls up some dough that then detaches and forms a slowly bending peak—if you don't get a peak, add another egg. And relax—even if you can't decide what to do, and use the maximum number of eggs, you'll still end up with a superior puff.

- Use the choux paste while it is still warm. Choux paste cannot be kept.

- Unfilled baked pastries can be well wrapped and frozen for a few weeks.

Pull up some dough. When finished, it should detach and form a slowly bending peak.

continued

This recipe produces a pastry with finesse. The crust of the choux is delicate—not in the least tough, a problem with lesser recipes—and the interior is soft, eggy, and almost custardy—in other words, perfect.

¹⁄₂ cup whole milk

¹⁄₂ cup water

7 tablespoons unsalted butter, cut into 7 pieces

1 tablespoon sugar

1 teaspoon salt

1¹⁄₂ cups all-purpose flour

5 to 6 large eggs, at room temperature

1 large egg beaten with 1 teaspoon cold water, for egg wash

Put the milk, water, butter, sugar, and salt into a 2-quart saucepan and bring to a full boil over medium heat, stirring frequently with a wooden spoon. At this point, the butter should be fully melted. Still stirring, add the flour all at once, and stir energetically and without stop until the flour is thoroughly incorporated. Then continue to cook and stir for another 30 to 45 seconds, or until the dough forms a ball and a light crust is visible on the bottom of the pan.

Remove the pan from the heat and scrape the paste into a medium bowl. Immediately, while the dough is still hot, beat in the eggs one at a time, stirring vigorously with a wooden spoon or spatula to incorporate each egg before adding the next. The first couple of eggs are the hardest to mix in, but as the mixture loosens, it softens, smoothes, and becomes easier to blend. (If you want, you can beat the eggs in with a mixer—hand-held, or standing with the paddle attachment—just keep the speed low and take care not to beat too much air into the dough.)

To pipe choux paste into eclairs, see page 433.

After you've incorporated 5 eggs, take a good look at the mixture—it might not need the last egg. You'll know the dough is perfect when, as you lift the wooden spoon, the spoon pulls up some of the dough that then detaches and forms a slowly bending peak. If the dough's too thick and doesn't peak, add the last egg.

The dough is now ready to be used in any recipe calling for choux paste. In fact, it must be used now, while it is still warm.

Contributing Baker **NORMAN LOVE**

Meringue

Makes enough meringue for about 5 dozen cookies ■ Master meringue—an easy feat—and everything you've ever wanted to know about airy whipped egg whites will be revealed. With a batch of meringue, you're ready to bake cookies (page 311), shape shells to fill with mousses and creams (page 395), stack a napoleon (page 393), top a pie (page 403), construct an elegant Viennese torte (page 286), whip up a chiffon cake (see page 241 for one version), or make a light buttercream (page 445).

Taking the Mystique Out of Meringue

- Separate eggs when they're cold—that's when the yolks and whites divide most easily—but whip the whites after they've been at room temperature for at least 5 to 10 minutes—that's when they'll puff most prodigiously.

- Always separate eggs one at a time: Drop the white into a small bowl so you can inspect it for any traces of yolk—if it's fine, pour it into the mixing bowl; if there's a speck of yolk, scoop it out or, to be cautious, save the egg for another use.

- Make sure the mixing bowl and whisk are impeccably clean, dry, and free of grease—if you want to be super-sure it's grease-free, rub your mixing bowl with white vinegar and then dry it thoroughly before you beat the egg whites.

- Use a heavy-duty mixer fitted with the whisk attachment, or a hand-held mixer, to get the most volume out of whites; if you're whipping by hand, use a whisk and copper bowl—the chemical reaction between the copper and the whites works to increase the amount of air you can beat into the whites.

- Add a pinch of salt or cream of tartar to stabilize the whites.

- Whip the whites to medium-soft peaks before adding the sugar.

- Don't whip your whites past the point of gloss—properly whipped whites are firm and shiny; overly whipped whites separate into small clumps.

- Use meringue immediately—if you need to leave it for a few minutes, keep the mixer going on low speed.

- Bake meringues at a temperature of between 175°F and 200°F until they are dry and crispy and can be lifted off the parchment paper without effort. Keep an eye on them—they shouldn't color.

- Don't even think about baking meringues on a humid day—they'll be as sticky as the weather.

continued

Here is a recipe for the basic egg white and sugar mixture on which dozens of creations depend.

4 large egg whites
Pinch of salt
1 cup sugar

Perfectly beaten
meringue holds
a firm peak.

Put the egg whites and salt in the bowl of a mixer fitted with the whisk attachment (or work with a hand-held mixer). Starting on the highest speed, beat the whites for about 3 minutes, until they increase in volume and form medium-soft peaks that hold their shape. With the mixer running, gradually add ¾ cup of the sugar and continue to beat on high speed for 5 minutes, at which point the peaks will be stiff. Add the remaining ¼ cup sugar and beat 2 to 3 minutes more. When the meringue is perfectly beaten, the whites will be firm and shiny. When you remove the bowl from the mixer, dip the whisk attachment into the meringue and lift it straight up—the meringue that adheres to the whisk should hold a firm peak if you turn the whisk upside down.

The meringue is now ready to pipe, swirl onto a pie, or fold into a batter and bake.

Three Types of Meringue

Plain: egg whites beaten with sugar, plain and simple; an uncooked meringue that is the least stable but easiest to make member of the meringue gang

Cooked: the egg whites and sugar are heated and then whipped to peaks; a more stable meringue, often used for buttercream, baked Alaska, or meringue pies

Italian: the egg whites are whipped with a sugar syrup that has been cooked to the soft-ball stage; the most stable meringue and the one used to make frozen desserts and soufflés

Contributing Baker **CHARLOTTE AKOTO**

Perfect Génoise

Makes enough batter for one 8-inch round cake ▪ The génoise is to the French baker what the sponge cake is to the American baker: a vital basic cake and a building block for fanciful confections. Sturdy, firm, adaptable, and amenable to almost any flavoring, the génoise is the first cake a French pâtissier learns to make, and the one he'll make most often in his career. It is drier than most American cakes and, for this reason, not every American's favorite, but its dryness is considered an asset by the French, who soak their génoises with sugar and liqueur syrups of every conceivable savor.

For those who don't know the cake, the process of making a génoise can seem intimidating. It shouldn't. It may look as if disaster will strike at every turn, but it rarely does because, at heart, the génoise is a very well behaved cake. Follow the directions and it will do just what it's supposed to do—even when you think it won't.

The génoise is worth mastering, because from it you can make gorgeous petits fours like miniature squares (page 268), rounds (page 271), and swirls (page 275), or a sleek French Strawberry Cake (page 273) and a showstopping Chocolate Ruffle Cake (page 263).

2 tablespoons unsalted butter, melted

1 cup sifted cake flour

½ cup sugar

⅛ teaspoon salt

4 large eggs, at room temperature

1 teaspoon pure vanilla extract

Pour the melted butter into a 1-quart bowl; reserve.

Return the sifted flour to the sifter or sieve and add 1 tablespoon of the sugar and the salt; sift onto a piece of waxed paper and set aside.

Put the eggs and the remaining sugar into the bowl of a heavy-duty mixer (or work with a hand-held mixer). Holding the whisk attachment from the mixer in your hand, beat the mixture to blend the ingredients. With the bowl and whisk attachment in place, whip the mixture on medium speed until it is airy, pale, and tripled in volume, like softly whipped cream, 4 to 5 minutes. You'll know that the eggs are properly whipped when you lift the whisk and the mixture falls back into the bowl in a ribbon that rests on the surface for about 10 seconds. If the ribbon immediately sinks into the mixture, continue whipping for a few more minutes. Pour in the vanilla extract during the last moments of whipping.

Forming "the ribbon."

continued

Top: Stop folding as soon as the last speck of flour has disappeared. *Bottom:* Pour the batter in a prepared pan and bake.

Detach the bowl from the mixer. Sprinkle about one third of the sifted flour mixture over the batter. Fold in the flour with a rubber spatula, stopping as soon as the flour is incorporated. Fold in the rest of the flour in 2 more additions.

Gently spoon about 1 cup of the batter into the bowl with the melted butter and fold the butter in with the rubber spatula. Fold this mixture into the batter in the mixer bowl. (This is the point at which the batter is at its most fragile, so fold gingerly.)

The batter should be poured into a prepared pan and baked immediately.

The Whys and Hows of Génoise

A génoise is a whole egg sponge cake. That is, it gets its lift not from chemical leavening or beaten egg whites, but from the air retained in a whole egg and sugar mixture that is beaten until it has tripled in volume.

Classically, the eggs and sugar are heated before they are beaten, an elegant method that is used to make the génoise in the magnificent Chocolate Ruffle Cake (page 225). Here, the technique departs from tradition—room-temperature eggs are beaten with sugar until they form the requisite ribbon. For the cakes made from this batter, as well as the sturdier batters for ladyfinger and sheet génoise (pages 41 and 42), this technique produces what the cake's name promises, perfect results.

Once the eggs have been beaten to triple their volume, a breathtaking sight to anyone with a passion for baking, their decline—and the baker's trepidation—begins. To this whipped cream–like concoction are added flour and salt. No matter how gently you fold in these dry ingredients, you're going to deflate the eggs and sugar. Don't worry—this deflation is built into the génoise equation. Work as delicately as you can and stop when the last speck of flour has disappeared—don't go any further.

Certainly, don't despair that you've deflated the mass—you're going to deflate it even further with the addition of melted butter. The easiest way to incorporate the heavy melted butter is to remove some of the batter and blend it with the butter, then fold the lightened butter back into the remaining batter. This is the most delicate operation you have to perform, but it's well within the reach of anyone who knows how to fold in ingredients. Most génoises withstand this operation very nicely. Even if they come out of the oven a little worse for the wear, they get spruced up with a splash of soaking syrup and a gloss of jam or icing, so relax. Make a few génoises in succession—the best training you can get—and you'll find them as easy to make as gingersnaps.

Contributing Baker **FLO BRAKER**

Ladyfinger Génoise

Makes enough batter for 6 dozen ladyfingers, 24 large madeleines, or 1 recipe petits fours ▪ The génoise is an inherently sturdy cake, but this génoise is even sturdier than the classic—it has a little more flour, giving it the body it needs to be piped into ladyfingers that will retain their shape, and additional egg yolks for moisture and even more structure. No matter that the proportions are different, the technique for making the batter is the same as that for Perfect Génoise (page 39).

Use this batter to make ladyfingers and madeleines (page 333) and the miniature pastries on pages 268 to 272.

> 3 tablespoons unsalted butter, melted
>
> 1¼ cups sifted cake flour
>
> ⅔ cup sugar
>
> ⅛ teaspoon salt
>
> 2 large eggs, at room temperature
>
> 4 large egg yolks, at room temperature
>
> 1 teaspoon pure vanilla extract

Pour the melted butter into a 1-quart bowl; reserve.

Put the sifted flour, 1 tablespoon of the sugar, and the salt into a sifter or sieve; sift onto a piece of waxed paper and set aside.

Put the eggs, yolks, and 1 tablespoon of the sugar into the bowl of a heavy-duty mixer (or work with a hand-held mixer). Holding the whisk attachment from the mixer in your hand, beat the mixture just to combine. Add the remaining sugar and whisk by hand to mix. With the bowl and whisk attachment in place, whip the mixture on medium speed until it is airy, pale, and tripled in volume, like softly whipped cream, 4 to 5 minutes. You'll know that the eggs are properly whipped when you lift the whisk and the mixture falls back into the bowl in a ribbon that rests on the surface for about 10 seconds. If the ribbon immediately sinks into the mixture, continue whipping for a few more minutes. Pour in the vanilla extract during the last moments of whipping.

For how to pipe ladyfingers, see page 333.

Detach the bowl from the mixer. Sprinkle about one third of the flour mixture over the batter. Fold in the flour with a rubber spatula, stopping as soon as the flour is incorporated. Fold in the rest of the flour in 2 more additions.

Gently spoon about 1 cup of the batter into the bowl with the melted butter and fold the butter in with the rubber spatula. Fold this mixture into the batter in the mixer bowl. (This is the point at which the batter is at its most fragile, so fold gingerly.)

The batter is now ready to be used and, in fact, must be baked immediately.

Contributing Baker **FLO BRAKER**

Sheet Génoise

Makes enough batter for one 10- by 15½- by ½-inch sheet ■ This is the most pliable génoise, a cake that can be made in a very thin sheet and either cut into strips to form multilayered cakes or spread with filling and rolled up jelly-roll style, as is done for the lovely little Raspberry Swirls (page 275).

1 tablespoon unsalted butter, melted

½ cup plus 1 tablespoon sifted cake flour

½ cup plus 1 tablespoon sugar

⅛ teaspoon salt

3 large eggs, at room temperature

2 large egg yolks, at room temperature

1 teaspoon pure vanilla extract

Pour the melted butter into a 1-quart bowl; set aside.

Put the flour, 1 tablespoon of the sugar, and the salt into a sieve and sift the ingredients onto a piece of waxed paper; set aside.

Put the eggs, yolks, and the remaining sugar into the bowl of a heavy-duty mixer (or work with a hand-held mixer). Holding the whisk attachment from the mixer in your hand, beat the mixture to blend the ingredients. With the bowl and whisk attachment in place, whip the mixture on medium speed until it is airy, pale, and tripled in volume, like softly whipped cream, 4 to 5 minutes. You'll know that the eggs are properly whipped when you lift the whisk and the mixture falls back into the bowl in a ribbon that rests on the surface for about 10 seconds. If the ribbon immediately sinks into the mixture, continue whipping for a few more minutes. Pour in the vanilla extract during the last moments of whipping.

Mixing batter into the melted butter makes it easier to incorporate.

Detach the bowl from the mixer. Sprinkle about one third of the sifted flour mixture over the batter. Fold in the flour with a rubber spatula, stopping as soon as the flour is incorporated. Fold in the rest of the flour in 2 more additions.

Gently spoon about 1 cup of the batter into the bowl with the melted butter and fold it in with the rubber spatula. Fold this mixture into the batter. (This is the point at which the batter is at its most fragile, so fold gingerly.)

The batter is now ready to be used and, in fact, must be baked immediately.

Contributing Baker **FLO BRAKER**

Brioche

Makes about 2¼ pounds dough ■ Brioche is an elegant yeasted dough, a cross between bread and pastry. It is rich with butter and eggs, just a little sweet, pullable—a gentle tug, and the bread stretches in long, lacy strands—and fine-textured, the result of being beaten for close to half an hour.

There is nothing difficult about making this perfect brioche, but you do need time and a heavy-duty mixer. Preparing this brioche will familiarize you with the texture and mixing pattern of other yeast doughs that include butter: Babas (page 413) and their sister, Savarin (page 416), Cranberry-Walnut Pumpkin Loaves (page 108), White Loaves (page 81), and Fruit Focaccia (page 196)—all of which come together like standard bread doughs, fall apart with the addition of butter (a sight that strikes panic into the hearts of first-timers), and come together once again.

Of course, you can use brioche to make the traditional topknotted têtes in fluted molds (page 188) or soft, golden loaves (page 189), which slice beautifully for breakfast toast or sandwiches and, when just past peak, make sublime French toast or Twice-Baked Brioche (page 198). But it is also the base of such glorious creations as plump Pecan Sticky Buns (page 190), custardy crème fraîche–topped Brioche Tart (page 386), and Savory Brioche Pockets (page 421), filled with mashed potatoes, goat cheese, and asparagus tips.

In this version, the brioche is made with a sponge, which gives the yeast a leisurely proofing period and deep flavor. You'll notice that the sponge instructions call for adding the dry yeast without a presoak to dissolve it. This is an unusual technique, one more commonly associated with the use of fresh yeast. If you have your doubts—have a bite.

THE SPONGE

- **⅓ cup warm whole milk (100°F to 110°F)**
- **2¼ teaspoons active dry yeast**
- **1 large egg**
- **2 cups unbleached all-purpose flour**

The flour coating erupts.

Put the milk, yeast, egg, and 1 cup of the flour in the bowl of a heavy-duty mixer. Mix the ingredients together with a rubber spatula, mixing just until everything is blended. Sprinkle over the remaining cup of flour to cover the sponge.

Rest Set the sponge aside to rest uncovered for 30 to 40 minutes. After this resting time, the flour coating will crack, your indication that everything is moving along properly.

continued

THE DOUGH

⅓ cup sugar

1 teaspoon kosher salt

4 large eggs, lightly beaten

1½ cups (approximately) unbleached all-purpose flour

1½ sticks (6 ounces) unsalted butter, at room temperature

Top: The dough comes together, wrapping itself around the hook. *Bottom:* But once you add the butter, the dough falls apart.

Add the sugar, salt, eggs, and 1 cup of the flour to the sponge. Set the bowl into the mixer, attach the dough hook, and mix on low speed for a minute or two, just until the ingredients look as if they're about to come together. Still mixing, sprinkle in ½ cup more flour. When the flour is incorporated, increase the mixer speed to medium and beat for about 15 minutes, stopping to scrape down the hook and bowl as needed. During this mixing period, the dough should come together, wrap itself around the hook, and slap the sides of the bowl. If, after 7 to 10 minutes, you don't have a cohesive, slapping dough, add up to 3 tablespoons more flour. Continue to beat, giving the dough a full 15 minutes in the mixer—don't skimp on the time; this is what will give the brioche its distinctive texture.

Warning Be warned—your mixer will become extremely hot. Most heavy-duty mixers designed for making bread can handle this long beating, although if you plan to make successive batches of dough, you'll have to let your machine cool down completely between batches. If you have questions about your mixer's capacity in this regard, call the manufacturer before you start.

Incorporating the Butter In order to incorporate the butter into the dough, you must work the butter until it is the same consistency as the dough. You can bash the butter into submission with a rolling pin or give it kinder and gentler handling by using a dough scraper to smear it bit by bit across a smooth work surface. When it's ready, the butter will be smooth, soft, and still cool—not warm, oily, or greasy.

With the mixer on medium-low, add the butter a few tablespoons at a time. This is the point at which you'll think you've made a huge mistake, because the dough that you worked so hard to make smooth will fall apart—carry on. When all of the butter has been added, raise the mixer speed to medium-high for a minute, then reduce the speed to medium and beat the dough for about 5 minutes, or until you once again hear the dough slapping against the sides of the bowl. Clean the sides of the bowl frequently as you work; if it looks as though the dough is not coming together after 2 to 3 minutes, add up to 1 tablespoon more flour. When you're finished, the dough should still feel somewhat cool. It will be soft and still sticky and may cling slightly to the sides and bottom of the bowl.

First Rise Transfer the dough to a very large buttered bowl, cover tightly with plastic wrap, and let it rise at room temperature until doubled in bulk, 2 to 2½ hours.

Second Rise and Chilling Deflate the dough by placing your fingers under it, lifting a section of dough, and then letting it fall back into the bowl. Work your way around the circumference of the dough, lifting and releasing. Cover the bowl tightly with plastic wrap and refrigerate the dough overnight, or for at least 4 to 6 hours, during which time it will continue to rise and may double in size again.

After this long chill, the dough is ready to use in any brioche recipe.

Storing If you are not going to use the dough after the second rise, deflate it, wrap it airtight, and store it in the freezer. The dough can remain frozen for up to 1 month. Thaw the dough, still wrapped, in the refrigerator overnight and use it directly from the refrigerator.

Working with Brioche and Other Egg-and-Butter-Rich Doughs

- Mix, mix, and then mix some more. Once all of the ingredients except the butter have been added, the dough must be beaten for a long time—sometimes as long as 25 minutes—to develop its fine texture.

- Listen for the slapping sound: The dough should wrap itself around the dough hook and visually and audibly slap the sides of the bowl. If the dough doesn't come together, add a few sprinkles of flour and continue to beat.

- Keep the butter smooth and cool. The butter and the dough it goes into should have a similar consistency—soft, smooth, and still cool (never oily). To get the butter to the right consistency, beat it with a rolling pin or smear it in pieces across a work surface.

- Add the butter bit by bit. The butter should go into the dough a few tablespoonfuls at a time while you mix at medium-low speed. Don't panic when your beautiful dough breaks up with the first few additions of butter—press on. The dough will come together and once again make that satisfying slapping sound (music to a baker's ears).

Contributing Baker **NANCY SILVERTON**

Puff Pastry

Makes 2½ pounds dough ■ Puff pastry is called *mille feuilles,* or "a thousand leaves" in French, but that's an exaggeration. In fact, there are only 944 layers of pastry, separated by 943 layers of butter, but no matter. This is still the queen of all pastries, the one that, once mastered, entitles you to whatever bragging rights you wish to claim.

What you learn making puff pastry also will apply to making croissants and Danish pastry. Although the doughs for croissants and Danish pastries are made with yeast, they are members of the roll-and-fold, or laminate, family of pastries—cut the dough after it's been given all its rolls, folds, and turns and you'll see the layers of dough and butter looking as though they've been pasted or laminated to one another.

While croissants and Danish pastries get extra lift from the inclusion of yeast, this pastry gets its puff power from the butter. Don't even think of using anything but butter—you won't get the full puff, and you'll never get the flavor. Cold, the butter holds a space that will be filled with air when it melts, and, of course, when it melts, the water in the butter turns to steam, pushing the layers of dough ever upward. This is the reason why how thinly and how evenly you roll the dough makes a big difference. To enable you to get thin, even layers, the butter and dough must be of similar consistencies. Not to put too poetic a point on it, they must move as one.

The way to keep any of the roll-and-fold doughs in good shape is to refrigerate them at the first sign of any problem. Soft dough, dough that sticks to the work surface, and/or butter peeping through the layers are the common, and quickly remedied, problems of laminates.

This puff pastry is one of the simplest ever developed. Unlike many traditional puff pastries, this one does not include butter in the initial dough. (Of course, as for all puff pastry, butter will be added during the subsequent rolling and folding.) The dough is made in a large food processor and, because it is butterless, it is unusually easy to roll. Since you'll be rolling a lot, it's nice to know that your effort will be rewarded with pastry that puffs so high you'll have to sit on it to keep it down.

With this dough, make glistening apricot pastries (page 192) or a large, rustic, savory tourte (page 423) layered with roasted peppers, ham, cheese, and herbed scrambled eggs. And with the scraps, you can fry Parmesan Puffs (page 427); create the Sunday supper of Alsace, a caramelized onion tart (page 426); and make pizzettes (page 428), bite-sized tartlets topped with whatever you have on hand, and myriad tidbits, sweet and savory, limited more by your pantry than your pastry prowess.

Simple Puff Pastry Dos and Don'ts

- Chill early and often—keep the pastry cold and you'll keep the layers.

- Be neat—fold the dough evenly.

- Stay away from the ends—don't roll over the ends of the pastry or you'll glue the layers together.

- Take your time—don't skimp on the number of turns or the chilling periods.

2½ cups unbleached all-purpose flour
1¼ cups cake flour
1 tablespoon salt
1¼ cups ice water
4 sticks (1 pound) very cold unsalted butter

Mixing the Dough Check the capacity of your food processor before you start. If it cannot hold the full quantity of ingredients, make the dough in two batches and combine them.

Put the all-purpose flour, cake flour, and salt in the work bowl of a food processor fitted with the metal blade and pulse a couple of times just to mix. Add the water all at once, pulsing until the dough forms a ball on the blade. The dough will be very moist and pliable and will hold together when squeezed between your fingers. (Actually, it will feel like Play-Doh.)

Remove the dough from the machine, form it into a ball, and, with a small sharp knife, slash the top in a tic-tac-toe pattern. Wrap the dough in a damp towel and refrigerate for about 5 minutes.

Meanwhile, place the butter between 2 sheets of plastic wrap and beat it with a rolling pin until it flattens into a square that's about 1 inch thick. Take care that the butter remains cool and firm; if it has softened or become oily, chill it before continuing.

Incorporating the Butter Unwrap the dough and place it on a work surface dusted with all-purpose flour. (A cool piece of marble is the ideal surface for puff pastry.) With your rolling pin (preferably a French rolling pin without handles), press on the dough to flatten it and then roll it into a 10-inch square. Keep the top and bottom of the dough well floured to prevent sticking and lift the dough and move it around frequently. Starting from the center of the square, roll out over each corner to create a thick center pad with "ears," or flaps.

Place the cold butter in the middle of the dough and fold the ears over the butter, stretching them as needed so that they overlap slightly and encase the butter completely. (If you have to stretch the dough, stretch it from all over—don't just pull the ends.) You should now have a package that is about 8 inches square.

continued

To make great puff pastry, it is important to keep the dough cold at all times. There are specified times for chilling the dough, but if your room is warm, or you work slowly, or you find that for no particular reason the butter starts to ooze out of the pastry, cover the dough with plastic wrap and refrigerate it. You can stop at any point in the process and continue at your convenience or when the dough is properly chilled.

Making the Turns Gently but firmly press the rolling pin against the top and bottom edges of the square (this will help to keep it square). Then, keeping the work surface and the top of the dough well floured to prevent sticking, roll the dough into a rectangle that is three times as long as the square you started with, about 24 inches. (Don't worry about the width of the rectangle; if you get the 24 inches, everything else will work itself out.) With this first roll, it is particularly important that the butter be rolled evenly along the length and width of the rectangle; check when you start rolling that the butter is moving along well, and roll a bit harder or more evenly, if necessary, to get a smooth, even dough-butter sandwich. With a pastry brush, brush off the excess flour from the top of the dough, and fold the rectangle up from the bottom and down from the top in thirds, like a business letter, brushing off the excess flour. You have completed one turn.

Rotate the dough so that the closed fold is to your left, like the spine of a book. Repeat the rolling and folding process, rolling the dough to a length of 24 inches and then folding it in thirds. This is the second turn.

Chilling the Dough If the dough is still cool and no butter is oozing out, you can give the dough another two turns now. If the condition of the dough is iffy, wrap it in plastic wrap and refrigerate it for at least 30 minutes. Each time you refrigerate the dough, mark the number of turns you've completed by indenting the dough with your fingertips. It is best to refrigerate the dough for 30 to 60 minutes between each set of two turns.

The total number of turns needed is six. (*When a recipe in this book calls for puff pastry, it means pastry that has been given the full six turns.*) If you prefer, you can give the dough just four turns now, chill it overnight, and do the last two turns the next day. Puff pastry is extremely flexible in this regard. However, no matter how you arrange the schedule, you should plan to chill the dough for at least an hour before cutting or shaping it.

Note on Freezing Puff Pastry

Although puff pastry can be chilled or frozen at any stage, it is really most convenient to give the puff pastry a full six turns, roll it out into a flat sheet, chill it on a parchment-lined baking sheet, and then, when it is cold, wrap it for the freezer. Rolling the dough into a sheet means it will defrost quickly and won't have to be rolled much before you cut and bake it. Thaw the dough, still wrapped, in the refrigerator.

Contributing Baker **MICHEL RICHARD**

Making Puff Pastry

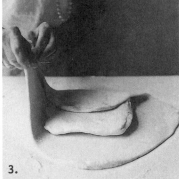

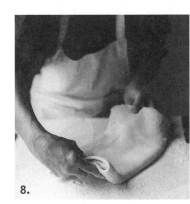
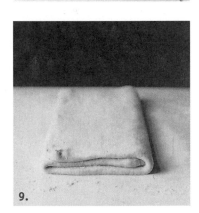

1. The dough is ready to work.
2. Press the dough to flatten, then roll it to a thickness equal to the butter square.
3. Each corner becomes a flap that is folded over the butter square.
4. Let the flaps overlap to encase the butter completely.
5. The butter moves as one with the dough, as the square is gently rolled to a rectangle three times its original length.
6. Fold the rectangle into thirds like a business letter.
7. The first turn is complete.
8. Rotate the dough and begin the next round of rolling, folding, and turning.
9. After six turns are completed, the finished puff pastry has 994 layers of dough and 993 of butter.

Danish Pastry

Makes 2 pounds dough ■ Traditionally, Danish pastry, a slightly sweet, very rich yeast dough, is made the way croissant dough or its unyeasted cousin, puff pastry, is made. That is, you make a dough that acts as a wrapper for a block of butter, then you roll and fold the dough several times to create layers. Here, in a quick method, the butter is cut into the dough in the food processor, making it easier and faster to work; the yeast and liquid are mixed into the dough and then the chilled dough is given the traditional rolls and folds. (Turn to page 48 for a lesson on rolling and folding.) Don't think you're cheating by taking the fast track—this is the way it's done these days all over Denmark, where they know great Danish when they taste it.

This is the recipe for the basic dough from which many pastries can be made. You'll find six different Danish shapes and five different fillings on pages 200 to 206.

¼ cup warm water (105°F to 115°F)

2½ teaspoons active dry yeast

½ cup milk, at room temperature

1 large egg, at room temperature

¼ cup sugar

1 teaspoon salt

2½ cups unbleached all-purpose flour

2 sticks (8 ounces) cold unsalted butter

Mixing the Dough Pour the water into a large bowl, sprinkle over the yeast, and let it soften for a minute. Add the milk, egg, sugar, and salt and whisk to mix; set aside.

Put the flour in the work bowl of a food processor fitted with the metal blade. Cut the butter into ¼-inch-thick slices and drop them onto the flour. Pulse 8 to 10 times, until the butter is cut into pieces that are about ½ inch in diameter. Don't overdo this—the pieces must not be smaller than ½ inch.

Empty the contents of the food processor into the bowl with the yeast and, working with a rubber spatula, very gently turn the mixture over, scraping the bowl as needed, just until the dry ingredients are moistened. Again, don't be too energetic—the butter must remain in discrete pieces so that you will produce a flaky pastry, not a bread or cookie dough.

Chilling the Dough Cover the bowl with plastic wrap and refrigerate the dough overnight (or for up to 4 days, if that better suits your schedule).

Rolling and Folding Lightly flour a work surface (a cool surface, such as marble, is ideal), turn the dough out onto it, and dust the dough lightly with flour. Using the palms of your hands, pat the dough into a rough square. Then roll it into a square about 16 inches on a side. (A French rolling pin, one without handles, is best here.) Fold the dough in thirds, like a business letter, and turn it so that the closed fold is to your left, like the spine of a book. (If at any time the dough gets too soft to roll, just cover it with plastic wrap and pop it into the refrigerator for a quick chill.)

Roll the dough out again, this time into a long narrow rectangle, about 10 inches wide by 24 inches long. Fold the rectangle in thirds again, turn it so the closed fold is to your left, and roll it into a 20-inch square. Fold the square in thirds, like a business letter, so that you have a rectangle, turning it so that the closed fold is to your left, and, once more, roll the dough into a long narrow rectangle, 10 inches wide by 24 inches long. Fold in thirds again, wrap the dough well in plastic, and chill it for at least 30 minutes, or for as long as 2 days. (Depending on what you plan to do with the dough, you might want to divide it in half now.)

The dough is now ready to be shaped, filled, and baked, following the recipes of your choice.

Storing The dough can be kept covered in the refrigerator for 4 days or wrapped airtight and frozen for 1 month; thaw overnight, still wrapped, in the refrigerator.

Contributing Baker **BEATRICE OJAKANGAS**

Croissant Dough

Makes enough dough for 20 to 24 croissants ■ Unless you've had a homemade croissant handcrafted by a patient, gifted baker, you may not recognize the real thing from the overblown confection you're accustomed to—the difference is that dramatic. Most croissants from bakeries and restaurants are more like cake than bread, more sweet than buttery, more shapely than flavorful. The real thing, a concoction that falls in that delicious middle ground between bread and pastry, is made with butter, and lots of it. It is light but not airy, a yeasted puff pastry that is one of the great glories of French bakers, although France is not where it was created. The croissant, or crescent, was invented to celebrate the Austrians' turning back of a Turkish siege in 1686—the shape of the multilayered roll mirrors the crescent on the Ottoman flag.

These directions for making croissants are long and detailed enough so that first-timers can be successful, but this is a dough that takes practice to perfect. Get it right and you'll produce croissants of a quality rarely found in the United States and rapidly disappearing in France. Make a good croissant and you'll know why it has been celebrated for more than three hundred years.

THE DOUGH

1 ounce compressed (fresh) yeast

3³/₄ cups unbleached all-purpose flour

¹/₃ cup sugar

2 teaspoons salt

1 cup (approximately) whole milk

Put the yeast, flour, sugar, salt, and 1 cup milk into the bowl of a mixer fitted with a dough hook. With the machine on its lowest speed, mix for 1 to 2 minutes, until a soft, moist dough forms on the hook. If the dough is too dry, add more milk, 1 tablespoon at a time. In most cases, if the dough needs more liquid, it won't need more than about 3 tablespoons, but check carefully, as you want all of the flour to be moistened. Stop the mixer and look into the bowl: If the hook has not picked up all of the flour from the bottom of the bowl, add a few drops more milk.

Set the mixer to its highest speed and work the dough until it is smooth, elastic, no longer sticky, and close to the consistency of soft butter, about 4 minutes. To make certain that the ingredients are perfectly blended, you can remove the dough from the mixer after 3 minutes and then, with the mixer on high speed, return plum-sized pieces of the dough to the bowl. The pieces will remain separate for a short while, then come together, at which time the dough is ready.

Remove the dough from the mixer, wrap it in plastic, and put the packet in a plastic bag, leaving a little room for expansion. Keep the dough at room temperature for 30 minutes to give the gluten a chance to relax, then refrigerate the dough for 8 hours, or overnight.

THE BUTTER

> 4½ sticks (1 pound 2 ounces) cold unsalted butter, cut into ½-inch cubes
>
> 2 tablespoons unbleached all-purpose flour

Attach the paddle to your mixer and beat the butter and flour on the highest speed until smooth and the same consistency as the croissant dough, about 2 minutes. Reach into the bowl and poke around in the butter to make sure that it's evenly blended—if you find any lumps, just squeeze them between your fingers. Scrape the butter onto a large piece of plastic wrap and give it a few slaps to knock the air out of it. Mold it into an oval 5 to 6 inches long and 1 inch thick, wrap tightly, and refrigerate until needed. *At this point, the dough and the butter can be frozen; defrost overnight in the refrigerator before proceeding with the recipe.*

Incorporating the Butter Place the croissant dough on a generously floured large work surface (marble is ideal) and sprinkle the top of the dough lightly with flour. Using a long rolling pin, roll the dough into an oval approximately 10 inches wide and 17 inches long. Brush the excess flour from the dough. Center the oval of chilled butter across the oval of dough and fold the top and bottom of the dough over the butter to make a tidy package. Gently and evenly stretch the folded layers of dough out to the sides and press the edges down firmly with your fingertips to create a neatly sealed rectangle.

If you have a French rolling pin (one without handles), now's the time to use it. Hold one side of the dough steady with your hand and strike the other side gently but firmly with the rolling pin to distribute the butter evenly. As you hit the dough, you'll see the butter moving out into the crevices. Strike the other side of the dough in the same way. After pounding, you should have a 1-inch-thick rectangle about 14 inches long and 6 inches wide.

Keeping the work surface and the top of the dough well floured, roll out the dough. If this is your first time working with croissant dough, you might want to roll out the dough just a little to distribute the butter, put it on a baking sheet lined with flour-dusted parchment paper, cover it with plastic, and chill it for 1 to 2 hours; this way you won't risk having the dough go soft or the butter seep out. (Each time you wrap the dough, make sure it's well covered—even a little air will cause the dough to form an unwanted skin.) If you're experienced, feeling courageous, or have dough that is still well chilled, go on to make the first turn.

Rolling and Folding Roll the dough into a rectangle 24 to 26 inches long by 14 inches wide, with a long side facing you. (You may feel as if you're rolling the dough sideways—and you are.) Brush off the excess flour and, working from the left and right sides, fold the dough in thirds, as you would a brochure, so that you have a package that's about 8 inches wide by 14 inches long. Carefully transfer the dough to a parchment-lined baking sheet, mark the parchment "1 turn" so you'll know what you've done, cover the dough with plastic, and refrigerate for at least 2 hours. *You can freeze the dough after this or any other turn. Thaw overnight in the refrigerator before proceeding.*

The dough needs two more turns. For the second turn, place the dough so that a 14-inch side runs from left to right. (You've given the dough a quarter turn.) Making certain that the work surface is well floured at all times, roll the dough as you did before into a rectangle 24 to 26 inches long by 14 inches wide. (When doing the second and third turns, you may find that the dough has cracked a little—that's natural—it's a result of the yeast; don't worry, just flour the dough and work surface and keep going.) As you did before, fold the dough in thirds. Place it on the parchment, mark the paper "2 turns," cover the dough with plastic, and refrigerate for at least 2 hours.

For the third turn, again start with a 14-inch side running from your left to your right. Roll the dough into a rectangle 24 to 26 inches long by 14 inches wide. Fold the left and right sides of the dough into the center, leaving a little space in the center, and then fold one side over the other as though you were closing a book. This is the famous double turn, also known as "the wallet."

Chilling the Dough Brush off the flour, wrap the dough in plastic, and refrigerate for 2 hours.

At this point, the dough is ready to be rolled, cut, and shaped into croissants.

The final fold is like closing a wallet or a book. Align the edges before proceeding.

Storing The dough can be frozen for up to 1 month. Thaw overnight, still wrapped, in the refrigerator.

Contributing Baker **ESTHER McMANUS**

BREADS

Sliced toasted White Loaf PAGE 81

Clockwise from top: Whole Wheat Loaf   PAGE 83, Bagels   PAGE 87, Onion Bialys   PAGE 90, Challah   PAGE 93, and Pumpernickel Loaf   PAGE 95

Pain fendu–shaped Mixed-Starter Bread   **PAGE 117**

Leaf–Shaped Fougasse **PAGE 146**

Forming the "veins"

59

Pebble Bread   PAGE 152

Sandwich made with Eastern European Rye

Matzos PAGE 160

Epi-shaped Mixed-Starter Bread **PAGE 113**

Sandwich made with Focaccia PAGE 143

Pita sandwich **PAGE 154**

Savory Wheat Crackers PAGE 163

Bagel with poppy seeds PAGE 87

Daily Loaves

NOTHING TASTES BETTER than homemade bread. However convenient it is to buy bread, however fine your neighborhood bakery, you'll never find another loaf that compares to the one you take from the oven, its warmth and yeasty aroma filling the kitchen. The common, simple, everyday breads presented in this chapter prove this to you beyond any doubt. With their full flavor, utter freshness, and the satisfaction they give in the making, they are worth every effort they demand.

For those who are new to bread baking or wary of its apparent complexities, these are the breads to start with. Their straightforward techniques and often relatively quick results (make the White Loaf in the morning and slice it for lunch) offer fundamental lessons that apply to all bread baking. You'll learn how to bring yeast to life, guide its growth, and bake a loaf to golden doneness. Try New York baker Craig Kominiak's pan loaves and you'll experience the essentials, literally firsthand.

These recipes also provide delicious examples of breads that have emerged from different traditions. Cookbook author Beatrice Ojakangas's Swedish Limpa and Finnish Pulla, one loaf dark, the other pale, are, like so many Scandinavian breads, slightly sweet and softly scented with the spices of the north countries. Baking teacher Nick Malgieri's golden yellow Semolina Bread is an Italian classic. And Lauren Groveman's dark, mysteriously sweet pumpernickel, egg-rich challah, and big bagels dusted with seeds and salt come from Eastern Europe.

White Loaves

COLOR PHOTOGRAPH, PAGE 56

Makes two 1¾-pound loaves ■ These mountainous loaves bake to a generous four and a half inches high, providing a large-enough slice for the most Dagwoodian sandwich. This is a basic, have-it-on-hand-at-all-times white bread with a difference—it's got full, rounded flavor and a substantial texture; not your average sandwich loaf. And it makes great toast—the little bit of butter in the dough browns nicely under heat. Since the dough belongs to the direct-rise family, meaning there are no starters, sponges, or unusually long rest periods, you can mix a batch after breakfast and eat still-warm-from-the-oven bread for lunch.

2½ cups warm water (105°F to 115°F)

1 tablespoon active dry yeast

1 tablespoon sugar

7 cups (approximately) bread flour or unbleached all-purpose flour

1 tablespoon salt

½ stick (2 ounces) unsalted butter, at room temperature

Mixing and Kneading Pour ½ cup of the water into the bowl of a heavy-duty mixer, sprinkle in the yeast and sugar, and whisk to blend. Allow the mixture to rest until the yeast is creamy, about 5 minutes.

Working in the mixer with the dough hook in place, add the remaining 2 cups water and about 3½ cups flour to the yeast. Turn the mixer on and off a few times just to get the dough going without having the flour fly all over the counter and then, mixing on low speed, add 3½ cups more flour. Increase the mixer speed to medium and beat, stopping to scrape down the bowl and hook as needed, until the dough comes together. (If the dough does not come together, add a bit more flour, a tablespoon at a time.) Add the salt and continue to beat and knead at medium speed for about 10 minutes, until the dough is smooth and elastic. If you prefer, you can mix the dough in the machine for half that time and knead it by hand on a lightly floured surface for 8 to 10 minutes. When the dough is thoroughly mixed (return it to the mixer if necessary), add the butter, a tablespoon at a time, and beat until incorporated. Don't be disconcerted if your beautiful dough comes apart with the addition of butter—beating will bring it back together.

First Rise Turn the dough out onto a lightly floured work surface and shape it into a ball. Place it in a large buttered or oiled bowl (one that can hold double the amount of dough). Turn the dough around to cover its entire surface with butter or oil, cover the bowl tightly with plastic wrap, and let the dough rest at room temperature until it doubles in bulk, about 45 minutes to 1 hour.

continued

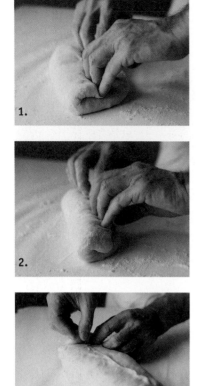

Shaping the Dough Butter two 8½- by 4½-inch loaf pans and set them aside.

Deflate the dough and turn it out onto a lightly floured work surface. Divide the dough in half and work with one piece at a time. Using the palms of your hands and fingertips, or a rolling pin, pat the dough into a large rectangle about 9 inches wide and 12 inches long, with a short side facing you. Starting at the top, fold the dough about two thirds of the way down the rectangle and then fold it again, so that the top edge meets the bottom edge. Seal the seam by pinching it. Turn the roll so that the seam is in the center of the roll, facing up, and turn the ends of the roll in just enough so that it will fit in a buttered loaf pan. Pinch the seams to seal, turn the loaf over so that the seams are on the bottom, and plump the loaf with your palms to get an even shape. Drop the loaf into the pan, seam side down, and repeat with the other piece of dough.

Second Rise Cover the loaves with oiled plastic wrap, and allow them to rise in a warm place (about 80°F) until they double in size again, growing over the tops of the pans, about 45 minutes.

While the loaves rise, center a rack in the oven and preheat the oven to 375°F.

Baking the Bread When the loaves are fully risen (poke your finger into the dough; the impression should remain), bake them for 35 to 45 minutes, or until they are honey-brown and an instant-read thermometer plunged into the center of the bread (turn a loaf out and plunge the thermometer through the bottom of the bread) measures 200°F. (If you like, 10 minutes or so before you think the loaves should come out, you can turn the loaves out of their pans and let them bake on the oven rack so they brown on the sides.) Remove the loaves from their pans as soon as they come from the oven and cool the breads on racks. These should not be cut until they are almost completely cool; just-warm is just right.

1. Press the dough into a rectangle with a width equal to the pan length. Fold the top third down and seal with your fingers.

2. Fold the dough over again and seal tightly.

3. Fold one end of the loaf in and pinch to form a neatly sealed package.

4. Fold in the other side.

Storing Once completely cool, the breads can be kept in a brown paper bag for a day or two. Once a loaf is sliced, turn it cut side down on the counter or a cutting board and cover with a kitchen towel. For longer storage, wrap the breads airtight and freeze for up to a month. Thaw, still wrapped, at room temperature.

Contributing Baker **CRAIG KOMINIAK**

Whole Wheat Loaves

COLOR PHOTOGRAPH, PAGE 57

Makes two 1¾-pound loaves ■ There's just enough honey and malt in this recipe to bring out the natural sweetness of the loaf's whole wheat flour. A tall crowned loaf with some chew and stretch in the crumb, this bread has the flavor and heft to stand up to strong cheeses and spicy cold cuts, making it first-class sandwich fare. Like the White Loaves (page 81), these are good loaves for bread-baking tyros: The techniques are basic, the rewards many.

2¼ cups warm water (105°F to 115°F)

1 tablespoon active dry yeast

¼ cup honey

3½ to 3⅔ cups bread flour or unbleached all-purpose flour

3 cups whole wheat flour

1 tablespoon canola oil

1 tablespoon malt extract

1 tablespoon salt *use a little less salt*

Mixing and Kneading Pour ½ cup of the water into the bowl of a heavy-duty mixer fitted with a dough hook and add the yeast and honey. Whisk to blend and allow the mixture to rest until the yeast is creamy, about 5 minutes.

Combine 3½ cups of the bread flour and the whole wheat flour and keep close at hand.

Working in the mixer with the dough hook in place, add the remaining 1¾ cups water, the oil, malt extract, and about half of the flour mixture to the yeast. Turn the mixer on and off a few times just to get the dough going without having the flour fly all over the counter and then, mixing on low speed, add the rest of the combined flours. Increase the mixer speed to medium and beat, stopping to scrape down the bowl and hook as needed, until the dough comes together. (If the dough does not come together, add up to 2 tablespoons more white flour.) Add the salt and continue to beat and knead at medium speed for about 10 minutes, until the dough is smooth and elastic. If you prefer, you can mix the dough in the machine for half that time and knead it by hand on a lightly floured surface for 8 to 10 minutes. As with many whole wheat doughs, this one will be a tad sticky even after proper and sufficient kneading.

First Rise Turn the dough out onto a lightly floured work surface and shape it into a ball. Place it in a large buttered or oiled bowl (one big enough to hold double the amount of dough). Turn the dough around to cover its entire surface with butter or oil, cover the bowl tightly with plastic wrap, and let the dough rest at room temperature until it doubles in bulk, about 1½ hours.

continued

Shaping the Dough Butter two 8½- by 4½-inch loaf pans and set them aside.

Deflate the dough and turn it out onto a lightly floured work surface. Divide the dough in half and, using the palms of your hands and fingertips, or a rolling pin, pat each half into a large rectangle about 9 inches wide and 12 inches long, with a short side facing you. Starting at the top, fold the dough about two thirds of the way down the rectangle, then fold again so that the top edge meets the bottom edge; seal the seam by pinching it. Turn each roll so that the seam is in the center of the roll, facing up, and turn the ends of each roll in just enough so that the rolls fit in the loaf pans. Pinch these seams to seal, turn the loaves over so that the seams are on the bottom, and plump the loaves with your palms to get an even shape.

Second Rise Drop the loaves into the buttered pans, seam side down, cover with oiled plastic wrap, and allow them to rise at room temperature until they double in size again, growing over the tops of the pans, about 1 hour.

While the breads rise, center a rack in the oven and preheat the oven to 375°F.

The plump shaped loaf is placed seam side down to rise in the loaf pan before baking.

Baking the Bread When the breads are fully risen (poke your finger into a bread; the impression should remain), bake for about 35 minutes, or until they are golden and an instant-read thermometer plunged into the center of the bread (turn a loaf out and plunge the thermometer through the bottom of the bread) measures 200°F. (If you like, 10 minutes or so before you think the loaves should come out, you can turn the loaves out of their pans and let them bake on the oven rack so they brown on the sides.) Remove the loaves from their pans as soon as they come from the oven and cool the breads on racks. These should not be cut until they are almost completely cool.

Storing Once completely cool, the breads can be kept in a brown paper bag for a day or two. Once a loaf is sliced, turn it cut side down on the counter or a cutting board and cover with a kitchen towel. For longer storage, wrap the breads airtight and freeze for up to a month. Thaw, still wrapped, at room temperature.

Contributing Baker **CRAIG KOMINIAK**

Buttermilk Bread in a Bread Machine

Makes 1 loaf or about 1 dozen rolls ■ An everyday bread that doesn't take a day to make. This is a basic bread-machine loaf made tender with buttermilk and sweet with maple syrup. Once you add the ingredients to the machine, you can go your merry way, or you can allow the dough to develop in the machine and then pull it out and shape it by hand. After the dough is made, the possibilities for shaping it are many: You can make a traditional loaf, rolls of any dimension and design, or long, twisty bread sticks. This is a malleable dough that's fun to form.

> 2½ **teaspoons active dry yeast, preferably SAF Instant (**not** rapid-rise)**
>
> 3 **tablespoons powdered buttermilk**
>
> 1 **teaspoon salt**
>
> 3 **cups (approximately) bread flour or unbleached all-purpose flour**
>
> 1 **tablespoon unsalted butter, at room temperature**
>
> 3 **tablespoons pure maple syrup**
>
> 1 **cup (approximately) room-temperature water**

Mixing and First Rise Be sure all the ingredients are at room temperature before putting them into the machine. Put the yeast, buttermilk, salt, 3 cups flour, butter, syrup, and 1 cup water into the bread machine, in that order (or in the order specified by your machine's manufacturer), and program the machine for "white bread," or the cycle on your machine for regular loaves. Press Start.

Look into the machine and check on your dough. If, after the first few minutes of kneading, the dough does not form a smooth, firm ball, add a few more tablespoons of water to the machine. If, on the other hand, the dough is sticky, sprinkle in a bit more flour. (Although this trick is not recommended by manufacturers, many bread machine mavens check their dough after 5 minutes in the machine by pulling out a piece and stretching it—it should be very smooth and elastic, an indication that the dough is developing properly.)

The dough can then be baked in the machine according to manufacturer's instructions or, if you want to shape the dough yourself, removed and baked in a conventional oven. If you do not want to bake the dough in the machine, set the machine for the "dough" cycle and remove the mixing container from the machine at the end of the final kneading cycle (or, if your machine does not have a "dough" cycle, at the end of the first rise). Cover the container with a cloth and allow the dough to rise at room temperature until doubled in bulk, about 45 minutes.

Butter a 9- by 5-inch loaf pan.

continued

Shaping and Second Rise When the dough has doubled, deflate it and turn it out onto a lightly floured work surface. Shape the bread into a loaf (see page 82 for shaping directions) and fit it into the buttered pan. Cover and let rise again until doubled, 40 to 60 minutes.

Meanwhile, preheat the oven to 425°F.

Baking the Bread Place the loaf in the oven, reduce the oven temperature to 375°F, and bake for 35 to 45 minutes, or until it is golden brown and an instant-read thermometer plunged into the center of the bread (turn the loaf out and plunge the thermometer through the bottom of the bread) measures 200°F. If you want a darker crust, remove the bread from the pan and let it bake directly on the oven rack for the last 10 minutes. Let the bread cool on a rack before serving.

Storing The bread and rolls can be kept, wrapped in plastic at room temperature for 2 days or frozen for up to 1 month. Thaw, still wrapped, at room temperature.

To Shape Sticks and Rolls

For Bread Sticks, pull off a piece of dough about the size of a Ping-Pong ball and, working on a lightly floured surface, roll it into a sausage. Press it down gently and then, holding it at each end, pull and twist the dough a few times to make a spiral bread stick of whatever length pleases you. Place on a parchment-lined baking pan, and continue shaping the rest of the dough. Allow the bread sticks to rise, covered, at room temperature for about 20 to 30 minutes, until doubled. If you want, brush the sticks with an egg glaze (beat 1 large egg with ½ cup heavy cream) and sprinkle with poppy or sesame seeds, or grated cheese. Bake in a preheated 425°F oven for 10 to 15 minutes, or until golden. Cool on a rack.

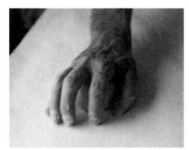

Tightly roll the dough against the work surface to form a ball.

For Cloverleaf Rolls, pull off a piece of dough about the size of a golf ball. Divide the piece into thirds and form each third into a tight ball by rolling it against the work surface. Place the 3 balls side by side in a buttered muffin cup. Repeat with remaining dough. Cover the muffin tin with a towel and allow the rolls to rise at room temperature until doubled in size, about 20 to 30 minutes. Brush with egg glaze and top with seeds if you want (see above). Bake in a preheated 425°F oven for about 15 minutes, or until golden. Cool on a rack.

For Knot Rolls, pull off pieces of dough about the size of Ping-Pong balls and roll them into sausages. Tie the sausages into knots and place them on a parchment-lined baking sheet. Cover the sheet lightly and let the rolls rise at room temperature for 20 to 30 minutes, until doubled. The knots can be brushed with egg glaze and sprinkled with seeds if desired (see above). Bake in a preheated 425°F oven for 15 minutes, or until golden. Cool on a rack.

Contributing Baker **LORA BRODY**

Bagels

COLOR PHOTOGRAPH, PAGE 78

Makes 10 large bagels ■ Like croissants, bagels have transcended their origins to become all-American. These are chubby bagels—boiled, then baked—with a cakey, open sponge; they are not heavy, stretchy, or chewy. They are made with high-gluten flour, the kind your local pizza maker uses. He might give you some, or you can order the flour by mail, but don't let not getting your hands on this stop you from bageling—you'll like what you get if you use bread flour or unbleached all-purpose flour.

Keep in mind that you can top your bagels with anything—one of the joys of making bagels at home—and you can bottom them too: Sprinkle the peel or baking sheet with any or all of your favorite toppings for around-the-bagel flavor.

THE BAGELS

2 tablespoons (approximately) unsalted butter, melted

2¼ teaspoons active dry yeast

2¼ cups tepid water (80°F to 90°F)

2 tablespoons (approximately) sugar

3 tablespoons solid vegetable shortening

1 tablespoon salt

1 to 2 teaspoons freshly ground black pepper (optional)

6 cups (approximately) high-gluten flour, bread flour, or unbleached all-purpose flour

Brush the inside of a large (about 8-quart) bowl with some of the melted butter; set aside. Reserve the remaining melted butter for coating the top of the dough.

Mixing and Kneading Whisk the yeast into ¼ cup of the tepid water. Add a pinch of sugar and let the mixture rest until the yeast has dissolved and is creamy.

Pour the remaining 2 cups water into a large bowl and add the shortening. Add the yeast mixture along with 2 tablespoons sugar, the salt, and the black pepper, if you're using it, and stir with a wooden spoon to mix.

Stirring vigorously with the wooden spoon, add the flour, ½ cup at a time, stopping when you have a soft, sticky dough that is difficult to stir. (You will probably use almost 6 cups of flour, but the dough will still be soft and sticky—and that's just the way it's supposed to be.) Turn the dough out onto a floured work surface and knead for 5 to 6 minutes, until it is smooth and elastic. Add additional flour as needed to keep the dough from sticking to your hands and the work surface.

continued

(To make the dough in a mixer, proof the yeast in ¼ cup of the warm water in the mixer's bowl. Fit the machine with the dough hook and add the remaining 2 cups water, the sugar, shortening, salt, and the pepper, if using it; mix on low to blend. With the machine still on low, gradually add 5½ to 6 cups of the flour, mixing for 2 to 3 minutes, or until the ingredients are blended. Increase the mixer speed to medium and knead for about 6 minutes, adding additional flour by the tablespoon until the dough is smooth and elastic. At this point, the dough may still be slightly sticky and it may not clean the sides and bottom of the bowl completely—that's OK.)

Rise Form the dough into a ball and transfer it to the buttered mixing bowl. Brush the top of the dough with a little melted butter, cover the bowl with buttered plastic wrap, and top with a kitchen towel. Let the dough rise at room temperature for about 1 hour, or until it doubles in bulk.

Chilling the Dough Deflate the dough, cover as before, and refrigerate for 4 hours, or, if it's more convenient, overnight. *At this point, the dough can be well wrapped and refrigerated for up to 2 days.*

When you're ready to make the bagels, position an oven rack in the lower third of the oven and preheat the oven to 500°F. If the bagels are to bake on a stone, preheat the baking stone too and generously dust a peel with cornmeal. If they will bake on baking sheets, brush the sheets with vegetable oil (or spray them) and dust them with cornmeal. For added flavor, use one or all of the suggested topping ingredients (see page 89) in combination with the cornmeal to dust the peel or the sheets. (To create steam in the oven, you'll be tossing ice cubes and water onto the oven floor. If you don't think your oven floor is up to this—it can be tricky with a gas oven—put a heavy skillet or roasting pan on the oven floor and preheat it as well.)

While the oven preheats, fill a stockpot with water and bring the water to a rapid boil.

Line 2 baking sheets or trays with kitchen towels. Rub flour into 1 of the towels and place both sheets close to your work surface.

Shaping the Dough Deflate the dough and transfer it to a lightly floured work surface. Divide the dough in half; cover and chill one piece of the dough while you work with the other. Cut the dough into 5 equal pieces; work with 1 piece at a time and cover the remaining pieces with a towel.

To form a bagel and develop the gluten cloak that will give it its structure, draw up the dough from the bottom, stretch it, and pinch it at the top. Keep pulling the dough up and pinching it until you have a perfectly round, tightly packed ball of dough with a little topknot or pleat at the top. Turn the dough over so that the knot is against the work surface and plunge your index finger into the center of the dough. Wiggle your finger around in the hole to stretch it, then lift the bagel, hook it over the thumb of one hand and the index finger of the other, and start rotating the dough, circling your thumb and finger and

Draw up the dough from the bottom and pinch it on top.

elongating the hole to a diameter of 2 to 2½ inches. (At this point, the dough will look more like a piece in a ringtoss game than a bagel, but it will soon boil to bagelhood.) Put the bagel on the baking sheet with the floured towel, and cover with another towel. Shape the remaining 4 pieces of dough into bagels. (You'll shape the refrigerated dough after you've completed boiling and baking these bagels.)

THE WATER BATH

¼ cup sugar

1 teaspoon baking soda

Add the sugar and baking soda to the boiling water. With a large slotted skimming spoon or slotted spatula, lower the bagels, one at a time, into the boiling water. Don't crowd them—the bagels should swim around in the water without touching one another; it's better to boil them in batches than to cram them into the pot all at one time. The bagels will sink to the bottom of the pot when you put them in, then rise to the top. Once the bagels have surfaced, boil for 1½ to 2 minutes on each side, flipping them over gently with the skimmer. Remove the bagels, shaking the skimmer over the stockpot to get rid of some of the excess water, and put them on the baking sheet with the unfloured towel, keeping the smoothest side of the bagel up. (Do not discard the sugar-water—you'll use it to boil the dough that is still in the refrigerator.)

Keeping the smoothest sides up, transfer the bagels to the peel or prepared baking sheet. (Work quickly, because the wet bagels have a tendency to stick to the towel.)

Top and bottom: Stretch the hole to enlarge it, then rotate it gently until it looks like a piece in a ringtoss game.

THE GLAZE AND TOPPINGS

2 large egg whites

1 teaspoon cold water

Sesame, poppy, and/or caraway seeds; kosher or sea salt; minced onions sautéed in vegetable oil; and/or dried garlic chips or dehydrated onions softened in hot water (optional)

Whisk the egg whites and cold water together until the whites are broken up, then push the glaze through a sieve and brush each bagel with the glaze. Try not to let the glaze drip onto the baking sheet or peel, or it will glue down the bagels. Don't worry if the bagels look wrinkled—they'll smooth out in the oven. Brush with another coat of glaze and, if you're using a topping, or more than one, sprinkle it, or them, evenly over the bagels now.

Baking the Bagels Put 4 ice cubes in a 1-pint measuring cup and add ¼ cup cold water. Put the bagels into the oven and immediately toss the ice cubes and water onto the oven floor (or into the hot pan). Quickly close the oven door to capture the steam produced by the ice, turn the oven temperature down to

450°F, and bake the bagels for 25 minutes. Turn off the oven and let the bagels remain in the oven for 5 more minutes. Open the oven door and leave the bagels in the oven for another 5 minutes. Transfer the bagels to a rack and cool. If you've used a baking stone, sweep the excess cornmeal from the stone. Before baking the next batch of bagels, be certain to bring the oven temperature back to 500°F.

While the first batch of bagels is baking, cut and shape the remaining dough. Boil, glaze, and bake these bagels just as you did the first batch.

Storing Cooled bagels can be kept for 1 day in a paper bag. For longer storage, pack into airtight plastic bags and freeze for up to 1 month. Thaw, still wrapped, at room temperature.

Bagel Chips

Cut stale bagels into ¼-inch-thick slices. Spread lightly with softened herb butter and sprinkle with coarse salt. Place on a wire rack set in a jelly-roll pan and bake in a preheated 375°F oven until uniformly crisp and golden brown. Start checking after 10 minutes; remove any chips that are crisp and brown and keep baking the others. The chips will probably need about 15 minutes in the oven, but some slow-crispers might take up to 20 minutes. Cool on a rack and store in an airtight tin.

Contributing Baker **LAUREN GROVEMAN**

Onion Bialys

COLOR PHOTOGRAPH, PAGE 70

Makes 12 bialys ■ The bialy, a culinary gift from Bialystok, Poland, is best known as the roll that keeps the bagel company at a New York brunch. It does, however, have a distinctive personality of its own. The bialy is a doughy roll, flat in the center and puffy around the rim (not unlike the Oasis Naan, page 149), that's sprinkled with sautéed onions. Few things smell better when they're toasting, and, oddly, the bialy is almost always toasted, even when it's at its freshest. For a taste of New York, split and toast a bialy, spread it with butter, and lay on a few pieces of kippered (hot-smoked) salmon, a slab of tomato, and a slice of red onion, or just slather it with Vegetable Cream Cheese (page 456).

THE SPONGE

2¼ cups warm water (105°F to 115°F)

2¼ teaspoons active dry yeast

2 teaspoons malt extract or sugar

2 tablespoons solid vegetable shortening

⅓ cup minced yellow onion

1 teaspoon freshly ground black pepper (optional)

3 cups high-gluten flour, bread flour, or unbleached all-purpose flour

Pour ¼ cup of the water into a small bowl; add the yeast and a drop of the malt extract or a pinch of sugar and whisk to combine. Allow the mixture to rest until the yeast dissolves and turns creamy, about 5 minutes.

Meanwhile, melt the solid shortening in a small skillet over medium heat. Add the onions and sauté until softened, about 3 minutes. Scrape the onions and the melted shortening into the bowl of a mixer fitted with the paddle attachment. Add the remaining 2 cups water and malt extract or sugar, and the black pepper, if you're using it.

Add the creamy yeast to the mixing bowl, making certain that the temperature of the ingredients already in the bowl doesn't exceed 110°F; if the mixture's too hot, give it a few minutes to cool to 110°F. With the mixer on low speed, add the flour in a steady stream, mixing until the flour is incorporated. Increase the speed to medium and beat for 3 minutes. Scrape down the bowl and paddle with a rubber spatula and remove the bowl from the mixer.

Rise Cover with plastic wrap and let the sponge rise at room temperature for 1¼ hours.

THE TOPPING AND DOUGH

2 tablespoons vegetable oil

1 cup minced yellow onions

2 teaspoons poppy seeds

Freshly ground black pepper to taste

2 tablespoons (approximately) unsalted butter, melted

The sponge (above)

1 tablespoon salt

3 cups (approximately) high-gluten flour, bread flour, or
   unbleached all-purpose flour

Heat the vegetable oil in a large skillet over medium heat and sauté the onions and poppy seeds until the onions are soft, 3 to 5 minutes. Season with pepper and let cool.

Brush the inside of a large mixing bowl with some of the melted butter; set aside. Reserve the remaining melted butter for coating the top of the dough.

continued

Mixing and Rising When the sponge is fully risen, return the bowl to the mixer. On low speed, working with the paddle or dough hook, beat in the salt and as much flour as needed to make a dough that cleans the sides of the bowl. Increase the speed to medium and knead for 3 to 5 minutes. Turn the dough out onto a floured work surface and knead briskly until the dough is smooth and elastic.

Form the dough into a ball and transfer it to the buttered mixing bowl. Brush the top of the dough with a little butter, cover the bowl with buttered plastic wrap, and top with a towel. Let the dough rise at room temperature for about 1½ hours, or until doubled in bulk.

Position a rack in the lower third of the oven and preheat the oven to 500°F. If you'll be baking the bialys on a baking or pizza stone, preheat it too and generously dust a peel with cornmeal; set aside. If they're going on baking sheets, brush the sheets with vegetable oil (or spray them) and dust them with cornmeal. Dust two kitchen towels with cornmeal. (To create steam in the oven, you'll be tossing ice cubes and water onto the oven floor. If you don't think your oven floor is up to this—it can be tricky with a gas oven—put a heavy skillet or roasting pan on the oven floor and preheat it as well.)

Shaping the Dough Divide the risen dough in half; work with one piece of dough at a time, keeping the other piece covered. Cut the dough into 6 equal pieces. Work with one piece of dough at a time, keeping the others covered with a towel. Shape the dough into a round and flatten the center to create a thick ½-inch-wide rim. Prick the center of the bialy with the tines of a fork and transfer it to a cornmeal-dusted towel; cover with another towel while you shape the other 5 bialys.

Prick the center of each shaped bialy again and transfer to the peel or a prepared baking sheet. Spoon a little of the onion–poppy seed filling into the center of each bialy and prick again to flatten.

Baking the Bialys Put 4 ice cubes in a 1-pint measuring cup and add ¼ cup cold water. Put the bialys into the oven and immediately toss the ice cubes and water onto the oven floor (or into the hot pan). Immediately close the oven door to trap the steam. Bake the bialys for 10 minutes, turn the oven down to 450°F, and bake for 5 minutes more. Transfer to a rack to cool. Brush off the baking stone, if necessary, and return the oven to 500°F.

While the first batch is baking, cut and shape the remaining bialys. Then bake them as you did the first batch. (When you are comfortable with this dough, you'll be able to work on a dozen bialys at once, baking them in one batch on a baking stone or two baking sheets.)

Storing Bialys are best the day they are made. To freeze them, cut them in half and wrap airtight. The bialys will keep in the freezer for a month and can be popped into the toaster directly from the freezer.

Contributing Baker **LAUREN GROVEMAN**

Challah

COLOR PHOTOGRAPH, PAGE 70

Makes 2 braided loaves ■ Think of challah as Eastern European brioche. It is a golden egg-and-butter-rich bread with a texture only slightly tighter than that of brioche. Braided challah is the traditional symbol of the Jewish sabbath, the bread over which grace is said. It is just a little sweet, just a little soft, and just this side of heavenly.

2 tablespoons (approximately) unsalted butter, melted

1½ tablespoons active dry yeast

½ cup tepid water (80°F to 90°F)

⅓ cup sugar

1 stick (4 ounces) unsalted butter, at room temperature

1 cup whole milk

1 tablespoon mild honey

2½ teaspoons salt

4 large eggs

6½ cups (approximately) high-gluten flour, bread flour, or unbleached all-purpose flour

Brush a large mixing bowl with some of the melted butter; set aside. Reserve the remaining melted butter for coating the top of the dough.

Mixing the Dough Whisk the yeast into the water. Add a pinch of the sugar and let rest until the yeast has dissolved and is creamy, about 5 minutes.

Cut the butter into small pieces and toss into a small saucepan with the milk; heat until the milk is very warm to the touch and the butter has melted. Pour the mixture into a large mixing bowl and add the remaining sugar, the honey, and salt, stirring with a wooden spoon to dissolve the sugar and salt. If necessary, let the mixture cool so that it is no warmer than 110°F.

Add the creamy yeast to the milk mixture, along with the eggs, and stir with the wooden spoon to mix. Stirring vigorously, add the flour, ½ cup at a time, stopping when you have a dough that cleans the sides of the bowl and is difficult to stir. Turn the dough out onto a floured work surface and knead, adding more flour as necessary to keep the dough from sticking to your hands and the counter, until the dough is smooth and elastic, about 10 minutes.

(You can make this dough in a heavy-duty mixer fitted with a dough hook. When the yeast, the milk mixture, and the eggs are combined, add about 5 cups of the flour, and beat on low speed for 3 minutes, or until the dough starts to come together. Beating on medium-low, add as much additional flour as needed to make a soft dough that will clean the sides of the bowl. Knead on medium-low for 8 to 10 minutes, until smooth, soft, and elastic.)

continued

First and Second Rises Form the dough into a ball and transfer it to the buttered mixing bowl. Brush the top with a little melted butter, cover the bowl with buttered plastic wrap, and top with a kitchen towel. Let the dough rise at room temperature for 1 to 1½ hours, or until doubled in volume. When the dough is fully risen, deflate it, cover as before, and let it rise until it doubles in bulk again, 45 minutes to 1 hour.

Shaping and Final Rise Line 2 baking sheets with parchment paper. Deflate the dough and turn it out onto a lightly floured work surface. Cut the dough in half and keep 1 piece of dough covered while you work with the other.

Braid the dough from the center to each end. When one half is braided, turn and braid the other half.

Divide the dough into 3 equal pieces. Roll each piece into a rope about 16 inches long; it should be thick in the center and tapered at the ends. Align the ropes vertically, side by side, and start braiding from the center down. When you've reached the end, turn the loaf around so that the braided half is on top; braid the lower half. Pinch the ends to seal and tuck the ends under the loaf. Transfer the loaf to a prepared baking sheet and gently plump it to get it back into shape; cover with a towel. Braid the second loaf, put it on a baking sheet, and cover. Let the loaves rise at room temperature for 40 minutes, or until soft, puffy, and almost doubled.

THE GLAZE AND TOPPING

1 large egg

1 large egg yolk

1 tablespoon cold water or heavy cream

Sesame, poppy, and/or caraway seeds (optional)

Coarse salt

Position the racks to divide the oven into thirds and preheat to 375°F.

Whisk the egg, yolk, and water together in a small bowl until broken up, then push the glaze through a sieve. Brush the tops and sides of the challahs with glaze; let the glaze set for 5 minutes, and brush again. Reserve the leftover glaze for brushing the loaves during baking. If you're topping the loaves, dust them with the seeds; sprinkle coarse salt over the loaves, topped or not.

Baking the Bread Bake for 20 minutes. The loaves will expand and expose some of the inner dough. Brush the newly exposed dough with the reserved glaze and bake 15 to 20 minutes longer, or until the loaves are golden and sound hollow when thumped on the bottom. If they start to brown too quickly, cover them with a piece of foil, shiny side up. Let cool before slicing.

Storing Once cut, challah should be kept in a plastic bag; it will keep for 2 days and then make excellent French toast. For longer storage, wrap the breads airtight and freeze for up to 1 month. Thaw, still wrapped, at room temperature.

Contributing Baker **LAUREN GROVEMAN**

Pumpernickel Loaves

COLOR PHOTOGRAPH, PAGE 57

Makes 2 large oval loaves ■ These oversize loaves are dark and sweet with the resilient texture of the best rye breads. Pumpernickel is, in fact, a member of the rye bread family, part of the German grainy black bread clan, but its chocolaty color and haunting sweetness make it seem like a very distant relation.

This bread delivers traditional taste using some untraditional ingredients—you probably won't be able to pick out the individual flavors, but it's the combination of espresso powder, chocolate, molasses, and lekvar (prune butter) that produces the beautifully browned crust and chocolate-colored crumb, and that haunting sweetness. The shaping method is also untraditional, but it's what gives you oversize, invitingly plump loaves, the kind you find lined up at the counter of an authentic, old-fashioned delicatessen. The slice is large, made for sandwiches. The bread is very good with any kind of cream cheese spread and great for the open-faced Reuben (page 101).

A note of caution to the less athletically inclined: Mixing and kneading this dough by hand replaces an hour at the gym pumping iron. However, the dough can be made in a heavy-duty mixer.

1 cup boiling water

1 tablespoon instant espresso powder

2½ ounces unsweetened chocolate, coarsely chopped

¼ cup unsulphured molasses

1 stick (4 ounces) unsalted butter, cut into small cubes

5½ teaspoons active dry yeast

Pinch of sugar

½ cup warm water (105°F to 115°F)

2 cups plain yogurt, at room temperature

¼ cup solid vegetable shortening

½ cup prune lekvar (also sold as prune butter in specialty markets and some supermarkets)

2 tablespoons ground caraway seeds (grind whole seeds in a spice or coffee grinder)

1½ tablespoons caraway seeds

1 tablespoon salt

3½ cups coarse rye meal or medium rye flour

6 cups (approximately) high-gluten flour, bread flour, or unbleached all-purpose flour

Melted butter, for greasing the mixing bowl

continued

Brush a large (about 8-quart) bowl with melted butter; set aside.

Mixing and Kneading Put the boiling water and espresso powder into a small heavy-bottomed saucepan and stir to dissolve the espresso. Add the chocolate, molasses, and butter and cook over low heat, stirring occasionally, until the butter and chocolate melt. Pour the mixture into another large (about 8-quart) bowl.

Meanwhile, whisk the yeast and pinch of sugar into the warm water; let rest until creamy, about 5 minutes.

Using a wooden spoon, stir the yogurt, shortening, lekvar, caraway seeds, and salt into the butter-chocolate mixture. When the ingredients are well blended and the mixture is just warm to the touch (no hotter than 110°F), stir in the yeast and the rye meal. Using lots of elbow grease, stir in enough of the high-gluten flour, ½ cup to 1 cup at a time, to make a very moist dough. (You'll probably use almost 6 cups of flour.)

When it is too difficult to stir the dough in the bowl, turn it out onto a work surface well dusted with high-gluten flour and knead until smooth and elastic but still soft and moist, about 10 minutes. The dough may seem a little pasty at first—because of the rye meal—but its texture will change with energetic kneading. While you're working, add only as much additional flour as you need to keep the dough from sticking to the table and your hands.

(You can make this dough in a heavy-duty mixer fitted with a dough hook. Once the yeast and rye meal have been added to the other ingredients, mix on low speed, scraping down the sides of the bowl as necessary, for about 2 minutes. Add about 5 cups of the high-gluten flour, 1 cup at a time, and beat on low speed for 3 to 4 minutes. Increase the speed to medium and beat in as much additional flour as needed to make a soft dough that will clean the sides of the bowl, then beat for about 8 minutes, until the dough is smooth and elastic.)

First Rise Form the dough into a ball and transfer it to the buttered bowl. Cover the bowl with buttered plastic wrap and top with a kitchen towel. Let the dough rise at room temperature for 1½ to 2 hours, or until it has doubled in volume.

Second Rise When the dough is fully risen, deflate it, turn it over, cover as before, and let it rise for about 1 hour, or until it doubles in bulk again.

Rolling and Shaping Deflate the dough, transfer it to a lightly floured work surface, and divide it in half. Work with 1 piece of the dough and keep the other covered with a towel or plastic wrap. Lay 2 clean kitchen towels on the counter and sprinkle them with flour; keep close at hand.

On a lightly floured surface, pat the dough into a rectangle about 8 inches by 14 inches. Starting at the short end farthest from you, roll the dough into a tight roll, pinching and sealing the seams you form with each roll as you go. Stand the roll on end and push your fingers down into the loaf, tucking some of the dough into the loaf as you burrow your fingers down into it. Then squeeze the end of the dough to elongate it, pinch it to seal, and fold each corner into the center, creating two triangles—it's like making hospital corners on a bed. Tuck the end under the bread, attaching it to the bottom seam, and repeat the burrowing, squeezing, folding, and tucking with the other end of the coil. Rotate and plump the dough to get a nicely shaped, rounded oval. Place the loaf, seam side up, diagonally on one of the floured kitchen towels and form a sling by joining the opposite corners of the towel that are farthest from the loaf. Punch a hole in the joined corners of the towel, slip an S-hook through the hole, and suspend the sling from a cupboard or doorknob (or tie the ends of the towel together to form a sling and suspend it). Shape the second piece of dough in the same manner and tuck it into a sling.

Rest The loaves should rest undisturbed in their slings for 40 minutes.

THE TOPPING AND GLAZE

Sesame and/or caraway seeds (optional)
1 large egg white
1 teaspoon cold water

Position a rack in the lower third of the oven and preheat the oven to 450°F. If the loaves are to bake on a baking or pizza stone, preheat the stone too and generously dust a peel with cornmeal. If they will bake on baking sheets, brush or spray one or two large, preferably dark steel, baking sheets with vegetable oil and sprinkle with cornmeal. For added flavor, use some sesame and/or caraway seeds in combination with the cornmeal to dust the peel or sheets. (To create steam in the oven, you'll be tossing ice cubes and water onto the oven floor. If you don't think your oven floor is up to this—it can be tricky with a gas oven—put a heavy skillet or roasting pan on the oven floor and preheat it as well.)

Whisk the egg white and water together and push the mixture through a sieve; reserve.

Release the slings and transfer the loaves, smooth side up, to the prepared peel or baking sheet(s), keeping the loaves at least 3 inches apart. These loaves are very big and unusually soft, so handle them carefully. Give the loaves a last plumping with your hands and, using a sharp serrated knife or a single-edge razor blade, slash the top of each loaf 3 times: The slashes should run horizontally across the loaf at a slight angle and should be about 1 inch deep. Paint each loaf with a generous coating of glaze, taking care not to paint the slashes. Sprinkle the loaves with caraway and/or sesame seeds, if you're using them.

Baking the Bread Put 4 ice cubes in a 1-pint measuring cup and add ¼ cup cold water. Put the loaves into the oven, immediately toss the ice cubes and water onto the oven floor (or into the pan), and quickly close the oven door to trap the steam produced by the ice. Bake the loaves for 10 minutes, then reduce the oven temperature to 350°F and bake for 35 to 40 minutes more, or until the loaves are deeply browned and the bottoms produce a hollow sound when rapped. (The internal temperature of the loaves should measure 200°F on an instant-read thermometer.) Remove the loaves and cool on a rack. The loaves must cool completely before they can be cut, so plan to wait 2 to 3 hours after baking.

Storing You can keep the bread in plastic bags at room temperature for 2 days or wrap the loaves airtight and freeze them for up to 1 month. Thaw, still wrapped, at room temperature.

Contributing Baker **LAUREN GROVEMAN**

Eastern European Rye
COLOR PHOTOGRAPH, PAGE 61

Makes 2 large oval loaves ▪ Brittle crusts, the kind that snap into small, sharp-edged flakes when the bread is cut, are one of the hallmarks of a great rye bread—and something you'll get from these loaves. The breads are large, studded and topped with fragrant caraway seeds, slashed in the authentic manner, and soft, slightly moist, and a little springy inside. They're perfect for a roast beef sandwich with "the works" or a bubbling hot Reuben (page 101).

> 1½ tablespoons active dry yeast
>
> 2¾ cups tepid water (80°F to 90°F)
>
> 1 tablespoon sugar
>
> 1 scant tablespoon salt
>
> ¼ cup solid vegetable shortening
>
> 3 cups medium rye flour
>
> 2 tablespoons finely ground caraway seeds (grind whole seeds in a spice or coffee grinder)
>
> 1½ tablespoons caraway seeds
>
> 3½ cups (approximately) high-gluten flour, bread flour, or unbleached all-purpose flour

Melted butter, for greasing the mixing bowl

Brush a large (about 8-quart) bowl with melted butter; set aside.

Mixing and Kneading Whisk the yeast into ½ cup of the water. Add a pinch of the sugar and let the mixture rest until the yeast dissolves and is creamy, about 5 minutes.

Pour the remaining 2¼ cups water into another large (8-quart) bowl and add the remaining sugar, the salt, shortening, and the creamy yeast. Working with a sturdy wooden spoon—and energy—stir in the rye flour and caraway seeds. When the mixture is smooth, start adding the high-gluten flour, ½ cup at a time, until the dough is difficult to stir (about 2½ to 3 cups).

When the dough is too hard to stir in the bowl, turn it out onto a work surface dusted with high-gluten flour and knead until smooth and elastic, 10 to 13 minutes. The dough may seem a little pasty at first—because of the rye flour—but its texture will change with kneading. While you're working, add only as much additional flour as you need to keep the dough from sticking to the table and your hands.

(You can make this dough in a mixer fitted with the dough hook. Once the rye flour and caraway seeds have been added, add 2½ to 3 cups of the high-gluten flour. Beat on medium-low for about 3 minutes, gradually adding as much additional flour as needed to make a soft dough that will clean the sides of the bowl. Increase the mixer speed to medium and beat the dough for about 8 minutes, until smooth and elastic.)

First Rise Form the dough into a ball and transfer it to the buttered mixing bowl. Cover the bowl with buttered plastic wrap and top with a kitchen towel. Let the dough rise at room temperature for about 1½ hours, or until it has doubled in volume.

Second Rise When the dough is fully risen, deflate it, turn it over, cover as before, and let it rise until it doubles in bulk again, about 45 minutes to 1 hour.

Rolling and Shaping Deflate the dough, transfer it to a lightly floured work surface, and divide it in half. Work with half the dough at a time, keeping the other half covered with a towel or plastic wrap. Lay two clean kitchen towels on the counter and sprinkle them with flour; keep close at hand.

Clockwise from top: challah (page 93), pumpernickel (page 95), and rye.

With a rolling pin or your hands, work the dough into a rectangle about 7 inches by 10 inches. Starting at the short end farthest from you, roll the dough into a tight roll, pinching and sealing the seams you form with each roll as you go. Stand the roll on end and push your fingers down into the loaf, tucking some of the dough into the loaf as you burrow your fingers down into it. Then squeeze the end of the dough to elongate it, pinch it to seal, and fold each corner into the center, creating two triangles—it's like making hospital corners on a bed. Tuck the end under the bread, attaching it to the bottom seam, and repeat the burrowing, squeezing, folding, and tucking with the other end of the coil. Rotate and plump the dough to get a nicely shaped, rounded oval. Place the loaf, seam side up, diagonally on one of the floured kitchen towels and form a sling by joining the opposite corners of the towel that are farthest from the loaf. Punch a hole in the ends of the towel, slip an S-hook through the hole, and suspend the sling from a cupboard or doorknob (or tie the ends of the towel together to form a sling and suspend it). Shape the second piece of dough in the same manner and tuck it into a sling.

Rest The loaves should rest undisturbed in their slings for about 30 minutes.

continued

THE GLAZE AND TOPPING

1 large egg white
1 teaspoon cold water
Caraway seeds (optional)
Kosher or coarse sea salt (optional)

Position a rack in the lower third of the oven and preheat the oven to 425°F. If you'll be baking the breads on a baking or pizza stone, preheat it too and generously dust a peel with cornmeal; set aside. If they're going on baking sheets, brush or spray one or two large, preferably dark steel, baking sheets with vegetable oil and sprinkle with cornmeal. (To create steam in the oven, you'll be tossing ice cubes and water onto the oven floor. If you don't think your oven floor is up to this—it can be tricky with a gas oven—put a heavy skillet or roasting pan on the oven floor and preheat it as well.)

Whisk the egg white and water together and push the mixture through a sieve; reserve.

Release the slings and gently transfer the loaves, smooth side up, to the prepared peel or baking sheet(s), keeping the loaves at least 3 inches apart. Give the loaves a last plumping with your hands and, using a sharp serrated knife or a single-edge razor blade, slash the top of each loaf 3 times: The slashes should run horizontally across the loaf at a slight angle and should be about 1 inch deep. Paint each loaf with a generous coating of glaze, taking care not to paint the slashes. Sprinkle the loaves with caraway seeds and salt, if you're using them.

Baking the Bread Put 4 ice cubes in a 1-pint measuring cup and add ¼ cup cold water. Put the loaves into the oven, immediately toss the ice cubes and water onto the oven floor, and quickly close the oven door to trap the steam

produced by the ice. Bake the loaves for 30 minutes, then reduce the oven temperature to 375°F and bake for 10 to 15 minutes more. (The internal temperature of the loaves should read 200°F on an instant-read thermometer.) Turn off the heat and let the loaves remain in the oven for 5 minutes more. Remove the loaves and cool on a rack. The loaves must cool completely before they can be sliced.

Storing Packed in plastic bags, the loaves will keep for 2 days at room temperature; wrapped airtight, they can be frozen for up to 1 month. Thaw, still wrapped, at room temperature.

Contributing Baker **LAUREN GROVEMAN**

Open-Faced Reuben Sandwich

Makes 6 servings ■ In the interest of slimmer sandwiches, here is a Reuben using only one slice of rye or pumpernickel but including all the rest of that unforgettable combination.

6 slices rye or pumpernickel

³/₄ stick (3 ounces) unsalted butter, melted

1 tablespoon fresh tomato sauce, chili sauce, or ketchup

1 tablespoon capers, chopped and patted dry

1 medium dill pickle, finely chopped and squeezed dry

²/₃ cup mayonnaise

Salt and freshly ground black pepper

18 or so slices pastrami or corned beef (¹/₈ inch thick)

3 tablespoons Dijon mustard

1¹/₂ cups sauerkraut, drained and squeezed dry

4 ounces or so Muenster or Swiss cheese, sliced ¹/₈ inch thick

Center a rack in the oven and preheat the oven to 450°F.

Toast the bread lightly on one side. Paint the untoasted side with the melted butter and place buttered side down on a baking sheet.

Blend the tomato sauce, capers, and pickle into the mayonnaise and season with salt and pepper. Spread this over the bread and cover with the slices of meat. Paint the meat with the mustard and cover with the sauerkraut, spreading it out to the edges of the bread (to prevent the bread from burning under the broiler). Arrange the cheese over the sauerkraut, covering it completely. *The sandwiches may be prepared to this point several hours ahead. Cover and refrigerate.*

Set the sandwiches on a baking sheet in the oven and bake until bubbling hot and the cheese has melted, 6 to 7 minutes. Then, watching closely, run the sandwiches under a hot broiler for a minute or two to brown the cheese lightly. Serve at once.

Contributing Baker **JULIA CHILD**

Semolina Bread

Makes 1 loaf ■ Golden semolina flour gives this loaf a warm, sunny color, a tender crumb, and a nutty taste. Semolina loaves are often associated with Italian baking—perhaps because semolina flour is milled from durum wheat, the flour used to make pasta—but their texture and flavor make them good companions to any type of fare. You can mix this dough by hand or in a heavy-duty mixer with a dough hook, but because it makes a single loaf and is mixed in a straightforward, uncomplicated way, it's quickly and easily mixed in the food processor.

THE SPONGE

1 cup warm water (about 110°F)

1 teaspoon active dry yeast

1 cup unbleached all-purpose flour

Pour the warm water into a medium bowl and whisk in the yeast. When the yeast has dissolved and is creamy, about 5 minutes, stir in the flour.

Rise Cover the bowl and let it rest at room temperature until the sponge doubles in volume, about 2 hours.

THE DOUGH

The sponge (above)

¹/₂ to ³/₄ cup unbleached all-purpose flour

³/₄ cup semolina flour

2 teaspoons salt

1 tablespoon olive oil

TO MAKE THE DOUGH IN A FOOD PROCESSOR, scrape the sponge into a processor fitted with the metal blade. Add ½ cup of the all-purpose flour and the rest of the ingredients and pulse on and off until the dough forms a ball on the blade. If the dough doesn't come together in a ball, add another ¼ cup of all-purpose flour, a tablespoon at a time, pulsing to mix it in. Let the dough rest in the work bowl for 5 minutes, then process for a full 20 seconds. The dough will be sticky.

TO MAKE THE DOUGH IN A MIXER FITTED WITH THE DOUGH HOOK, scrape the sponge into the bowl and add ½ cup of the all-purpose flour and the remaining ingredients. Mix on medium speed until you have a dough that is smooth and elastic but still somewhat sticky, about 5 minutes. If the dough is too soft, add up to ¼ cup more all-purpose flour, a tablespoon at a time.

First Rise Turn the dough into an oiled bowl, cover the bowl with plastic wrap, and let the dough rest at room temperature until it doubles in volume, about 2 hours.

Shaping and Second Rise Turn the dough onto a floured work surface and deflate it by flattening it with your palms. Pat the dough into a rough oval shape and then roll it, from one long side to the other, to form a plump loaf. Tuck the ends under, and transfer the loaf to a parchment paper–lined baking sheet. Cover it lightly with oiled plastic wrap and allow it to rest until it doubles in bulk again, about 2 hours.

Baking the Bread Preheat the oven to 400°F.

Holding a single-edge razor blade at a 30-degree angle to the loaf, slash lines on each side of the loaf from top to bottom: The slashes should be at an angle, and each should be about 1 inch away from the last. Make sure the lines don't meet in the center of the loaf.

Bake for about 35 minutes, until deeply golden or until an instant-read thermometer inserted into the bottom of the bread reads 210°F. Transfer the bread to a rack and cool completely before cutting.

Storing The bread can be kept at room temperature for a day; cover it loosely with plastic wrap. For longer storage, wrap it airtight and freeze for up to 1 month. Thaw, still wrapped, at room temperature.

Contributing Baker **NICK MALGIERI**

Swedish Limpa

Makes 2 round loaves ■ Limpa is a Swedish rye bread, but not at all like the Eastern European ryes with which you may be familiar. It is an extremely dark loaf, somewhat sweet because of the molasses and brown sugar, and somewhat spicy thanks to the typically Scandinavian addition of caraway, fennel, and anise seeds. Traditionally, this bread, baked in a round cake pan, is served at Christmas as part of a buffet of cold meats and cheeses. Once you taste the bread, you'll see how the licoricelike anise and fennel and the slight sweetness of the molasses lend themselves to cured meats and savory holiday foods.

2 cups milk
1 teaspoon caraway seeds
1 teaspoon fennel seeds
1 teaspoon anise seeds
1 tablespoon active dry yeast
1 teaspoon sugar
¼ cup warm water (about 110°F)
¼ cup molasses
1 stick (4 ounces) unsalted butter, melted
¼ cup (packed) dark brown sugar
1½ teaspoons salt
Grated zest of 1 orange
1½ cups light or medium rye flour
5 to 6 cups bread flour

Light or dark molasses, for glaze

Mixing the Dough Pour the milk into a small saucepan and heat until scalded; that is, until a ring of small bubbles is visible at the edge of the pan. Remove from the heat and let the milk cool.

Using a mortar and pestle, a spice grinder, or a coffee mill, coarsely grind the caraway, fennel, and anise seeds. Don't grind them to a powder—you're aiming to crush them just enough to release their flavor. Keep close at hand.

Working in a large bowl, whisk the yeast and sugar into the water, stirring until the yeast is dissolved. Let the mixture rest for 5 minutes, or until it turns creamy, then stir in the cooled milk, the molasses, butter, brown sugar, salt, crushed seeds, and grated orange zest. Whisk in the rye flour and stir until smooth. Add 1 cup of the bread flour and whisk until the mixture is very smooth. Switch to a wooden spoon and mix in as much additional bread flour, 1 cup at a time, as it takes to make a stiff dough. (You can also make this dough in a mixer fitted with the dough hook. Follow the procedure for hand mixing, adding the ingredients in the same order.)

Rest Cover the bowl and let the dough rest for 15 minutes.

Kneading the Dough Dust a work surface with bread flour and turn the dough out onto the flour. Knead the dough for 5 to 10 minutes, or until it is smooth and elastic and there are small blisters visible on the surface of the dough. (If you are working in a mixer, knead the dough at medium speed, adding additional flour as needed. To get a feel for the dough, remove it from the mixer before it is completely kneaded and, working on a lightly floured surface, knead it until smooth by hand.)

First Rise Rinse out the bowl, rub it with a little oil, and place the dough in it. Cover the bowl tightly with plastic wrap and let the dough rise at room temperature until it doubles in bulk, about 1 hour.

Shaping the Dough Grease two 8- or 9-inch cake pans. Deflate the dough by folding it over on itself a few times and turn it out onto a work surface. Divide the dough in half and shape each half into a round loaf that will fit into a prepared cake pan. This is most easily done by working each half of dough into a tight ball between your cupped hands. Keep turning the ball between your hands and then, when it's tight, place it in one of the pans, smooth side up, flattening the dough as necessary to fit the pan.

Second Rise Cover the dough with oiled plastic wrap and allow to rise at room temperature until the loaves almost double in volume, about 1 hour.

Baking the Bread Center a rack in the oven and preheat the oven to 375°F.

Bake the loaves for about 35 minutes, or until a wooden skewer inserted into the top of the bread comes out clean. As soon as you remove the loaves from the oven, turn the loaves out of their pans and brush their tops with molasses. Cool the loaves on a wire rack.

Storing The breads will keep at room temperature, wrapped in plastic, for 2 days. For longer storage, wrap airtight and freeze for up to 1 month. Thaw, still wrapped, at room temperature.

Contributing Baker **BEATRICE OJAKANGAS**

Finnish Pulla

COLOR PHOTOGRAPH, PAGE 69

Pulla baked as a
braided wreath.

Makes 1 wreath ■ Like brioche and challah, Finnish pulla is a butter-and-egg-rich bread. Although it can be served at any time, it is often a celebration loaf. In this version, it is braided, rounded into a wreath, and finished with a bow, lending it a look quickly linked with Christmas. The traditional flavoring for a pulla is cardamom, which is best bought in the pod—powdered cardamom is invariably lackluster. Crack the pod, empty out the seeds, and crush them, using a mortar and pestle, spice mill, or coffee grinder. If you crush the cardamom in your coffee grinder and then grind coffee, the residual cardamom will flavor the beans and your next pot of coffee in an authentically Scandinavian way.

1 cup milk

1 tablespoon active dry yeast

¼ cup warm water (about 110°F)

½ cup sugar

1 teaspoon crushed cardamom seeds (from about 7 pods)

1 teaspoon salt

2 large eggs, lightly beaten, at room temperature

4½ to 5 cups unbleached all-purpose flour

1 stick (4 ounces) unsalted butter, melted

1 large egg beaten with 1 tablespoon milk, for glaze

Sliced or slivered almonds, for topping

Pearl sugar, for topping

Mixing the Dough Put the milk in a small saucepan and scald it (heat it until a ring of small bubbles is visible around the sides of the pan). Remove the pan from the heat and cool the milk to a temperature of between 105°F and 115°F.

In a large bowl, whisk the yeast into the warm water. Set aside for 5 minutes, or until the yeast has dissolved and is creamy. Whisk in the milk, sugar, cardamom, salt, and eggs. Switch to a wooden spoon, add 2 cups of the flour, and beat the mixture until smooth. Beat in the butter and then add as much additional flour, ½ cup at a time, as you can until the dough is stiff but not dry. (You can also make this dough in a mixer fitted with the dough hook. Follow the procedure for hand mixing, adding the ingredients in the same order.)

Rest Cover the bowl with plastic wrap and allow the dough to rest for 15 minutes.

Kneading the Dough Turn the dough out onto a lightly floured work surface and knead until it is smooth and satiny, about 10 minutes. (If you are working in the mixer, knead the dough at medium speed; you might want to stop just short of a satiny dough and knead the dough by hand for the last few minutes—it will give you a feel for the dough.)

First Rise Shape the dough into a ball. Place it in a lightly greased bowl, turn it around in the bowl to grease the top, and cover the bowl tightly with plastic wrap. Let the dough rise at room temperature until it doubles in bulk, 45 minutes to 1 hour.

Line a 14-inch pizza pan or a large baking sheet with parchment paper and set aside. Lightly oil a cool work surface; marble would be ideal. (If your kitchen is very hot, fill a metal pan with ice cubes and run the bottom of the pan over your work surface to cool it.)

Shaping the Dough Turn the dough out onto the oiled surface and knead it lightly and briefly, just to deflate it and release the air. Divide the dough into thirds and roll each third into a rope about 36 inches long. Braid the three strands, braiding as far down to the bottom of the strands as you can. Lift the long braid onto the parchment-lined pan, shaping it into a circle as you place it on the pan. Snip about 1 inch of dough off each end of the braid and fuse the ends together, pressing and pinching them (if necessary) to fit. Roll the trimmings into a rope about a foot long and twist the rope into a bow shape. Place the bow over the seam you created when you fused the ends.

Second Rise Cover the wreath with a kitchen towel and allow it to rise at room temperature until it is puffy but not doubled, about 45 minutes.

Pulla baked as a braided loaf.

Baking the Bread Center a rack in the oven and preheat the oven to 375°F.

Brush the egg glaze over the bread. Sprinkle the wreath with sliced almonds and pearl sugar.

Bake for 20 to 25 minutes, until golden, taking care not to overbake the wreath. Transfer the loaf to a rack to cool to room temperature before cutting.

Storing The bread will keep for a day at room temperature, lightly covered with plastic. If you want to keep the bread longer, wrap it airtight and freeze it for up to 1 month. Thaw, still wrapped, at room temperature.

Contributing Baker **BEATRICE OJAKANGAS**

Cranberry-Walnut Pumpkin Loaves

COLOR PHOTOGRAPH, PAGE 68

Makes 3 small loaves ■ These loaves are small, beautifully crowned, and the color of fall's golden leaves. Never mind that the combination of pumpkin, cranberry, walnut, and raisin may set you thinking of a baking powder–raised quick bread with a biscuit or butter cake texture, this bread is a yeast bread, albeit one that's slightly sweet, just a little spicy, and even a bit savory. Although the bread is of the direct-rise family, meaning there's no starter or sponge, it is given an overnight rest in the refrigerator, a dormant period that builds both character and texture in the finished loaf.

$2^{2}/_{3}$ **to 3 cups bread flour**

1 teaspoon cinnamon

$^{1}/_{2}$ **teaspoon grated nutmeg**

$^{1}/_{2}$ **teaspoon salt**

2 tablespoons tepid water (80°F to 90°F)

2 teaspoons active dry yeast

5 tablespoons unsalted butter, at room temperature

$^{1}/_{3}$ **cup sugar**

8 ounces (1 cup) puréed cooked pumpkin or butternut squash, fresh or canned solid packed (see Note)

1 large egg, at room temperature

$^{3}/_{4}$ **cup walnut pieces, toasted**

1 cup plump golden or dark raisins

$^{2}/_{3}$ **cup cranberries (if frozen, thaw and pat dry)**

Mixing and Kneading Whisk $2^{2}/_{3}$ cups of the flour, the cinnamon, nutmeg, and salt together in a large bowl just to mix; set aside until needed.

Pour the water into a small bowl, sprinkle in the yeast, and whisk to blend. Allow the yeast to rest until it's creamy, about 5 minutes.

In a mixer fitted with the paddle attachment, beat the butter and sugar at medium speed until creamy. Add the pumpkin and egg and beat until blended. Don't be concerned if the mixture looks curdled; it will come together when you add the dry ingredients.

Set the mixer speed to low and add the yeast, then begin to add the dry ingredients, about $^{1}/_{2}$ cup at a time. As soon as the mixture starts to form a dough that comes together, scrape the paddle clean and switch to the dough hook. If your dough does not come together (it might be because your pumpkin purée was liquidy), add a few more tablespoons of flour.

Mix and knead the dough on medium-low speed for 10 to 15 minutes, scraping the sides of the bowl and the hook now and then with a rubber spatula. At the start, the mixture will look more like a batter than a dough, but as you continue to work, it will develop into a soft, very sticky dough that will just ball up on the hook. (This dough develops much the way brioche does.)

With the machine on low speed, add the walnuts and raisins, mixing only until incorporated, about 1 minute. Add the cranberries and mix as little as possible to avoid crushing them. (Inevitably, some cranberries will pop and stain a patch of dough red; think of this as charming, and proceed.)

First Rise Scrape the dough into a lightly buttered large bowl, cover tightly with plastic wrap, and set aside at room temperature to rise until nearly doubled in bulk, about 2 hours.

Chilling the Dough When the dough has doubled, fold it over on itself a couple of times to deflate it, wrap it tightly in plastic, and refrigerate overnight.

Shaping the Dough At least 6 hours before you want to begin baking, remove the dough from the refrigerator. Leave the dough, covered in its bowl, until it reaches at least 64°F on an instant-read thermometer. (This will take as long as 3 to 4 hours—don't rush it.) If you don't have an instant-read thermometer, look for the dough to be slightly cool and just a little spongy.

Lightly butter three 5¾- by 3¼- by 2-inch loaf pans.

Working on a lightly floured surface, divide the dough into thirds and pat each piece of dough into a 5- by 7-inch rectangle; keep a short end facing you. Starting at the top of each rectangle, roll up the dough toward you and seal the seam by pressing it with your fingertips. Seal the ends, then place each roll, seam side down, in a prepared pan.

Second Rise Cover the pans lightly with a kitchen towel and allow to rise at room temperature for 1½ to 2 hours, or until the dough has nearly doubled— it will rise to just above the rim of the pans.

Baking the Bread Center a rack in the oven and preheat the oven to 350°F.

Bake the loaves for about 35 minutes, or until deeply golden. Remove the pans to a cooling rack; after a 5-minute rest, turn the breads out of their pans and allow them to cool to room temperature on the rack.

Storing The breads can be kept at room temperature for a day or two or frozen, wrapped airtight, for up to 1 month. Thaw, still wrapped, at room temperature.

Note To use fresh pumpkin or butternut squash, split the squash, remove the seeds, and place, cut side down, on a baking sheet. Roast in a preheated 350°F oven for about 1 hour, or until meltingly tender. Scoop the softened pulp out of the shell and cool completely. One pound of squash yields about 12 ounces of cooked pulp.

Contributing Baker **STEVE SULLIVAN**

Artisanal Breads
CRUSTY AND RUSTIC

TIME IS THE KEY to successful bread baking, and today, a new generation of professional American bakers has turned back—or at least slowed down—the clock. Rejecting the hurry-up methods of commercial baking, they've adopted the long, slow-rising techniques of old-time artisanal bakers and are creating loaves in the best European traditions.

From coast to coast, American artisanal bakers are using sourdoughs, *levains,* and sponges to develop doughs with the earthy, full flavor of grain. Baking on stone and brick hearths, many of them wood-fired, they're producing loaves of unsurpassed quality: hand-shaped, deeply browned breads with crackling crusts and supple, moist interiors. And you will too, as you follow the recipes and time-tested techniques of some of the country's most talented bread bakers and discover the incomparable joy of handcrafting traditional, artisanal loaves.

With these recipes, you will learn to give each bread the time it needs. It will take you just a couple of hours to make Leslie Mackie's golden, fine-crumbed Rustic Potato Loaves, and an afternoon to make Danielle Forestier's just-like-Paris baguettes. But you'll spend a weekend creating Berkeley baker Steve Sullivan's breathtaking couronne, and Joe Ortiz's Pain de Campagne will capture your attention for four days. During these hours and days, you'll come to know the breads, their textures and tastes, intimately, and you'll understand the wisdom of slowing down the pace. You'll also realize that with these breads, the working time is short and the waiting time is long—but always worth it.

Mixed-Starter Bread

COLOR PHOTOGRAPH, PAGE 62

Makes about 2½ pounds dough; enough for 1 very large or 4 small loaves ■ Unless you are an accomplished professional baker, it is unlikely that you will ever have made a bread this splendid. Everything about the way the bread is made is designed to develop depth of flavor, perfect texture, and polished looks—and it all succeeds. This is an extraordinary dough, one that might be softer, tackier, and more fluid than any you're accustomed to working with, but it is these characteristics that produce professional-quality loaves with a crumb that's chockablock with stretchy holes of all different sizes, each edged with an almost opalescent tinge, the sign of an exceptionally well developed bread. Its taste is sweet, wheaty, complex; its texture chewy; and its crust thick, dark, crackly, tasty, and not the least bit tough.

Wheat-stalk loaves, called *épis*, made from Mixed-Starter dough.

It will take practice to get this dough right, but not only will it be worth it, you'll probably find that even your not-so-perfect trials are better than many store-bought loaves. You'll be making two consecutive starters for the dough—the first, a mixture of old dough (make the pizza on page 157 and pull off a small piece of dough to start this bread), flour, and water; the second, a sponge based on the first starter—and when you mix the final dough, you'll add just a smidgen of yeast.

This is, for the most part, a naturally fermented dough, its fermentation similar to the chef-levain method used in Pain de Campagne (page 128), and not entirely unlike a sourdough method—but for this bread, the fermentation is arrested before the flavor becomes sour.

continued

A Bread-Making Plan

The starters and long fermentation periods require that you stretch your bread making over two days. With experience, you'll come up with your own plan of action, but here's a way to start Saturday and have fresh, fabulous bread for Sunday:

DAY ONE	DAY TWO
11 A.M.	**7 A.M.**
Make the first starter	Mix the final dough
Let rise 8 hours	First rise 1½ hours
7 P.M.	**9:30 A.M.**
Make the second starter	Shape the dough
Let rise 4 hours	Final rise 1½ hours
Chill 8 hours	**12:00 noon**
	Bake the loaves

You can use this dough to form baguettes, wheat stalks, pain fendu, and/or couronnes, or make it the base of the wonderful Walnut Bread on page 121.

THE FIRST-STAGE, OR OLD-DOUGH, STARTER

A walnut-sized (¹/₂-ounce) piece of fully risen dough (pizza, page 157, or other white-flour bread dough)

¹/₄ cup warm water (105°F to 115°F)

²/₃ cup unbleached all-purpose flour

You can make the starter easily by hand, but you can use a mixer with a dough hook or paddle if you prefer. No matter which method you use, cut the dough into small bits, drop them into a bowl with the warm water, and let them soften for about 5 minutes.

Using a sturdy wooden spoon, gradually mix in the flour. You'll be producing a very stiff dough, one that will soon become too stiff to mix with the spoon, so reach into the bowl and mix the dough with your hands; if that becomes too difficult, and it may, turn the dough out onto a counter and knead. You're not looking to develop the gluten in the dough, just to get the ingredients well incorporated. (Working by machine, just mix in the flour and beat on low speed for 2 to 3 minutes.)

First Rise Put the dough in a bowl, cover with plastic wrap, and allow the dough to rise in a warm place (between 80°F and 85°F) for about 8 hours, after which it will be soft and sticky, bubbly, and springy.

THE SECOND-STAGE STARTER

The first-stage starter (above)

¹/₄ cup warm water (105°F to 115°F)

³/₄ cup unbleached all-purpose flour

This second-stage starter, or sponge, is made like the first. Again, it is made easily by hand or can be made in a mixer fitted with the dough hook. To work by hand, scrape the fully developed first-stage starter onto a cutting board and cut it into 4 pieces. Put the pieces into a bowl, add the water, and allow the dough to soften for about 5 minutes. Working with a wooden spoon, and then your hands if you need to, mix in the flour and stir until the dough comes together. This second-stage starter will be softer than the first. (Working by machine, just mix in the flour and beat on low speed for 2 to 3 minutes.)

Second Rise and Chilling Transfer the sponge to a large bowl, cover with plastic wrap, and let it rest in a warm place (between 80°F and 85°F) for 4 hours, during which time it will more than double.

After this rise, the sponge, when stretched, will show long, lacy strands of gluten and smell sweet and yeasty (even though you haven't added yeast yet—the aroma's the result of the starter's natural fermentation). Chill the risen sponge for at least 1 hour, but no more than 8 hours, before proceeding.

THE FINAL DOUGH

1¼ cups cool water (about 78°F)

½ teaspoon SAF instant yeast (*not* rapid-rise) or ¾ teaspoon active dry yeast

The second-stage starter (above)

3⅓ cups unbleached all-purpose flour

1 tablespoon kosher salt

The final dough is worked in a mixer with the dough hook. Put the water into the bowl of the mixer, sprinkle in the yeast, and stir by hand to mix. Deflate the second-stage starter, break it into pieces, add it to the bowl, and allow it to soften for 5 minutes.

Add the flour and pulse the machine on and off a few times to start mixing in the flour without having it fly out of the bowl. Mix on low speed only until the flour is incorporated, then let the dough rest in the bowl for 10 minutes—this gives the flour time to absorb the water.

Kneading the Dough With the machine running at low speed, sprinkle the salt onto the dough; increase the mixer speed to medium-high and mix and knead the dough for 5 to 8 minutes. The dough will be very soft and moist and may ride up the dough hook. If you are working in the kind of mixer that allows you to lower the bowl, here's a neat trick: Lower the bowl and at the same time speed up the mixer—the dough will be thrown off the hook. If you're working with another kind of mixer, push the dough down with a rubber spatula as necessary.

Third Rise Transfer the dough to a clean bowl, cover with plastic wrap, and allow to rest in a warm place (between 80°F and 85°F) for about 1½ hours. The dough will probably double in bulk and it should have a network of bubbles visible under the surface.

Final Rise Fold the risen dough down on itself a few times in order to deflate it and to redistribute the yeast, then cover again and let rise for 45 minutes. (Don't punch the dough down; you don't want to lose the open, bubbly structure that's been developed.)

After this last rise, you must shape and bake the dough. If you refrigerate the dough now, or do anything else to retard it, you will have a sourdough bread, which is not what this dough is meant to be. Choose the shapes you want and follow the instructions for forming and baking each type of loaf.

Shaping Long Loaves

1. Form all long loaves, like baguettes and bâtards, by first pressing the measured dough into a flat rectangular shape.
2. Starting at the top of the rectangle, fold down the top third of the dough and press gently to seal with your fingertips.
3. Fold down again (tucking in the sides of the rectangle if they are uneven) and seal the seam with your fingertips. Repeat this process of folding and sealing once or twice to form a short log shape with a tight skin.
4. Roll the log under both palms, cupping your hands to gently press the loaf against the work surface while pushing it forward and back.
5. Elongate the loaf gradually by working your hands out to the ends while rolling. Do not tear the skin.
6. Place the long loaves in the pleats of a heavy floured cloth (or *couche*) for rising.

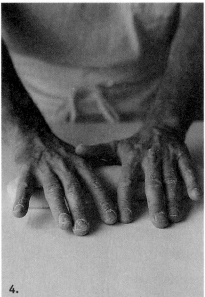

Baguettes, Wheat Stalks, and Pain Fendu
COLOR PHOTOGRAPH, PAGE 58

These are some of the classic French bread shapes whose forming starts with a long roll or sausage. The baguette is the basic long loaf; the wheat stalk is a baguette that's been snipped and its resulting rolls turned to create a regal sheaf of wheat; and the pain fendu, or "split bread," is a shorter, squatter bread that looks like two side-by-side mini-baguettes. One batch of dough yields about two and a half pounds (forty ounces) of dough. Here are the amounts of dough you'll need for each type of bread:

Baguette	10 ounces (about ¼ batch dough)
Wheat Stalk	10 ounces (about ¼ batch dough)
Pain Fendu	6 ounces

To shape the breads and transfer them from the peel to the oven, you'll need some rice flour; either brown or white will do.

Cover a baking sheet with a linen or cotton kitchen towel, rub the towel well with rice flour, and set the sheet aside. (This will be the dough's resting place.)

Preliminary Shaping Each shape starts like a baguette. Divide the dough into the number of pieces you need, and, being careful not to mash the dough, pat each piece into a rough rectangle. Working with one piece at a time, starting at the top of the rectangle, fold down about a third of the dough and press it gingerly into the middle of the dough with your fingertips. If the rectangle is really ragged, fold in the sides to even them, then fold everything down to the bottom and, once again, gingerly press the dough into place, creating a seam where the dough meets. Not pressing down too hard, roll the dough, seam side up, back and forth under your palms to form a short sausage. Cover the dough with a towel and let it rest for 5 to 10 minutes.

TO MAKE EITHER A BAGUETTE OR A WHEAT STALK (called an *épi* in French), roll each piece of the rested dough gently under your palms to make a 15-inch-long baguette with slightly tapered ends. (The wheat stalk cuts will be made right before the bread goes into the oven.) Place the loaves seam side up on the floured towel, lifting a bit of the towel up to form a pleat between each loaf.

Dividing the pain fendu.

TO FORM A PAIN FENDU, make a smaller baguette shape from the piece of dough. Handling the dough gently, dredge it in rice flour, covering both sides. Make a pile of rice flour on the work surface and put the dough seam side up on the flour. Press a dowel or a broom-stick along the seam to divide the dough in half the long way. Rock the dowel back and forth into the dough, but do not cut through the dough. The piece of dough between the two almost-separated mini-baguettes should be very thin.

Grasp a mini-baguette in each hand, thumbs in the center, and fold the dough under itself so that the mini-baguettes are on the underside and the side of the dough facing up is smooth. Lay the loaf split side down on the towel-lined baking sheet.

Rise Cover the loaves with another towel and let rise at room temperature for 1½ hours. The loaves are properly risen when the dough is soft all the way through (if you gently squeeze a small piece, it will be spongy) and a depression made with your finger does not spring back quickly.

Baking the Bread Position a rack in the lower third of the oven, line it with quarry tiles or a baking stone (leaving about 1 inch free all around), and preheat the oven to 450°F. Put a cast-iron or other very heavy skillet on the floor of the oven if it is a gas oven, or directly on the heating element if it is an electric oven. Rub a peel with rice flour.

Pour about 1 cup of warm water into a long-necked bottle, preferably plastic. About 2 minutes before you're ready to put the loaves into the oven, open the oven door, stand back, and pour the water into the hot skillet. Immediately close the oven door to trap the steam.

Flip the baguette(s) and/or pain fendu onto the peel so that the seam of the baguette(s), or the flat side of the pain fendu, is against the peel. The baguettes need to be slashed: Hold a razor almost parallel to each and make 3 cuts diagonally across the width of the bread (see page 127 for a fuller description of slashing a baguette); the pain fendu can go into the oven without further fuss (unless the mini-baguettes have stuck together; if so, trickle a teaspoon of water between them to separate the split pieces). For the wheat stalks, dust the loaves with rice flour, flip them over onto the peel, and, using small sharp scissors, make cuts every 2 inches, snipping along the center and cutting on a diagonal about three quarters of the way into the loaf. Lift up a snipped piece and move it to the right, turning it so that the cut portion is face up, move the next piece to the left, turn it, and continue until you've worked your way down the loaf and have created the stalk.

Snipping the *épi*.

Slide the loaves onto the hot tiles or baking stone. Try to do this quickly so that you lose neither the oven's heat nor its humidity. Bake the loaves for about 20 minutes, or until deeply and beautifully brown. Plunge an instant-read thermometer into the center of the bread—it should read 200°F, the guarantee of fully baked bread.

Transfer the breads to a rack to cool completely before cutting.

Couronne

COLOR PHOTOGRAPH, PAGE 72

The couronne, or crown, is a large ring of bread, a classic French shape that is often decorated with a deep slash around the edge of the bread or, as in this one, a string of pearls, an elegant bread necklace. Because the shape is so popular, French bakers have *bannetons*, or "rising baskets," meant solely for this bread—these linen-lined baskets have a raised center, like a tube pan, and can be quite large. In fact, the couronne pictured here was raised in a banneton that measured sixteen inches across the top. You can simulate such a banneton by inverting a small bowl in the center of the largest springform pan you have. Since it will probably be no more than twelve inches in diameter, you might have to use a smaller amount of dough and adjust the rising and baking times accordingly. Cover the bowl and the inside of the springform with a well-floured linen kitchen towel and you're ready to proceed. Or, you can try using a ring mold that is at least ten inches across and three or more inches high, with a three-inch center. Again, adjust the amount of dough for the mold so that you have enough room for it to double in volume during its rise, and keep an eye on it during baking.

Three couronnes made from Mixed-Starter dough.

The couronne uses 2 pounds 5 ounces of dough; the leftover 3 ounces of dough (a little more than ½ cup) can be used to make a small roll or saved for your next batch of this bread.

Preliminary Shaping Cut off a piece of dough that weighs 5 ounces (about 1 cup of dough) and pat it out into a rectangle. Fold a third of the dough down to the center of the rectangle and then fold that portion of dough down to the bottom; repeat the patting and folding three times more, giving the dough a quarter turn each time. The last time, pinch the dough so that you make a seam where the folds meet. Try to be as gentle as you can with the dough, since you want to maintain the bubble structure that's been developing all this time. Roll the dough into a rope and let it rest, covered, while you shape the couronne.

Plunge your elbow into the center of the dough to make a hole.

TO MAKE THE COURONNE, rotate the 2-pound piece of dough against the work surface and between your hands to form a ball. Roll up your sleeves and plunge one of your elbows into the center of the dough, wiggling it around a bit to make a hole. Flour the fingers of your right hand (if you're a righty—reverse if you're left-handed) and stick them, tips down, into the hole. Set the dough spinning around your fingers until the center hole expands. It doesn't have to be as large as the center hole of your rising basket—you'll enlarge it again later. Cover and let the dough rest for 15 minutes.

continued

1. Form the string of pearls.

2. Gently transfer the pearls to the basket.

3. Widen the hole a second time and place the dough in the basket.

TO MAKE THE STRING OF PEARLS, roll the rope under your palms until it is about ½ inch thick and measures 2 to 2½ feet long, depending on the size of your banneton or mold. (Keep in mind that the dough will lengthen as you make the pearls, so roll it to a length about 3 inches smaller than your banneton's circumference.) The pearls are going to be shaped with the side of your hand, actually your pinky: Position your hand, pinky perpendicular to the dough, about ½ inch from one end of the rope. Slide your finger back and forth very gently across the dough to form a pearl; continue making pearls at ½-inch intervals, each connected by a little twist of dough, the result of your pinky's sawing motion. Carefully lift the string of pearls up and into the floured basket, placing it slightly off center, closer to the outer edge.

Final Shaping Again using floured fingers, widen the center hole of the couronne, keeping the dough round and opening it up so that the outer circumference is about the same size as the rising basket. Working carefully and quickly, turn the dough over into the basket, on top of the pearls.

Rise Cover the basket and allow the bread to rise at room temperature for about 1½ hours, until the dough is soft and spongy all the way through and a depression made with your finger does not spring back quickly.

Baking the Bread Position a rack in the lower third of the oven, line it with quarry tiles or a baking stone (leaving about 1 inch free all the way around), and preheat the oven to 450°F. Put a cast-iron or other very heavy skillet on the floor of the oven if it is a gas oven, or directly on the heating element if it is an electric oven. Rub a peel with rice flour. Pour about 1 cup of warm water into a long-necked bottle, preferably plastic.

About 2 minutes before you're ready to put the loaf into the oven, open the oven door, stand back, and pour the water into the hot skillet. Immediately close the oven door to trap the steam.

Turn the couronne over onto the peel. Slide the bread onto the hot tiles or stone and quickly close the oven door. Immediately reduce the oven temperature to 425°F. Bake the loaf for 35 to 45 minutes, or until very brown (the edges of the pearls may even be really black, which is terrific) and the internal temperature measures 200°F on an instant-read thermometer. Transfer to a rack to cool completely before cutting.

Storing The large couronne will keep at room temperature for 2 to 3 days, the baguettes, wheat stalks, and fendus for only a day. Keep the sliced breads cut side down on a board or the counter. For storing for up to a month, wrap the breads airtight and freeze. Thaw, still wrapped, at room temperature.

Contributing Baker **STEVE SULLIVAN**

Walnut Bread

COLOR PHOTOGRAPH, PAGE 66

Makes one 3-pound round loaf ■ This bread is made from a batch of Mixed-Starter dough but because of the hefty amount of walnuts, the color, texture, and flavor of the bread are changed. This large, round, heavily crusted bread has the warm, rustic look of the loaves stacked on provincial bakers' shelves throughout France—it's got the taste too.

Here are the instructions for incorporating the walnuts and shaping and baking the bread. For everything else you need to know about the base dough, its starters, stages, and rising times, read the recipe for Mixed-Starter Bread (page 113).

1 recipe Mixed-Starter Bread dough (page 113), fully kneaded

8 ounces walnuts, coarsely chopped

After you have finished kneading the dough, turn it out onto a work surface. Press the dough down to flatten it. Sprinkle the walnuts over the dough and fold the dough over on itself a few times. Press it down again and fold it twice more, then knead the dough for a minute or two, just to make certain the walnuts are evenly incorporated.

First Rise Turn the dough into a large bowl, cover, and let rise in a warm place (between 80°F and 85°F) for 1½ hours. The dough will probably double in bulk and it should have a network of bubbles visible under the surface.

Second Rise Fold the dough down on itself a few times and then cover again and let rise for 45 minutes before deflating and shaping.

Shaping the Dough To shape the dough into a *boule*, or ball, fold the fully risen dough over on itself a few times, turn it out onto a work surface, and gather it together gently between your rounded palms. Work the dough around between your palms, using the unfloured work surface to create tension, until you have a smooth ball.

Final Rise The dough can rise in a well-floured large banneton or in a large colander lined with a well-floured linen towel. Sprinkle the inside of the banneton or towel-lined colander with rice flour and turn the walnut dough over into it; the dough's smooth side will be down. Cover and let the dough rise at room temperature for 1½ hours, or until it is soft and spongy all the way through.

Baking the Bread Position a rack in the lower third of the oven, line it with quarry tiles or a baking stone (leaving about 1 inch free all the way around the tiles), and preheat the oven to 450°F. Put a cast-iron or other very heavy skillet on the floor of the oven if it is a gas oven, or directly on the heating element if

Slashing the
sunburst pattern.

it is an electric oven. Rub a peel with rice flour. Pour about 1 cup of warm water into a long-necked bottle, preferably plastic.

About 2 minutes before you're ready to put the loaf into the oven, open the oven door, stand back, and pour the water into the hot skillet. Immediately close the oven door to trap the steam.

Invert the bread onto the peel and, using a single-edge razor blade, quickly slash the bread by cutting a cross in the center and making one short slash from the center out in each of the resulting quadrants—the pattern should look like a sunburst. (Alternatively, you can slash a circle in the dough. Immediately slide the bread onto the hot quarry tiles or baking stone and turn the oven temperature down to 400°F. Bake the bread for 40 to 50 minutes, or until deeply browned and the internal temperature of the bread registers 200°F on an instant-read thermometer. Remove to a rack to cool completely before cutting.

Storing The sliced bread will keep for 2 to 3 days cut side down on a board or the counter. For storage of up to 1 month, wrap airtight and freeze. Thaw, still wrapped, at room temperature.

Basic Boule

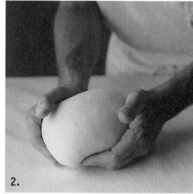

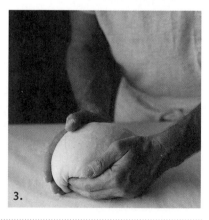

1. Tuck the dough in on itself to stretch the outer skin, or "gluten cloak," as you bring the edges into the middle.
2. To form the round or *boule*, rotate the bottom of the loaf against the work surface.
3. Use the bottom edges of your hands to tighten the skin of the loaf and seal the bottom as it rotates. Place the round on a prepared surface or in a banneton to rise.

Contributing Baker **STEVE SULLIVAN**

Classic French Bread

Makes 3 to 4 loaves ■ A baguette is often called a crispy loaf of French bread, but a good loaf is so much more. Crispy, although part of the package, is not the point. In addition to a crisp crust on these long, thin loaves, you want an elastic texture, a sweet taste, and something to chew on—all of which this bread delivers.

CLockwise from left: a large boule, a bâtard, and two rolls.

There are no starters or sponges in this French bread. The flavor and texture come from good mixing, enough kneading, a double rise at the right temperature, proper shaping, and a closely timed bake in a hot, humid oven—techniques and conditions within the reach of an American home baker in an average home kitchen.

Although the recipe is, as its name indicates, a classic, and it has been tested over time, it, like all other yeast recipes, will vary according to any number of conditions: the weather, the temperature in your kitchen, the quality of a particular sack of flour, and, who knows, maybe even your mood. Like other artisanal breads, a French loaf takes patience to create and practice to perfect.

Temperature and timing, the Siamese twins of the bread baker's kitchen, are the major players in the Classic French Bread drama. The temperature of your kitchen, the dough's rising place, and the temperature of the dough will affect the timing of each rise, often by as much as 50 percent. In fact, since the dough contains a relatively small amount of yeast (a condition that always calls for long rising times) and spends a lot of time exposed to room temperature during kneading, hydration, and relaxation periods, room and dough temperatures become critical. The ideal temperature for this dough is 78°F, as measured by an instant-read thermometer. If your dough is the magical temperature, life is easy. But, since the world is rarely perfect, you'll have to find a cooler rising place for a dough that is warmer, or a warmer place for a cooler dough, and deal with the fact that rising times will vary. You won't succeed if you're a slave to the clock—you must look for and learn from the changes in the dough. All the information necessary to make the right decisions is in the body of the recipe, so read through the directions a couple of times before setting off.

One last note: Making the dough by hand using the "fountain" method, i.e., working the liquid into the flour on the counter with your fingers, is as classic as the loaves themselves and puts you on intimate terms with the dough, but the process is messy and unwieldy for the uninitiated. It's certainly worth a try, but keep in mind that you can make this dough in a heavy-duty mixer (instructions follow those for hand mixing). That is, in fact, how it is done all over France today.

continued

5 cups bread flour

2 cups cool water (about 78°F)

One 0.6-ounce cube compressed (fresh) yeast

2½ teaspoons salt

TO MAKE AND KNEAD THE DOUGH BY HAND, pour the flour onto a smooth work surface, one that is appropriate for kneading bread and amenable to being roughed up with a dough scraper. Pile the flour in a mound and use your fingers to burrow a well in the center. Pour the water into the well, a very little bit at a time, while using your fingertips to draw in the flour closest to the water. Work in increasingly larger circles, adding water and drawing in flour to form a medium-soft dough. Don't worry about it being homogeneous—even after all of the flour is moistened, you'll probably find a few dry spots.

The fraisage.

With the help of your dough scraper, pull the mass of dough toward you. Starting with the dough farthest from you, put a small (golf-ball size) piece of dough under the heel of your hand and smear it across the work surface. When you have worked through all the dough (this technique is called *fraisage* in French), you'll have a thoroughly mixed, firmly supple dough. Transfer the dough to a floured board, cover it lightly with a towel, and allow it to rest at room temperature for 15 minutes. (This rest period, called the *autolyse,* is an opportunity for the flour to hydrate completely.)

Flatten the dough as best as you can with your fingers and palms. Crumble the compressed yeast and sprinkle it, bit by bit, over the dough, folding the dough over on itself to mix in the yeast. Keep folding and incorporating all the bits of yeast, then continue to fold for about a minute, so that the yeast, which can be tricky to incorporate, is fully blended into the dough. Repeat the flattening and folding process, this time gradually adding the salt.

Using any method of kneading with which you are comfortable, knead the dough for 10 to 15 minutes, flouring the counter, your hands, and the dough as necessary, until the dough is very smooth and its gluten cloak, or surface, is as beautifully stretched as the skin of a balloon.

One Baker's Knead

Grab the dough at one end with either hand—this becomes a real workout, so you may want to switch hands at some point—and lift it about shoulder-high. Throw it down onto the work surface with a good slam, and roll the flattened dough over on itself, using the heels and fingers of both hands. The dough will naturally roll into thirds. Now grab either end of the roll of dough—the coiled part—in one of your hands and prepare to slam it down again. You'll find you have given the dough a quarter turn. Repeat the slamming, rolling, and turning motion for 10 to 15 minutes, until the dough is smooth and elastic, flouring your hands, the counter, and the dough as necessary.

TO MAKE AND KNEAD THE DOUGH IN A HEAVY-DUTY MIXER, fit the mixer with the dough hook and put all the flour and water in the bowl. Mix on low speed for 3 to 4 minutes, or until the dough just comes together in a shaggy, sticky mass. Turn the machine off, cover the bowl, and let the dough rest for 15 minutes; this is the *autolyse*, or hydration period.

Turn the mixer speed to low and, bit by bit, add the yeast; this should take about a minute. Increase the speed to medium and knead the dough for about 2 minutes. Return the speed to low and sprinkle in the salt, mixing until it is incorporated. Increase the mixer speed to medium and knead the dough for about 5 minutes, until it is smooth and elastic and just cleans the sides and bottom of the bowl. Turn it out onto a lightly floured work surface and knead by hand for a minute or two to bring the dough to completion.

Rest Form the dough into a tight ball by pulling the dough from the corners down under the center, and let it rest on the counter, covered with a floured towel, for 15 minutes, just long enough for the gluten to relax a bit.

First Rise Turn the dough over and, using the palms of your hands, slap and press the dough to flatten it slightly. Grab the dough on either side and pull it out in a long stretch; fold the stretched ends back to the center. Do the same pull, stretch, and fold from the top and bottom of the dough. Work the dough into a tight ball again and put it on a floured baker's peel, a floured cutting board, or floured work surface, cover with a floured towel, and let it rise at room temperature for 1½ to 3 hours, or until the dough is nearly doubled in bulk. (Here is where the temperature of the dough and the room come into play so dramatically: The dough will probably need at least 2 hours to double, but it might need 3, or even 3½ if it or the room is cool, so be prepared and patient.)

Shaping the Dough You will have about 42 ounces of dough, enough to make four 10-ounce bâtards (shorter baguettes) or three 12-ounce bâtards with a couple of rolls thrown in for good measure. Full directions follow for shaping bâtards, but you can shape the dough into boules (round loaves) or dinner rolls if that suits your needs better. Boules can weigh 1 pound, 1¼ pounds, or 1½ pounds, and dinner rolls (really baby boules) are nice when they're about 2½ ounces (in which case, you can get about 16 rolls from one batch of dough). You'll find instructions for shaping a boule in the recipe for Walnut Bread, on page 122.

Turn the dough out onto the work surface and deflate it by slapping it authoritatively with the palms of both hands. Divide the dough into thirds or quarters with your dough scraper. (Each piece of dough should be between 10 and 12 ounces, a good weight for either a bâtard or a baguette.) Form the pieces of dough into balls, cover them lightly, and allow them to relax on the counter for 5 minutes.

Rub some flour into a large cotton or linen towel and lay the towel on a board or peel. Make one fold or stand-up pleat at one of the short ends of the towel, and keep it handy; this is where the formed loaves will have their last rise before baking.

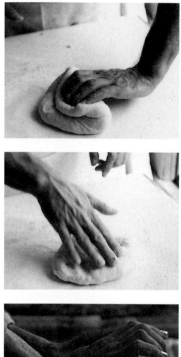

Top and center: To start shaping the dough, roll it over in thirds. Then slap the dough onto the work surface to flatten. *Bottom:* After marking and folding the fully worked dough, push to seal the seam with the heel of your hand.

Working with one ball of dough at a time, and dusting the work surface, your hands, and the dough as necessary with flour, form the bâtards. (If your oven is big enough, you can make baguettes—the technique is the same, the length is about 2 feet.) Turn the dough smooth side down and hit it with the flat of your hand to expel the gases. Lift the dough with one hand, rolling it over into thirds, and grab it again with your other hand. Slap the roll of dough onto the surface, flattening it into an even rectangle. Roll and flatten two more times. During this and the subsequent forming, dust your hands with flour as necessary.

Put the dough seam side up on the work surface and, using the heel of your hand, make a groove across the dough to mark the mid-point. Start with one side of the heel of your hand and rock to the other end. Lift the top edge of the dough and fold it two thirds of the way down the dough. Use the heel of your hand to seal the seam. Again, fold the dough down at the two-thirds mark and seal the seam with the heel of your hand. Finally, fold the top edge of the dough down to the bottom edge, seal the seam with the heel of your hand, and turn the dough seam side up.

Scrape the work surface clean of flour and, working with one piece of dough at a time, turn the dough seam side down on it. Cup your right hand over the center of the dough and place your cupped left hand over your right. Start rolling the dough back and forth along the counter, separating your hands and widening the space between them as the dough extends; keep your hands cupped and your fingertips and the heels of your hands touching the counter. Push the dough forward with the heels of your hands and pull it back with your fingertips. Ideally, the flat counter, not your hands, should be doing the majority of the shaping. When the dough is about 14 inches long, the right length for a bâtard, press down slightly on the ends of the dough to taper them.

As each piece of dough is shaped, lift it up, seam side up, onto the floured towel and pull a pleat of towel up to cradle it.

Final Rise When all the pieces are shaped and on the towel, fold the end of the towel over the loaves and let them rest at room temperature for between 1 and 2 hours, or until the dough has risen markedly and barely springs back when you prod it gently with your finger. Again, the range of time needed to rise the dough properly is a function of the dough's temperature and that of the room.

Baking the Bread Position an oven rack in the lower third of the oven and line the rack with a baking stone or quarry tiles, leaving a border of at least 1 inch all around. You are going to have to make steam in the oven and you can do this in one of two ways: You can either throw water directly onto the floor of the oven—often a risky business if you have a gas oven—or pour it into a heavy skillet (cast-iron is ideal) placed directly on the floor of a gas oven or on the heating element of an electric oven. Preheat the oven (with the skillet in place, if using it) to 425°F. Flour a baker's peel.

You need to work quickly now. Humidify the oven by carefully tossing ½ cup water onto the oven floor or into the preheated skillet; immediately close the oven door. Flip one bâtard onto the floured baker's peel and slash it with a single-edge razor. Hold the razor almost parallel to the loaf and make 3 cuts: The first should extend one third of the way down the loaf, starting from the center of one tip; the second should start about halfway down the first slash and ¼ inch below it and be 3 to 4 inches long; and the third slash should start halfway down the second, beginning ¼ inch below it, and reach the center of the opposite tip of the loaf. Put the loaf into the oven as soon as it is slashed. Slash the others and get them into the oven as quickly as possible. (If this has taken a bit too long and the steam seems to have dissipated, toss ¼ cup more water into the oven before putting in the last loaf.)

Slashing the bâtard.

Bake the loaves for 20 to 25 minutes, or until they are brown all over and reach an internal temperature of 200°F as measured on an instant-read thermometer plunged into the center of the bread. (Putting the loaves into the oven one by one, you may have cooled down the oven at the start of the baking period, in which case the baking time may be even a little longer than 25 minutes.) Pull the loaves from the oven and put them, slashed side down, on a counter. As long as the loaves are not resting on their flat bottoms, there is no need to put them on a rack. The loaves must cool for at least 20 minutes before you can cut them, and are best eaten as soon as possible after they've reached room temperature.

Storing The breads will be at their best for about 6 hours and fine for a day. They should be kept uncovered at room temperature until serving time; for longer storage, wrap airtight and freeze for up to a month. Thaw, still wrapped, at room temperature.

Contributing Baker **DANIELLE FORESTIER**

Pain de Campagne
COLOR PHOTOGRAPH, PAGE 71

Makes one 2-pound round loaf ■ If you were the type of student who never minded when the teacher sent you back to the drawing board for the third time, this recipe is for you. Because this loaf is made by the centuries-old chef-levain method, which depends on capturing and nurturing airborne wild yeast, it's an iffy project that comes with no guarantees. You might work on this bread for four days and get a loaf as flat as a pizza—or the bread of your dreams. Wild yeast is like that.

If this isn't for you, turn to page 136 and set to work on the Country Bread—it's a similar loaf, but it's made with yeast and can be prepared in one long day or worked on over two days. But if you persevere with this bread, it is likely you will learn to coax wild yeast and bacteria from the air and harness their energy into a tasty loaf—a challenge worth the effort. And, as you might expect, the more baking you do in your kitchen, the more yeast you'll find hovering there, and, hence, the greater your chances of success in the future.

To straighten out terminology, the *chef,* or chief, is a mixture primarily of flour and water that is allowed to ferment over a period of two days, after which it is "fed" with more flour and water and allowed to develop for another twelve hours or more. When it is fed, or "refreshed" (the baker's traditional term), it becomes the *levain,* or leavening. Together, without the aid of commercial yeast, they produce a natural sourdough.

As with the Classic French Bread (page 123), the Pain de Campagne can be made using the fountain method or by machine, and directions for both methods are given. The large round loaf can sport an outer braid and a decorative bouquet of wheat stalks, but if you're new to this method of bread making, it's best to concentrate on developing a healthy levain and then, when you've got the method down pat, move on to the braid-and-wheat-stalk decorations or the grape-cluster and star-shaped breads, all of which are described following the recipe.

THE CHEF

> ½ **cup (approximately) whole wheat flour**
> 3 **tablespoons warm water (105°F to 115°F)**
> ½ **teaspoon milk**
> ⅛ **teaspoon cumin**

Measure ½ cup flour out onto a work surface and shape it into a mound. Use your fingers to make a volcanolike well, or fountain, in the center and add the water, milk, and cumin. (This minuscule amount of cumin will add flavor to the dough but, in the end, will not be distinguishable as cumin.) Use the index finger of one hand to start mixing the ingredients in the center of the fountain, slowly drawing in the flour. You're aiming for a firm dough. At first the mixture will be pasty, but as you fold and knead the little piece of dough for about 5 minutes, it should firm up, become springy, and bounce back when prodded. (If you're having trouble getting a springy dough, add a few sprinkles more of whole wheat flour.)

If you're not comfortable working with the fountain, mix the chef, by hand or with a wooden spoon, in a bowl—the results will be the same.

First Rise Put the chef in a bowl, cover with plastic wrap, and let rest at room temperature for 2 days, during which time it will develop a light crust. Remove the plastic and take a whiff—it should already smell like a pleasantly sour, wheaty bread. The chef will have risen a little and the consistency will be spongy and moist.

REFRESHMENT 1

2 tablespoons chef (above)
¾ cup (approximately) whole wheat flour
⅓ cup (approximately) warm water (105°F to 115°F)

Pull aside the outer crust of the chef and scoop out 2 tablespoons of the moist dough, discarding what remains. Cut or pinch the chef into small pieces.

Make a mound on the work surface with ¾ cup whole wheat flour and form a fountain in the center with an opening between 3 and 5 inches across—it's got to hold the water. Put the pieces of chef in the center and pour over the water. Let the chef soften in the water for a couple of minutes before you start to draw the flour into the water as you did to make the chef, making first a paste and then a dough that you fold and knead. At this point, the dough is officially called the levain. If you can't get all of the flour into the levain, you may leave aside a tablespoon or so. If the levain is too wet, add a little more flour; too dry, add a drop of water. You're aiming for a springy, firm dough that is slightly sticky. When you roll the dough into a ball, it should hold its shape and spring back when poked with a fingertip.

(To make this stage by machine, put the water and the pieces of levain in the mixer bowl and set aside for a couple of minutes. Working with the paddle attachment in place, add the flour and mix on low speed for 2 to 3 minutes, until the dough comes together with uniform consistency. Scrape the dough out of the bowl onto a work surface and knead by hand for 2 minutes or so, adding more whole wheat flour if necessary to achieve a firm, springy ball of dough that is just slightly sticky.)

Second Rise Turn the levain into a bowl, cover with plastic wrap, and let it proof at room temperature for 18 hours, during which time it should show some signs of having risen. It may, in fact, rise and then fall again, which is fine. If your levain doesn't show signs of movement after 18 hours, check back in another 6 hours. When you uncover the levain and remove the crust, you'll be struck by a sweet, alcoholic aroma. Pull on a piece of the dough, and it will be bubbly and stretchy. *At this point, the levain can be frozen; bring it to room temperature before carrying on.*

REFRESHMENT 2

½ cup (4 ounces; a piece the size of a tangerine) levain (above)

¾ cup whole wheat flour

½ cup unbleached all-purpose flour

½ cup warm water (105°F to 115°F)

Avoiding the top crust, measure out the ½ cup of levain (it may be the entire piece except the crust); discard the rest. Pull the levain into small pieces.

Just as you did before, make a mound with the two flours, create a fountain, drop in the pieces of levain, and moisten with the water. Because you have a greater quantity of ingredients, you'll find yourself working in bigger and bigger circles as you draw in the flour and develop the levain. This time, you want to get all of the flour incorporated, so add more water by drops if that's what it takes to get everything mixed. Once again, you're looking for a firm dough.

You'll notice that the dough is more elastic at this stage. This is due in part to the addition of white flour (which has more gluten than whole wheat flour does) and in part to the developed chef-levain.

(To continue making the dough by machine, soften the pieces of levain in the water, as you did before. Using the dough hook this time, set the mixer to low speed, gradually add the flours, and mix for 4 to 5 minutes, or until the dough is firm and easily removed from the dough hook and bowl. Turn the dough out onto the work surface and knead briefly by hand, adding more flour if necessary to form a very firm ball of dough.)

Third Rise Put the levain in a bowl, cover with plastic, and let rise at room temperature for 5 to 8 hours, until it mounds. You want to try to catch the levain at its highest point, when it has risen to a definite round.

THE DOUGH

3⅓ cups unbleached all-purpose flour

1½ cups (12 ounces; a piece the size of a large orange) levain (above)

1 cup (approximately) warm water (110°F to 115°F)

2½ teaspoons salt

This step is most easily done in a heavy-duty mixer fitted with a dough hook. Measure out the 1½ cups levain (this will probably be all of the levain), and pull it into small pieces. Soften the levain in the water for a few minutes. Then, with the dough hook in place and the mixer set at low speed, gradually add the flour and mix until the dough comes together in a shaggy mass, about 2 minutes. Still mixing, add the salt. Raise the speed to medium and mix and knead until the dough is smooth and elastic, about 6 minutes. Finish with a brief kneading by hand to firm up the dough.

(To continue making the dough by hand, put the flour on the work surface and arrange it so that it forms a large dike or dam around what will become a wide pool. Put the levain in the center of the moat, and pour ¾ cup of the water around the levain, keeping it within the walls of the dike. Sprinkle the salt on the water, keeping it close to the flour. Squish the levain with the fingers of one hand, softening it with some of the water, and then start, as you did before, to draw the flour into the water and levain. Work slowly and carefully, drawing in the flour and taking care to keep the dike intact until the last possible moment. This is a long process—it may take you between 10 and 15 minutes to fully incorporate the flour. You want a firm dough, but one that is not dry, so add as much of the remaining water as necessary. When you've incorporated all the flour, knead the dough for about 3 to 5 minutes, until it is smooth and very elastic.)

The fountain.

Fourth Rise Put the dough in a large bowl and cover with plastic wrap. Allow the dough to rise at room temperature for about 5 hours. The dough will not necessarily double in bulk, but it may rise slightly and it definitely will hold an indentation when you prod it gently with your fingertip. (If you want to start a new batch of pain de campagne now, cut off a piece of dough about the size of a large walnut; this becomes your new chef. Using 2 tablespoons of this dough, begin your next batch of bread with the first refreshment.)

Shaping the Dough Prepare a resting place for the loaf. Traditionally, a pain de campagne is formed in a linen-lined basket called a banneton. The banneton for this loaf is round and measures about 8 inches across at the base (the top will be wider) and 4 inches in height. If you do not have a banneton, you can use a large basket or a colander; line it with a linen towel. Rub flour into the liner of the banneton or basket and set aside until needed. (If you are going to make the braid-and-wheat-stalk pain de campagne, follow the shaping directions on pages 132 to 133.)

Turn the dough out onto a work surface that's been very lightly dusted with flour and pat it into a flat round with your fingers and palms. Fold the edges in and press them down with the heel of your hand, then turn the dough over and, using your cupped hands, work the dough against the counter to form a tight, somewhat flat, ball that's about the same size as your banneton or basket. Turn the round over and lay it smooth side down into the banneton.

Final Rise Cover the dough and set it at room temperature to rise for 4 hours, during which time it should rise perceptibly.

Baking the Bread About 30 minutes before you're ready to bake the loaf, position a rack in the lower third of your oven and line it with a baking stone or quarry tiles, leaving a border of at least 1 inch free all around. Preheat the oven to 425°F. Pour some water into a spray bottle and set aside.

continued

When the dough is fully risen, rub a baker's peel or baking sheet with cornmeal and carefully invert the loaf onto it. Spray the oven walls with water and immediately close the oven door to trap the steam. Using a single-edge razor blade, slash the loaf in a pattern that appeals to you—3 long slashes or a broad tic-tac-toe pattern would be nice—cutting about ½ inch into the loaf. Slide the bread onto the hot baking stone or tiles, turn the oven heat down to 400°F, and immediately spray the oven walls again; close the door as quickly as you can. Bake the bread for 50 to 60 minutes, or until the crust is deeply golden, the loaf sounds hollow when thumped on the bottom, and the internal temperature of the loaf is 200°F as measured by an instant-read thermometer plunged into its center.

Remove the loaf to a rack and allow it to cool for at least 20 minutes, preferably longer, before cutting. (It is really best to allow the bread to cool to room temperature before slicing it.)

Storing The bread should remain reasonably fresh at room temperature for at least 4 days, or up to a week. Turn the cut side of the bread against a wooden board and leave the bread uncovered. Cooled fresh bread can be wrapped airtight and frozen for up to a month; thaw, still wrapped, at room temperature.

Braid-and-Wheat-Stalk
Pain de Campagne
COLOR PHOTOGRAPH, PAGE 71

1 recipe Pain de Campagne (page 128), risen and ready for shaping

Left to right: Starshaped pain de campagne (page 134) and braid-and-wheat-stalk pain de campagne.

When you are ready to shape the loaf, use a metal dough scraper to divide the dough in half. Keep one half intact and cut off one quarter of the other piece to use for the wheat stalks.

TO SHAPE THE WHEAT STALKS, cut the small piece of dough into quarters and form each little piece into a baguette or sausage. Let the pieces relax for a few minutes, then roll each piece under your fingers so that the upper half to two thirds of each stalk is thicker than the bottom, which will become the stem. Place two of the pieces in the center of the banneton, leaving a little room between them. Bend one wheat stalk to the left, the other to the right. Place the remaining stalks in the basket, nestling one beneath each of the bent stalks; bend these stalks out too. (You'll snip the stalks to make them truly look like wheat after they've risen.)

Working on a surface that has been very lightly dusted with flour, shape the large piece of dough into a round, somewhat flat, loaf, folding and pressing the dough as described on page 131. Try to make the loaf about an inch smaller than the base of your banneton or basket. Turn the loaf over and lay it smooth side down in the banneton over the wheat.

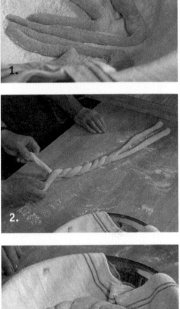

TO FORM THE BRAID, cut the remaining piece of dough in half and shape each half as you would a baguette or a sausage. Let the dough relax for a couple of minutes and then roll each piece under your palms, applying some pressure, until it is 25 to 26 inches long. (You'll probably find it easier to elongate the sausages if you work on a surface that does not have a dusting of flour.) Line the pieces up next to each other and make a braid by starting in the middle and laying the right piece over the left and then lifting the left piece over the right; when you reach the end, turn the braid around so that the unbraided portion is closest to you and braid that section. Leave 2 to 3 inches unbraided at one end. Lift up part of the round loaf that's in the basket (a good place to lift would be the center of the top of the loaf as determined by where the tops of the center wheat stalks are) and tuck the unbraided portion of the braid neatly under the loaf. With the open piece secured, lay the rest of the braid around the bread. Looking down on the banneton, you'll see that the braid encircles the loaf and sits on top of it, touching the sides of the banneton.

First Rise Cover the loaf and allow to rise at room temperature about 2 hours in the banneton.

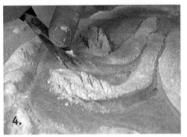

Second Rise Carefully invert the loaf onto a cornmeal-dusted peel or a parchment-covered baking sheet. Cover and allow to rest another 2 hours, at which point it should have risen perceptibly.

Baking the Bread Position a rack in the lower third of your oven and line it with a baking stone or quarry tiles, leaving a border of at least 1 inch free all around. Preheat the oven to 425°F. Pour some water into a spray bottle and set aside.

When you are ready to bake the loaf, beat 1 large egg white with ½ cup cold water to use as a wash. Use an awl or a barbecue skewer to poke some air holes into the bread (these replace the slashes you would normally make in a bread this size), then brush off any flour that might still be on the "background" of the loaf; if there's flour on the wheat stalks and braid, leave it.

Brush the loaf with the egg wash or, if you want, brush just the braid and stalks or just the background. Using small pointed scissors, clip the wheat stalks one at a time: With the tip of the scissors pointed toward the stem, make snips down each side and in the center of the thick part of each stalk. As you snip, pull the scissors up so that you lift the snipped piece of dough. Bake as directed on page 131.

1. The bent wheat stalks ready to rise.

2. Begin braiding in the middle.

3. Place the braid over the dough to encircle it.

4. Before baking, snip the stalks to make them look like wheat.

continued

Star-Shaped Pain de Campagne
COLOR PHOTOGRAPH, PAGE 71

1 recipe Pain de Campagne (page 128), risen and ready for shaping

A ready-to-glaze
star-shaped pain de
campagne.

TO SHAPE THE DOUGH INTO STAR BREADS, divide it into thirds. Shape each third into a baguette (follow the directions on page 117 as a guide) and use a long sharp pair of scissors to cut each baguette into 6 equal pieces: Hold the scissors above the baguette and cut down into the loaf on a diagonal. (The action is similar to that used to make a wheat stalk loaf, or *épi*, page 132, but here you are cutting all the way through the loaf.) Arrange 5 of the pieces on a floured baking sheet to form a star, pinching together the ends of the pieces that meet in the middle and leaving space between each piece to allow for rising. Shape the sixth piece into a ball and place it in the center of the star. Repeat with the other pieces, forming 3 stars.

Glazing and Rising Glaze the stars with egg wash (1 large egg white beaten with ½ cup cold water; reserve the remaining egg wash), cover with a towel, and allow to rise at room temperature for 1 hour.

Baking the Bread Preheat the oven to 425°F. Line one or two baking sheets with parchment paper and flour the parchment.

Before baking, adjust the shapes if needed, pinching the ends of the dough to get better points on the stars, reglaze the breads, and, if you want, sprinkle the breads with a mixture of poppy, sesame, and fennel seeds. Bake for 20 to 25 minutes, or until golden and the internal temperature of the loaves is 200°F as measured by an instant-read thermometer. Cool before cutting.

Grape-Cluster Pain de Campagne

1 recipe Pain de Campagne (page 128), risen and ready for shaping

TO SHAPE THE DOUGH INTO GRAPE-CLUSTER BREADS, cut the dough in half. Shape each half into a baguette (follow the directions on page 117 as a guide) and cut each baguette into 7 pieces with a dough scraper. Working on an unfloured work surface, form 6 of the pieces into tight balls, working the dough under your cupped palm and applying pressure with the heel of your hand. Arrange the balls in a triangular shape on the baking sheet, leaving a little space for rising between each piece: The triangle should have one ball on top, two in the middle, and three at the base. Form the seventh piece of dough into a sausage. Using the dough scraper or a small knife, slit the sausage down the center, going about three quarters of the way up. Separate the slit portion and put this piece, which will become the grape leaf tendril, on the baking sheet. Repeat with the remaining pieces of dough.

Grape cluster and tendrils set to rise.

Glazing and Rising Glaze the two grape clusters and tendrils with egg wash (1 large egg white beaten with ½ cup cold water; reserve the remaining egg wash), cover with a towel, and allow to rise at room temperature for 1 hour.

Baking the Bread Preheat the oven to 425°F. Line one or two baking sheets with parchment paper and flour the parchment.

When you're ready to bake, lift one tendril from the baking sheet and, holding it by the unsplit stem, place it on the center of the middle ball of the three-ball base of one grape cluster. Let one of the split tendril pieces drift down the grape cluster; twist the other a couple of times and arrange it along the cluster. Repeat with the second tendril. Reglaze the breads and, if you want, sprinkle them with a mixture of poppy, sesame, and fennel seeds. Bake for 20 to 25 minutes, or until golden and the internal temperature of the loaves is 200°F as measured by an instant-read thermometer. Cool before cutting.

Contributing Baker **JOE ORTIZ**

Country Bread

Makes 1 large round bread ■ With this loaf, you get the look of the Pain de Campagne (page 128) without the uncertainty that comes from dealing with a chef-levain. Here, the bread gets its flavor and character from a yeasted sponge, made from white, rye, and whole wheat flours, that ferments for eight hours. If you're looking to give the bread an extra kick of sourdough flavor, you can tuck the sponge into the refrigerator and let it do its fermenting there overnight.

Follow the directions on page 132 if you want to decorate this loaf with an outer braid and a centerpiece of wheat stalks. The instructions for making star (page 134) and grape-cluster (page 135) breads are also applicable.

THE SPONGE

1½ cups warm water (105°F to 115°F)

2½ teaspoons active dry yeast

1 cup bread flour or unbleached all-purpose flour

½ cup rye flour

½ cup whole wheat flour

Put about ¼ cup of the warm water into the bowl of a mixer and sprinkle over the yeast, stirring to mix. Allow the yeast to rest for about 5 minutes, until it turns creamy, before adding the rest of the water. Stir the 3 flours together and gradually add them to the yeast mixture, stirring them in with a wooden spoon and mixing until the sponge has the consistency of a pancake batter.

First Rise Cover the bowl with a towel and let the sponge rest at room temperature for 6 to 8 hours, during which time it will rise and fall, or put it in the refrigerator overnight. *If you've chilled the sponge, pull it out of the refrigerator about an hour before you're ready to continue with the recipe and, just to be on the safe side, use warm water in the next step.*

THE DOUGH

1 teaspoon active dry yeast

1 cup water

The sponge (above)

3 to 3½ cups bread flour or unbleached all-purpose flour

1 cup whole wheat flour

1 tablespoon salt

Dissolve the yeast in ½ cup of the water; pour another ½ cup water into the bowl with the sponge. Combine 3 cups of the white flour and the 1 cup of whole wheat flour.

Working in the mixer with the dough hook in place, gradually add 2 cups of the flour to the sponge, mixing at medium-low speed. After mixing for about

3 minutes, add the yeast mixture and beat to incorporate. Sprinkle the salt over the dough and mix it in. Now work in the remaining flour mixture and enough additional white flour to produce a dough that starts to clean the sides of the bowl. Increase the mixer speed to medium and knead for about 10 minutes. The dough should be moist and satiny, even a bit sticky.

Second Rise Turn the dough into a bowl and cover with plastic wrap. Allow the dough to proof at room temperature for 1½ to 2 hours, or until it doubles in volume.

Shaping the Dough Prepare a resting place for the loaf. A banneton that measures 8 inches across the base would be good, as would a large basket or colander lined with a linen towel. Rub flour into the liner of the banneton or basket and set aside until needed.

Turn the dough out onto a work surface that's been very lightly dusted with flour and pat it into a flat round with your fingers and palms. Fold the edges in and press them down with the heel of your hand, then turn the dough over and, using your cupped hands, work the dough against the counter to form a tight ball that's about the same size as your banneton or basket. Repeat this process of folding, flattening, and tightening into a ball four more times. Turn the loaf over and lay it smooth side down into the banneton.

Final Rise Cover the dough and set it at room temperature to rise for 1 to 1½ hours.

Baking the Bread About 30 minutes before you're ready to bake the loaf, position a rack in the lower third of your oven and line it with a baking stone or quarry tiles, leaving a border of at least 1 inch free all around. Preheat the oven to 425°F. Pour some water into a spray bottle and set aside.

When the dough is fully risen, rub a baker's peel or baking sheet with cornmeal and carefully invert the loaf onto it. Spray the oven walls with water and immediately close the oven door to trap the steam. Using a single-edge razor blade, slash the loaf in a pattern that appeals to you—3 long slashes or a broad tic-tac-toe pattern would be nice—cutting about ½ inch into the loaf. Slide the bread onto the hot baking stone or tiles, turn the oven heat down to 400°F, and immediately spray the oven walls again; close the door as quickly as you can. Bake the bread for 60 to 70 minutes, or until the crust is deeply golden, the loaf sounds hollow when thumped on the bottom, and the internal temperature is 200°F as measured by an instant-read thermometer plunged into its center.

Remove the loaf to a rack and allow it to cool for at least 20 minutes, preferably longer, before cutting. (It is really best to allow the bread to cool to room temperature before cutting.)

Storing The loaf will keep for about 3 days at room temperature. Store it cut side down on your counter—its thick crust will be fine exposed to the air. For storage of up to a month, wrap the loaf airtight in plastic and freeze it. Thaw, still wrapped, at room temperature.

Contributing Baker **JOE ORTIZ**

Rustic Potato Loaves
COLOR PHOTOGRAPH, PAGE 65

Makes 2 loaves ■ A yeast-raised bread with a dough that's half flour, half mashed potatoes, and entirely satisfying. The crust is deep and dark, the moist crumb is tender and open here, tightly grained there, and the flavor is haunting and not easily placed, almost a little nutty. It is an odd and interesting dough to work with, a reverse dough—it comes together quickly and then softens and falls apart, defying what's expected of bread dough. The breads, two free-form rustic-looking loaves, each with a jagged, flour-encrusted crease running down its center, are easy to make and quick to rise—they proof for just twenty minutes before shaping and twenty minutes after, making them good candidates for baking on a whim.

1½ pounds russet potatoes (about 3)

4 teaspoons salt

½ cup tepid reserved potato water (80°F to 90°F)

1 tablespoon active dry yeast

2 tablespoons extra-virgin olive oil

4¾ cups unbleached all-purpose flour

Cooking the Potatoes Scrub the potatoes and cut them into quarters, peel and all. Toss them into a 2-quart pot, cover with water, add 2 teaspoons of the salt, and boil until the potatoes are soft enough to be pierced easily with the point of a knife. Dip a measuring cup into the pot and draw off ½ cup of the potato water; reserve. Drain the potatoes in a colander and then spread them out, either in the colander or on a cooling rack over a jelly-roll pan, and let them cool and air-dry for 20 to 30 minutes. It's important that the potatoes be dry before they're mashed.

Mixing the Dough When the potatoes are cool, stir the yeast into the reserved potato water (if the water is no longer warm, heat it for a few seconds in a microwave oven—it should feel warm to the touch) and allow it to rest for 5 minutes; it will turn creamy.

Meanwhile, turn the cooled potatoes into the bowl of a mixer fitted with the paddle attachment and mash them. With the mixer on low speed, add the dissolved yeast and the olive oil and mix until the liquids are incorporated into the potatoes.

Replace the paddle with the dough hook and, still mixing on low speed, add the flour and the remaining 2 teaspoons salt. Mix on low speed for 2 to 3 minutes, then increase the speed to medium and mix for 11 minutes more. The dough will be firm at first and soft at the finish. At the start, it will look dry, so dry you'll think you're making a pie crust. But as the dough is worked, it will be transformed. It may even look like a brioche, cleaning the sides of the bowl but pooling at the bottom. Have faith and keep beating.

First Rise Cover the mixing bowl with plastic wrap and allow the dough to rise at room temperature for 20 to 30 minutes, at which point the dough will have risen noticeably, although it may not have doubled.

While the bread is proofing, position a rack in the bottom of the oven and fit it with a baking stone or quarry tiles, leaving a border of at least 1 inch all around. Preheat the oven to 375°F. Place a linen towel on a baking sheet, rub the towel with flour, and set aside; this will be the resting place for the bread's final rise. Rub a baker's peel or baking sheet with cornmeal or flour. Fill a spray bottle with water; set aside.

Shaping the Dough Turn the bread out onto a lightly floured surface and, using a dough scraper, cut the dough in half. To shape each half into a torpedo shape, first shape it into a ball and then flatten it into a disk. Starting at the end farthest from you, roll up the dough toward you. When you're on your last roll, stop and pull the free end of dough toward you, stretching it gently, and dust its edge with flour. Finish the roll and, if necessary, rock the loaf back and forth a little to taper the ends and form a torpedo, or football.

Second Rise Place the loaves on the floured towel, seam side down, and cover them with the ends of the towel (or another towel). Let the breads rise at room temperature for 20 minutes.

Baking the Bread When you're ready to bake, spray the oven walls with water and immediately close the oven door to trap the steam. Turn the breads out, seam side up, onto the peel or baking sheet and transfer them to the oven. Spray the oven with water again and bake the loaves for 45 to 50 minutes, or until the crust is very brown, the loaves sound hollow when thumped on the bottom, and, the most important test, the interior temperature measures 200°F when an instant-read thermometer is plunged into the center of the loaves. Remove the loaves from the oven and cool on a rack for at least 20 minutes before slicing. While you should wait for the bread to firm up in the cooling process, slathering this bread with butter while it's still warm is a great treat.

Storing The breads should be stored at room temperature. Once sliced, the bread should be turned cut side down on a cutting board; it will keep at room temperature for about 2 days. For longer storage, wrap the breads airtight and freeze them for up to a month. Thaw, still wrapped, at room temperature.

Contributing Baker **LESLIE MACKIE**

Flatbreads

PIZZA TO PITA

IN THIS GLOBAL COLLECTION of flatbreads are the familiar and the foreign, the simple and the simple to dress up. Here are pizza, made with Steve Sullivan's trademark precision, and focaccia, the bread that has forever changed the way we think about sandwiches, made with Craig Kominiak's amazingly active dough and shaped in various ways, none more beautiful than the open-pattern leaf nor more practical than the large square, an invitation to create a colorful grilled-vegetable sandwich.

From Jeffrey Alford and Naomi Duguid, culinary explorers, come flatbreads like the Persian Naan, long, striated, and sculptural; round and puffed scallion-topped Oasis Naan; and savory Eastern Mediterranean Pizzas, a meal in themselves. There are the truly flat breads such as Beatrice Ojakangas's Norwegian lefse, a crêpelike bread made with a potato dough, and Lauren Groveman's matzos, the dry, bumpy-topped crackers eaten to commemorate Passover. And there are flatbreads that don't look flat at all, such as Alford and Duguid's pitas that puff up as they bake. Make one and you'll never want to forgo the taste or the pleasure of preparing these at home.

Indeed, the techniques of forming and baking these flatbreads are simple and satisfying. Whether you're dotting a naan with dozens of fingerprints, running a pizza cutter across a cracker dough, unfurling a matzo dough onto a hot stone, or lifting a lefse from the griddle with a stick, you'll find yourself as pleased with the process as with the prize.

Focaccia

COLOR PHOTOGRAPH, PAGE 63

Makes 3 focaccias ■ The dough for these focaccias is so active and bubbly it squeaks. Indeed, every step in working with this dough is designed to keep the bubbles that will give the breads their beautiful inner open weave and speckled, oil-glistened crust.

Focaccia and pizza, cousins in the Italian flatbread family, were often the baker's snack, the midwork nibble between ovenloads of breads. But these focaccias are so gorgeous—sunny-gold, oiled, topped with herbs or fruited, and spectacularly sculptural—that you'll want to make them the main event.

This dough is mixed quickly in a heavy-duty mixer, allowed to rise, and then refrigerated for at least twenty-four hours, the time it needs to set that bubbly structure in place. Once developed, it can be used to make a plain herb-topped focaccia (this recipe), a sweet fougasse (page 194) topped with streusel, or a savory fougasse (page 146). You can use the full recipe to make any of these shapes and flavors or you can divide this recipe in thirds and make all three kinds of bread.

Once the focaccias are made, the serving possibilities are limitless. Try the grilled vegetable sandwich (page 145), or use the focaccia as a pizza, baking it with any of your favorite toppings. And don't toss away stale focaccia—it makes flavorful bread crumbs or a great stuffing for a roasted chicken.

> 2¼ to 2½ cups tepid water (about 90°F)
> 2 tablespoons active dry yeast
> ¼ cup olive oil
> 6½ cups unbleached all-purpose flour
> 4 teaspoons salt

Mixing the Dough Whisk ½ cup of the water and the yeast together in the bowl of a mixer. Set the mixture aside for 5 minutes, until the yeast dissolves and turns creamy.

Meanwhile, pour 1¾ cups warm water into a large measuring cup, add the olive oil, and whisk to blend; set aside. Whisk the flour and salt together in a large bowl and set this aside as well.

Pour the water-oil mixture over the yeast and stir with the whisk to blend. Add about half of the flour and stir with a rubber spatula just to mix. Attach the dough hook, add the remaining flour, and mix on low speed for about 3 minutes, or until the dough just starts to come together. If the dough appears dry and a little stiff, add a few drops of warm water, scraping the bowl and hook if necessary to incorporate the water and create a soft dough. Increase the mixer speed to medium-high and continue to mix for about 10 minutes, scraping

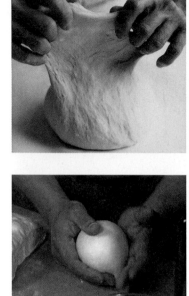

down the hook and sides of the bowl as needed, until you have a soft, slightly moist, extremely elastic dough that cleans the sides of the bowl. You will know that the dough is properly mixed when a piece can be stretched, without tearing, to create a "window," an almost transparent patch of dough.

First Rise Transfer the dough to a work surface and form it into a ball. Place the dough in an oiled bowl, turn it around to cover it with oil, and cover the bowl tightly with plastic wrap. Allow the dough to rise at room temperature until doubled in bulk, 1 to 1½ hours.

Second Rise Fold the dough down on itself to deflate it and let it rise again until doubled and billowy, 45 minutes to 1 hour.

Shaping and Resting Fold the dough over on itself again to deflate it (as you do this, you can hear the bubbles squeak and pop) and turn it out onto a work surface. Using a metal dough scraper or a knife, cut the dough into 3 equal pieces. Shape each piece into a ball.

The dough needs to be refrigerated for between 24 and 36 hours. (It is this long refrigerated rest that gives the focaccia its characteristic chewy texture and surface bubbles.) Place each ball in an oiled gallon-size lock-top plastic bag and refrigerate.

About 1½ hours before you plan to bake, remove the dough from the refrigerator and gently take the balls out of the oiled bags. (If you have a problem, cut the bags open with scissors to release the dough.) Place the dough on a lightly floured surface, dust the tops of the balls with flour, and cover loosely but completely with plastic (to avoid having the tops go crusty). Let rest for 1 hour, until the dough reaches a cool room temperature and feels spongy when prodded.

Top: The "window."
Bottom: Shape each piece into a ball.

THE TOPPING

Herb-infused or other olive oil

Chopped fresh herbs, such as rosemary and/or thyme (2 to 3 tablespoons), and coarse sea salt

Position an oven rack in the lower third of the oven and preheat the oven to 450°F. If you have a baking stone, place it in the oven and preheat it too; dust a peel with cornmeal. Or line two baking sheets with parchment paper and dust the paper with cornmeal; set the baking sheets aside. Fill a spray bottle with water and set it aside as well.

Pull and stretch dough into a square.

Shaping the Dough Use your palm to press down gently on each piece of dough, causing bubbles to appear on the sides, then slit the bubbles with a single-edge razor blade to release the gases. Gently pull and stretch each piece of dough into a square about 10 inches across, taking care not to overwork the dough or handle it too roughly—you don't want to knock out the bubbles you've worked so hard to create. Let the dough relax, covered, for about 10 minutes, then tidy up the edges with your hands.

Baking the Bread Transfer the foccacias to the cornmeal-dusted peel or the parchment-lined baking sheets. Use a single-edge razor blade to slash each square, cutting a tic-tac-toe pattern, or making 3 slashes in the center of the dough and enclosing them in 4 slashes to form a square with open corners. Brush the foccacias with olive oil, sprinkle with fresh herbs and coarse sea salt, and put them into the oven.

Slash and top with olive oil, herbs, and salt.

Bake the breads for 15 to 20 minutes, or until they are golden with a heavy speckling of small surface bubbles, spraying the oven with water three times during the first 8 minutes of baking. As soon as you remove the foccacias from the oven, brush them with a little additional olive oil and transfer them to a rack to cool before serving.

Storing The foccacias are best the day they are baked, but once cooled, they can be wrapped airtight and frozen for up to 2 weeks. Thaw the breads, still wrapped, at room temperature and warm them in a 350°F oven before serving.

Grilled Vegetable Focaccia Sandwich

You can use any vegetables, in any amount, you choose; this is just a suggestion. Split a square of focaccia in half and brush the cut sides with olive oil. Layer grilled and fresh vegetables, each nicely seasoned, in the following order: grilled zucchini or summer squash, ripe red tomatoes, grilled eggplant, grilled red peppers, fresh basil, ripe yellow tomatoes, and crumbled goat cheese. Put the top of the bread in place and, if you want, warm the sandwich in a 450°F oven to melt the cheese before serving.

Contributing Baker **CRAIG KOMINIAK**

Leaf-Shaped Fougasse

COLOR PHOTOGRAPH, PAGE 59

Makes 2 large or 3 medium breads ■ A tradition in southern France and many regions of Italy, the leaf-shaped fougasse is a stunning, sculpted bread, scented with olive oil and herbs and lovely served with savory spreads, soft cheeses, or hearty soups and stews. You can make the fougasse any size you want, but the bigger it is, the more impressive, and the shape is easier to make than appearance would have you believe. One batch of focaccia dough will make two large or three medium fougasse, any or all of which can be placed in the center of the table as decoration. Intersperse the fougasse with bunches of fragrant herbs, and you can forget the flowers.

1 recipe Focaccia dough (page 143), chilled for at least 24 hours
Olive oil, for brushing
Fresh herbs or dried herbes de Provence, for topping
Coarse sea salt, for sprinkling

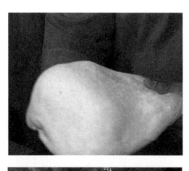

Top: Lift the dough around your fist.
Bottom: Cut ³/₄-inch nicks on the edge of the dough, then cut the interior pattern.

Position the oven racks to divide the oven into thirds and preheat the oven to 450°F. Line two baking sheets with parchment paper and dust the paper with cornmeal; keep the sheets close at hand. Fill a spray bottle with water and set it aside.

Shaping the Dough Working with one piece of dough at a time (keeping the other[s] covered), and working with the dough as you do with all focaccias—that is, gently, taking care not to knock out all the air you've worked into it—put the dough over your left fist (your right if you are left-handed) and lift and circle it around your fist with your other hand. Pull it a little and pinch the edges slightly as you work your way around—you're aiming for a teardrop or triangular shape about a foot long and 10 inches across at the base. Put the dough on a cornmeal-dusted baking sheet and cover it while you work the other piece(s) into shape.

Use a single-edge razor blade or a sharp serrated knife, held perpendicular to the dough, to create the leaf pattern in the dough: Position the teardrop with the broad base parallel to you and cut 3 vertical slashes in a line down the center of the teardrop, plunging the razor straight down into the dough. With these as your guide, cut 3 slanted cuts in both halves of the teardrop, angling the cuts between the slashes that clip the long sides. Nick the sloping sides, cutting at an angle and cutting only about half the length of the razor blade into the dough. Starting with the diagonal slashes on either side of the vertical cuts, work your fingers into all of the openings and stretch them evenly to double or triple their original size. (They must be opened now so that the holes won't close when the dough rises.)

Rest Brush the loaves with olive oil, sprinkle with herbs, and dust with coarse salt. Let rest for about 10 minutes before baking.

Baking the Bread Bake the fougasse for 15 to 18 minutes, or until they are golden and speckled with small surface bubbles, spraying the oven with water three times during the first 8 minutes of baking. If the breads aren't browning evenly, rotate the pans, top to bottom and front to back, halfway through the baking period. As soon as you remove the fougasse from the oven, brush them with a little more olive oil, and transfer them to a rack to cool before serving.

Use your fingers to stretch the openings.

Storing The fougasse are best the day they are baked, but once cooled, they can be wrapped airtight and frozen for up to 2 weeks. Thaw the breads, still wrapped, at room temperature and warm them in a 350°F oven before serving.

Contributing Baker **CRAIG KOMINIAK**

Persian Naan

Makes 4 long narrow breads ▪ The look of this bread is at once dramatic and rustic. Long—snowshoe-shaped, actually—and dimpled from stem to stern with fingerprints that give it an undulating appearance and an interesting crisp-here-chewy-there texture, this thin flatbread of Central Asia is traditionally baked in a tandoor, a deep clay oven. But you need no out-of-the-ordinary equipment to turn out authentic breads at home. The making of the dough follows standard techniques for mixing and rising—it's the shaping that's odd and fun. The breads are stretched, wet to just this side of soaked, pummeled with your fingertips, and tossed onto hot quarry tiles (or a baking sheet) to bake for a mere five minutes, finishing with a firm, toasty bottom crust and a crumb that's soft but stretchy, warm, and wheaty. Don't even think about slicing these breads; they're meant to be stacked on the table, an edible centerpiece, and torn into pieces big and small. This same dough makes Oasis Naan (page 149), a round bread speckled with scallions.

continued

2¹/₂ cups tepid water (80°F to 90°F)

2 teaspoons active dry yeast

5 to 6 cups bread flour or unbleached all-purpose flour

1 tablespoon salt

4 teaspoons sesame seeds

Put the water and yeast in a large bowl and stir to blend. Add 3 cups of the flour, about a cup at a time, stirring in one direction with a wooden spoon. Beat for 1 minute, or about 100 strokes, to develop the gluten. Sprinkle the salt over the mixture and start adding the remaining flour, again about a cup at a time, stirring after each addition and then stirring until the dough is too stiff for you to work. You may not need to use it all.

Turn the dough out onto a lightly floured work surface and knead it vigorously, adding more flour as necessary, until it is smooth and easy to handle, about 10 minutes.

Rise Transfer the dough to a lightly oiled bowl, turning to cover the entire surface with oil, cover the bowl with plastic wrap, and let the dough rest at room temperature until it has more than doubled in bulk, about 2 hours. Don't worry if it goes longer—it will be just fine. *If it's more convenient, you can put the bowl in the refrigerator and let the dough rise overnight; bring the dough to room temperature before continuing.*

When you're ready to bake, line the center rack of your oven with quarry tiles or a baking stone, leaving a 1-inch air space all around, and preheat the oven to 500°F. (If you do not have tiles, place an inverted baking sheet on the oven rack and preheat it with the oven.)

Top: Dimple the dough.
Bottom: Then stretch the dough by slowly pulling your hands apart.

Shaping the Dough Deflate the dough, turn it out onto a lightly floured work surface, and divide it into 4 pieces. Flatten the pieces and shape them into ovals, each about 6 inches wide and 8 inches long. Cover the ovals with plastic wrap and let them rest for a few minutes to relax the gluten.

Start shaping the first bread a few minutes after the oven reaches 500°F. Fill a small bowl with cold water, dip your fingers into the water, and, starting at one end of the oval, press your fingertips into the dough to make deep, closely spaced rows of indentations all across the dough. (Don't be timid—the impressions have to be deep enough to remain after you've stretched the dough.) Keep moistening your fingers as you work so that the dough's surface remains wet— really wet. In fact, it may look a little sloppy to you, but that's the way it's supposed to be.

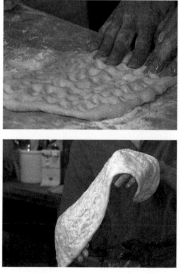

Lift the dough, drape it over your hands, and stretch it by slowly pulling your hands apart. You will need to drape and stretch a couple of times in order to get the right shape—you're aiming for an oval that is about 5 inches wide and between 16 and 18 inches long. Don't worry if there are a few holes in the dough—carry on.

Baking the Bread Put the dough down on the work surface and sprinkle with a teaspoon of the sesame seeds. Then carefully lift the dough with both hands and place it on the baking stone (or baking sheet). (If you are adept at using a peel, transfer the bread to the oven on a cornmeal-dusted peel.) Bake until the bread has golden patches on top and is brown and crusty on the bottom, about 5 minutes. Remove the bread from the oven, let it cool on a rack for 5 minutes, and then wrap it in a cotton towel to keep it soft and warm.

While one bread is baking, shape the next bread. When you've had some practice shaping, you'll become fast enough to slip a second bread into the oven by the time the other is halfway through its bake time.

Serve warm or at room temperature.

Storing The breads are best eaten shortly after they're baked, but they'll keep, wrapped in a towel, for a day. For longer storage, wrap the breads airtight and freeze for up to a month. Keep the breads in their wrappers while they thaw at room temperature and then warm them for a few minutes in a 400°F oven before serving.

Contributing Bakers **JEFFREY ALFORD**
AND NAOMI DUGUID

Oasis Naan

COLOR PHOTOGRAPH, PAGE 74

Makes 8 round breads ■ The dough for these naan is the same as that for Persian Naan, but it is shaped differently. These breads are formed into rounds, their centers flattened and sprinkled with scallions, salt, and a pinch of cumin, and their edges left full, to expand like the crust of a Neapolitan pizza.

    1 recipe Persian Naan dough (page 147), fully risen
    1 tablespoon coarse salt
    2 scallions, trimmed and chopped (white and tender green
       parts only)
    1 teaspoon (approximately) cumin or caraway seeds

Center a rack in the oven and line it with quarry tiles or a baking stone, leaving a 1-inch air space all around. (If you do not have tiles or a stone, place an inverted baking sheet on the oven rack.) Preheat the oven to 500°F. Set aside a baker's peel or dust a baking sheet with flour.

Shaping the Dough Divide the dough into 8 equal pieces and roll each piece into a ball; flatten each ball with lightly floured palms. Roll out the dough into circles about ¼ inch thick and 5 to 6 inches across and sprinkle with water. (You don't want these to be as wet as Persian breads.) Each circle needs to be well pricked all over, with the exception of a 1- to 2-inch border. Traditionally, this is done with a dough stamp, a round utensil with concentric circles of thin spikes. Alternatively, you can use a roller pricker (also known as a pastry docker), the tines of a fork, or the pointy metal loop at the bottom of a whisk. Whatever you choose, you want to prick the dough with determination, flattening the center of each circle. Sprinkle each center with coarse salt, chopped scallions, and a pinch of cumin or caraway seeds.

Baking the Bread Slide the breads onto the hot quarry tiles using the baker's peel (or slide onto the baking sheet), and bake for 6 to 8 minutes, or until the tops start to color. Remove the breads and cool on a rack for about 5 minutes before wrapping them in a cotton towel. These are best served warm.

Storing The breads are best eaten shortly after they're baked, but they'll keep, wrapped in a towel, for a day. For longer storage, wrap the breads airtight and freeze for up to a month. Keep the breads in their wrappers while they thaw at room temperature and then warm them for a few minutes in a 400°F oven before serving.

Contributing Bakers **JEFFREY ALFORD AND NAOMI DUGUID**

Ka'kat

Makes 32 bread rings ▪ Throughout the Eastern Mediterranean, ka'kat are a staple—and satisfying—street food, seemingly available everywhere and anytime. Sesame-seed–encrusted and sized for snacking, they're about two and a half inches across and reminiscent, if not in taste, then certainly in mood, of soft American pretzels. This bread is often flavored with mahleb, the ground kernels of a type of black cherry found in the region. Mahleb is available in Middle Eastern groceries, and a quarter teaspoon mixed into the dough will add an exotic aroma to the baked breads.

2 tablespoons sugar

2 teaspoons active dry yeast

2 cups warm water (105°F to 115°F)

4 to 5 cups bread flour or unbleached all-purpose flour

1½ teaspoons salt

¼ teaspoon ground mahleb (optional)

1 large egg beaten with 1 tablespoon cold water, for egg wash

3 to 4 tablespoons sesame seeds

Whisk the sugar, yeast, and water together in a medium bowl. Stirring in one direction with a wooden spoon, add 2 to 3 cups of flour, a cup at a time, mixing until incorporated. Stir for a minute, about 100 strokes. Let this sponge rest, covered, for 10 minutes.

Stir the salt and mahleb into the sponge. Continuing to stir with the wooden spoon, and still stirring in one direction, gradually add as much additional flour as the dough can incorporate. Then turn it onto a lightly floured work surface and knead it for 8 to 10 minutes, adding more flour only if necessary. The dough should be smooth and elastic.

First Rise Transfer the dough to an oiled bowl, cover with plastic wrap, turn to coat the dough with oil, and allow it to rise at room temperature until doubled in volume, 1½ to 2 hours.

Shaping and Second Rise Lightly oil two baking sheets and keep them close to your work space. Punch the dough down, turn it out onto a work surface, and cut it into 32 pieces. Lightly flour the work surface, then use your palms to roll each piece of dough into a rope 6 to 7 inches long. Pinch the ends of each one together to form a circle and place the circles on the oiled baking sheets, leaving at least ½ inch between them. Cover and allow to rise for 30 minutes.

Baking the Bread Set the oven racks in the upper part of the oven and preheat the oven to 400°F.

Brush the ka'kat with the egg wash and sprinkle with sesame seeds. Bake until nicely browned, about 20 minutes. To ensure that the breads bake evenly, rotate the baking sheets top to bottom and front to back halfway through the baking time. Transfer the baked breads to racks and cool for about 5 minutes before wrapping in a cloth to keep warm. These are best served warm.

Storing These can be kept in a plastic bag at room temperature for a day or two or wrapped airtight and frozen for a month. Thaw, still wrapped, at room temperature and crisp in a hot oven before serving.

Contributing Bakers **JEFFREY ALFORD AND NAOMI DUGUID**

Pebble Bread

COLOR PHOTOGRAPH, PAGE 60

Makes 8 round breads ■ In Morocco, this bread is baked on hot pebbles, some of which usually get baked into the bread and have to be shaken out. At home, you can get the same pitted texture with your fingertips, and the same tender, soft-from-steam texture by soaking the dough and cooking it first in a skillet and then under the broiler. Pebble Bread's rich, full flavor comes from the use of barley flour and the effects of a twenty-four-hour rest, a period that allows the dough to sour a little.

THE SPONGE

> 3 cups lukewarm water (95°F to 105°F)
> ½ teaspoon active dry yeast
> 2 cups bread flour or unbleached all-purpose flour

Stir the water and yeast together in a large bowl until the yeast is dissolved. Stirring in one direction with a wooden spoon, add the bread flour and stir 100 times, about 1 minute.

First Rise Cover the bowl with plastic wrap and allow the sponge to rest at room temperature for 24 hours, during which time it will develop a pleasantly—and characteristically—sour flavor.

THE DOUGH

> 1½ cups barley flour
> 1 tablespoon salt
> 4 cups bread flour or unbleached all-purpose flour
>
> 1 tablespoon (approximately) vegetable oil, for cooking

The next day, you'll find that the sponge is bubbly and the extra water will have separated from it. Fold and stir the water back into the batter before continuing.

Mixing and Kneading Using a wooden spoon and always stirring in one direction, stir in the barley flour. Stir in the salt. Gradually add the 4 cups bread flour, stirring and folding the flour into the dough until it becomes too stiff to stir. Turn the dough out onto a lightly floured work surface and knead it for 8 to 10 minutes, or until it is smooth and elastic.

Second Rise Wipe the bowl clean and return the dough to it; cover with plastic wrap and let the dough rise at room temperature for 3 hours, or until it almost doubles in bulk.

Shaping the Dough Use your fingertips to pull the dough away from the sides of the bowl and turn it out onto a lightly floured work surface, then cut the dough into 8 pieces and shape each into a ball. Lightly flour the palm of one hand and use it to gently flatten each ball. Cover the balls with a towel and let them rest for 10 minutes.

Meanwhile, position an oven rack or the broiler rack 4 to 6 inches from the broiler element and turn on the broiler. Lightly oil a large (about 12-inch diameter) skillet that can be used under the broiler and set it over medium heat. Place a large shallow bowl or pan containing at least an inch of water near your work surface.

Final Shaping and Baking Roll a ball of dough into a 9- to 10-inch round that is less than ¼ inch thick. Lift the round and put it into the bowl of water, pressing it down gently to immerse it. Transfer the dough to a work surface and use your fingertips to create deep, rounded indentations all over the dough. Place the dough in the hot skillet (it will sizzle and steam) and cook for about 3½ minutes, or until the bottom surface firms. (As the bread begins to cook, it may lose some of its indentations—press in some more while it is in the skillet.) Sprinkle a little more water over the bread and lift it from the skillet to the oven rack. Broil for 4½ to 5 minutes, or until golden.

Remove the bread from the oven and wrap immediately in a cotton cloth to preserve the bread's warmth and suppleness. Continue with the remaining balls of dough. When you've done several batches of this bread, you may be able to work out a rhythm that will allow you to roll out a bread or cook a bread in the skillet while another bread is baking under the broiler—it takes practice. You'll know you're proficient when you can work with two skillets.

Storing These breads should be eaten the day they are made.

Contributing Bakers **JEFFREY ALFORD AND NAOMI DUGUID**

Pita Breads

COLOR PHOTOGRAPH, PAGE 76

Makes about 16 pitas ■ Pita breads are a testament to the magic of yeast and heat. They start out flat, innocent little disks of dough tossed onto a hot surface, but minutes later they puff almost to the bursting point. During their short baking time—they're only in the oven for about five minutes—they expand to create a pocket roomy enough to fill with grilled vegetables, cool greens, savory spreads, or chunky salads. They also make great scooper-uppers for mixes like lentil or chickpea salad, herbed yogurt cheese, or dips (pages 454 to 456).

As versatile as the breads are in terms of serving, that's how versatile they are in terms of preparation. They can be made entirely of whole wheat or white flour, but a mix gives the pita an appealing sweetness. And while they get an additional flavor boost from being made with a sponge (a mini-batch of dough that rests for eight hours and intensifies the character of the bread), they can be made more quickly—just let the initial mix of dough rest for ten to thirty minutes. Finally, if sixteen pitas are more than you can use, you can make the dough and refrigerate it for up to a week, cutting off as much as you need for the day. In summer, skip the oven and bake them on a griddle.

1 teaspoon active dry yeast

2½ cups tepid water (80°F to 90°F)

2½ cups whole wheat flour

1 tablespoon salt

1 tablespoon olive oil

2½ to 3½ cups unbleached all-purpose flour

Top: A well-developed sponge.

Bottom: Turn the dough out and knead.

Mixing and Resting Stir the yeast and water together in a large bowl. Using a wooden spoon and stirring in one direction, stir in the whole wheat flour about a cup at a time; then stir 100 times, or until the mixture looks smooth and silky. This is the sponge and it needs to rest, covered with plastic wrap, for at least 30 minutes, although it's best if it can rest for as long as 8 hours in a cool place, a rest that will give it a fuller flavor.

Mixing and Kneading Sprinkle the salt over the sponge and then stir in the olive oil, mixing well, again stirring in the same direction. Add the all-purpose flour about a cup at a time, mixing until the dough is too stiff to stir with the spoon. Turn the dough out onto a lightly floured work surface and knead it mixing until it is smooth and elastic, 8 to 10 minutes. The dough will be moderately firm and have a slight sheen.

Rise Clean the mixing bowl, dry it, and coat it lightly with oil. Transfer the dough to the bowl, turn the dough around to oil its surface, and cover tightly with plastic wrap. Let the dough rise at room temperature for 2 to 3 hours, or until it doubles in bulk.

If you want, you can make the dough ahead to this point and keep it refrigerated for up to a week. Pack the dough into a plastic bag that is at least three times as big as the dough; seal the bag at the very end, to leave as much room as possible for expansion. When you're ready to bake, cut off as much dough as you need, transfer it to a bowl, cover, and bring it to room temperature before proceeding with the recipe. Don't be concerned if the aroma of the bread changes as it remains in the refrigerator. This aroma, reminiscent of sourdough, is the result of the dough's natural fermentation.

TO BAKE THE BREADS IN THE OVEN If you have quarry tiles or baking stones, use them to line the bottom rack of your oven, leaving a 1-inch border free around the tiles so that the heat can circulate properly. You can simulate the quality of a tiled oven by lining the rack with two small baking sheets, leaving a similar border. Preheat the oven to 450°F.

Shaping the Dough Deflate the dough by kneading it briefly. Divide it in half and keep one half under plastic or a cloth while you work with the other. Cut the dough into 8 equal pieces and, with lightly floured cupped hands, form the pieces into tight balls; keep the balls under plastic as you work on the others. On a well-floured surface, flatten the balls of dough with your fingertips and then, using a rolling pin, roll each piece of dough into a circle 8 to 9 inches in diameter and less than ¼ inch thick. Cover but do not stack the rolled-out breads.

Place as many of the rolled-out breads as will fit onto the preheated tiles or baking sheets—you'll probably be able to bake 4 to 6 breads at a time—and bake for 3 to 5 minutes, or until the breads resemble well-blown-up balloons. Don't worry if you get seams or dry spots or less-than-full balloons (your tiles might not have been hot enough); the breads will still taste good. As the breads come from the oven, wrap them together in a large kitchen towel. Finish baking this batch of bread, roll out the remaining dough, and continue baking.

TO BAKE THE BREADS ON THE STOVE TOP Preheat a 9-inch griddle or cast-iron skillet over medium-high heat, and lightly oil the griddle. Bake one rolled-out circle at a time on the griddle, putting the pita top side down on the griddle and cooking for 15 to 20 seconds before turning the bread over gently. Cook for another minute, or until big bubbles appear. Turn the bread again and cook until it balloons fully. Pressing a towel on those areas where bubbles have formed will push air into the flat areas. The breads should bake for no more than 3 minutes. Oil the griddle after every 4 or 5 breads.

Storing Pita is best the day it is made, but it can be wrapped airtight and frozen for 1 month. Thaw and reheat on a baking sheet in a 350°F oven before serving.

Contributing Bakers **JEFFREY ALFORD AND NAOMI DUGUID**

Eastern Mediterranean Pizzas
COLOR PHOTOGRAPH, PAGE 75

Makes 8 round breads ■ The base of these lamb and tomato breads is a pita dough, thinly rolled and flattened in the center. The dough's natural ballooning action is kept at bay by the weight of the unusual topping, a mixture made aromatic with cinnamon and allspice. If you prefer, you can omit the lamb and increase the proportions of tomatoes and shallots. Add a soft crumbled cheese, like goat cheese, to the topping and the breads will remind you of pizza.

THE TOPPING

1 teaspoon olive oil

¼ cup finely chopped shallots

2 to 3 cloves garlic, peeled and finely chopped

¼ pound finely ground lean lamb

8 ripe plum tomatoes, chopped (or use well-drained canned tomatoes)

⅛ teaspoon cinnamon

⅛ teaspoon allspice

½ teaspoon salt, or more to taste

¼ teaspoon freshly ground black pepper

Heat the olive oil in a heavy skillet over medium heat. Add the shallots and garlic and cook, stirring, for 2 to 3 minutes, or until softened. Add the lamb and, still stirring, cook until it loses its raw color. Turn the heat down to medium-low, add the tomatoes, and cook until soft, 2 to 3 minutes. You want the filling to be moist but not watery, so pour off any excess liquid now. Stir in the cinnamon, allspice, salt, and pepper and set the pan aside.

The topping can be made several hours or up to a day or two ahead and stored, tightly sealed, in the refrigerator. It is best to bring the topping to room temperature before putting it on the breads.

THE BREAD

½ recipe Pita Breads dough (page 154), fully risen

1 to 2 tablespoons pine nuts

Preheat the oven to 450°F. Lightly oil 2 large baking sheets.

Shaping the Dough Deflate the dough by kneading it briefly. Divide it in half and keep one half under plastic or a cloth while you work with the other. Cut the dough into 4 equal pieces and, with lightly floured cupped hands, form the pieces into tight balls, rolling them around under your hand and using some pressure; keep the finished balls under plastic as you work on the others. On a well-floured surface, flatten the balls of dough with your fingertips and then, using a rolling pin, roll each piece of dough into a thin circle 6 to 8 inches in diameter and less than ¼ inch thick. Cover but do not stack the rolled-out breads as you finish them.

Topping and Baking Place 1½ to 2 tablespoons of the topping in the center of one bread, leaving a ½-inch border free around the edge. Sprinkle a few pine nuts over the topping and put the bread on one of the lightly oiled baking sheets. Continue to prepare breads in this way, filling one baking sheet and setting it into the oven before starting on another. Bake for about 7 minutes, or until the crusts of the breads are lightly browned. Cool on a rack for a few minutes and then, to keep the breads warm for serving, wrap them in a cotton towel. Continue to bake the remaining breads. These are best served hot, but they can be eaten at room temperature.

Storing Both the topping and the pita dough can be made ahead. (See page 154 for make-ahead instructions.) However, the topped and baked pizzas should be served the day they are made.

Contributing Bakers **JEFFREY ALFORD AND NAOMI DUGUID**

Pizza with Onion Confit

Makes 2 large pizzas ■ Here's a dough that has enough texture and flavor to hold its own under any topping you choose, whether it's the classic tomato and cheese or this Provençal-inspired onion confit. Opt for the confit, and you might want to make it as soon as you set the sponge aside to rise, since it needs to cook for about an hour and then cool. Of course, you can prepare it a couple of days ahead and store it in the refrigerator until needed.

If you're planning to make the Mixed-Starter Bread (page 113), save a piece of this fully risen dough to serve as the "old dough" in the first of the starters.

THE SPONGE

> 1½ **teaspoons active dry yeast**
> 1½ **cups tepid water (about 80°F)**
> 2 **tablespoons olive oil**
> 2¼ **cups unbleached all-purpose flour**

Place the yeast in a medium bowl (you can use the bowl from your mixer) and add the water, stirring to dissolve the yeast. Allow the yeast to rest for about

5 minutes, until it turns creamy. Stir the oil into the mixture and then gradually stir in the flour, mixing until well incorporated.

First Rise Scrape down the sides of the bowl, cover, and let the sponge rest in a warm place (about 85°F) for about 1½ hours, or until the sponge is very bubbly and has risen to about double its volume.

While the sponge is rising, make the onion confit.

THE CONFIT

3 tablespoons unsalted butter

4 medium onions (about 2½ pounds total), peeled, halved, and sliced ⅛ to ¼ inch thick

Salt and freshly ground black pepper to taste

1 tablespoon sugar

Fresh thyme sprigs or leaves to taste

1¼ to 1½ cups red wine

¼ cup red wine vinegar

Crème de cassis to taste (optional)

Melt the butter in a large heavy skillet and stir in the onions. Season with salt and pepper, stir, cover the pan, and cook the onions over low heat until they are soft, about 5 minutes. Sprinkle the sugar over the onions, stir, cover, and cook for another 5 minutes.

Add the thyme, 1¼ cups red wine, the vinegar, and a tablespoon or two of crème de cassis, if you want to use it. Stir well and cook the mixture over the lowest possible heat, stirring from time to time, for about 1 hour, until just about all the liquid has evaporated. If the liquid has cooked off in half an hour or less, add a bit more wine. Turn the onions out onto a flat plate and let them cool to room temperature.

The onions can be made up to 2 days ahead and kept covered in the refrigerator. They should be brought to room temperature before they're spread on the pizza.

THE DOUGH

The sponge (above)

2 to 2¼ cups unbleached all-purpose flour

2 to 3 teaspoons salt (depending on your taste)

If you didn't make the sponge in your mixer bowl, transfer it to that bowl now. Use a rubber spatula to deflate the sponge, which will be sticky and loose, and fit the mixer with the dough hook. Add 2 cups of the flour and the salt to the sponge and mix on low speed for 2 to 3 minutes. Increase the mixer speed to medium and, if the dough isn't coming together nicely and cleaning the sides of the bowl, sprinkle in a little more flour by spoonfuls. Continue to knead on medium speed for another 4 to 5 minutes, until the dough is smooth and elastic. Although the dough may remain moist and a little sticky, you should be able to grip it without having it stick uncomfortably to your fingers.

Second Rise Place the dough in a lightly oiled large bowl, turn the ball of dough over so that its entire surface is moistened with oil, cover, and allow to rest in a warm place (about 85°F) for 1½ hours, or until it has doubled in bulk and holds an impression for a few seconds when you prod it gently with your finger.

TO FINISH THE PIZZA

The onion confit (above) with olives, goat cheese, and/or Parmesan cheese (optional)—or any other topping you desire

Position a rack in the lower third of the oven, fit the rack with a baking stone or quarry tiles, leaving a border of at least 1 inch free all around, and preheat the oven to 475°F. Rub a baker's peel with cornmeal and set aside until needed.

Shaping the Dough Turn the dough out onto a lightly floured work surface (snip off a small piece of dough to save for the Mixed-Starter Bread if you want) and divide it into 2 pieces. You'll probably have to bake the pizzas one at time, so keep one piece covered while you work with the other. *If you do not want to make two pizzas at this time, wrap one piece of dough tightly in plastic and store it in the refrigerator, where it will keep for a day or two, or wrap it airtight and freeze it for up to a month. Thaw frozen dough, still wrapped, overnight in the refrigerator. Bring chilled dough to cool room temperature before shaping.* Shape the dough into a ball and then flatten it into a disk. To form the pizza, you can either turn and stretch the dough, stopping to allow the dough to rest for a few minutes if it springs back readily, or roll it out with a rolling pin. Either way, work the dough until it is about ¼ inch thick (you can make it a little thinner if you prefer) and transfer it to the peel.

Topping and Baking Top with half the cooled onion confit and any or all of the optional ingredients, or the topping of your choice, leaving a 1-inch border around the rim of the pizza, and slide the pizza into the oven. Bake for 13 to 15 minutes, or until the topping is bubbling and the uncovered rim is puffed and beautifully golden. Repeat with the remaining dough and topping.

Storing Pizza is at its prime piping hot from the oven—don't even think about reheating it.

Contributing Baker **STEVE SULLIVAN**

Matzos

COLOR PHOTOGRAPH, PAGE 61

Makes 12 large crackers ■ Matzos are the unleavened bread that the Jewish people carried out of Egypt when they fled the pharaoh. With no time to bake the dough they had made, the Jews packed it on their backs, and it was baked to a cracker crispness by the sun. This matzo bears little relation to what must have been the not-too-tasty bread that sustained them on their exodus. It is neither traditional nor religious, but it is both wonderful to eat and fun to make.

The quickly made dough is rolled to an even thickness—actually, an even thinness—sprinkled with coarse salt, and literally unfurled into a very hot oven. The results are large, bumpy, irregularly shaped crackers that look stunning piled in the center of a buffet. They are great with cocktails, full-flavored enough to be served solo, and accommodating enough to take almost any spread—try a piece with soft goat cheese, a drizzle of olive oil, and some freshly cracked black pepper.

> 4 cups unbleached all-purpose flour
> ¼ cup sesame seeds (optional)
> Freshly ground black pepper to taste (optional)
> 2 teaspoons coarse salt, plus additional salt for the tops of the matzos
> 1½ cups warm water (105°F to 115°F)

Position a rack in the lower third of the oven, remove the other rack, and preheat the oven to the highest setting below broil, probably 550°F. Invert a large baking sheet (not a black one) onto the oven rack and preheat it with the oven.

Mixing and Kneading Put the flour and the sesame seeds and pepper, if you're using them, into a large bowl; whisk just to combine the ingredients. Whisk the salt into the warm water, make a well in the center of the dry ingredients, and pour the water into the well. Using your hands, mix the wet and dry ingredients together until you get a dough that cleans the sides of the bowl. The dough may seem a little dry and shaggy, but some kneading will improve its looks. Turn the dough out onto a lightly floured work surface and knead until smooth, about 3 minutes.

Shaping the Dough Divide the dough into 12 pieces and keep all but the piece you're working with covered. Roll the dough out on the floured surface until it is as thin as you can possibly roll it. You can aim for a rectangle that's about 8 inches by 12 inches, but you're likely to end up with an oval, a circle, or a trapezoid of some sort. The irregular shapes you create are part of the charm. What's most important is that you roll the dough to an even thinness. Use as much flour as you need to keep the dough moving and turn the dough over occasionally as you roll to help you get the thinnest, most even sheet. Prick the dough all over with a docker or the tines of a fork and sprinkle the top lightly with coarse salt. Run your hands over the dough to help the salt stick to the surface, but don't press down.

Baking the Crackers Open the oven door, hold the sheet of dough by one end, and flip or fan it onto the hot baking sheet, as you would unfurl a beach towel, so that the portion of the dough that goes in first is near the back of the oven. Try to do this as quickly as you can—you don't want to lose too much oven heat. (Don't worry about the salt that slides off the top.) Close the oven door and set a timer for exactly 1 minute. At the end of the minute, turn the matzo over (fingers work best here, but be very careful—this is an extremely hot oven), and bake for another (precisely timed) minute. The matzo is done when it is golden, blistered, and crisp. If the matzo needs a little more time, continue to bake it, turning it often, for 20-second intervals, until it is lightly golden and crisp. Keep your eye on it—don't even think about leaving the kitchen or answering the telephone when you make these, since each matzo needs close attention and not all the matzos will bake for the same amount of time. When baked, transfer the matzo to a cooling rack and continue with the rest of the batch.

Storing The matzos will keep for several days at room temperature. Cover them lightly with foil and, if the weather's humid, heat them in a moderate oven for a minute or two before serving—their crisp will come back.

Contributing Baker **LAUREN GROVEMAN**

Swedish Oatmeal Hardtack

Makes about 6 dozen crackers ■ The word *hardtack* will make you think of last-forever crackers, and rightly so. Hardtack were, in fact, the kind of crackers packed on long voyages, prized more for their indestructibility than their tastiness. Not so these crackers from Sweden. Flavored with oatmeal and buttermilk, ruffle-edged, honey-brown, and baked to a crisp, they are fun to make and great to have on hand. In Sweden, they're served at breakfast, but give them a try at cocktail time with Smoked Trout Spread (page 458) and aquavit.

¼ cup solid vegetable shortening

2 tablespoons unsalted butter, at room temperature

¼ cup sugar

1½ cups unbleached all-purpose flour

1 cup quick-cooking oats

¾ teaspoon salt

½ teaspoon baking soda

¾ cup buttermilk

Mixing the Dough Put the shortening, butter, and sugar in a large bowl and blend, using a sturdy rubber spatula, until smooth and creamy. In another bowl, whisk the flour, oats, salt, and baking soda together. Add the buttermilk and the dry ingredients to the creamed mixture all at once and stir with the spatula. You will have a dough that will remind you of a cookie dough, firm but malleable.

Cover the bowl and chill for 30 minutes.

Center a rack in the oven and preheat the oven to 325°F. Lightly grease a large baking sheet or the back of an inverted jelly-roll pan and set aside.

Shaping the Dough Remove the dough from the refrigerator and divide it into thirds. Work with one third at a time and keep the remaining dough covered in the refrigerator. Place the dough in the center of the greased pan and press it down with the heel of your hand, just to soften and flatten it a bit. Using a rolling pin covered with a pastry sock or rubbed with flour, roll the dough into a rectangle, working to make the rectangle as large and as thin as possible; getting the dough to within an inch of the pan's edges is ideal. Don't worry if the dough tears or the rectangle is a little uneven—you can cut and patch as you go.

At this point, it is traditional to roll over the dough with a hardtack rolling pin, a wooden pin with small carved points, like hobnails. The hardtack pin gives the dough a pebbly texture and keeps it from rising in the oven. If you don't have one, use the tines of a fork or a docker to prick the dough all over, making the holes about ¼ inch apart to give the crackers a rough texture.

Using a pastry or ravioli wheel (a crimped one is nice), a knife, or a pizza cutter, cut through the dough to make 2- by 4-inch rectangles, but don't move the dough around: The crackers will separate by themselves during baking.

Baking the Crackers Bake the crackers for 10 to 12 minutes, until crisp and golden; check them at the 7-minute mark to make sure they're not baking too quickly—it's better to take the crackers out sooner than later. Transfer the baking sheet to a cooling rack; within minutes, the crackers will shrink and separate. Remove the crackers to the rack to cool to room temperature, and continue with the remaining dough.

Storing Once cooled, the crackers should be stored in an airtight container at room temperature. The crackers will keep for at least a week.

Contributing Baker **BEATRICE OJAKANGAS**

Savory Wheat Crackers
COLOR PHOTOGRAPH, PAGE 77

Makes at least 12 dozen crackers ■ The dough for these irresistible crackers is made in minutes in the food processor. The rolling and baking can take a bit longer and is best attacked in assembly-line fashion: Roll and bake, roll and bake, nibble and nibble, roll and bake. Here, the ingredients for topping the crackers have a Central Asian tang, but anything goes with these little crunchies. You can top them with hot chili powder, grated cheese, or even a sprinkling of coconut. In fact, since you'll be rolling out many sheets of crackers from one batch of dough, you can change the topping from sheet to sheet.

   2 teaspoons sesame seeds
   1 teaspoon anise seeds
   ½ teaspoon nigella seeds (see Sources, page 467)
   ½ teaspoon coarse salt
   3 cups (approximately) whole wheat flour
   1 teaspoon salt
   1½ cups (approximately) warm water (105°F to 115°F)

Mixing the Dough Stir together the sesame, anise, and nigella seeds and the coarse salt; set aside.

continued

Place 3 cups flour and the teaspoon of salt in a food processor fitted with the metal blade and whirl for a few seconds, just to mix. With the machine running, add 1½ cups water in a steady stream, processing for 10 seconds. You should have a large ball of dough. If the dough has not come together, remove the top of the processor and poke around with your fingers to get a feel for the dough. If the dough is very sticky, add 3 to 4 tablespoons more flour and process to form a ball; if it's dry, add 2 to 3 tablespoons more water while the motor is running.

When you have a ball of dough, process for 1 minute more. Remove the dough to a lightly floured work surface and knead it for 30 seconds, to evenly distribute the ingredients.

Rest Cover the dough with plastic wrap and let it rest at room temperature for 30 minutes.

Position a rack in the center of the oven and preheat the oven to 500°F. Ready a couple of large baking sheets, inverted jelly-roll pans, or pizza pans and a spray bottle filled with water.

Shaping the Dough Cut the dough into 8 pieces. You'll be working with one piece of dough at a time; the remaining pieces should be kept covered at room temperature. Dust a work surface with flour and lightly flour your hands. Press a piece of dough down on the work surface with your hands to flatten it, then switch to a rolling pin and roll the dough into a large, very thin rectangle, trying to roll it to an even thickness. Gently roll up the dough around your rolling pin and unroll it onto one of the baking pans. (If you find rolling and unrolling the dough with your pin tricky, make the next batch by rolling the dough directly on the baking sheet rather than the work surface.)

Use a pizza cutter or a thin sharp knife to cut the dough into rectangles—there's no need to separate the crackers, and don't worry if they're not all the same size. Sprinkle the dough with about ½ teaspoon of the spice mixture and spray it lightly with water.

Baking the Crackers Bake the crackers for 2½ to 3 minutes. As soon as the thinnest crackers start to brown, remove them with a metal spatula; continue to bake the others until they are golden. It is better to bake these too little than too much. Once the crackers start browning, check them every 30 seconds to be certain they're not burning.

When the crackers come out of the oven, some will already be crisp and others will crisp in the air. Put the crackers in a large bowl, breaking up any that did not separate during baking. Roll, season, and bake the remaining dough.

Storing Cooled crackers can be stored in tins or well-sealed plastic bags for up to 1 month.

Contributing Bakers **JEFFREY ALFORD AND NAOMI DUGUID**

Potato Lefse

Makes about 12 crêpes ■ Technically a flatbread, a lefse will look more like a crêpe to the uninitiated. It is a rich potato-based dough, a Norwegian specialty, rolled to crêpe thinness and baked on a griddle. Although lefse can be made successfully with the equipment found in most home kitchens, it has its own traditional *batterie de cuisine*. It is customarily rolled out on a slightly raised canvas round, a contraption that looks like an embroidery hoop fitted with fine white canvas. The pin is a grooved rolling pin, once only hand-carved by craftsmen for their favorite lefse makers, now commercially produced. And the finished lefse is lifted off its large round griddle with a lefse stick, a cross between a crêpe stick and a paint stirrer, which makes a fine substitute. (See Sources, page 467.)

Lefse tastes the way it smells, profoundly soothing, like a buttered baked potato, and it can be served as either a sweet or a savory. Most often it is slathered with butter and sugar, cinnamon sugar, honey, or jam, but there are those who use lefse as a wrapper for small sausages or frankfurters. Experiment.

> 4 cups peeled and diced russet potatoes (1½ pounds, about 3 medium potatoes)
> ½ stick (2 ounces) unsalted butter, melted
> ½ cup heavy cream
> 2 tablespoons sugar
> 1 teaspoon salt
> 1½ cups (approximately) all-purpose flour

Cooking the Potatoes Put the potatoes in a medium saucepan with enough water to cover. Bring the water to a boil and cook the potatoes until they are fork-tender but not mushy, 10 to 13 minutes; you should be able to pierce the potatoes easily with a skewer. Drain the potatoes and turn them out onto a large platter, spreading them out in a single layer and allowing them to air-dry for a minute or two before you continue with the recipe.

Using a potato ricer (an old-fashioned, inexpensive, and effective utensil), press the potatoes into a large bowl. With a sturdy rubber spatula, mix the potatoes with the butter, cream, sugar, and salt, stirring them until they are very smooth.

Chilling the Potatoes The potatoes now need to be chilled for at least 8 hours, or overnight. Do not cover the potatoes—you want them to dry out further in the refrigerator.

When you're ready to make the lefses, prepare your work space. You need a good rolling surface that can be kept well floured. If you have a canvas-covered rolling round or board, set it up and flour it. If not, you can tack or tape a muslin or linen cloth to your counter or wrap a large cutting board with a cloth. Pull the cloth very taut and rub it well with flour. Rub flour over a grooved lefse rolling pin or a standard rolling pin (cover your standard pin with a well-floured pastry sock, if you have one).

Mixing the Dough Remove the potatoes from the refrigerator and break them up with a rubber spatula. Add 1 cup of the flour and mix it in with your hands. Add about another ¼ to ½ cup flour, a heaping tablespoon at a time, and mix that in with your hands. Your goal is to have a real dough—not stiff mashed potatoes—and to achieve it, you might have to add a bit more flour. When you can pinch a piece of the dough between your fingers without having it stick, you're there.

Preheat an ungreased electric griddle to between 475°F and 500°F, or place a griddle over medium-high heat on your stove. Clear a place near the griddle and lay out a terry-cloth towel to be used to stack the baked lefses under plastic wrap.

Shaping the Dough Divide the dough into quarters and the quarters into thirds. Working with one piece of dough at a time and keeping the remaining dough under a towel, form the dough into a ball with your hands. Put the dough on the well-floured rolling surface and pat it out into a round, just to get the shaping started. Now, using light pressure, work with the rolling pin to roll the dough into a large round that is as thin as you can possibly roll it. Keep everything well floured at all times, lifting the lefse and flouring under it a few times, flouring the top of the dough, and flouring the pin.

Baking the Lefse Carefully slide a lefse stick, paint stirrer, or dowel under the round, wrapping it around the stick just enough to lift it off the rolling board and onto the hot griddle; unroll it onto the hot dry griddle. Bake the lefse until the top bubbles and the underside is speckled with brown, 1 to 2 minutes. Slide the stick under the lefse and flip it over. As with a pancake, the second side will bake faster than the first. As soon as the lefse is baked, take it off the griddle, place it on the terry-cloth towel near the griddle, and cover with plastic. Roll out the next lefse. Brush the griddle with a pastry brush to rid it of any flour before baking the lefse.

This is a great job for two people—one to roll and one to bake. If you're working solo, you might try to roll the next lefse while the last one is baking—or not; everything will wait.

Serve the lefses warm, spread with butter and sugar or cinnamon sugar and rolled up. If you want to roll the lefses around hot dogs, brush with butter and mustard and change their name—served with franks, they're called lumpa.

Storing When the lefses have cooled completely, they can be stacked between sheets of waxed paper, wrapped airtight, and frozen for 2 weeks. Thaw the lefses in their wrappers and reheat them in a microwave oven or a hot conventional oven.

Contributing Baker **BEATRICE OJAKANGAS**

MORNING PASTRIES
and Quick Breads

Blueberry Muffins PAGE 208 and Buttermilk Crumb Muffins PAGE 207

Popover PAGE 213

Sweet Berry Fougasse PAGE 194

Irish Soda Bread PAGE 214

Twice-Baked Brioche PAGE 198

Pecan Sticky Buns PAGE 190

Danish Braid PAGE 205

Slice of Danish Braid

175

Fruit Focaccia PAGE 196

Sunny-side-up Apricot Pastry PAGE 192

Shaping Croissants

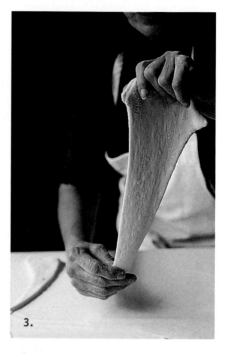

1. Cut a doubled sheet of croissant dough into triangles.

2. Unfold the triangles carefully; cut along the fold line to separate.

3. Gently stretch each triangle to twice its original length.

4. Enclose a piece of scrap dough to plump the middle.

5. and 6. Roll the dough toward you, gently moving your hands down and out to the sides.

7. Curve the pointed ends of the rolled croissant to form the traditional shape.

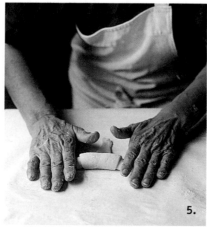

Assorted Croissants PAGE 185

179

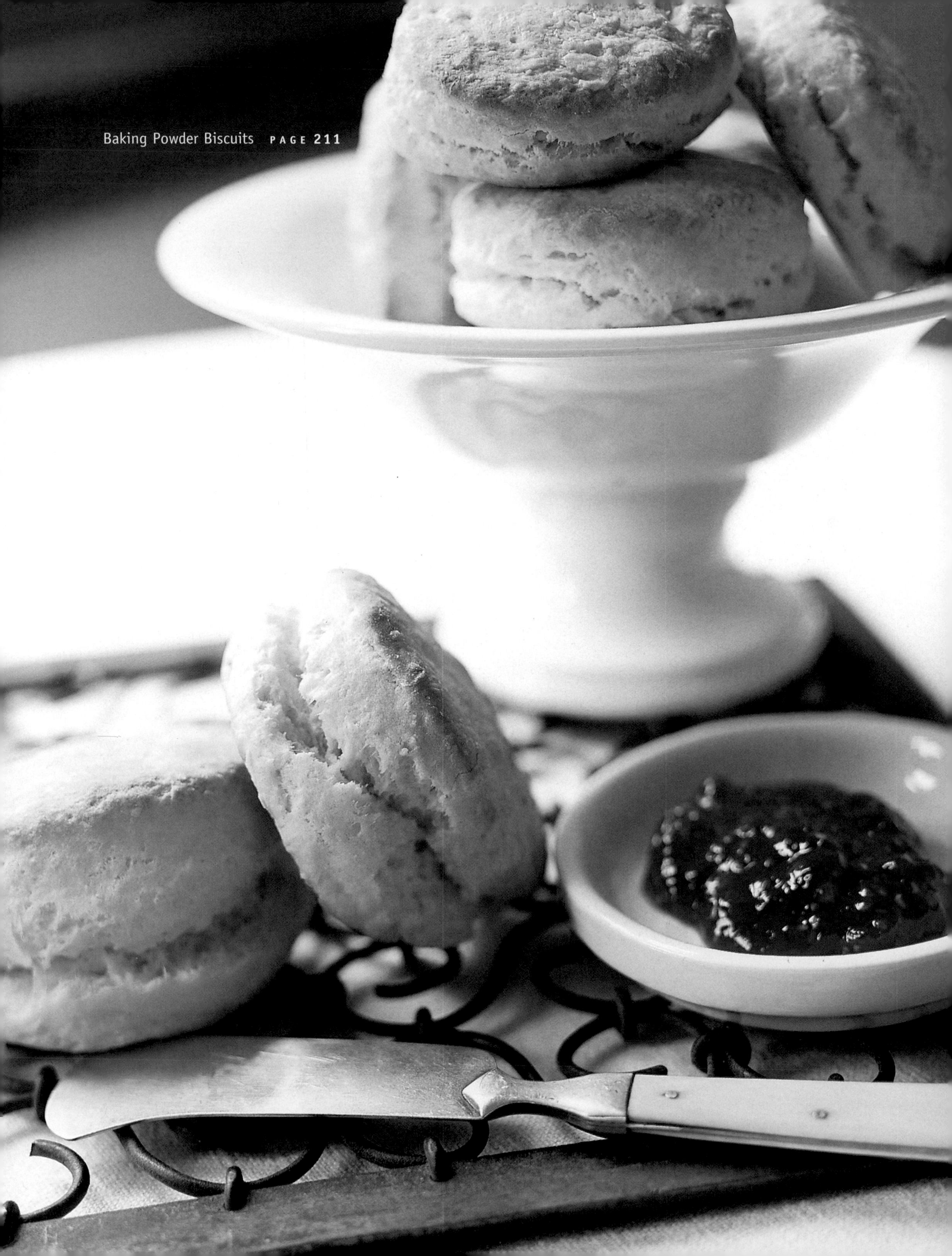
Baking Powder Biscuits PAGE 211

Pinwheel Danish PAGE 200

Morning Pastries
AND QUICK BREADS

IN BUSY TIMES, few things make us feel as

pampered as a leisurely breakfast with

homemade pastries, and no pastries could

be more welcome than the sweet breads,

fruit pastries, muffins, and scones in this

sumptuous collection. The morning classics

in this chapter set the gold standard for richness and excellence.

From Esther McManus, whose croissants are better than most

found in France today, you'll learn to fold and roll flaky dough to

perfection before forming it into traditional crescents or shaping

it into rolls plumped with chocolate, almond cream, or even a

little pâté. Beatrice Ojakangas teaches all you want to know about

baking fruit-filled Danish (in pockets, pinwheels, and braids), and

Michel Richard, a French pastry chef who knows what Americans love, enchants with his Sunny-side-up Apricot Pastries (ovals of buttery pastry hugging vanilla cream and two apricot orbs).

Brioche, the croissant's traditional companion, is also tucked into this chapter—look for Nancy Silverton's buttery, decadent brioche-based Pecan Sticky Buns—as are tempting sweet focaccia, jam-packed with dried cranberries and golden raisins, and streusel-topped sweet fougasse.

Only a tad more restrained but no less delightful are the quick breads that reflect baking traditions inherited from Britain and Ireland. From Marion Cunningham, the well-known chronicler of American baking, come delectable, easy-to-make muffins, scones, biscuits, and soda bread—recipes that provide all the encouragement you'll ever need to rise, and bake.

Croissants

COLOR PHOTOGRAPH, PAGE 179

Makes 20 to 24 croissants ■ With one batch of dough you can shape and bake a variety of croissants to take you from dawn to dusk. Start the day with plump, buttery crescent-shaped croissants; take your first coffee break with almond-filled croissants; at mid-afternoon have square chocolate croissants the way French schoolchildren do; and then finish the day with a pudgy pâté-filled croissant.

No matter which croissant you want to make, it's important to read through the directions for these plain croissants—they'll give you the foundation techniques applicable to all other types of croissants and instructions for glazing, rising, and baking.

1 recipe Croissant Dough (page 52), well chilled

1 large egg beaten with 1 tablespoon cold water, for egg wash

Rolling the Dough Generously flour a work surface. Position the dough so that it resembles a book, with the spine to your left and the opening to your right. For easy handling, cut the dough in half horizontally so that you have two pieces about 7 inches long and 6½ inches wide; wrap and chill one half while you work with the other half. Flour the dough and roll it into a rectangle that's 20 to 24 inches long and 15 to 18 inches wide. This takes a lot of rolling. Keep the work surface and the dough well floured, and have patience.

If necessary, turn the dough so that a long side runs from left to right along the counter. Carefully fold the top half of the dough down to the bottom. The dough is now ready for cutting.

Cutting the Dough Working with a pizza cutter or a large, very sharp knife, cut triangles from the dough. This is done most easily by making a diagonal cut on the lefthand side to get the pattern started; save the uneven pieces of dough. Measure off a 3- to 4-inch base and begin cutting the triangles, always cutting from bottom to top. You'll have another scrap when you reach the other end—you'll use these scraps when you shape the croissants. Unfold each pair of triangles and cut them in half to separate. You should have 10 to 12 (maybe 14) triangles; set them aside while you clear your work surface of all flour.

Line two large baking sheets with parchment paper.

Shaping the Croissants (For an illustrated lesson in shaping, see page 178.) Moisten your hands with a wet towel. Working with one triangle at a time, gently stretch the base to widen it slightly, then, holding the base of the triangle firmly in one hand, run the fingers of your other hand down to the point of the triangle. Use your

Stretch the dough until it's twice the original length.

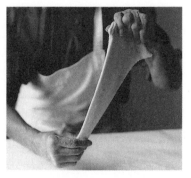

thumb to help you pull and stretch the dough until it's almost twice its original length—have courage and tug; the extra length is what will allow you to make a large croissant with sufficient rolls to show off its layers of dough.

Place the triangle, point toward you, at arm's distance on the work table (this will give you enough space to roll the croissant into shape without having to lift it in mid-roll). Pull off a little piece of the reserved scrap dough, mold it into a small football shape, and center it on the wide top part of the triangle—

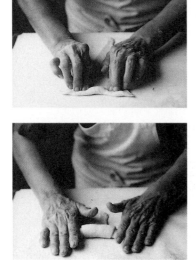

this will help make the "belly" of the croissant plump. Fold about ½ inch of this wide end over itself and press the ends down once to secure. With your palms and fingers positioned over the flattened ends of the croissant and the heels of your hands flat on the work surface, roll the croissant toward you—try to keep your hands moving down and out to the sides as you roll—ending with the point of the triangle tucked under the croissant. A well-shaped croissant—and it takes practice to achieve one—will sport at least six clearly countable sections, or ridges, from rolling. Place the croissants on one of the baking sheets, leaving space for them to triple in size without touching one another. Repeat with the other half of the dough.

Top: Tuck in a scrap of dough to make the croissant plump.
Bottom: Pull the dough toward you, gently moving your hands down and out to the sides.

Glazing and Rising Give the croissants a last gentle plumping, carefully turning their ends down and in toward the center to produce the classic crescent shape. Brush the croissants with egg wash and allow them to rise, uncovered, at room temperature for 3 to 4 hours, until tripled in size and spongy. (Reserve the egg wash, covered, in the refrigerator.) The ideal place for rising is a turned-off oven (one with a pilot light is fine) containing a pan of hot, steamy water. To test that they are properly risen, wet your fingers and squeeze the end of a croissant: It should offer no resistance and feel almost hollow.

Baking the Croissants Arrange the oven racks to divide the oven into thirds and preheat the oven to 350°F.

Brush the croissants once again with egg wash and bake for 12 minutes. Rotate the baking sheets top to bottom and front to back and bake another 4 to 6 minutes, until the croissants are deeply bronzed. Cool on racks. As tempting as they are, croissants should not be eaten as soon as they come from the oven. The dough—and the layers—needs time to set.

Storing The croissants are best eaten the day they are made. If you must keep them, freeze them, wrapped airtight. Thaw the croissants overnight in the refrigerator or at room temperature (still wrapped) and reheat in a 350°F oven for about 8 minutes.

Almond Croissants

COLOR PHOTOGRAPH, PAGE 179

Almond croissants are made exactly like plain croissants, except that instead of tucking a scrap of dough into the belly of the croissant, you use a spoonful of almond filling. After giving the croissants their second coating of egg wash, you can sprinkle a few sliced almonds over the top for decoration.

THE FILLING

½ **stick (2 ounces) unsalted butter, at room temperature**

¾ **cup finely ground almonds, preferably a combination of blanched and unblanched**

½ **cup confectioner's sugar**

1 tablespoon cornstarch

1 teaspoon pure almond extract

Put the butter, almonds, and confectioner's sugar in the work bowl of a food processor fitted with the metal blade and pulse and process until creamy and blended. Add the cornstarch and almond extract and pulse until the filling forms a ball that rides on the blade. Scrape the filling out of the bowl, wrap in plastic, and chill until firm, an hour or two.

When ready to use, instead of scraps of dough, fill each croissant with 1 tablespoon of almond filling molded into a football shape, and proceed to shape the rest of the croissants and allow to rise. Bake following the instructions on page 186.

Pâté Croissants

Croissants can be filled with any kind of pâté. While a soft liver pâté is lovely, you could even use small pieces of meat loaf.

1 tablespoon soft pâté or 1 small strip of firm pâté for each croissant

When the croissant dough is ready to cut, measure off 3- to 4-inch-wide pieces and cut in a straight line from bottom to top; unfold each strip and cut crosswise in half. Position a spoonful or strip of pâté at the top of each strip of dough and then roll the dough into a coil, finishing seam side down. Give the rolls a pat to flatten them a bit, and proceed to shape the rest of the croissants and allow to rise. Bake following the instructions on page 186.

continued

Chocolate Croissants

COLOR PHOTOGRAPH, PAGE 179

Roll the dough around the chocolate, finishing seam side down.

This is the traditional late-afternoon snack for French school-children. Because these are not formed into crescent shapes, their French name is *petits pains au chocolat,* or chocolate rolls, and, indeed, their shape is that of a club roll. For authenticity, try to find thin, bittersweet chocolate sticks for the filling (see Sources, page 467); if they're not available, chopped chocolate will do just fine.

1 ounce bittersweet chocolate (preferably 2 bâtons) for each croissant

When the dough is ready to be cut, measure off 3- to 4-inch-wide pieces, or pieces as wide as a chocolate bâton is long, and simply cut the dough from bottom to top in straight lines; unfold each strip and cut crosswise in half. Position 2 bâtons or 1 ounce chopped chocolate at the top of each strip of dough—it's not necessary to press or seal it—and roll the dough into a coil around the chocolate, finishing seam side down; then give it a pat to flatten it ever so slightly. Proceed to shape the rest of the croissants and allow to rise. Bake following the instructions on page 186.

Contributing Baker **ESTHER McMANUS**

Brioche

Makes 3 têtes or 3 loaves ▪ In France, brioche is baked in several forms and used for everything from keeping the morning's cafe au lait company to serving with foie gras and Sauternes or caviar and Champagne. While function often follows form, the two most popular forms, the Parisienne, or tête, and the Nanterre, or loaf, provide enough flexibility to allow them to function deliciously in just about any situation. The tête is perhaps the most familiar shape; made in a fluted mold, it sports a topknot of golden dough and can be either large, the true Brioche Parisienne, or small. Its cousin, the loaf-shaped Nanterre, is elegantly designed, made by positioning six balls of dough in a loaf pan so that when they rise they touch one another but maintain their inviting knobby shape. (This is the bread that makes the most extraordinary French toast. Don't wait for a loaf to go stale to whip up this treat—set aside a loaf for this purpose alone.) Each recipe of brioche will make either three large Parisiennes or three loaves à la Nanterre.

TÊTES (PARISIENNE)

1 recipe Brioche dough (page 43), chilled
1 large egg beaten with 1 tablespoon cold water, for egg wash

Butter 3 large fluted brioche pans, using a pastry brush to make certain you get into the flutes; set aside.

Shaping the Têtes Divide the dough into thirds. Keep the remaining dough covered in the refrigerator while you work with one piece at a time. Put one piece of the dough on a lightly floured work surface and, using your dough scraper, cut off a hunk of dough that is a scant one third of the piece. Work the larger piece of dough gently and quickly between your hands and against the work surface to form a smooth ball. Drop the ball into a buttered mold.

Roll the smaller piece of dough into a pear shape. Use your fingers to make a depression in the center of the dough that's in the mold and fit the narrow top of the pear-shaped piece of dough into the depression. Pinch and press the dough together as needed to make certain that the seam between the large and small pieces of dough is sealed. Repeat with the remaining dough.

Rise Cover the pans with a piece of buttered plastic wrap and allow the dough to rise at room temperature for about 2 hours, or until doubled in size.

Baking the Têtes Preheat the oven to 375°F.

Lightly brush the brioche with the egg wash, taking care not to let the glaze dribble into the mold (it will impair the dough's rise in the oven). Working quickly, use the ends of a pair of sharp scissors to snip 2 or 3 slits in each larger ball of dough. Bake the brioche for about 30 minutes, or until they are deeply golden and an instant-read thermometer plunged into the center of the bread (plunge from the bottom) reads 200°F. If the breads appear to be browning too quickly, cover them loosely with an aluminum foil tent. Cool to room temperature on a rack.

LOAVES (NANTERRE)

1 recipe Brioche dough (page 43), chilled
1 large egg beaten with 1 tablespoon cold water, for egg wash

Butter three 8½- by 4½- by 2½-inch loaf pans; set aside.

Shaping the Loaves Divide the dough into thirds. Keep the remaining dough covered in the refrigerator while you work with one piece at a time. Using a dough scraper, divide the piece of dough into 6 equal pieces and, on a lightly floured work surface, shape each piece into a ball. Place the balls in a loaf pan side by side so that you have three short rows, each with two balls of dough. Repeat with the remaining dough.

Rise Cover the pans with a piece of buttered plastic wrap and allow the dough to rise at room temperature for about 2 hours, or until doubled in size.

Baking the Loaves Preheat the oven to 375°F.

Lightly brush the brioche with the egg wash, taking care not to let the glaze dribble into the pan (it will impair the dough's rise in the oven). Working quickly, use the ends of a pair of sharp scissors to snip a cross in each ball of dough. Bake the brioche for about 30 minutes, or until they are deeply golden and an instant-read thermometer plunged into the center of the bread (plunge from the bottom) reads 200°F. If the breads appear to be browning too quickly, cover them loosely with an aluminum foil tent. Cool to room temperature on a rack.

Storing The brioche, whether têtes or loaves, are best the day they are made, but they can be kept nicely at room temperature for a day or two; wrap them in plastic. Wrapped airtight, they can be frozen for a month. Thaw, still wrapped, at room temperature.

Pecan Sticky Buns

COLOR PHOTOGRAPH, PAGE 172

Makes 14 buns ■ The ne plus ultra of sticky bundom. Not only do you start with the best possible brioche dough, you fold as much butter between the layers of dough as you have already beaten into the dough. Then you fill the buns with sugary pecans and line the pans with caramel, sweet, gooey, and irresistible, so that when the buns are turned out the caramel lightly glazes their tops. The technique of folding butter into the dough and giving the dough two turns, as you would with puff pastry, enriches an already-rich dough and produces beautiful, buttery layers. These bear no resemblance to anything store-bought.

THE DOUGH

1 recipe Brioche dough (page 43), chilled
1½ sticks (6 ounces) unsalted butter, at room temperature

Divide the dough in half and keep one half covered in the refrigerator while you work with the other.

On a lightly floured work surface (cool marble is ideal), roll the dough into a rectangle that's 11 inches wide, 13 inches long, and ¼ inch thick. Try to work quickly, because the dough is so active that even the warmth of your hands may be enough to get it rising again. Dot the surface of the dough evenly with half of the softened butter and fold the dough in thirds, as though you were folding a business letter. Turn the dough so that the closed fold is to your left and then roll it out again, taking care not to roll over the edges—you don't want to crush the layers you're creating by folding and rolling.

Chilling the Dough Fold the dough in thirds again, wrap well in plastic, and refrigerate for 30 minutes so that it can relax. Repeat the rolling, folding, and chilling with the second piece of dough and the remaining butter.

THE FILLING

¼ cup sugar

¼ teaspoon cinnamon

1 large egg, lightly beaten

1 cup chopped pecans

Mix the sugar and cinnamon together in a small bowl and keep it close at hand.

Remove the first piece of dough from the refrigerator and, on a lightly floured work surface, roll it into a rectangle 11 inches wide, 13 inches long, and ¼ inch thick, just as you did at the start. Using a pastry brush, paint the surface of the dough with the beaten egg. Leaving the top quarter of the dough bare, sprinkle over half of the cinnamon sugar and half of the chopped pecans; spread everything around with your fingers so that the filling is evenly distributed. Very lightly roll the rolling pin over the dough to press in the filling. Starting from the base of the rectangle, roll the dough up into a log.

Chilling the Logs Wrap the log in plastic and freeze until firm, 45 minutes to an hour, so it will be easy to cut. Repeat with the second piece of dough. *The sticky bun logs can now be double-wrapped and kept in the freezer for up to a month. If left to freeze solid, the rolls should be allowed to rest at room temperature for 15 minutes before you continue with the recipe.*

THE TOPPING

2 sticks (8 ounces) unsalted butter, at room temperature

1 cup (packed) light brown sugar

42 pecan halves

While the logs are chilling, prepare the pans. You'll need two 9-inch round cake pans with high sides. Using your fingers, press a stick of butter evenly over the bottom of each pan; sprinkle the brown sugar evenly over the butter.

Shaping the Buns Remove a log of dough from the freezer and, if the ends are ragged, trim them. Using a long sharp serrated knife and a gentle sawing motion, slice the log into seven 1½-inch-wide slices. Lay each slice on one of its flat sides, press the slice down with the palm of your hand to flatten it slightly, and then, with cupped hands, turn the slice around on the work surface two or three times to reestablish its round shape. Press 3 pecans, flat side up, into the top of each slice so that the nuts form a triangle. Holding on to the nuts as best as you can, turn the slices over into a prepared pan, placing the buns in a circle and putting the last slice in the center; the seams of the buns should face the outside of the pan. Repeat with the second log of dough.

Allow the pans of sticky buns to rest, uncovered, at room temperature for 1½ to 2 hours, or until the slices rise and grow to touch one another.

continued

Baking the Buns Arrange the oven racks so that one rack is in the middle of the oven and the other is just below it and preheat the oven to 350°F.

Put the pans of sticky buns on the middle rack and slip a foil- or parchment-lined jelly-roll pan onto the lower rack, at the ready to catch any drips. Bake the buns for 35 to 40 minutes, or until golden brown. As soon as you remove the sticky buns from the oven, invert them onto a serving dish. (If you leave the buns in the pan for a few minutes, the sugar may harden and they'll be difficult to unmold. If this happens, soften the sugar by putting the pan over a flame or in a pan of hot water.) Serve the sticky buns at room temperature or just slightly warm—never serve them straight from the oven, because the caramelized topping is dangerously hot.

Storing Sticky buns should be served the day they are made.

Contributing Baker **NANCY SILVERTON**

Sunny-side-up Apricot Pastries
COLOR PHOTOGRAPH, PAGE 177

Makes 8 pastries ■ Generous ovals of buttery puff pastry are rolled in sugar and topped with a dollop of silk-smooth vanilla pastry cream (made from a quick and foolproof recipe) and two perfectly poached apricot halves, the "sunny-side-ups" of this inviting package. The ends of the pastry not covered with cream and fruit puff to extraordinary heights, nestle the fruit cozily, and turn golden when the sugar caramelizes—an altogether beguiling breakfast pastry or mid-afternoon treat.

The pastries can, of course, be made with store-bought puff pastry.

THE APRICOTS

> 2 cups water
>
> 1 cup sugar
>
> Juice of ½ lemon
>
> 8 apricots, halved and pitted

A few hours (or as long as 2 days) ahead poach the apricots: Bring the water and sugar to a boil in a 3- to 4-quart saucepan over medium heat, stirring to dissolve the sugar. Add the apricots and simmer for 8 to 10 minutes, or until they offer just a little resistance when pierced with the tip of a sharp knife. Take the pan off the heat and let the apricots cool in the syrup. Drain and pat the apricots dry before using. If keeping the apricots for longer than a few hours, cover and refrigerate them.

THE PASTRY CREAM

1 cup milk

¼ cup sugar

Pinch of salt

2 large egg yolks

2½ tablespoons cornstarch

½ vanilla bean or 1½ teaspoons pure vanilla extract

Put the milk, sugar, salt, egg yolks, and cornstarch in a 2-quart saucepan. If you're using a vanilla bean, split it in half lengthwise, scrape the soft, pulpy seeds into the pan, and toss in the pod. If you're using vanilla extract, keep it in reserve until the cream is cooked. Stir with a wire whisk to blend, bring to the boil, whisking constantly, and let the pastry cream boil for 30 to 60 seconds, at which point it will have thickened and the whisk will leave tracks as you stir. Take the pan off the heat and scrape the pastry cream into a strainer set over a bowl.

Push the cream through the strainer into the bowl and discard the vanilla bean, if you used it; if you're using extract, stir it in now. Cover the bowl with plastic wrap, pressing the plastic against the surface of the pastry cream, and top the plastic with a layer of ice cubes. Leave the ice cubes in place until the cream cools. *The cream can be made up to 3 days in advance and kept tightly covered in the refrigerator.*

THE PASTRY

½ recipe Puff Pastry (page 46), chilled, or 1¼ pounds store-bought puff pastry

2 cups (approximately) sugar

½ cup apricot jam

2 teaspoons water

Center a rack in the oven and preheat the oven to 350°F.

Working on a lightly floured work surface (cool marble is ideal), roll the puff pastry to a thickness of between ⅛ and ¼ inch. Flour the edges of a 4-inch round cookie cutter and cut 8 rounds from the dough. Stack the puff pastry scraps neatly, trying to keep the layers in line, wrap in plastic, and refrigerate to use in Parmesan Puffs (page 427), Alsatian Onion Tart (page 426), pizzettes (page 428), or other recipes.

Clean the work surface and sprinkle it generously with the sugar. While you work on one round, keep the others covered with plastic wrap. Rest a puff pastry round on the sugar and dust the top of the round lightly with flour to facilitate the rolling. Roll out the round until it elongates into an oval about 8 inches long. Don't roll all the way to the ends—you want the ends to be a little thicker so that they'll puff up higher around the apricots (also, if you roll over the ends, you risk pasting the layers together). Brush the flour off the top and put the oval on a large unbuttered baking sheet, sugar side up. Repeat with the remaining pieces of puff pastry, leaving just a little room between each pastry on the baking sheet—these are going to puff up, not out.

Baking the Pastries Spoon a walnut-sized dollop of pastry cream onto the center of each oval and set 2 apricot halves side by side on the cream so that they resemble eggs sunny-side-up. Bake the pastries for about 35 minutes, rotating the pan once from front to back during baking. The pastries should be golden and beautifully puffed, and the sugar should have caramelized.

Glazing the Pastries While the pastries are baking, heat the apricot jam with the water in a small saucepan over low heat just until the glaze comes to the boil. Remove from heat and push through a strainer; keep warm until ready to use. (Alternatively, heat the jam and water in a microwave oven; strain before using.)

As soon as the pastries are baked, transfer them from the baking sheet to a cooling rack. Brush the pastries all over with the apricot glaze, then let them cool and set a bit before serving. These can be served warm or at room temperature.

Storing Although the apricots and pastry cream can be prepared ahead, the finished pastries should be eaten the day they are made.

Contributing Baker **MICHEL RICHARD**

Sweet Berry Fougasse
COLOR PHOTOGRAPH, PAGE 170

Makes 1 dozen squares ■ The Focaccia dough (page 143) that is usually brushed to glistening with olive oil and dusted with fresh herbs is transformed into a breakfast treat in this recipe. Here, the dough is cut into small squares and topped with juicy berries and cinnamon streusel. One recipe makes a dozen pastries, enough to include several toppings: In winter, top the fougasse with very thinly sliced apples or pears or poached dried fruits; in fall, plums or even grapes; and, for a fruitless treat, just dust the pastries generously with turbinado sugar—it will caramelize in the oven and give the fougasse a nice shine and a light sweetness.

1³/₄ cups all-purpose flour

1 tablespoon cinnamon

1 teaspoon grated nutmeg

¹/₂ cup granulated sugar

¹/₂ cup (packed) light brown sugar

1 stick (4 ounces) cold unsalted butter, cut into small pieces

1 recipe Focaccia dough (page 143), chilled for at least 24 hours

1 to 2 pints fresh blueberries and/or raspberries

Making the Streusel Stir the flour, cinnamon, and nutmeg together just to mix; set aside.

Place the granulated and brown sugars and the cut-up butter in a large bowl; toss to coat the butter with the sugar. Add the flour mixture and work with your fingertips to break up the butter and create a crumbly mixture that, if pressed, is moist enough to hold together. (If you prefer, you can make the streusel in the food processor. Put all of the ingredients except the butter in the work bowl of a food processor fitted with the metal blade and pulse to mix. Add the pieces of butter and pulse and process until the mixture forms coarse crumbs.) Set the streusel aside until needed.

Position the oven racks to divide the oven into thirds and preheat the oven to 425°F. Line two baking sheets with parchment paper and dust the paper with cornmeal. Fill a spray bottle with water.

Shaping and Topping the Fougasse Working with one piece of dough at a time, gently shape each of the three pieces of dough into a square about 10 inches across, taking care not to deflate the bubbles you've worked to create, and cut each square into quarters. Transfer the pastries to the baking sheets. Use a single-edge razor blade to cut a cross-hatch pattern in the center of each piece.

Lightly press a few berries into each piece and top with a generous amount of streusel. Delicately press the streusel down to keep it from flying off the fougasse as it bakes. Allow the fougasse to rest for 10 minutes.

Baking the Fougasse Bake the fougasse for 20 to 25 minutes, spraying the oven with water three times during the first 8 minutes of baking; the pastries should be golden brown. Transfer to a rack and cool before serving.

Storing The fougasse are best eaten the day they are made, but they can be wrapped airtight and frozen for up to 2 weeks. Thaw, still wrapped, at room temperature.

Contributing Baker **CRAIG KOMINIAK**

Fruit Focaccia

COLOR PHOTOGRAPH, PAGE 176

Makes 1 very large focaccia; about 12 servings ■ This is, in fact, a focaccia, but probably one unlike any you've ever tasted. Caught somewhere between a yeasted coffee cake and a fruit bread, it is definitely delectable. Although you can choose to vary the fruits, the recipe calls for dried cranberries and moist golden raisins, a combination that provides just the right mix of tangy and sweet. The fruits are soaked for a few hours to plump them appealingly, and the soaking juice, now a raspberry red, becomes the dough's liquid. A little honey, some butter, and a scraping of orange zest add to the bread's full flavor and its come-and-get-it aroma. This very unusual bread wins fans easily. If you have any left over, use it in a stuffing for pork chops, or whir it in the blender or food processor to produce large, coarse crumbs and include them in your favorite recipe for homemade granola.

Plan ahead for this bread—like brioche, it needs to be refrigerated for twenty-four hours before baking. In fact, you might want to review brioche basics (see page 45), because even though this dough is eggless, it behaves very much like brioche.

2⅓ cups (12 ounces) dried cranberries

1⅓ cups (8 ounces) golden raisins

3½ cups hot water (115°F to 120°F)

3¾ cups unbleached all-purpose flour

1 teaspoon salt

5 teaspoons active dry yeast

¼ cup mild honey

2 tablespoons grated orange zest

2 tablespoons unsalted butter, cut into 4 pieces, at cool room temperature

1 large egg yolk beaten with 2 tablespoons heavy cream, for glaze

Turbinado sugar, for topping

Macerating the Fruit Put the dried cranberries, raisins, and water in a large bowl. Cover with plastic wrap and allow to macerate at room temperature for at least 3 hours, or as long as overnight.

Mixing the Dough When you are ready to make the dough, drain the fruit in a colander, pressing against the fruit to remove as much liquid as possible; reserve 1¼ cups of the fruit juice. Mix the flour and salt together; set aside.

Put ¼ cup of the reserved fruit juice and the yeast into the bowl of a heavy-duty mixer and whisk to combine; allow the mixture to rest for 5 minutes, until it becomes creamy. Stir in the rest of the reserved fruit juice along with the honey and orange zest.

Add about half of the flour to the liquid and stir with a rubber spatula to blend. Attach the dough hook, add the remaining flour, and mix on low speed to incorporate the ingredients, 2 to 3 minutes, or until the dough comes together. Increase the mixer speed to medium and continue to mix, scraping down the hook and sides of the bowl occasionally, for approximately 10 minutes, or until the dough is smooth and shiny. The dough will be extremely soft and, although it will clean the sides of the bowl, it will pool at the bottom. (The machine will get hot during this period, but most heavy-duty mixers can handle this. If you have questions about your mixer, contact the manufacturer before you attempt this recipe.)

Turn the mixer speed down to medium-low and add the butter bit by bit. The dough may come off the hook and separate—just continue to add the butter and mix, scraping the sides of the bowl from time to time. Increase the mixer speed to medium and beat for 3 to 5 minutes, until the dough comes together and slaps the sides of the bowl.

Now comes the messy part. With the machine on medium-low speed, add the macerated fruits in 2 batches. The dough will have a hard time accepting the fruit and you'll have to incorporate it by alternately mixing with a rubber spatula and the mixer. The addition of the fruits will break up the dough again and cause it to look rough, but don't get discouraged. Work in the fruits as best you can—it should take about 5 minutes—and don't worry about getting an even distribution. While the mixture may now look more like a batter than a dough, if you stir it a bit with your spatula, you'll see that the dough is smooth and shiny and very stretchy—pull a little of the dough and you'll see a webby network of dough enveloping the fruit.

First Rise Scrape the dough into a large buttered bowl, cover tightly with plastic wrap, and allow the dough to rest at room temperature until doubled in bulk, 3 to 3½ hours.

Chilling the Dough Lift the plastic wrap, stir the dough down with a rubber spatula (it will still be very sticky), cover again with plastic wrap, and chill for 24 hours.

Fit the bottom of a jelly-roll pan with parchment paper; butter the paper and the sides of the pan.

Shaping and Second Rise Turn the chilled dough out onto a lightly floured work surface, flour the top of the dough, and gently roll, pull, and stretch the dough into a rectangle the size of your baking pan. As you work, lift the dough up off the work surface and dust with additional flour as needed to keep the dough from sticking. Lift the dough into the prepared baking pan, pulling and pushing the dough gently here and there if necessary to get an even fit. Lightly butter a piece of plastic wrap and place it, buttered side down, over the dough—just lay it gently on the surface; don't press down and don't try to wrap the pan. Let the dough come to room temperature and then start to rise, a process that will take about 3 hours. The dough is ready when it feels spongy to the touch.

Glazing, Topping, and Baking Position a rack in the lower third of the oven and preheat the oven to 400°F.

Brush the dough with the egg glaze and sprinkle with turbinado sugar. Bake for 25 to 30 minutes, or until the top is a deep golden brown. If the focaccia starts to brown too quickly, cover it with a foil tent. Invert the focaccia onto a cooling rack, remove the parchment, and turn the bread over to cool right side up.

Storing The focaccia can be kept, well wrapped, at room temperature for 2 days or frozen for up to a month. Thaw, still wrapped, at room temperature.

Contributing Baker **CRAIG KOMINIAK**

Twice-Baked Brioche
COLOR PHOTOGRAPH, PAGE 171

Makes 10 small loaves ■ Twice-baked brioche, the biscotti of the brioche world, was once a tasty baker's trick, a way to turn a profit on a product, stale brioche, that would otherwise be a loss. But the trick was so appealing that many bakers began to make fresh brioche just for the purpose of baking them again. In this recipe, you make ten mini-loaves of brioche and (if you don't down them immediately) soak them in orange syrup, butter them with almond cream, and bake them to a toasty brown. This technique, whether used with fresh or stale bread, is also terrific with croissants—split and soak them and fill and top with the almond cream—or challah—use a thick slice, soaked and slathered with the cream.

THE BRIOCHE

½ **recipe (1 pound 2 ounces) Brioche dough (page 43), chilled**
¾ **cup dried sour cherries**

Butter 10 mini-loaf pans, each measuring about 4 inches by 2 inches by 1¼ inches. Divide the dough into 10 equal pieces and press the dried cherries into the dough. Working on a smooth surface, roll each piece into a rectangle a few inches larger than the loaf pans. Starting at the top, with a short end, roll the dough into a tight coil, pinching and sealing the seams you form. Turn in the ends of the coil just enough so that it fits into the pan. Pinch the seams at the ends to seal and drop the loaf, seam side down, into the pan.

Rise Cover the pans with oiled plastic wrap and let rise at room temperature until the dough doubles in size, 45 minutes to 1 hour.

Baking the Bread Center a rack in the oven and preheat the oven to 325°F.

Bake the loaves for 15 to 20 minutes, just until they are lightly browned. (If you want to eat these loaves once-baked, brush them with an egg wash before they go into the oven and bake them a little longer, waiting for them to turn a golden brown.) As soon as the loaves come out of the oven, turn them out of the pans and let them cool to room temperature on a rack.

THE SYRUP

> 1½ cups sugar
> 1 cup water
> ½ cup fresh orange juice
> 1 vanilla bean

Put the sugar, water, and orange juice into a medium saucepan. Split the vanilla bean lengthwise and scrape the soft, seedy pulp into the pan. Toss in the vanilla pod and bring the mixture to the boil over medium heat, stirring to dissolve the sugar. Boil the syrup for 1 minute, then remove the pan from the heat; cool completely. When the syrup is cool, discard the vanilla pod. *The syrup can be made up to a week in advance and kept covered in the refrigerator.*

THE CREAM

> 1 stick (4 ounces) unsalted butter, at warm room temperature
> ½ pound almond paste, at room temperature
> ½ cup ground almonds
> 2 large eggs, at room temperature
> ½ cup all-purpose flour
> ¼ teaspoon pure almond extract
>
> Sliced blanched almonds, for garnish
> Confectioner's sugar, for garnish

Working at low speed in a mixer fitted with the paddle attachment (or using a hand-held mixer), beat the butter, almond paste, and ground almonds together until creamy. Add the eggs one at a time, and mix until fully blended. Add the flour and mix for another minute, until incorporated. Remove the bowl from the mixer and stir in the almond extract with a rubber spatula. *The cream can be made up to 3 days in advance and kept covered in the refrigerator.*

Position a rack in the center of the oven and preheat the oven to 325°F. Set a cooling rack over a waxed paper–lined jelly-roll pan to be used for draining the syrup-soaked loaves and set it aside. Line another baking sheet or jelly-roll pan with parchment paper for baking the loaves and set it aside.

Slice the tops off the loaves so that the tops are level.

Pour the orange syrup into a deep wide bowl. One by one, submerge the loaves in the syrup, turning them around so that each of the sides is well moistened. Lift the loaves out of the syrup and onto the rack to drain. When the last loaf has been submerged, start working on frosting the first loaf you submerged. Spread a thin layer of the almond cream over the top and sides of each loaf. Place the loaf on the parchment-lined pan and press a few blanched almonds into the cream. Repeat with the remaining loaves.

Baking the Loaves Bake the loaves about 20 minutes, until the almond cream is golden brown. Transfer them to racks to cool. Just before serving, dust the loaves with confectioner's sugar.

Storing Twice-baked, the brioche will keep uncovered for 1 day at room temperature.

Contributing Baker **NANCY SILVERTON**

Danish Pastry Pockets
COLOR PHOTOGRAPH, PAGE 181

Pinwheel Danish.

Makes 16 pastries ▪ Here are four different pastry shapes, each made by cutting Danish Pastry dough into five-inch squares. With just a twist of the dough, you can create the Spandauer, which wraps the filling the way a baby is wrapped in a blanket; the three-corner, a turnover; the packet, a little pastry purse with a topknot; or the pinwheel. Each pastry has a dollop or two of filling at its center. Use any flavor filling that pleases you, or do as the Danes do—use two: Include a spoonful of fruit filling and another of either confectioner's cream or almond filling.

1 recipe Danish Pastry dough (page 50), chilled
1 recipe Apricot, Prune, or Fresh Berry Jam Filling (pages 203 to 204)
1 recipe Confectioner's Cream (page 204) or Almond Filling (page 202)
1 large egg white, beaten
Pearl sugar or crushed sugar cubes, for sprinkling

½ cup confectioner's sugar, sifted, for glaze
2 to 3 teaspoons milk, for glaze

Line a baking sheet with parchment paper and set aside.

Flour the top of the dough and place it on a lightly floured work surface. Roll the dough into a square that is 20 inches on a side. Using a ruler and a long wet knife or a pizza cutter, trim the edges to even them, if needed. Score each side at 5-inch intervals, then cut through the dough, using the ruler as your guide, to make sixteen 5-inch squares.

TO MAKE THE SPANDAUER, place a pastry square on the work surface with one of the points aimed at you. Place a tablespoon of fruit filling and a tablespoon of cream or almond filling in the center of the pastry, one filling over the other, and brush the left- and right-hand points with a little of the beaten egg white. Fold the sides of the diamond into the center, with the points overlapping, and press down gently so that you create a pointed rectangular pastry with a little filling peeking out from the top and the bottom of the overlap.

TO MAKE THE THREE-CORNER, put a pastry square on the work surface with a point facing you. Spoon a tablespoon of fruit filling onto the center of the pastry and spoon a tablespoon of either almond or cream filling on top of it. Brush the edges of the pastry with some of the beaten egg white. Fold the bottom half of the pastry over the top to form a triangular turnover and press the edges to seal. You can crimp the edges with the tines of a fork if you want, or decorate the top of the turnover with a scrap of pastry. Glue the decoration to the three-corner with egg white.

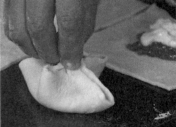

TO MAKE THE PACKET, place a pastry square on the work surface, spoon on a tablespoon of fruit filling, and top with a tablespoon of either cream or almond filling. Brush the edges of the pastry with some of the beaten egg white and, with both hands, lift the four corners of the pastry off the counter and in toward the center of the square. Squeeze the corners together in the center and give them a little pinch and a twist to create a small topknot.

TO MAKE THE PINWHEEL, place a pastry square on the work surface and spoon a tablespoon of fruit filling onto the center of the square. Spoon a tablespoon of either cream or almond filling on top of it. Using a pizza cutter or a thin sharp knife, cut a slash from the center to each corner. Brush every other pastry point with a little beaten egg white and lift those points off the counter and in toward the center, pressing the dough lightly against the filling and overlapping the points to create a pinwheel.

Top: For the Spandauer, fold the sides of the square into the center.
Below: For the packet, draw up the corners.
Below center and bottom: For the pinwheel, cut slashes from center to corners. Then lift every other point in toward the center.

Rise Lift the pastries onto the parchment-lined baking sheet, cover with a kitchen towel, and allow the pastries to rise at room temperature for 30 minutes. (Reserve the remaining beaten egg white.) Although the pastries won't double, they will look and feel puffy.

Baking and Glazing Position a rack in the center of the oven and preheat the oven to 400°F.

Brush the risen pastries with the reserved beaten egg white, sprinkle with pearl sugar, and bake for 8 to 10 minutes, or until lightly golden. Transfer the pastries from the baking sheet to a wire rack to cool slightly while you prepare the glaze.

continued

Mix the confectioner's sugar and milk together in a small bowl, adding enough milk to produce a glaze that is smooth and can be piped. Scrape the glaze into a small plastic bag with a zipper lock, and seal. Snip a corner of the bag to create a small opening (your piping tip) and squeeze the glaze through the bag onto the pastries in attractive squiggles. Serve the pastries warm or at room temperature.

Storing Danish pastries are best served the day they are made—the closer to just baked, the better. If necessary, the pastries can be kept tightly covered at room temperature for several hours.

· *Contributing Baker* **BEATRICE OJAKANGAS**

Five Fillings

These nut, fruit butter, jam, and cream fillings are the little jewels of the baker's pantry. A spoonful here, a dollop there, and plain pastries take on polish. While these were created for Danish and other pastries, they make excellent bases for tartlets, fillings for cookies, or spreads for morning toast. The almond cream is whirred in the food processor and the fruit fillings and confectioner's cream are made in the microwave oven, which makes fast work of the fillings while preserving the fresh, brilliant colors of the fruit. You may never boil jam again.

Almond Filling

Makes 1 cup

- **1 cup blanched almonds, toasted**
- **1/2 cup confectioner's sugar**
- **2 tablespoons unsalted butter, at room temperature**
- **1/2 teaspoon pure almond extract**
- **1 large egg white, lightly beaten**

Put the almonds, sugar, and butter in the work bowl of a food processor fitted with the metal blade. Process until the almonds are finely ground, stopping to scrape the bowl as needed. Add the almond extract and 2 tablespoons of the beaten egg white and process to mix. Pack the filling into an airtight container and store in the refrigerator until needed. Bring to room temperature before using. *The filling can be made up to a week ahead and kept chilled.*

Apricot Filling

Makes about 1⅓ cups

> 1 cup (packed) dried apricots
>
> 1 cup water
>
> 1 cup sugar
>
> 2 tablespoons fresh lemon juice, or more to taste
>
> ½ teaspoon pure almond extract

Stir the apricots, water, and sugar together in a large microwave-safe bowl or a 1-quart glass measuring cup. Put the bowl in a microwave oven set to full power and cook, stirring a few times, for 10 minutes, or until the apricots are soft and puffed and have absorbed almost all of the liquid. Turn the mixture into the work bowl of a food processor fitted with the metal blade and process until smooth, scraping the bowl as needed. Transfer the purée to a bowl, add the lemon juice and almond extract, and stir to mix. Scrape the filling into a small container and cool to room temperature. Seal the container and chill. *The filling will keep in the refrigerator for up to 2 weeks.*

Prune Filling

Makes about 1⅓ cups

> 1 cup (packed) pitted prunes
>
> 1 cup water
>
> 1 cup sugar
>
> 2 tablespoons fresh lemon juice
>
> ½ teaspoon pure vanilla extract
>
> ½ teaspoon cinnamon (optional)

Stir the prunes, water, and sugar together in a large microwave-safe bowl or a 1-quart glass measuring cup. Put the bowl in a microwave oven set to full power and cook, stirring a few times, for 10 minutes, or until the prunes are soft and puffed and have absorbed almost all of the liquid. Turn the mixture into the work bowl of a food processor fitted with the metal blade and process until smooth, scraping the bowl as needed. Transfer to a bowl and add the lemon juice, vanilla extract, and the cinnamon, if you're using it, and stir to mix. Scrape the filling into a small container and cool to room temperature. Seal the container and chill. *The filling can be refrigerated for up to 2 weeks.*

continued

Fresh Berry Jam Filling

Makes about 2 cups

> 2 cups crushed fresh berries, such as strawberries, raspberries, or other seasonal berries (use one type of berry or several types in combination)
>
> 1 cup sugar
>
> 1 to 2 tablespoons fresh lemon juice

Stir the berries and sugar together in a large microwave-safe bowl or a 1-quart glass measuring cup. Put the bowl in a microwave oven set to full power and cook for 10 minutes. Stir the mixture and cook for 5 to 8 minutes longer, or until most of the liquid has been absorbed and the filling is glossy. Stir in the lemon juice. Scrape the filling into a small container and cool to room temperature. Seal the container and chill. *The filling will keep in the refrigerator for up to 1 week.*

Confectioner's Cream

Makes 1 cup

> 1 cup half-and-half or heavy cream
>
> 1½ tablespoons cornstarch
>
> 2 tablespoons sugar
>
> 1 large egg yolk
>
> 1 teaspoon pure vanilla extract

Whisk the half-and-half, cornstarch, and sugar together in a large microwave-safe bowl or a 1-quart glass measuring cup. Put the bowl in a microwave oven set to full power and cook for 1 minute. Stir the mixture and cook for 2 to 3 minutes more, a minute at a time, or until the mixture comes to the boil and thickens slightly.

While the liquid is heating, whisk together the yolk and vanilla in a small bowl.

Slowly whisk a little of the hot liquid into the yolk. Pour the yolk mixture into the boiled mixture, whisk well, and return the bowl to the microwave oven. Cook the cream for 30 seconds longer, then remove the bowl from the oven and stir again. The cream's consistency is like that of lemon curd. Scrape the cream into a small container, press a piece of plastic wrap against the surface of the cream to prevent a skin from forming, and cool to room temperature. Seal the container and chill. *The cream can be made up to 3 days ahead and kept refrigerated.*

Contributing Baker **BEATRICE OJAKANGAS**

Danish Braid

COLOR PHOTOGRAPH, PAGE 174

Makes 1 long braid; 6 to 8 servings ■ What looks like a braid is actually just a crisscross of pastry strips, made in minutes but giving the impression of being complex to construct. The braid is packed with two fillings (your choice) and decorated with a coffee-sugar glaze.

½ recipe Danish Pastry dough (page 50), chilled

1 recipe Apricot, Prune, or Fresh Berry Jam Filling (pages 203 to 204)

1 recipe Confectioner's Cream (page 204) or Almond Filling (page 202)

1 large egg white, beaten

Pearl sugar or crushed sugar cubes, for sprinkling

Sliced unblanched or chopped blanched almonds, for garnish (optional)

2 to 3 teaspoons cold strong coffee, for glaze

½ cup confectioner's sugar, sifted, for glaze

Shaping the Dough Working on a lightly floured surface, roll the chilled dough into a rectangle 10 inches wide and 16 inches long. Lift onto a sheet of parchment, and position lengthwise on the work surface. Spread some of the fruit filling down the length of the center third of the dough, then top with some of the cream or almond filling (you might not need the entire amount of either filling), spreading it so that a little of the fruit filling peeks out on either side. Using a pizza cutter or the point of a sharp knife, cut 12 to 14 slanting lines down each side, angling the cuts from the center of the pastry to the edge and cutting strips about ¾ inch wide. Fold the strips of pastry into the center, crisscrossing the filling by alternating one strip from the left side of the pastry with one from the right. Lightly press the ends together to seal and run your hands along the sides of the pastry to straighten them.

Rise Brush the pastry with the beaten egg white and sprinkle with pearl sugar and almonds. Cover with a kitchen towel and allow it to rise at room temperature for 30 minutes, until it looks and feels puffy; it will not double.

Baking the Braid Center a rack in the oven and preheat the oven to 400°F. Slide the braid, paper and all, onto a baking sheet; bake for 15 to 20 minutes, or just until golden. Transfer the pastry onto a cooling rack and make the glaze.

Glazing the Braid Stir the coffee into the confectioner's sugar, adding just enough coffee to produce a smooth, shiny glaze. Spoon the glaze into a small zipper-lock plastic bag, seal the top, and snip a bottom corner to create a little decorating tube. Squeeze squiggles of the glaze over the pastry, allow it to set for a few minutes, and serve while the pastry is still warm.

Contributing Baker **BEATRICE OJAKANGAS**

Danish Slices

Makes 2 long pastries; about 16 servings ■ A traditional shape and an easy one to make. The dough is rolled into a long rectangle and the edges are folded over the filling, leaving some of the filling exposed and glistening. Think of this as the Danish version of the rustic galette or fruit croustade.

1 recipe Danish Pastry dough (page 50), chilled
1 cup Confectioner's Cream (page 204) or Almond Filling (page 202)
½ cup Apricot, Prune, or Fresh Berry Jam Filling (pages 203 to 204)

1 cup confectioner's sugar, sifted, for glaze
2 to 3 teaspoons milk, for glaze

Line a baking sheet with parchment paper and set aside.

Shaping the Dough Working on a lightly floured surface, roll the chilled dough into a rectangle 10 inches wide by 24 inches long. Using a pizza cutter or a long sharp knife, cut the dough crosswise into two strips, each 10 inches by 12 inches.

Spread the cream or almond filling down the center of each piece of dough, leaving a 2-inch-wide border along each of the long sides. Spread the fruit filling over the layer of cream or almond filling. Carefully lift the bare edges of each pastry with your fingers and fold them over the filling, leaving about 1 inch of the filling peeking out down the center. Press the edges down gently over the filling.

Rise Carefully lift the pastries onto the parchment-lined baking sheet (two wide metal spatulas will do the trick here) and cover with a kitchen towel. Allow the pastries to rise at room temperature for about 30 minutes, until they look and feel puffy; they will not double.

Baking the Pastry Center a rack in the oven and preheat the oven to 400°F. Bake the pastries for 18 to 20 minutes, or until they are lightly browned. Transfer the pastries to a rack to cool slightly while you make the glaze.

Making the Glaze Stir the sugar and enough of the milk together to produce a shiny glaze that falls easily from the tip of a spoon. Drizzle the glaze over the pastries. Allow the glaze to set for a few minutes before cutting the pastries into slices, each about 1½ inches wide.

Storing You can keep the pastries covered at room temperature for a few hours, but they should be served the day they are made. Cut the pastries just before serving.

Contributing Baker **BEATRICE OJAKANGAS**

Buttermilk Crumb Muffins

COLOR PHOTOGRAPH, PAGE 207

Makes 14 to 16 muffins ■ These sweet, tender muffins have a light, open crumb, rather like a moist, soft butter cake. Before the spices are added to the batter, a little is spooned off and reserved to be used as the crumb topping, providing a gentle crunch atop the cinnamon- and-nutmeg-laced, flat-top muffins.

2½ **cups unbleached all-purpose flour**

2 **cups (packed) light brown sugar**

⅔ **cup solid vegetable shortening**

2 **teaspoons baking powder**

½ **teaspoon baking soda**

½ **teaspoon cinnamon**

¼ **teaspoon grated nutmeg**

½ **teaspoon salt**

1 **cup buttermilk**

2 **large eggs, well beaten**

Position a rack in the center of the oven and preheat the oven to 350°F. Spray or grease two 12-cup muffin tins, or, if you have them, use a 12-cup and a 6-cup tin.

Mixing the Batter and Topping Put the flour and brown sugar into a large bowl and stir with your fingers or a fork to mix well. Break the shortening into a few pieces, drop them into the flour mixture, and, using your fingertips, lightly rub the shortening and flour together. When the mixture looks like coarse bread crumbs, you've mixed enough—don't worry about any little lumps. Measure out ½ cup of the mixture and set it aside to use later as the crumb topping.

Add the baking powder, baking soda, cinnamon, nutmeg, and salt to the flour mixture and stir with a fork to mix well. Add the buttermilk and beaten eggs and, using a large spoon, mix until the ingredients are well blended and the batter is thick and shiny.

Spoon the batter into the muffin tins, filling each cup at least two-thirds full. Sprinkle the top of each muffin with a rounded teaspoon of the reserved crumb mixture and pat it gently onto the batter. Half-fill any empty muffin molds with water—this will help the muffins bake evenly.

Baking the Muffins Bake for 25 to 30 minutes, or until a toothpick inserted into the center of a muffin comes out clean. Serve warm.

Storing The muffins are best the day they are made, but will keep in a plastic bag or closed container for a day; reheat for 5 to 8 minutes in a 350°F oven.

Contributing Baker **MARION CUNNINGHAM**

Blueberry Muffins

COLOR PHOTOGRAPHS, PAGE 168

Makes 18 muffins ■ There is an ineffable lightness about these muffins. Savored while still warm, the texture is melt-on-your-tongue light; only the plump blueberries seem substantial. The next day, when they have settled down, literally, they are more conventionally muffiny and a different kind of wonderful. That is the day you might want to slice them, toast them, and let a little butter melt into them.

One reason these muffins are so light is their leavening: home-made baking powder—a combination of baking soda and cream of tartar. The other reason is the way they're mixed—which is minimally. Although the butter is whipped to whiteness and then fluffed with sugar and eggs, the dry and liquid ingredients are folded in only enough to barely mix them. The blueberries, which are tossed with a few spoonfuls of the dry ingredients so they don't all sink to the bottom of the muffins, are mixed even less.

> $1^{3}/_{4}$ cups cake flour
>
> 2 teaspoons baking soda
>
> 1 teaspoon cream of tartar
>
> 1 teaspoon salt
>
> 1 pint fresh blueberries
>
> $^{3}/_{4}$ cup milk
>
> $^{1}/_{4}$ cup sour cream
>
> 1 stick (4 ounces) unsalted butter, at room temperature
>
> $^{2}/_{3}$ cup sugar
>
> 1 large egg, at room temperature
>
> 1 large egg yolk, at room temperature

Position a rack in the center of the oven and preheat the oven to 400°F. Butter or spray 18 muffin cups or line them with paper bake cups. (These muffins are best made in standard tins in which the cups are 2½ inches in diameter.) If you have 2 muffin tins with 12 cups, fill the 6 cups that will be empty in one of the tins with water—this will help the muffins bake evenly.

Mixing the Batter Sift the cake flour, baking soda, cream of tartar, and salt together twice, and leave the sifted dry ingredients in the sifter or strainer; set it on a piece of waxed paper. Remove a tablespoon or two of the dry ingredients and toss with the blueberries. In a separate bowl, stir the milk and sour cream together and set aside until needed.

In a mixer fitted with the paddle attachment (or work with a hand-held mixer), beat the butter on medium speed until white and pale, about 3 minutes. Add the sugar and beat until the mixture no longer feels grainy, about 3 minutes, scraping down the paddle and the sides of the bowl as needed. Add the eggs and yolk and beat until the mixture is fluffy, about 2 minutes.

Remove the bowl from the mixer and sift half of the dry ingredients into the bowl. Add half of the milk and sour cream mixture and, using a large rubber spatula, delicately fold the ingredients together, stopping when barely combined. Add the remaining dry and liquid ingredients and fold in only until just mixed—don't be concerned about getting everything evenly incorporated. Sprinkle over the blueberries and fold them in only to the just-mixed stage.

Baking the Muffins Spoon the batter into the prepared muffin tins, filling each cup at least two-thirds full, and bake for 18 to 20 minutes, or until the tops, which will be flat, are golden and spring back when lightly pressed. Turn the muffins out onto a cooling rack and allow them to cool for 10 to 15 minutes before serving.

Storing The muffins will stay light and lovely for a day. If you are not going to serve them within a few hours of baking, pack them into a plastic bag; they'll keep for 1 more day and will then be best sliced and toasted. For longer storage, wrap airtight and freeze for up to a month. Thaw, still wrapped, at room temperature.

Contributing Baker **RICK KATZ**

Buttermilk Scones

Makes 12 triangular or 24 rolled scones ■ Think of scones as British biscuits. They are made in a manner similar to biscuits and, in fact, share biscuits' buttery-layered texture, but their name, their shape, and the fact that they're served with tea rather than gravy lift them to the level of fancier fare.

Here are scones two ways: the traditional triangle and the rolled—tender buttermilk dough rolled around chopped fruits, nuts, and/or jam. Whichever way you choose, they're luscious: à la the British, with tea and whipped cream, or served the American way, with coffee and a gloss of jam.

THE SCONES

3 cups all-purpose flour

1/3 cup sugar

2 1/2 teaspoons baking powder

1/2 teaspoon baking soda

3/4 teaspoon salt

1 1/2 sticks (6 ounces) cold unsalted butter, cut into small pieces

1 cup (approximately) buttermilk

1 tablespoon grated orange or lemon zest

1/2 stick (2 ounces) unsalted butter, melted, for brushing

1/4 cup sugar, for dusting

4 tablespoons jam or jelly and/or 4 tablespoons diced or small
plump dried fruits, such as currants, raisins, apricots, or figs,
for filling (optional)

Position the oven racks to divide the oven into thirds and preheat the oven to 425°F.

Mixing and Kneading In a medium bowl, stir the flour, sugar, baking powder, baking soda, and salt together with a fork. Add the cold butter pieces and, using your fingertips (the first choice), a pastry blender, or two knives, work the butter into the dry ingredients until the mixture resembles coarse cornmeal. It's OK if some largish pieces of butter remain—they'll add to the scones' flakiness.

Pour in 1 cup buttermilk, toss in the zest, and mix with the fork only until the ingredients are just moistened—you'll have a soft dough with a rough look. (If the dough looks dry, add another tablespoon of buttermilk.) Gather the dough into a ball, pressing it gently so that it holds together, turn it out onto a lightly floured work surface, and knead it very briefly—a dozen turns should do it. Cut the dough in half.

TO MAKE TRIANGULAR-SHAPED SCONES, roll one piece of the dough into a ½-inch-thick circle that is about 7 inches across. Brush the dough with half of the melted butter, sprinkle with 2 tablespoons of the sugar, and cut the circle into 6 triangles. Place the scones on an ungreased baking sheet and set aside while you roll out the rest of the dough.

TO MAKE ROLLED SCONES, roll one piece of dough into a strip that is 12 inches long and ½ inch thick (the piece will not be very wide). Spread the strip with half of the melted butter and dust with half of the sugar. If you want to spread the roll with jam and/or sprinkle it with dried fruits, now's the time to do so; leave a narrow border on a long edge bare. Roll the strip up from a long side like a jelly roll; pinch the seam closed and turn the roll seam side down. Cut the roll in half and cut each piece into six 1-inch-wide roll-ups. Place the rolled scones cut side down on an ungreased baking sheet, leaving a little space between each one. Repeat with the remaining dough.

Baking the Scones Bake the scones for 10 to 12 minutes, until both the tops and bottoms are golden. Transfer the scones to a rack to cool slightly. These are best served warm but are just fine at room temperature.

Storing If you're not going to eat the scones the day they are made, wrap them airtight and freeze; they'll stay fresh for a month. To serve, defrost the scones at room temperature in their wrappers, then unwrap and reheat on a baking sheet for 5 minutes in a 350°F oven.

Contributing Baker **MARION CUNNINGHAM**

Baking Powder Biscuits
COLOR PHOTOGRAPH, PAGE 180

Makes about 14 biscuits ■ Among bakers, one hears the expression "She has a good biscuit hand." Like pie crusts, biscuits are a measure of a baker's talents and a pastry in which bakers take particular pride.

To have a good biscuit hand is to have a light touch and restraint—a biscuit dough is so soft that it invites poking and prodding, kneading and mashing, when it should be just barely worked. The golden rule with biscuits is to stop doing whatever you're doing to them two beats before you have to. So, when you're rubbing the shortening and flour together and there are still some chubby chunks of shortening—stop. When you're tossing the flour-and-butter mixture with the milk and the dough looks only just moistened—stop. And when you turn the dough out onto the counter and knead it just to work it into a mass, count each knead, get to ten, and—stop.

2 cups all-purpose flour
1 tablespoon baking powder
1 teaspoon salt
$1/3$ cup solid vegetable shortening
1 cup milk

Position a rack in the center of the oven and preheat the oven to 425°F. Grease a 9- by 12-inch baking pan and set it aside.

Mixing the Dough Put the flour, baking powder, and salt into a large bowl and stir with a fork just to mix. Add the shortening, roll it around in the flour mix to coat it, and break it into 4 or 5 pieces. Rub the flour and shortening together with the tips of your fingers, making little crumbs and letting the crumbs fall back into the bowl. Keep rubbing the flour and shortening together and tossing the contents of the bowl until most of the shortening is mixed with the flour. Don't worry if you still have a few largish pieces. Add the milk and stir with a fork to moisten the flour. Again, don't worry about getting everything thoroughly or evenly mixed. You'll have a sticky mass of dough.

Kneading the Dough Flour a work surface and your hands, scoop the dough out of the bowl, and drop it onto the counter. Knead the dough ten times—no more, even if its malleable texture tempts you. Pat the dough into a circle about 9 inches across and, using a 2-inch round biscuit or cookie cutter, cut out the biscuits. (You can, of course, make the biscuits larger or smaller to meet your needs. And you can always press the scraps together into a $1/4$-inch-thick circle and cut out additional biscuits.)

Baking the Biscuits Transfer the biscuits to the baking pan, allowing them to touch each other if you want biscuits with soft sides, and placing them apart if you want crisper sides. (The biscuits can be brushed with melted butter before baking, an optional but nice touch.)

Bake the biscuits for 12 to 15 minutes, or until they are golden on top. Serve them warm.

Storing Biscuits are best just out of the oven, but they can be kept covered at room temperature for a few hours and warmed for about 5 minutes in a 350°F oven before serving.

Contributing Baker **MARION CUNNINGHAM**

Popovers

COLOR PHOTOGRAPH, PAGE 169

Makes 9 large or 10 medium popovers ■ From their name, which inspires smiles, to their puffing power, popovers have magical appeal. Many of us have fond memories of the messy thrill of eating popovers dripping with butter and honey. Here's a method that turns out beautifully puffed popovers with golden crowns, crispy crusts, and custardy interiors.

1 cup all-purpose flour

1 cup whole or 2% milk, at room temperature

½ teaspoon salt

3 large eggs, at room temperature

2 tablespoons unsalted butter, melted

Melted butter, for greasing the popover cups

Position a rack on the lowest rung of the oven and preheat the oven to 425°F. Butter or spray nine ¾-cup glass custard cups or ten ½-cup muffin cups. If you're using custard cups, place them on a jelly-roll pan, leaving space between each cup. If you're using muffin pans, you'll need to use two 12-hole muffin tins because, to give the popovers ample air circulation, you won't be filling all of the holes.

Pour all the ingredients into the container of a blender and whirl until smooth. (This can also be done in a food processor or in a bowl, using a rotary or hand-held beater.) Strain the batter if it is at all lumpy.

Baking the Popovers For the custard cups, pour ⅓ cup of batter into each cup, dividing any extra batter among the cups. For the muffin cups, use ¼ cup of batter for each cup, filling alternate cups in each tin so that every popover has puffing space. Bake, without opening the oven door, for 25 minutes, until the popovers are puffed, nicely browned, and crisp on the exterior. Turn the temperature down to 350°F and bake for another 15 to 20 minutes to help dry out the interior, which, no matter what you do, will always be a little doughy in the center. (Some people love this part, others pull it out.) Serve immediately.

Storing Popovers are at their puffiest right out of the oven. You can hold them at room temperature for a few minutes, or wrap them airtight, freeze them for up to a month, and reheat them in a 350°F for 10 to 15 minutes, and they'll taste good—but never as good as just baked.

Contributing Baker **MARION CUNNINGHAM**

Irish Soda Bread

COLOR PHOTOGRAPH, PAGE 170

Makes one 8-inch round loaf ■ This is a very basic loaf made with just four ingredients, ingredients every household in Ireland traditionally had on hand. The bread gets its remarkable texture and lift from just one leavener—its namesake baking soda. In combination with the tangy buttermilk, it produces a loaf that tastes pleasingly wholesome and plain. Both the taste and the tight-crumbed texture lend themselves to spreads and dunking. Irish soda bread is a good accompaniment to tea, Irish or not.

A nice nontraditional touch is to add a cup of raisins, currants, or diced dried fruits to the dough.

> 4 cups unbleached all-purpose flour
> 1 teaspoon baking soda
> 1½ teaspoons salt
> 2 cups buttermilk

Position a rack in the center of the oven and preheat the oven to 375°F. Grease an 8-inch glass pie plate or a baking sheet; set aside.

Mixing and Kneading Put the flour, baking soda, and salt in a medium bowl and stir with a fork to blend. Add the buttermilk and stir vigorously until the dough comes together.

Turn the dough out onto a lightly floured work surface and knead gently for a minute. The dough will be soft and malleable, but, tantalizing as it is, it should not be overworked. Pat the dough into a disk about 6 inches across, slash an X across the top, cutting it about ½ inch deep, and place the dough in the greased pan (it won't touch the sides of the pan—that's OK) or on the baking sheet.

Baking the Bread Bake for about 50 minutes, or until the slash has widened and the bread is golden brown. Transfer to a rack to cool completely, then slice or wrap in a moist towel until ready to serve. Allow the bread to cool completely before slicing.

Storing The bread can be kept for a few hours, wrapped and at room temperature, but by the end of the day, with just the wee bit of fat that's in the buttermilk, it will turn as hard as the Blarney Stone.

Contributing Baker **MARION CUNNINGHAM**

CAKES

Vanilla Chiffon Roll   **PAGE 251**

Gingerbread Baby Cake PAGE 247

Assorted Meringue Cookies   PAGE   311

Boca Negra   PAGE 253

Sage Upside-down Baby Cake PAGE 247

Hazelnut Baby Loaf PAGE 420

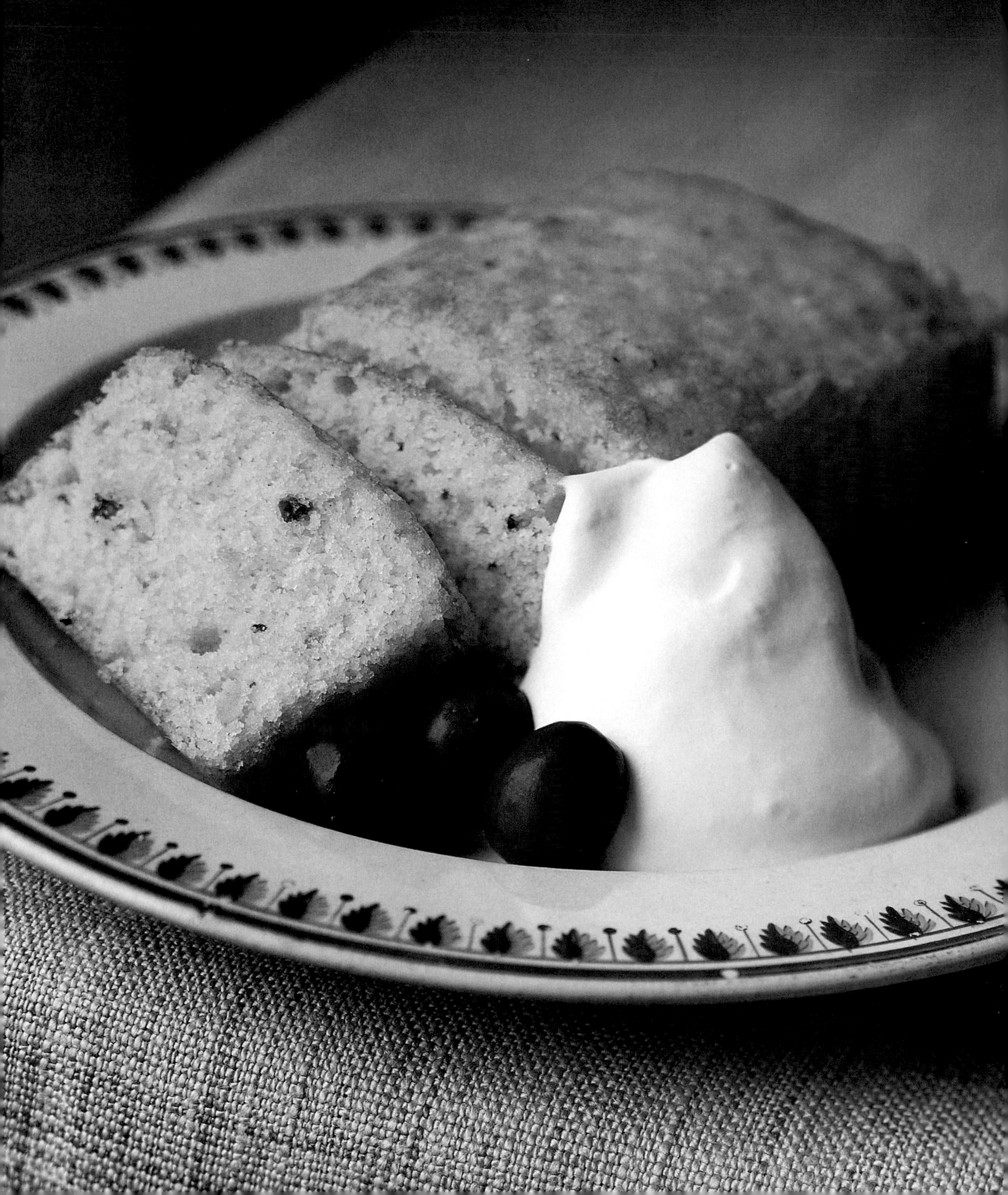

Hazelnut Biscotti PAGE 315

X Cookies PAGE 318, Cornmeal-Currant Biscotti PAGE 316, and Cantuccini PAGE 313

Vanilla-Hazelnut Cheesecake   **PAGE 216**

Chocolate Ruffle Cake PAGE 263

Cardinal Slice PAGE 286

Miniature Florentine Squares PAGE 268, a Raspberry Swirl PAGE 275, and Glazed Mini-Rounds PAGE 271

Rugelach PAGE 325

Oven-Roasted Plum Cakes PAGE 255

Poppy Seed Torte PAGE 258

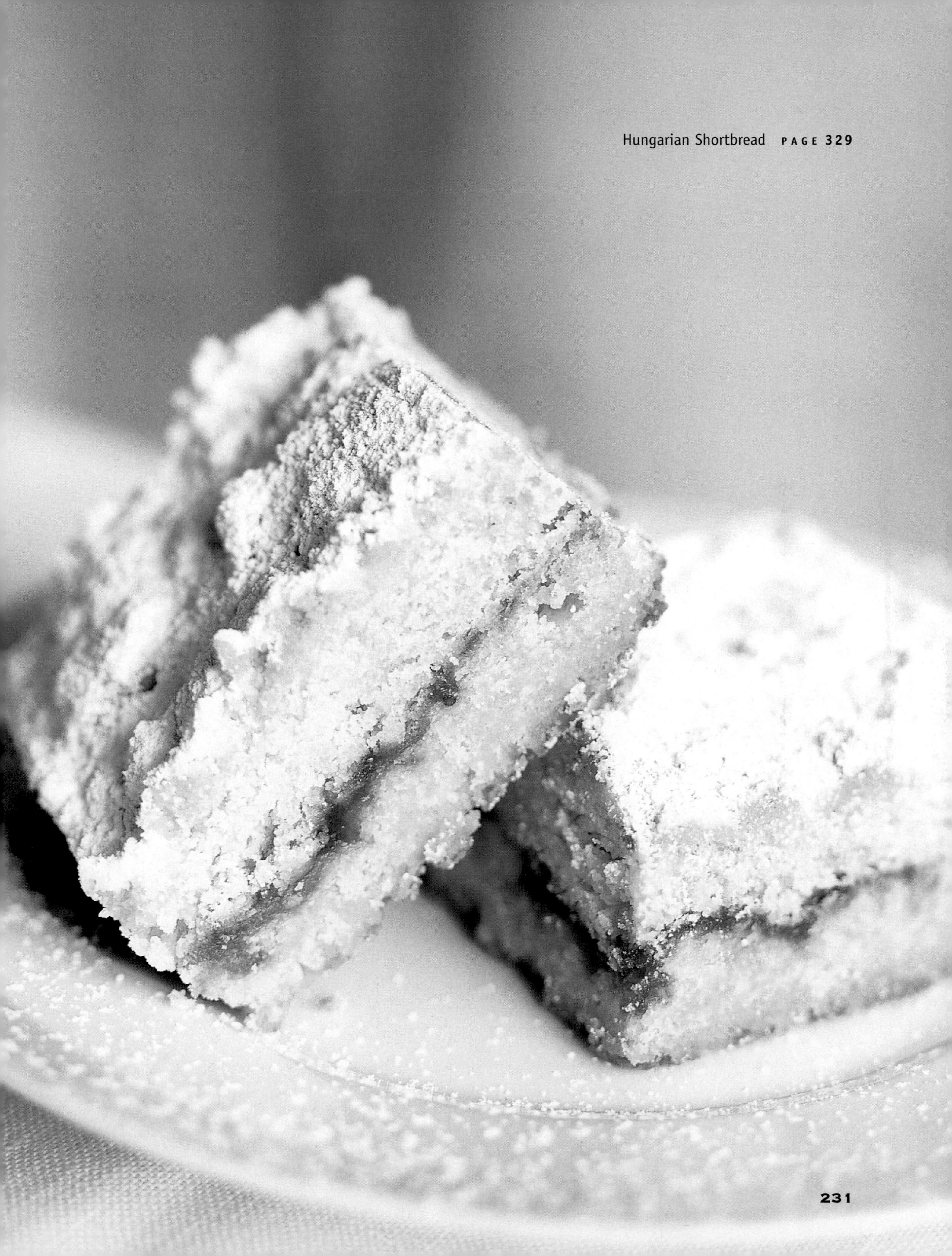

Hungarian Shortbread PAGE 329

A Glorious Wedding Cake PAGE 391

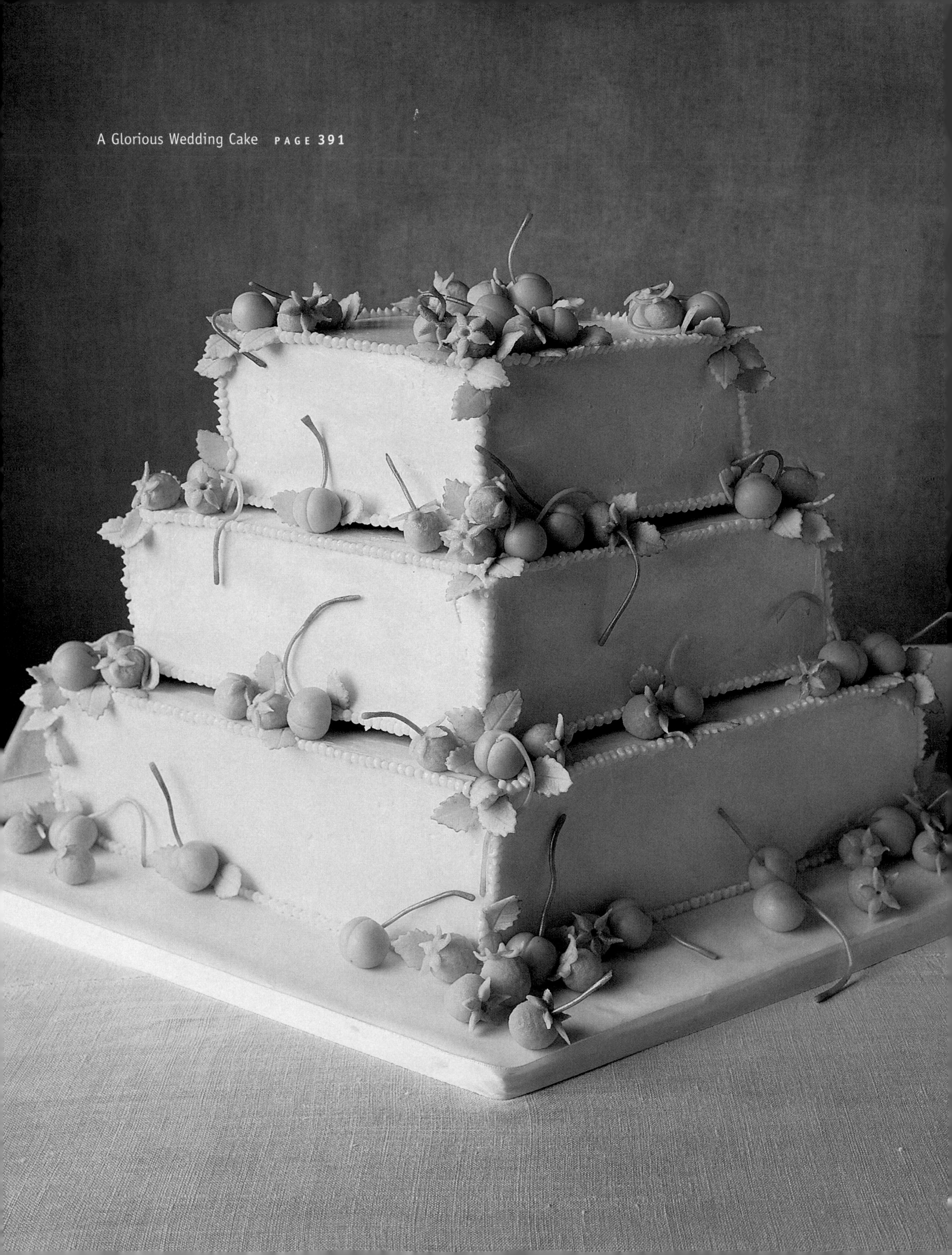

Marzipan fruits PAGE 300

233

A Glorious Wedding Cake

1. To make the dacquoise for each cake layer, trace the outline of the cake pan onto a sheet of parchment.

2. Start the dacquoise layer by piping a thick ribbon of meringue that follows the traced outline. Continue to pipe meringue within the diamond shape to fill the layer.

3. Smooth the piped lines of meringue with an offset spatula to create an even layer before baking.

4. To cut each cake layer accurately, measure the midpoint and mark with toothpicks on all sides.

5. Using toothpicks as guides, slice the cake in half horizontally with a long serrated knife.

6. Pipe a border of buttercream on the bottom layer of the cut cake and spread apricot jam evenly over the surface.

7. Lay the baked dacquoise over the cake and trim the edges to even the sides.

8. Pipe more buttercream on the dacquoise, spread more jam, and carefully replace the top half of the sliced cake.

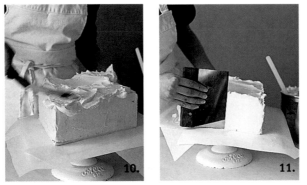

9. Lightly coat each of the three filled cake tiers with a thin veneer of buttercream. This is the crumb coat.

10. Cover the chilled crumb coat with a thick layer of buttercream, icing across the top of the cake layer and down the sides.

11. Use a bench scraper to smooth the buttercream over the sides of the tiers.

12. Use an offset spatula to complete the finish coat of buttercream icing.

13. Place support columns of drinking straws and wooden skewers into the bottom cake tier. Cut supports at even heights with heavy-duty shears. Repeat with the middle tier.

14. Carefully center and set the middle tier on the bottom tier. Then set the top tier in place.

15. Gently hammer a long wooden dowel through all three cake tiers to prevent the assembled cake from toppling.

16. Pipe buttercream beads along all horizontal and vertical edges of each cake tier.

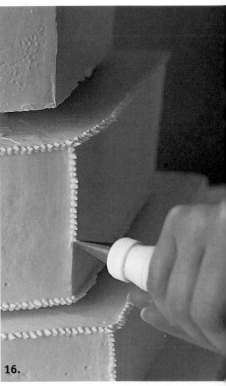

Making Marzipan Fruit

1. Pinch off a small piece of marzipan and roll it between your fingers and palms to form a ball.

2. Roll the blunt edge of a candymaker's knife into one side to make a cherry's crease.

3. Cut leaves for fruit with star-shaped and oval leaf cutters and press with a latex mold to make the leaf veins.

4. To give the raspberries texture, roll marzipan balls over the smallest holes of a box grater.

5. Apply dry food colors, or petal dust, to shaped fruits with a paintbrush. Cherries are blushed with a mixture of buttercup and mango colors.

6. Highlight just the edges of the cherry leaves with moss green petal dust.

7. Create your fruit decorations well ahead of the wedding and store in plastic containers lined with bubble wrap.

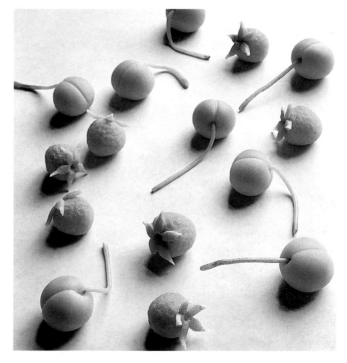

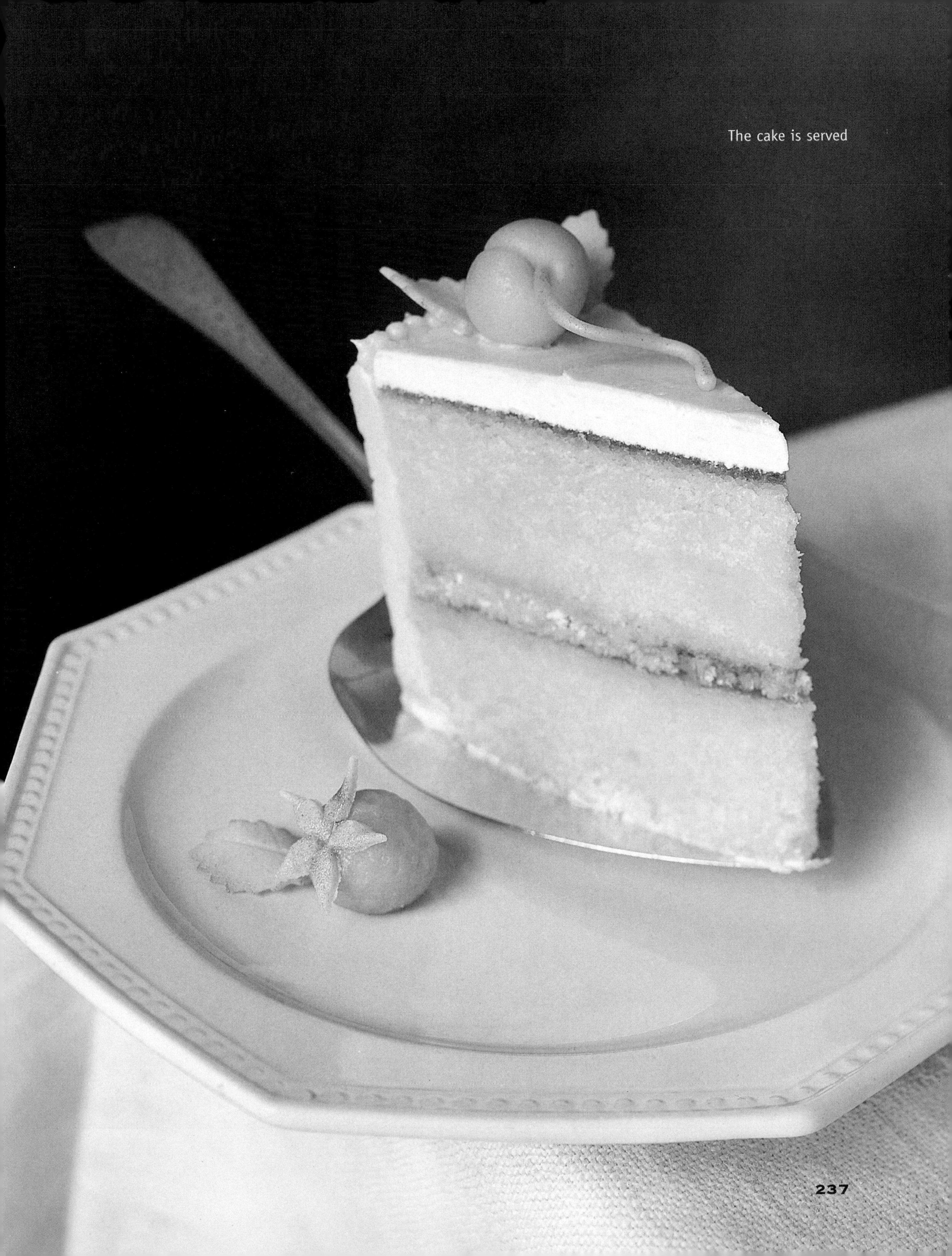

The cake is served

Nectarine Upside-down Chiffon Cake   PAGE 241

Everyday Delights

THIS IS THE CHAPTER bound to become speckled with flour and fingerprints, the resource you'll turn to repeatedly for simple sweets you can make without fuss and serve again and again.

With no frostings, a few fruits, and only a scoop of whipped cream to dress them up, these simple and sturdy cakes stand on their flavor. Some are so easy to make that you can bake them on a whim. For example, the lemon loaf from Norman Love, a pastry chef best known for his elaborate dessert constructions, is a five-minute wonder. You need nothing more than a whisk, a bowl, and ingredients that are usually at hand to turn out this sweet with its fine, pound-cakish texture, puckery lemon tang, and commendable keeping qualities—you can nibble it all week. The profoundly fudgy Boca Negra from Lora Brody, who can simplify the most complicated concoctions, can be made in the food processor by neophytes who've never wielded a whisk. Other cakes, like the little plum cakes from the Trellis Restaurant's Marcel Desaulniers, or the baby cakes—in three flavors—from Al Forno's Johanne Killeen, a pastry chef whose simple desserts are deeply delicious, are easy-to-make treats of the old-fashioned kind. Chock-full of fruit, just a little sugary, and more than a little homey, they have a handmade look that is a sign of warmth and welcome.

Most of the cakes in this chapter, even the grand Poppy Seed Torte from teacher Markus Farbinger, are made using the time-honored cream-the-butter-and-sugar-together technique. Learn to make one and you'll understand them all.

Nectarine Upside-down Chiffon Cake

COLOR PHOTOGRAPH, PAGE 238

Makes 8 to 10 servings ■ Named for the billowy, gossamer fabric that was flapper wear, chiffon cake is a fully American creation, almost certainly from the 1920s and most probably, as was later boasted, the first new cake to be created in a hundred years. A chiffon cake is delicate, light-textured, springy, moist, and not as fragile as its sponge-cake cousins. It's a cross between an angel food cake and a butter cake; its distinguishing characteristic is that it's made with vegetable oil.

Because vegetable oil, unlike solid shortening or butter, cannot be whipped and therefore will not trap air, a chiffon cake needs to rely on other leavenings, usually baking powder, sometimes baking soda, and always meringue, so you might want to read more about meringue (page 37).

With its springy texture and sprightly flavor, this chiffon cake is a fine foil for the caramely brown sugar and nectarine topping. It's a large cake—it's baked in a tall ten-inch springform, the better to show off the rings of baked fruit— and in the center is a layer of crunchy, crumbly oatmeal and almond streusel. The lemon base is a versatile palette—you can top it with ripe juicy pears, tart apples, sweet apricots, dark plums, or even bananas.

THE TOPPING

- ½ **stick (2 ounces) unsalted butter**
- **1 cup (packed) dark brown sugar**
- **3 to 4 ripe medium nectarines (the number will depend on the size), each cut into 8 pieces**

Center a rack in the oven and preheat the oven to 350°F.

Cut the butter into 3 or 4 chunks and toss them into a 10-inch-diameter springform pan that's 3 inches high. Place the pan directly over medium-low heat and melt the butter, tilting the pan so that the butter covers the bottom evenly. Remove the pan from the heat and scatter the brown sugar evenly over the butter, patting it down with your fingertips. Arrange the nectarine pieces in concentric circles over the sugar. For a fancier effect, alternate the way the nectarines face from circle to circle. Wrap the bottom of the pan in aluminum foil to catch any butter that might drip during baking and set the pan aside.

continued

THE STREUSEL

¼ **cup unblanched whole almonds**

⅓ **cup all-purpose flour**

¼ **cup (packed) dark brown sugar**

1 **teaspoon cinnamon**

1 **teaspoon ginger**

½ **stick (2 ounces) cold unsalted butter, cut into small pieces**

½ **cup quick-cooking (*not* instant) oats**

Put the almonds on an ungreased jelly-roll pan and bake them until golden brown and fragrant, 10 to 15 minutes, stirring frequently so that they toast evenly. To test for toastiness, break one open—it should be light brown in the center. Cool the almonds before proceeding.

Line the jelly-roll pan with parchment paper and keep at the ready.

Put all of the streusel ingredients, including the almonds, into the work bowl of a food processor fitted with the metal blade and pulse just to mix the ingredients and chop the almonds and butter. The mixture will be rough and crumbly. Spread the streusel out on the pan and, if you'd like to have a few largish lumps for textural interest (a nice touch), squeeze some of the streusel lightly between your hands and then break the big clumps into smaller bits.

Baking the Streusel Bake the streusel for 10 to 15 minutes, stirring once or twice, until golden brown. Transfer the pan to a rack and cool while you make the cake. (Keep the oven at 350°F.)

THE CAKE

1½ **cups sugar**

1 **cup all-purpose flour**

1 **teaspoon baking powder**

1 **teaspoon baking soda**

¼ **teaspoon salt, preferably kosher**

4 **large eggs, separated**

½ **cup vegetable or safflower oil**

½ **cup fresh lemon juice**

2 **large egg whites**

Ice cream or lightly sweetened whipped cream, for serving (optional)

Sift together 1 cup of the sugar, the flour, baking powder, and baking soda onto a sheet of parchment or waxed paper; add the salt.

In a large bowl, whisk together the yolks, oil, and lemon juice until blended. Gradually add the dry ingredients to the yolk mixture, whisking all the while; set aside.

Beat the 6 egg whites in the bowl of a mixer fitted with the whisk attachment, or work with a hand-held mixer. At low speed, beat the whites until they're foamy and form very soft peaks. Increase the mixer speed to medium-high and gradually add the remaining ½ cup sugar, beating until the whites are thick and shiny and hold peaks. (If you run a finger through the whites, it should leave a smooth, even path.) Fold about one third of the whipped egg whites into the yolk mixture to lighten it, then turn the yolk mixture into the whites and fold it in gently but thoroughly.

Baking the Cake Pour and scrape half of the batter into the fruit-lined pan. Smooth the top, using an offset spatula, and sprinkle over the streusel, keeping a little in reserve for decorating the finished cake. Top with the remainder of the batter, smoothing it with the spatula, and place the pan on a jelly-roll pan. Bake in the 350°F oven for 45 to 50 minutes, or until golden and a toothpick inserted in the center comes out clean. Remove the cake to a cooling rack and let it cool for at least 25 minutes before inverting it onto a cardboard cake round or a serving platter.

Serve the cake with ice cream or lightly sweetened whipped cream if desired and a dusting of the remaining streusel.

Storing The cake is best served just warm or at room temperature the day it is made. However, you can cover the cake and keep it at room temperature overnight.

Contributing Baker **MARY BERGIN**

Fresh Rhubarb Upside-down Baby Cakes

COLOR PHOTOGRAPH, PAGE 219

Makes 8 small cakes ■ Here's a tender, soft-crumbed butter cake, a classic of the genre, made as individual upside-down cakes. The baby cake pans, each four inches across (see Sources, page 467), are lined with a mixture of melted butter, brown sugar, and pecans and decorated with slices of rhubarb before the bourbon-boosted butter cake batter is poured in. It is a sassy take on the old pineapple upside-down cake (a cake worthy of revival if made without the once-obligatory maraschino cherry). In fact, there's nothing sacred about rhubarb; you can vary the fruit as you choose. Try using mangoes, apples or pears, apricots, plums, or bananas, and vary the liqueur or flavoring to match the fruit. (For ideas about making this cake with rose geranium leaves or herbs, turn to page 247.)

If the urge to bake these lovely cakes strikes and you haven't a set of baby cake pans at hand, make these in muffin tins or custard cups, or make the recipe as one large cake. The batter is perfect for an eleven- or twelve-inch cast-iron skillet or a twelve-inch round cake pan, and, turned out, the large cake is impressive.

These baby cakes, as well as the Gingerbread Baby Cakes (page 247), Hazelnut Baby Loaves (page 249), Oven-Roasted Plum Cakes (page 255), Vanilla Pound Cake (page 251), Lemon Loaf Cake (page 252), and the grand and glorious Wedding Cake (page 232), are members of the same large and universally appealing family, the butter cake clan.

1⅔ cups all-purpose flour

2 teaspoons baking powder

1 teaspoon salt, preferably kosher or fine sea salt

2 teaspoons pure vanilla extract

1 cup crème fraîche, homemade (page 447) or store-bought, or
   sour cream

1½ sticks (6 ounces) unsalted butter, at room temperature

½ cup (lightly packed) dark brown sugar

1 tablespoon bourbon

2 tablespoons chopped pecans

6 to 7 stalks (12 ounces) fresh rhubarb, trimmed and cut into
   ¼-inch-thick slices

1 cup granulated sugar

2 large eggs, at room temperature

Melted butter, for greasing the pans
Lightly sweetened whipped cream, for serving (optional)

Butter Cake Basics

The basics of building a lovely butter cake are few and simple, but, like all things in the baker's repertoire, they should be attended to with care. Concentrate on the following pointers and you'll be on your way to success.

■ Cream the butter and sugar well. Whether you're working by hand with a rubber spatula or with a mixer, the butter and sugar should be blended together perfectly, a process called creaming. Beat the softened butter and sugar together until they lighten in texture, turn pale, and no longer feel grainy when you rub a little of the mixture between your fingers.

■ Add the eggs one at a time and give each one a good beating. In a butter cake, the eggs provide some of the cake's fat and a lot of its volume, so you need to make certain they get whipped into shape—literally. Beat the batter after each egg is added and then beat it for a minute or so after the last egg goes in. (Some recipes may require that you beat a little less, others a little longer, but, in general, the rule is to beat the eggs in and then give them a final whirl-around.)

■ Slow down and add the dry and liquid ingredients alternately. After you've created that wonderful bubble structure with the butter, sugar, and eggs, you don't want to do anything that will knock the air out of it, so slow down. If you're working with a mixer, some recipes will tell you to turn the mixer to its lowest speed, others will tell you to switch from the mixer to a rubber spatula. Just keep in mind that no matter which method you use, you want to be gentle. The dry ingredients are usually added to the batter in three additions, the liquid in two, which means you add one third of the dry ingredients, follow it with half of the liquid, then add half of the remaining dry, the rest of the liquid, and the last of the dry. Mix only as much as is needed to incorporate these ingredients and stop as soon as the last speck of dry ingredients disappears.

■ Test early and often for doneness. Butter cakes aren't shy when it comes to telling you they're done. Take a look at the cake five minutes before the recipe says it might be ready. With butter cakes, you want a toothpick inserted in the center of the cake to come out clean—meaning it may catch a couple of dry crumbs but it shouldn't be wet—and you want to see the cake start to pull away from the sides of the pan. These are the two primary tests that work for just about every butter cake, although, with that said, exceptions come to mind: Some cakes can be poked lightly in their centers and they'll spring back, a sign that they're done, and then there are those butter cakes that are meant to be underbaked and left kind of soft in the center so the toothpick test is a washout and the pulling-away-from-the-sides-of-the-pan test might or might not apply. If a cake is an exception to the norm, the recipe will tell you.

continued

Position a rack in the center of the oven and preheat the oven to 350°F. Brush the insides of 8 mini- or baby cake pans, each 4 inches across and 1 inch deep, with a light coating of melted butter, dust with flour, and tap out the excess. Whisk or stir the flour, baking powder, and salt together just to blend; reserve. In a separate bowl, stir the vanilla into the crème fraîche and set aside until needed.

Melt the ½ stick of butter in a heavy skillet. Add the brown sugar and bourbon and cook over medium heat, stirring with a wooden spoon, until the sugar melts. Stir in the pecans to coat with the caramel and turn off the heat. Divide the caramel evenly among the pans, working quickly to get it to the edges of the pans before it sets (cooked sugar cools rapidly). Arrange the rhubarb in circles over the sugar, and set aside while you make the batter.

Put the remaining stick of butter and the granulated sugar in the bowl of a mixer fitted with the paddle attachment, or use a hand-held mixer, and beat on medium-high speed until the mixture is smooth and creamy, scraping down the sides of the bowl with a rubber spatula as needed. The butter and sugar must be beaten until they are light, fluffy, and pale, so don't rush it—the process can take 3 to 4 minutes with a heavy-duty mixer and 6 to 8 minutes with a hand-held mixer. Reduce the speed to medium and add the eggs one at a time, beating well after each addition.

Working with a rubber spatula, carefully fold in the dry ingredients and the crème fraîche alternately—3 additions of dry ingredients, 2 of crème fraîche. You'll end up with a thick batter.

Baking the Cakes Spoon the batter over the rhubarb and smooth the tops by rotating the pans while you run a rubber spatula over the batter. Put the pans on a jelly-roll pan and bake for 20 to 25 minutes, or until a toothpick inserted in the center of a cake comes out clean. (Test a couple of the cakes to be certain.) As soon as the cakes are removed from the oven, turn them out of their pans onto a rack.

Serve with whipped cream if desired.

Storing The cakes can be kept wrapped in plastic at room temperature overnight.

Large Upside-down Cake

Make the caramel in a heavy 11- or 12-inch skillet that can go into the oven—cast-iron is ideal for this. Arrange the rhubarb over the caramel, spoon in the batter, and bake the cake for 45 to 50 minutes. If you do not have a skillet, butter and flour a 12-inch cake pan, pour in the caramel, top with the rhubarb and batter, and bake. If, when you turn out the cake, some of the caramel and fruit sticks to the bottom of the pan, scrape it onto the top of the cake, smoothing the top with a blunt knife.

Rose Geranium Upside-down Cake

By varying the batter slightly, you can produce upside-down cakes with a very different look and taste. For making a rose geranium cake, a sage cake (which appears in the photograph on page 219), or any other kind of herb cake, choose plants that have not been sprayed. Butter and flour the cake pans, but do not make the caramel. To prepare the batter, substitute 2 teaspoons of rose water for the vanilla. Arrange a few geranium leaves on the bottom of each pan, spoon in the batter, and bake. The rose geranium or any other baby cakes can be made as a large cake; just use a 12-inch round cake pan and bake for 45 to 50 minutes.

Contributing Baker **JOHANNE KILLEEN**

Gingerbread Baby Cakes
COLOR PHOTOGRAPH, PAGE 217

Makes 8 small cakes ■ This gingerbread is spicy, robust, and bursting with the heat of ginger and black pepper. Its texture is soft and moist, its color, dark and mysterious. It looks like a sweet chocolate cake, but it delivers a punch. Wonderful with lightly whipped cream and candied lemon peel, it's a good match with ice cream of various flavors. Although the cakes are adorable made in baby cake pans (see Sources, page 467), the recipe can be made successfully as one large cake.

Gingerbread Baby Cakes and Hazelnut Baby Loaves (page 249).

2 cups unbleached all-purpose flour

¼ cup instant espresso powder

3 tablespoons unsweetened cocoa powder

1 tablespoon ground ginger

½ teaspoon baking powder

1 teaspoon salt, preferably kosher or fine sea salt

1 teaspoon freshly ground black pepper

2 sticks (8 ounces) unsalted butter, at room temperature

1 cup (packed) dark brown sugar

4 large eggs, at room temperature

2½ tablespoons peeled and finely chopped fresh ginger

2 cups unsulphured molasses

Melted butter, for greasing the pans

Sweetened whipped cream, for serving

Candied lemon peel (optional)

continued

Position a rack in the center of the oven and preheat the oven to 350°F. Brush the insides of 8 mini- or baby cake pans, each 4 inches across and 1 inch deep, with a light coating of melted butter, dust with flour, and tap out the excess.

In a small bowl, whisk the flour, espresso powder, cocoa, ground ginger, baking powder, salt, and black pepper together just to mix; reserve.

Put the butter and brown sugar in the bowl of a mixer fitted with the paddle attachment, or use a hand-held mixer, and beat on medium-high speed until the mixture is smooth and creamy, scraping down the sides of the bowl with a rubber spatula as needed. The butter and sugar must be beaten until they are very light and fluffy, so don't rush it—the process can take 6 to 8 minutes with a hand-held mixer, 3 to 4 minutes with a heavy-duty mixer. Reduce the speed to medium and add the eggs one at a time, beating on high speed for 30 seconds to a minute after each addition. The mixture may look curdled, but that's OK—it will smooth out as you continue to mix the batter. Beat in the fresh ginger and add the molasses, mixing on medium speed for 1 to 2 minutes, until completely smooth.

With a rubber spatula, fold in the dry ingredients, mixing only until they are incorporated.

Baking the Cakes Divide the batter among the prepared pans and rotate the pans a couple of times to level. Bake the cakes for 20 to 25 minutes, or until the cakes

are springy to the touch and the tops crack. Take care not to overbake these cakes; they should remain moist.

Transfer the cakes to a rack and cool for 10 minutes, then run a thin knife around the edges of the pans to loosen and unmold the cakes. Turn the cakes over so they cool right side up.

Serve the cakes warm or at room temperature with a generous dollop of lightly whipped cream and a shower of chopped candied lemon peel if desired.

Storing These moist cakes will keep covered at room temperature for 3 days or, wrapped airtight, can be frozen for up to a month. Thaw, still wrapped, at room temperature.

Large Gingerbread Cake

Butter and flour a 10-inch round cake pan, fill with the batter, and bake for 50 to 60 minutes, until the top is springy and a toothpick inserted in the center comes out clean. Transfer the cake to a rack and cool for 10 minutes, then run a thin knife around the edge of the pan to loosen and unmold the cake. Turn the cake over so it cools right side up.

Contributing Baker **JOHANNE KILLEEN**

Hazelnut Baby Loaves

COLOR PHOTOGRAPH, PAGE 220

Makes 8 individual loaves ■ These small loaf cakes develop a thin, light, sugary crust and a soft, tender inner crumb due to the addition of cream to the batter. The loaves are beautifully flavored and scented with ground hazelnuts, and accompanied by a grappa-mascarpone cream that you'll find yourself making often. The cream is outstanding with these loaves and just as lovely with Tuiles (page 321) or spicy Gingerbread Baby Cakes (page 247).

THE CREAM

- ¾ cup heavy cream
- 2 tablespoons sugar
- ¾ cup mascarpone
- 1 teaspoon grappa

Whip the heavy cream with the sugar until it forms soft peaks. Scrape the mascarpone into a medium bowl and stir it briefly with a rubber spatula to loosen it. (Don't get carried away—the mascarpone is so rich that if you stir it too much, you'll have butter.) Stir in the grappa, then fold in the whipped cream. Cover the cream and chill until needed. *The cream can be made ahead and chilled for up to 4 hours.*

THE CAKES

- ⅓ cup hazelnuts, peeled (see page 315 for information on peeling hazelnuts)
- 1 cup sugar
- 1⅔ cups all-purpose flour
- 2 teaspoons baking powder
- 1 teaspoon salt, preferably kosher or fine sea salt
- ½ teaspoon pure almond extract
- 1 cup crème fraîche, homemade (page 447) or store-bought, or heavy cream, at room temperature
- 1 stick (4 ounces) unsalted butter, at room temperature
- 2 large eggs, at room temperature

Melted butter, for greasing the pans
Sliced peaches or other fresh fruit, for garnish

Position a rack in the center of the oven and preheat the oven to 350°F. Brush a light coating of melted butter over the insides of 8 mini-loaf pans, each 4¼ by 2½ by 2 inches (see Sources, page 467). Dust the inside of each pan with a little flour and tap out the excess.

continued

Place the hazelnuts and 1 tablespoon of the sugar in the work bowl of a food processor fitted with the metal blade. Process until the nuts are finely ground, taking care not to overdo this or you'll end up with hazelnut butter. Whisk or stir together the ground hazelnuts, flour, baking powder, and salt just to combine; set aside. In a separate bowl, add the almond extract to the crème fraîche and stir to blend and loosen the crème fraîche; reserve.

Put the butter and the remaining sugar in the bowl of a mixer fitted with the paddle attachment, or use a hand-held mixer, and beat on medium-high speed until the mixture is smooth and creamy, scraping down the sides of the bowl with a rubber spatula as needed. The butter and sugar must be beaten until they are light, fluffy, and pale, so don't rush it—the process can take 3 to 4 minutes with a heavy-duty mixer or 6 to 8 minutes with a hand-held mixer. Reduce the speed to medium and add the eggs one at a time, beating well after each addition.

Working with a rubber spatula, carefully fold in the dry ingredients and the crème fraîche alternately—3 additions of dry ingredients, 2 of crème fraîche. You'll have a thick batter.

Baking the Cakes Divide the batter evenly among the prepared pans, filling the pans between half and two-thirds full, then give each pan a couple of raps

against the countertop to settle the batter. Put the pans on a jelly-roll pan and bake for about 30 minutes, or until a toothpick inserted in the center of a cake comes out clean. (Test a couple of the cakes to be certain.) As soon as the cakes are removed from the oven, turn them out of their pans onto a rack. Invert the cakes and cool right side up.

The loaves can be served warm or at room temperature. Serve one loaf to a person, either slicing the loaves in half diagonally or cutting them into thin slices; garnish with the grappa-mascarpone cream and sliced fruit.

Storing The cakes can be kept covered at room temperature for about 2 days or wrapped airtight and frozen for a month. Thaw, still wrapped, at room temperature.

Contributing Baker **JOHANNE KILLEEN**

Vanilla Pound Cake

Makes 16 to 20 servings ■ The pound cake, so called because of its original pro-portions—a pound of flour, a pound of butter, a pound of sugar, and a pound of eggs—is a tight-grained, moist, good-keeping cake that holds its flavor. This cake has all of those qualities plus the heady fragrance and warm, full flavor of vanilla. The method is textbook, easy-to-make butter cake, but the form, a tube or Bundt cake, is different from the cracked-down-the-middle loaf shape most often associated with pound cakes. (For a more traditionally shaped cake, made in a less traditional way, have a look at the Lemon Loaf Cake, page 252.)

3 cups all-purpose flour

2 teaspoons baking powder

½ teaspoon salt

2 sticks (8 ounces) unsalted butter, at room temperature

2 cups sugar

3 large eggs, at room temperature, whisked to blend

1 cup milk, at room temperature

2 teaspoons pure vanilla extract

Position a rack in the lower third of the oven and preheat the oven to 350°F. Butter and flour a 10-inch tube pan or other 12-cup decorative pan with a center tube.

Sift the flour, baking powder, and salt together onto a sheet of waxed or parchment paper; reserve.

Put the butter into the bowl of a mixer fitted with the paddle attachment (or work with a hand-held mixer) and beat at medium speed until smooth. With the machine running, add the sugar in a steady stream. Stop the machine and scrape down the paddle and the sides of the bowl with a rubber spatula. Continue to beat at medium speed until the mixture is very light and fluffy, about 4 to 5 minutes.

With the mixer still at medium speed, begin to add the eggs in small addi-tions, about a tablespoon at a time. If the mixture becomes watery or shiny, stop adding the eggs and beat at an increased speed just until it smooths out. When the batter has come together again, decrease the speed to medium and continue adding the eggs, scraping down the paddle and sides of the bowl from time to time; it will take 3 to 4 minutes to incorporate the eggs. The mixture is prop-erly combined when it appears white, fluffy, and increased in volume.

Reduce the mixer speed to low and add the flour mixture and the milk alter-nately—4 additions of flour, 3 of milk—scraping the paddle and bowl fre-quently and mixing until the batter is smooth after each addition. Add the vanilla and mix just to blend.

continued

Baking the Cake Spoon the batter into the prepared pan and smooth the top with a spatula. Bake for 55 to 65 minutes, or until a wooden toothpick inserted in the center of the cake comes out clean. Transfer the cake to a cooling rack and allow it to cool in the pan for 10 minutes. Invert the cake onto a rack, remove the pan, and cool to room temperature. The cake is best served in very thin slices.

Storing The cake can be kept covered at room temperature for about 3 days or wrapped airtight and frozen for a month. Keep in mind that stale pound cake is excellent lightly toasted and used as the base for ice cream sundaes.

Contributing Baker **FLO BRAKER**

Lemon Loaf Cake

Makes 12 to 15 servings ■ This cake is a fooler: Its texture is that of a classic pound cake, moist, firm, and tightly knit, but it's made in just five minutes using the same sponge technique you'd draw on for almost-weightless génoise. Like most pound cakes, this lemon loaf is rich enough to serve in thin slices and dense enough to take nicely to a light toasting.

- **4 large eggs, at room temperature**
- **1⅓ cups sugar**
- **Pinch of salt**
- **Grated zest of 3 large lemons**
- **1¾ cups cake flour**
- **½ teaspoon baking powder**
- **½ cup heavy cream, at room temperature**
- **5½ tablespoons unsalted butter, melted and cooled to room temperature**

Position a rack in the center of the oven and preheat the oven to 350°F. Butter a 9- by 5-inch loaf pan and dust with flour, shaking out the excess.

Working in a large bowl, whisk together the eggs, sugar, and salt for just a minute, until foamy and smoothly blended; the mixture should not thicken. Whisk in the grated zest.

Spoon the flour and baking powder into a sifter and sift about a third of the dry ingredients over the foamy egg mixture. Whisk the flour into the eggs, mixing lightly—there's no need to beat. Sift the flour over the eggs in two more additions and whisk only until everything is incorporated. Whisk the heavy cream into the mixture. Switch to a rubber spatula and gently and quickly fold in the melted butter.

Baking the Cake Pour and scrape the batter into the prepared pan—it will level itself—and bake for 50 to 60 minutes, or until the center of the cake crowns and cracks and a toothpick inserted in the center comes out clean. Remove the cake to a cooling rack to rest for 10 minutes before unmolding. Cool to room temperature right side up on a rack.

You can serve this cake as soon as it cools, although there are those who believe that a pound cake needs a day to ripen. Make a taste test for yourself. In any case, the cake should be sliced with a serrated knife and served in thin slices, a pair to a plate.

Storing Once cooled, the cake should be wrapped tightly in plastic wrap. It will keep at room temperature for 3 or 4 days or, if double-wrapped, can be frozen for a month. Thaw, still wrapped, at room temperature.

Contributing Baker **NORMAN LOVE**

Boca Negra

COLOR PHOTOGRAPH, PAGE 218

Makes 12 servings ■ A *boca negra*, or black mouth, is what you'll have after one bite of this intensely chocolaty cake—you'll also have a smile on your face. A chocolate craver's ideal, this cake calls for twelve ounces of bittersweet chocolate and you'll taste every ounce, so choose chocolate you love. The cake is meant to be served warm or at room temperature, when it is as moist, dense, and dark as the chocolate you use to make it. Chilled, it has all the appeal of fudge. The white chocolate cream, which is made a day ahead, is one you can use with other desserts, and neither the cake nor the cream is a challenge for beginner bakers. In fact, if you make it in the food processor, it takes only five minutes.

THE CREAM

12 ounces white chocolate, finely chopped

1 cup heavy cream

¼ cup bourbon (or more to taste)

Prepare the white chocolate cream at least 1 day in advance. Put the white chocolate into the work bowl of a food processor fitted with the metal blade or a blender container. Heat the heavy cream in a small saucepan until small bubbles form around the edge of the pan. Pour the cream over the chocolate and process until completely smooth. Add the bourbon, taste, and add up to a tablespoon more if you want. Turn into a container with a tight-fitting lid and chill overnight. *The cream can be kept covered in the refrigerator for a week or frozen for up to a month. If you've frozen the cream, thaw it overnight in the refrigerator.*

continued

THE CAKE

12 ounces bittersweet chocolate, coarsely chopped

1⅓ cups sugar

½ cup bourbon

2 sticks (8 ounces) unsalted butter, cut into 10 pieces, at room temperature

5 large eggs, at room temperature

1½ tablespoons all-purpose flour

Position a rack in the center of the oven and preheat the oven to 350°F. Lightly butter a 9-inch round cake pan and line the bottom with parchment or waxed paper; butter the paper. Put the cake pan in a shallow roasting pan and set aside until needed.

Put the chopped chocolate in a medium bowl and keep close at hand. In a 2-quart saucepan, mix 1 cup of the sugar and the bourbon and cook over medium heat, stirring occasionally, until the sugar dissolves and the mixture comes to a full boil. Immediately pour the hot syrup over the chocolate and stir with a rubber spatula until the chocolate is completely melted and the mixture is smooth. Piece by piece, stir the butter into the chocolate mixture. Make certain that each piece of butter is melted before you add another.

Put the eggs and the remaining ⅓ cup sugar in a medium bowl and whisk until the eggs thicken slightly. Beating with the whisk, add the eggs to the chocolate mixture and whisk until well blended. Gently whisk in the flour.

(If you want to make the cake batter in a food processor, put the chocolate in the work bowl of the processor. Bring all of the sugar and the bourbon to a full boil and pour the syrup into the work bowl; process until the mixture is completely blended, about 12 seconds. With the machine running, add the butter in pieces, followed by the eggs, one at a time, and then the flour. Process an additional 15 seconds before turning the batter into the prepared pan.)

Baking the Cake Pour and scrape the batter into the prepared pan, running your spatula over the top to smooth it. Pour enough hot water into the roasting pan to come about 1 inch up the sides of the cake pan. Bake the cake for exactly 30 minutes, at which point the top will have a thin, dry crust. Remove the cake pan from its water bath, wipe the pan dry, and cover the top of the cake with a sheet of plastic wrap. Invert the cake onto a flat plate, peel off the parchment, and quickly but gently invert again onto a serving platter; remove the plastic.

Serve the cake warm or at room temperature with the chilled white chocolate cream.

Storing Once cooled, the cake can be covered with plastic and kept at room temperature for 1 day or refrigerated for up to 3 days; bring to room temperature before serving. For longer storage, wrap the cake airtight and freeze it; it will keep for up to a month. Thaw overnight, still wrapped, in the refrigerator.

Contributing Baker **LORA BRODY**

Oven-Roasted Plum Cakes

COLOR PHOTOGRAPH, PAGE 229

Makes 12 servings ■ These little cakes are traditional cream-the-butter-and-sugar-together cakes, but baked in small custard cups and showered with brown sugar, they take on a caramely flavor and develop a sugary crust that set them apart from other fine-crumbed butter cakes. Each cake takes just two tablespoons of batter and half of a ripe, juicy plum—not much—but they bake into sweets with the appeal of shortcakes and the warmth of fruit tarts. They're winning on their own and special with ice cream, unsweetened whipped cream, or Bittersweet Chocolate Sauce (page 446).

> **1 stick (4 ounces) unsalted butter, at room temperature**
> **2/3 cup (packed) light brown sugar**
> **1/2 cup granulated sugar**
> **2 large eggs**
> **1 teaspoon minced orange zest**
> **1/2 teaspoon pure vanilla extract**
> **1 cup all-purpose flour**
> **3/4 teaspoon baking soda**
> **1/4 cup buttermilk**
> **4 large ripe plums, halved and pitted**
>
> **Melted butter, for coating the custard or soufflé cups**

Position a rack in the center of the oven and preheat the oven to 350°F. Coat the insides of twelve 8- or 9-ounce custard or soufflé cups with melted butter and set them on a jelly-roll pan; reserve.

Working in a mixer fitted with the paddle attachment or with a hand-held mixer, cream the butter, 2 tablespoons of the brown sugar, and the granulated sugar together on medium speed for 3 minutes. Scrape down the sides of the bowl and continue to beat for 3 minutes more, or until the sugar is dissolved and the mixture whitens. Add one of the eggs, increase the speed to high, and beat for about half a minute; scrape down the bowl and paddle, add the second egg, and beat again for 30 seconds. Add the zest and vanilla and, still on high, beat until incorporated, about 30 seconds more. Reduce the mixer speed to low, add the flour and baking soda, and beat for just 15 seconds. Pour in the buttermilk and mix for just 30 seconds more. Finish blending the ingredients with a rubber spatula (a precaution to avoid overmixing the batter).

Baking the Cakes Spoon about 2 tablespoons of batter into each of the prepared cups. Place a half plum, cut side up, into each cup, pushing the plum down only a little. (Try to leave some of the plum above batter level so that when the cake rises, the plum will still show.) Sprinkle an equal amount of the remaining brown sugar over the cut surface of each of the plums. Place the baking pan with the filled soufflé cups on the center rack of the oven and bake for about 25 minutes, or until golden brown and a toothpick inserted in the cake part of the dessert comes out clean. Remove the pan from the oven and cool the cakes in their cups for 8 to 10 minutes before unmolding.

Unmolding the Cakes To unmold the cakes, run a short icing spatula or blunt knife around the edge of the cakes; if necessary, work it under the cakes to release the bottoms. Lift the cakes out with the spatula and, keeping them right side up, place them in the center of individual dessert plates. Serve the cakes warm (although they are great at room temperature), accompanying them with ice cream, whipped cream, or chocolate sauce if desired.

Storing Wrapped airtight, the cakes can be kept at room temperature for a day.

Contributing Baker **MARCEL DESAULNIERS**

Chocolate-Mascarpone Cheesecake

Makes 12 to 16 servings ■ Serious cheesecake lovers will take this luscious version to their hearts: It contains cream cheese, mascarpone cheese, sour cream, and eggs—and it's chocolate to boot. The batter is mixed for a longish time on slow speed, a process that keeps the creaminess in and extra air out. It is poured crustless into a high-sided cake pan, baked in a water bath, and then turned out and spread with crumbs before it is turned right side up. You can use any kind of crumb that appeals to you. Traditional graham cracker crumbs are good, but so are chocolate cookie, amaretti, or biscotti crumbs. In fact, if you use an interesting crumb, you might even want to make a slightly thicker padding or press some around the edge of the cake.

Plan to make the cake at least a day before you want to serve it; it needs time to come to room temperature before it can be unmolded and then several hours, if not a day, in the refrigerator to chill and set.

1½ **pounds cream cheese, at room temperature**

¾ **cup sugar**

¼ **cup all-purpose flour**

1 **teaspoon pure vanilla extract**

½ **pound mascarpone, at room temperature**

3 **large eggs, at room temperature**

½ **cup sour cream**

6 **ounces bittersweet chocolate, melted and still very warm**

½ **cup (approximately) cookie crumbs**

Center a rack in the oven and preheat the oven to 350°F. Butter the bottom, sides, and rim of an 8-inch cheesecake pan, one that is 3 inches high (see Sources, page 467). Have ready a roasting pan that is large enough to hold the cheesecake pan.

Put the cream cheese in the bowl of a mixer fitted with the paddle attachment (or work with a hand-held mixer) and beat on medium-low speed until it is perfectly smooth, about 4 minutes, scraping the bowl and the paddle a few times during the process. Add the sugar and continue to beat until the sugar is dissolved and a little of the batter rubbed between your fingers feels smooth, about 4 minutes more. Scrape down the bowl and paddle as needed. Add the flour, vanilla extract, and mascarpone and beat just until incorporated.

Add one of the eggs and beat the mixture for a minute. The egg will loosen up the ingredients in the bowl and give you a good opportunity to really get your rubber spatula down to the bottom of the bowl and scrape around to ensure that everything is being well mixed. Add the remaining eggs one at a time, and continue to beat until blended, scraping down the bowl after each addition. Add the sour cream and mix just until incorporated.

Remove about 1 cup of the cheesecake mixture and stir it into the warm melted chocolate, then mix the chocolate into the cake batter, either continuing to use the paddle or switching to your rubber spatula. When you no longer see white streaks, pour and scrape the batter into the prepared pan, rotating the pan briskly a couple of times to level the batter..

Baking the Cake Set the cake pan in the roasting pan and place on the center rack of the oven. Pour hot water into the roasting pan until it comes halfway up the sides of the cake pan. Bake the cake for 50 to 60 minutes. The cake will puff around the edges and the top will turn dry and a little blistery. You're looking for the cake to set the way a custard sets—just enough so that when you shake the pan, it sends a quivering wave across the cake. Remove the pans from the oven and transfer the cake to a rack to cool to room temperature. *If it's more convenient, you can leave the cake out overnight and unmold it in the morning. Once it's cool, you can also cover the pan and chill the cake until needed, although this will make it a little trickier to unmold.*

Unmolding and Chilling the Cake When you want to unmold the cake, ready a cutting board and a large flat serving platter, or two cutting boards, and the crumbs. Turn the cake over onto a cutting board and coat the bottom of the cake with the crumbs. (If the cake has been chilled, you will need to dip the bottom of the pan into a basin of hot water, letting the water come up as high as the top of the cake, but taking care not to get the cake wet. Wipe the pan before you unmold the cake.) Invert the cake onto the serving platter or the second cutting board and chill for at least 6 hours, or up to 2 days. *If you are going to keep the cake in the refrigerator for more than a few hours, cover it, once it is set, with plastic wrap.*

Serve the cake directly from the refrigerator. Use a long thin knife to cut the cake, dipping the knife into a glass of hot water and wiping it dry before each cut. To state the obvious—this is rich, so you needn't be overly generous; on the other hand, don't be surprised when there are requests for seconds.

Storing The cheesecake will keep, covered, in the refrigerator for about 4 days and wrapped airtight for a month in the freezer. Thaw, still wrapped, in the refrigerator.

Contributing Baker **DAVID OGONOWSKI**

Poppy Seed Torte

COLOR PHOTOGRAPH, PAGE 230

Makes 12 servings ■ Tortes are typically Eastern European and quintessentially Viennese. Often thought of as a multilayered cake, like a Dobostorte (known as a Seven-Layer Cake), the torte lends its name to the tartlike Linzertorte, to substantial single layer cakes, like the Sachertorte, and to this pound-cakeish beauty with the exotic flavor of poppy seeds and a trim of poached apricots.

Poppy seeds, which do, in fact, come from the opium poppy (but only taste addictive), are so tiny that you need almost a million of them to make a pound. Buy your poppy seeds from a reliable supplier with high turnover (see Sources, page 467) and, if you're not going to use them immediately, store them in the freezer. And taste a seed or two before you start—these steely-gray, crunchy seeds are sublime when fresh, but rank when rancid, a state they fall into easily.

Take note of the neat trick of baking poached apricots with the cake and then topping the baked—and subsequently wrinkled—fruit with fresh, still-pert poached apricots. If you want to give the cake a little extra sparkle, brush the "new" apricots and the rest of the cake with a gloss of heated red currant jelly or heated and strained apricot jam.

THE APRICOTS

12 apricots

3 cups water

1½ cups sugar

½ vanilla bean

1 chunk peeled fresh ginger (the equivalent of 3 pieces the size of a quarter)

To peel the apricots, bring a few cups of water to the boil in a medium saucepan; have a bowl of ice water close at hand. Make a small X cut in the top of each apricot and, one by one, drop the apricots into the boiling water. Boil for 10 seconds, lift with a slotted spoon, and drop into the cold water. The skins should slip off easily. If you have a few recalcitrant apricots, pop them back into the boiling water for a couple of seconds.

Put all of the poaching ingredients—the 3 cups water, the sugar, vanilla bean, and ginger—into a large saucepan. Cover the pan and bring to a full boil, then reduce the heat so that the syrup is just below a simmer; you don't want it to boil again. Drop the apricots into the syrup, cover the pan, and cook until the apricots are tender and can be pierced easily with the tip of a knife, between 5 and 20 minutes, depending on the ripeness of the apricots. Remove the pan from the heat and leave it, covered, at room temperature until needed. *To poach the apricots a few days ahead, double the quantity of sugar and pack the apricots, submerged in the syrup, into a tightly sealed jar or container; refrigerate until needed.*

THE CAKE

2 cups poppy seeds

1⅓ cups cake crumbs (see Note)

1 tablespoon brewed espresso, cold

Juice of ½ lemon

2 sticks (8 ounces) unsalted butter, at room temperature

½ cup confectioner's sugar, sifted

1 tablespoon cinnamon

Grated zest of 1 lemon

7 large eggs, separated

7 tablespoons granulated sugar

Center a rack in the oven and preheat the oven to 350°F. Coat a 10-inch round cake pan with vegetable oil spray and line the bottom with a round of parchment paper. (You can also use a 10-inch springform pan.)

Grind the poppy seeds in a clean coffee grinder and sift them through a fine strainer. (Or, if you buy the poppy seeds at a specialty or spice store, you can have them ground there.) Mix the seeds with the cake crumbs, push through the strainer, and fluff the mixture with a fork; set aside.

Stir together the espresso and lemon juice, and reserve.

Put the butter in the bowl of a mixer fitted with the paddle attachment (or work with a hand-held mixer) and beat on medium speed for 1 minute. Add the confectioner's sugar and beat for 30 seconds. Add the cinnamon and lemon zest and continue to beat on medium speed for 2 minutes, scraping down the sides of the bowl and the paddle as needed.

The egg yolks should be added 2 at a time: Add the first 2 yolks and beat on medium speed for half a minute. Add the next 2 and beat on medium-high for 30 seconds. Add 2 more and beat on medium for 30 seconds, then add the last yolk and beat on medium-high for half a minute. Lower the speed to medium and beat for another minute, stopping to scrape down the bowl and paddle as needed. The mixture should be smooth and shiny. (If your butter and eggs were cold, the mixture might not come together and may have a dull look. If this happens, either put the bowl over low heat for a couple of seconds, stirring all the while, or pull out your trusty blowtorch and hit the sides of the bowl with a few blasts—a pro's trick.) Transfer the mixture to a large bowl.

Wash and dry the mixer bowl and pour in the egg whites and granulated sugar. Holding the mixer's whisk attachment in your hand, use it to stir the whites and sugar together just to combine. Attach the whisk to the mixer and beat the mixture on medium speed to break up the whites. Increase the speed to high and whip the meringue until it is shiny and holds medium peaks. (Alternatively, you can whip the whites with a hand-held mixer.)

Using a large rubber spatula, fold one quarter to one third of the meringue into the cake batter, then fold in about one quarter of the reserved poppy seed mixture. Fold in the rest of the meringue, not being overly thorough, but just mixing until you have a marbleized batter. Fold in the rest of the dry ingredients in 3 more additions, then fold in the espresso–lemon juice combination.

Baking the Cake Pour and scrape the batter into the prepared pan, rotating the pan gently to level the batter. Hold a metal dough or bench scraper at a slight angle against the top of the batter, barely touching it, and spin the pan to get a really flat top. Now hold the scraper perpendicular to the top of the cake and use it to mark off 12 portions. Remove 6 apricots from the syrup, pat them dry, cut them in half, and place 1 apricot half, cut side down, in the center of the wide end of each portion, circling the cake.

Bake the cake for 35 to 45 minutes, or until the cake pulls away from the sides of the pan and a toothpick inserted in the center comes out clean. Transfer the cake to a cooling rack and let it cool for 10 minutes before unmolding.

Unmolding the Cake Run a knife around the sides of the pan and invert the cake onto a parchment or waxed paper–covered cardboard cake round or cutting board; invert the cake onto a serving platter. (If the cake was baked in a spring-form, remove the ring, invert the cake, and remove the base of the pan.) Remove the remaining apricots from the syrup, pat them dry, cut them in half, and top each baked apricot with a "new" poached apricot. This is done as much for looks as for taste—the poached fruit looks fresher and perkier than its baked counterpart. The cake is best served tepid, but it is delicious at room temperature.

Note You can use any kind of cake except angel food or meringue to make the crumbs, and the cake can be either chocolate or vanilla. If the cake is dry, scrape against a strainer or the fine holes of a grater to produce crumbs, or put pieces of the cake in a food processor fitted with the metal blade and process to form crumbs.

Storing The cake can be kept covered at room temperature for 2 days.

Contributing Baker **MARKUS FARBINGER**

Cakes for Occasions

RUFFLES, ROLLS, AND SWIRLS

WORKS THAT SHOW OFF the pastry chef's art and craft, the stunning cakes in this collection are often constructed, component upon component, and then finished with flair and more than a few flourishes. Impossible to hurry, these cakes are prepared slowly and should be savored in the same way.

From one of America's most acclaimed chocolatiers, Alice Medrich, comes the Chocolate Ruffle Cake. At once sophisticated and playful, this cake has a sleek chocolate band, dense chocolate layers, and a halo of crinkly-edged chocolate ruffles that conceals a luxurious crème fraîche filling. But if you're craving a fancy chocolate cake and haven't yet worked your way up to ruffles, turn to Mary Bergin's Bundt cake, a simple chiffon cake dressed up with a drizzle of satiny crème brûlée. Or consider Marcel Desaulniers's White Chocolate Patty Cake with red raspberry crush, perfect after any meal.

In this collection, you'll also find small cakes from the mistress of miniatures, Flo Braker; a jelly roll and a cheesecake, neither the usual; and an extraordinary pastry from Markus Farbinger's native Austria, the Cardinal Slice. A combination of sponge and meringue, the layers are both chewy and crunchy, a lovely foil for the exquisitely flavored espresso cream that swathes them.

Chocolate Ruffle Cake

COLOR PHOTOGRAPH, PAGE 225

Makes 12 to 16 servings ■ A majestic cake and one of many parts: a dark chocolate génoise moistened with an intoxicatingly aromatic framboise syrup, a filling of satiny crème fraîche and brilliantly red raspberries, a wrapper of dark chocolate, and a profusion of magnificent chocolate ruffles. The technique for making ruffles does take some practice, but fortunately, the mistakes are not only edible, they're usually usable—irregularly shaped pieces still produce a knock-out confection. And the chocolate wrapper or ribbon is also eminently doable—it is made by a method that reproduces the quality of tempering without the fuss. Professionals use acetate or Mylar as the form on which to shape the wrapper, but a trip to the hardware store will turn up ridged plastic shelf liners, the perfect material for the job.

Each part of the cake can be made ahead, so that you have only the assembly to finish on the day the cake is to be served. And don't pass up the opportunity to make this cake if you haven't the time to tackle the ruffles. You can pile the cake high with fresh raspberries, irregularly shaped pieces of chocolate, or chocolate shards, and it will still be great. Think of this cake as a format rather than a precise, can't-vary-a-thing formula: Substitute another kind of cake for the génoise, use whipped cream instead of crème fraîche, or omit the soaking syrup—the basic idea is yours to embellish.

THE CAKE

3 tablespoons hot clarified unsalted butter (see page 5)

1 teaspoon pure vanilla extract (optional)

⅓ cup plus 1 tablespoon sifted all-purpose flour

⅓ cup plus 1 tablespoon sifted unsweetened cocoa powder, preferably Dutch-processed

4 large eggs

⅔ cup sugar

1 pound bittersweet or semisweet chocolate, finely chopped, for ruffles

Position a rack in the lower third of the oven or just below the center of the oven and preheat the oven to 350°F. Fit the bottom of an 8-inch round cake pan, one at least 2 inches high, with parchment paper and set aside.

Pour the clarified butter into a 1-quart bowl and stir in the vanilla extract, if you're using it. The butter must be hot when it is added to the batter, so either keep the bowl in a skillet of hot water or reheat it at the last moment.

Although the flour and cocoa were sifted before they were measured, they need to be triple-sifted together. Sift or sieve the flour and cocoa together three times, then set the sifter on a plate or piece of waxed paper and return the dry ingredients to the sifter. Keep close at hand.

Whisk the eggs and sugar together in a large heatproof bowl or the bowl of a heavy-duty mixer. Set the bowl over direct heat or in a pan of barely simmering water and heat the eggs, whisking constantly, until they are warm to the touch. Remove the bowl from the heat and, working with a heavy-duty mixer fitted with the whisk attachment (or using a hand-held mixer), beat the eggs at high speed until they are cool, have tripled in volume, and hold a ribbon when the whisk is lifted.

Sift one third of the dry ingredients over the eggs and, using a large rubber spatula, fold in gently but thoroughly. When the color of the batter is almost uniform, fold in the rest of the flour-cocoa mixture.

Spoon about 1 cup of the batter into the hot clarified butter and fold together until well blended. Spoon this over the batter and, using the large rubber spatula, gently fold it in.

Baking the Cake Spoon the batter into the pan; there's no need to smooth the top or rap the pan on the counter, as is sometimes done with foam-based cakes. Bake the cake for 25 to 30 minutes, or until the top of the cake springs back when pressed gently. Transfer the pan to a rack and let the cake cool in the pan.

When the cake is completely cool, run a small knife around the sides of the pan to release the cake and unmold onto a rack; invert right side up onto a piece of parchment paper. *The cake can be made ahead to this point, wrapped well, and kept in the refrigerator for up to 2 days or frozen for up to 3 months. Thaw, still wrapped, at room temperature.*

Ruffle Cake Equipment

- 8-inch round cake pan, at least 2 inches high

- 8-inch round cake pan with removable bottom or 8-inch springform pan

- untreated heavy-duty jelly-roll pans

- rubber spatula, offset spatula, and flexible 8-inch metal icing spatula

- decorating turntable, lazy Susan, or inverted round cake pan

- ridged plastic shelf liner, freezer paper, or 005 Mylar

- parchment paper and waxed paper

Preparing the Chocolate The chocolate is going to be spread and then scraped into ruffles from four baking pans; if you don't have enough pans, you can make the ruffles in two batches. Choose heavy-duty jelly-roll pans that are neither warped nor dented, neither nonstick nor treated with special coatings. Keep them close at hand.

Melt the chocolate in a heatproof bowl set in a skillet of barely simmering water, in the top of a double boiler over an inch of simmering water, or in a microwave oven set at medium power. Stir the chocolate regularly until it is fully melted, smooth, and 115°F to 120°F. (You can test the temperature with an instant-read thermometer or by putting a drop on your top lip—it should feel warm.)

Hold the bottom of one of the baking pans over a burner (either gas or electric) and, moving it back and forth, heat it until it is warm but not hot enough to burn your fingers. Put the baking pan upside down on a flat surface and pour on about ⅓ cup of the chocolate. Use an offset spatula to spread the chocolate thinly and evenly over the bottom of the baking pan; the chocolate will only be about 1/16 inch thick. Refrigerate the pan for at least 30 minutes, or for as long as several hours, depending on your schedule. (It is better to chill the pans for a long time and let them come up to ruffling temperature—in which case they'll stay at temperature longer—than to catch them the moment they turn cool enough to ruffle.) Repeat with the rest of the chocolate and the other baking pans.

Shaping the Ruffles To shape the ruffles, work with one baking pan of chocolate at a time. Remove a pan of chocolate from the refrigerator and leave it at room temperature to warm gradually until it is pliable enough to be scraped.

Place the baking pan on a counter in front of you, a short side braced against your body. Hold the end of the blade of a thin, flexible 8-inch metal icing spatula in your left hand (reverse these procedures if you're left-handed) and, with your right hand, grab the blade close to the handle. You should have 4 to 5 inches of blade exposed and available for ruffling.

Using the top left corner of the pan as your starting point and imagining that corner of the pan as 12 o'clock, position your left hand in that corner, and your right at 2 o'clock. Press the edge of the blade against the chocolate at a very shallow angle, as if you were going to slide the spatula blade under the chocolate. Now slide the blade forward, moving your right hand down to 5 o'clock and then pivoting the blade to the left, all the way to the edge of the pan. As your right hand is moving down, so is your left, although not as far—your left hand will move down 4 to 5 inches. This is an important point—if you don't move your left hand down, you'll end up with tight curls of chocolate rather than ruffles. As you scrape and ruffle the chocolate against the blade and then make the pivot, the chocolate will gather against the blade—use your left hand to pinch the chocolate so that the ruffles form a fan and the pinched part is a little handle. You've completed one ruffle.

Top: To start the ruffle, press the blade against the chocolate at a shallow angle.
Bottom: As you pivot the blade, pinch the "tail" of the ruffle to form a fan.

As you make each ruffle, place it on a parchment or waxed paper–lined baking sheet and refrigerate. When the ruffles harden, you can layer them between sheets of waxed paper. *Store them in a container in the refrigerator; they'll keep for a few days.*

Make two more ruffles across the top of the pan, using the previously scraped area as your guide—the left-hand corner of chocolate will be your 12 o'clock point and the cleaned-off section of the pan your edge, or end point. Make the next three ruffles just below, then turn the pan around to get to the chocolate on the bottom and make three more. With practice—and ruffling takes lots of practice—you'll get nine ruffles from each pan. Don't worry if you get fewer at the start.

If, as sometimes happens, your ruffles crack or you get rolls of chocolate, not ruffles, it might be because the chocolate is too cold—give it a few more minutes at room temperature before you try again. If the chocolate melts and gets gooey against the spatula, it's too soft and needs a minute or two more in the refrigerator. When the temperature is just right—smooth and pliable—but you still can't get a nicely fanned ruffle, angle the blade differently as you scrape.

THE SYRUP

⅓ cup water

⅓ cup sugar

¼ to ⅓ cup eau-de-vie de framboise or white rum

Bring the water and sugar to the boil in a small saucepan, stirring to dissolve the sugar, and simmer for 2 to 3 minutes. Remove from the heat and cool. Add ¼ cup of the eau-de-vie. Taste the syrup and decide if you'd like a little more of the liqueur; set aside.

THE FILLING

3 cups crème fraîche, homemade (page 447) or store-bought

2 teaspoons pure vanilla extract

2 to 3 tablespoons sugar

5 ounces semisweet or bittersweet chocolate, finely chopped

3 tablespoons boiling water

Two 5-ounce containers fresh raspberries

3 ounces bittersweet or semisweet chocolate, finely chopped, for the wrap

Beat the crème fraîche with the vanilla extract to soft peaks, then add 2 tablespoons of the sugar, beating until thickened. Taste and add more sugar if you want it, then continue to beat until the cream just begins to stiffen. Cover and keep refrigerated until needed.

Assembling the Cake Cut the cooled génoise into 3 even layers with a long serrated knife. Fit one layer into the bottom of a high-sided 8-inch round cake pan with a removable bottom or an 8-inch springform pan and brush the layer with some framboise syrup.

Put the chopped chocolate in a small bowl and whisk in the boiling water, whisking until the chocolate is fully melted and smooth. Switch to a rubber spatula and fold ¼ cup of the crème fraîche into the chocolate. Fold in another ½ cup of the crème fraîche and then quickly, before it hardens, spread the chocolate crème fraîche evenly over the génoise layer in the pan.

Moisten the second layer of génoise with framboise syrup and set it, moistened side down, in the pan, pressing it gently to level it on the chocolate crème fraîche. Moisten the top of the layer with some of the syrup and top with an even layer of fresh raspberries, leaving just a bit of space between each berry. Keep 1 perfect berry in reserve.

Beat the remaining crème fraîche until it holds its shape. Spoon 1½ to 2 cups of the crème fraîche over the berries and, using an offset spatula, delicately smooth the crème fraîche over and between the berries.

Moisten the remaining layer of génoise with framboise syrup and set it, moistened side down, into the pan, again pressing lightly to set it in place.

Chilling the Cake Cover the cake and the remaining crème fraîche with plastic and refrigerate for at least 2 to 3 hours, or up to 24 hours.

Run a knife around the sides of the cake, then release and remove the pan or the ring of the springform pan. Put the cake, still on its pan bottom, on a large piece of parchment paper and set the cake on a decorating turntable, a lazy Susan, or a large inverted round cake pan.

Making the Wrap Using ridged plastic shelf liner (available in hardware and housewares stores), freezer paper, or 005 Mylar (from an art supply store), cut a strip 26 inches long and ⅜ inch wider than the height of the finished cake, about 3 inches. Place a larger piece of waxed paper on the counter in front of you—this is your drip sheet—and put the strip on the waxed paper. (If you're using ridged plastic or Mylar, put the smooth glossy side facing up.)

Melt the chocolate in the top of a double boiler set over an inch of barely simmering water or in a microwave oven set at medium power, stirring the chocolate once or twice until melted and smooth. The chocolate should be between 115°F and 120°F. Pour the chocolate down the center of the plastic strip, spreading it with an offset spatula across the entire strip and beyond—let it run over a bit onto the waxed paper. (You can scrape up the chocolate from the waxed paper later and remelt it when you need a dollop of chocolate to finish the cake.)

Slip the point of a small knife under one edge of the chocolate-coated strip and grab the edges of the strip with your fingers. Slide your free hand under the strip and grab the other end. Lift the strip and fit it neatly around the cake, positioning it so that the chocolate side is against the cake. Press one end against the cake and leave the other end standing away from the cake at the point where it would overlap if you pressed it closed. Slip a small piece of waxed paper into this spot, just to hold your place.

Wrap the chocolate-coated strip around the cake, keeping the chocolate side against the cake.

continued

Chilling the Wrapped Cake Refrigerate the cake for at least 1 hour, until the chocolate hardens.

Finishing the Wrapped Cake Place the cake on the decorating turntable and spread the remaining crème fraîche over the top, spreading it out to the edge of the band.

Remove the chocolate ruffles from the refrigerator and, beginning at the outside edge, arrange the ruffles in a circle, planting them gently in the crème fraîche and allowing their frilly edges to extend beyond the cake's rim. Continue to arrange the ruffles in slightly overlapping concentric circles until the crème fraîche is covered. Put the reserved perfect raspberry in the center of the cake and chill the cake for about 15 minutes, until firm (or up to 6 hours, if necessary), before removing the plastic and serving.

To remove the plastic on the chocolate band, discard the waxed paper "place keeper" and peel away an inch of the plastic from the end of the band attached to the cake. Put a dollop of melted chocolate on that end to act as glue and overlap the other end of the band, pressing lightly to seal it. Carefully remove the plastic. If the plastic sticks, put the cake back in the refrigerator for about 10 minutes, then try again.

Top: Starting at the cake's rim, place the chocolate ruffles in concentric circles covering the crème fraîche.

Bottom: Gently pull away the paper or plastic strip.

To cut the cake, dip a long sharp serrated knife into hot water, wipe it dry, and cut straight down. Since the first piece is often difficult to remove, it's best to make it a generous, easier-to-maneuver slice.

Storing Although the parts of the cake can be made well in advance, the assembled cake should be served the day it is made.

Contributing Baker **ALICE MEDRICH**

Miniature Florentine Squares
COLOR PHOTOGRAPH, PAGE 227

Makes thirty-six 1½-inch squares ■ If you've never attempted fancy miniatures before, you'll be amazed at how polished a petit four you can produce. The base of these mini-cakes is the Ladyfinger Génoise, the sturdiest génoise in the repertoire. It is brushed with a gloss of sweet wine syrup and currant jelly and glazed with a white chocolate ganache. But its prettiest and most ingenious touch is the way it is decorated, a technique you'll pull from your baker's bag of tricks to use again and again. By piping randomly spaced lines of milk and dark chocolate over the white glaze and running a pick across the surface, you'll create a marbleized design that echoes the intricate patterns celebrated by Florence's master papermakers.

1 recipe Ladyfinger Génoise batter (page 41)

¼ cup sweet dessert wine, such as a muscat

1 tablespoon sugar

⅔ cup red currant jelly, pushed through a strainer

Position a rack in the lower third of the oven and preheat the oven to 350°F. Grease a 9-inch square cake pan with solid shortening, dust with flour, and tap out the excess. Fit the bottom of the pan with a parchment or waxed paper square.

Baking the Cake Pour the batter into the prepared pan and smooth the top, creating a slight ridge of batter around the edges. Bake for 20 to 25 minutes, or until the top springs back when lightly prodded and the cake starts to come away from the sides of the pan. Transfer the cake to a rack and let rest for 5 to 10 minutes.

To remove the cake from the pan, first test its readiness: Tilt and rotate the pan, then gently tap it on the counter. If it doesn't seem as if the cake is releasing from the pan, run a thin blade between the cake and the sides of the pan, freeing the sides and letting a little air get under the cake. Invert the cake onto a rack and remove the pan. Slowly peel off the paper liner, turn it over, and put it back on the cake. Cover the cake with another rack and invert again. Remove the top rack and let the cake cool completely right side up. *The cake can remain uncovered at room temperature for a day, but it should be wrapped in plastic if you won't be using it within 2 days. For longer storage, wrap it well and freeze it; it will keep for 10 days.*

Miniature Florentine Squares, Glazed Mini-Rounds (page 271), and Raspberry Swirls (page 275).

Making the Syrup Stir the sweet wine and sugar together in a small bowl until the sugar dissolves, and keep at hand.

Filling the Cake Carefully, using a gentle sawing motion, cut the cake in half horizontally. Place the bottom layer, cut side up, on a cardboard cake round or the removable bottom of a tart pan. Brush the sweet wine syrup over the cut side of the layer. Spread a thin layer of jelly over the cake and cover with the top layer.

Keeping the cake on its cardboard, place it on a wire rack and place the wire rack on a jelly-roll pan.

THE GLAZE

12 ounces white chocolate, finely chopped

⅔ cup heavy cream

2 ounces milk chocolate, melted and still warm, for decoration

2 ounces semisweet chocolate, melted and still warm, for decoration

continued

Put the chopped chocolate into a medium bowl and pour the cream into a heavy-bottomed 1½-quart saucepan. Heat the cream just to the boil and then pour it over the chocolate, stirring constantly with a rubber spatula. The chocolate may look lumpy, but it will smooth out as you stir it. When the glaze is creamy smooth, push it through a strainer into a bowl.

You want to use the glaze while it's still warm and liquid. To test, spread a little of the glaze over a piece of white bread; it should seep in just a bit. (If the glaze has cooled and is no longer spreadable—it thickens as it stands— heat it over a pan of hot water.)

Glazing the Cake Pour the warm glaze over the cake and spread it evenly across the top, using a flexible metal icing spatula. Don't be concerned if some of the glaze dribbles down the sides of the cake.

Decorating the Cake Spoon the melted chocolate into 2 small parchment paper piping cones or a zipper-lock plastic bag with the smallest possible opening snipped from the corner (see page 18 for directions). Test to see that the chocolates flow easily from the cones. (If the chocolates have cooled, pop them into a microwave oven for 3 to 5 seconds.)

Draw the prongs across the glaze to create a Florentine pattern.

Immediately pipe several lines of milk chocolate across the surface of the cake; don't be concerned about spacing them just so or keeping them perfectly straight—even squiggles will come out fine in the end. Pipe semisweet chocolate lines in the same fashion. Draw a multipronged tool (a clean hair pick is perfect for this), or a slender nail or the tip of a very thin knife, across the lines, pulling the chocolate just a little to create a marbled effect. Let the glaze dry at room temperature for 1 hour, or chill until set.

Cutting the Cake When you're ready to cut the cake, have a long serrated knife, a small glass of hot water, paper towels, and a 12-inch ruler at hand. Trim a sliver of cake from each side. Using the ruler as a guide and the tip of the knife as a marker, mark small notches in the glaze every 1½ inches across the top and bottom of the cake. (Depending on how much the cake has shrunk or been trimmed, you may have to measure off a scant 1½ inches.) Repeat this procedure down the sides, making sure that the notches line up directly across from one another.

Dip the knife into the hot water, wipe it with a paper towel, and, using just the tip of the knife and the ruler as your guide, score the glaze (don't cut through the cake) in straight lines from one notch to another so that the pattern for cutting squares is formed. Now cut through the scored lines, heating and cleaning your knife between cuts.

Storing Once glazed and cut, the cake should be served within an hour or two, but if you cut it and don't separate the pieces, you can keep the cake for several hours.

Contributing Baker **FLO BRAKER**

Glazed Mini-Rounds

COLOR PHOTOGRAPH, PAGE 227

Makes about 24 mini-rounds ■ Essentially the same ingredients as those used for the Florentine squares (page 268) and just about the same techniques, but the change of shape and a bevy of different decorations, including small polka dots and darling tiny hearts, give you delightfully different petits fours.

1 recipe Ladyfinger Génoise batter (page 41)

¼ cup fruity white wine

1 tablespoon sugar

⅔ cup apricot jam, strained

Position a rack in the lower third of the oven and preheat the oven to 350°F. Grease a 9-inch round cake pan with solid shortening, dust with flour, tap out the excess, and fit the bottom of the pan with a parchment or waxed paper circle.

Baking the Cake Pour the batter into the prepared pan and smooth the top, working across the surface with a rubber spatula and creating a slight ridge of batter around the edges. Bake for 22 minutes, or until the center of the cake springs back when lightly prodded. Transfer the cake to a rack and let rest for 5 to 10 minutes.

To remove the cake from the pan, first test its readiness: Tilt and rotate the pan, then gently tap it on the counter. If it doesn't seem as if the cake is releasing from the pan, run a thin blade between the cake and the sides of the pan, freeing the sides and letting a little air get under the cake. Invert the cake onto a rack and remove the pan. Slowly peel off the paper liner, turn it over, and put it back on the cake. Cover the cake with another rack and invert again. Remove the top rack and let the cake cool completely right side up. *The cake can remain uncovered at room temperature for a day, but it should be wrapped in plastic if you won't be using it within 2 days. For longer storage, wrap it well and freeze it; it will keep for 10 days..*

Making the Syrup Mix the wine and sugar together in a small bowl until the sugar dissolves; set aside.

Filling the Cake Carefully, using a gentle sawing motion, cut the cake in half horizontally. Place the bottom layer, cut side up, on a cardboard cake round or the removable bottom of a tart pan and brush the wine syrup over the cut side of the layer. Spread a thin layer of jam over the cake (there may be some jam left over) and cover with the top layer.

Cutting the Rounds Use a 1½-inch round biscuit or cookie cutter to cut as many rounds from the cake as you can, about 24. Put the small rounds on wire racks, leaving an inch between each one, and place the racks on a waxed paper–lined jelly-roll pan.

continued

THE GLAZE

12 ounces white chocolate, finely chopped
²/₃ cup heavy cream

1 ounce semisweet chocolate, finely chopped, for decoration
24 crystallized violets (optional), for decoration

Put the chopped white chocolate into a medium bowl and pour the cream into a heavy-bottomed 1½-quart saucepan. Heat the cream just to the boil and then pour it over the chocolate, stirring constantly with a rubber spatula. The chocolate may look lumpy, but it will smooth out as you stir it. When the glaze is creamy smooth, push it through a strainer into a bowl.

You want to use the glaze while it's still warm and liquid. To test, spread a little of the glaze over a piece of white bread; it should seep in just a bit. (If the glaze has cooled and is no longer spreadable—it thickens as it stands—heat it over a pan of hot water.)

Top: Piping polka dots.
Center: Using prongs to marbleize glaze.
Bottom: Piping chocolate glaze.

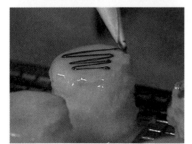

Glazing the Cake Ladle about 2 tablespoons of the glaze over each little cake, allowing it to run over the top and down the sides to cover the cakes completely. When you've gone through your batch of glaze, scrape up whatever has dripped onto the jelly-roll pan, push it through a sieve (since some cake crumbs may have gotten mixed in), and reheat over hot water. When the glaze is warm, continue coating the remaining cakes.

Inevitably, some of the glaze will have glued the cakes to the wire racks, so run a small metal spatula under the cakes to cut any drips from the underside (this will give you a neat finish) and carefully move the cakes to another position on the rack.

Decorating the Cake Melt the dark chocolate in a bowl set over a saucepan filled with hot water. Half fill a small parchment paper piping cone or a zipper-lock plastic bag with the smallest possible opening snipped from the corner (see page 18 for directions) with the dark chocolate and, while the white chocolate glaze is still warm and hasn't set, decorate the cakes by piping several tiny dots on each cake with the dark chocolate, piping one dot and drawing a toothpick through it to create a heart, or piping lines or squiggles. You can make these even more decorative by topping each round with a crystallized violet. (You can even use unsprayed rose petals.)

Allow the glaze and decorations to set (this will take about 1 to 2 hours, depending on the temperature of the room) and then, with a small metal spatula, carefully lift the cakes onto a serving platter.

Storing If you're not going to serve the cakes immediately, transfer them to a foil-lined cake box and store in a cool room for up to a day.

Contributing Baker **FLO BRAKER**

French Strawberry Cake

Makes 8 to 10 servings ■ This French rendition of a strawberry shortcake is a charmer. A génoise is layered with sugared berries and a velvety blend of whipped sweet cream and sour cream, topped with swirls and rosettes of cream, and finished with fresh berries, their frilly hulls adding additional color to the cake. This is the classic version of the cake, the one you find in the best Parisian pâtisseries, but the berries and cream mixture can be used with Vanilla Pound Cake (page 251), Lemon Loaf Cake (page 252), or chocolate chiffon Bundt cake (page 280).

1 recipe Perfect Génoise batter (page 39)

2 pints ripe fresh strawberries, hulled and sliced
¼ to ⅓ cup sugar (depending on the sweetness of the fruit)

Position a rack in the lower third of the oven and preheat the oven to 350°F. Grease the bottom and sides of an 8-inch round cake pan with solid shortening, dust with flour, and tap out the excess. Fit the bottom with a parchment or waxed paper circle.

Baking the Cake Carefully pour the batter into the prepared pan, smoothing the top with a rubber spatula, working from the center outward and creating a slightly raised ridge around the sides. Bake for 25 to 27 minutes, or until the top springs back when lightly prodded and the cake starts to come away from the sides of the pan. Transfer the cake to a rack and let it rest for 5 to 10 minutes.

To remove the cake from the pan, first test its readiness: Tilt and rotate the pan, then gently tap it on the counter. If it doesn't seem as if the cake is releasing from the pan, or you are the cautious type, run a thin blade between the cake and the sides of the pan, freeing the sides and letting a little air get under the cake. Invert the cake onto a rack and remove the pan. Slowly peel off the paper liner, turn it over, and put it back on the cake. Cover the cake with another rack and invert again. Remove the top rack and let the cake cool completely right side up. *The cake can remain uncovered at room temperature for a day, but it should be wrapped in plastic if you won't be using it within 2 days. For longer storage, wrap it well and freeze it for up to 10 days. Thaw, still wrapped, at room temperature.*

Preparing the Berries Toss the sliced berries with the sugar in a large bowl and leave them, uncovered, at room temperature for at least 2 hours.

Coarsely mash the berries with the tines of a fork and toss them again; let them stand for 1 hour longer. *You can do this the day before, but the berries should be refrigerated after they are mashed.*

continued

THE CREAM

    1¼ cups cold heavy cream

    2 tablespoons sour cream

    2 tablespoons sugar

    1 teaspoon pure vanilla extract

    5 large strawberries (with hulls)

Using a mixer fitted with the whisk attachment or a hand-held mixer, whip the heavy cream, sour cream, sugar, and vanilla together until the mixture forms soft peaks. The cream is the proper consistency when the tracks made by the whisk close slowly and almost disappear. Cover and refrigerate the cream until you're ready to frost the cake. Just before using the cream, give it a turn or two by hand with a whisk to bring the mixture together again.

Finishing the Cake Using a serrated knife and a gentle sawing motion, cut the cake horizontally into 3 layers. Place the bottom layer cut side up on a cardboard round or the removable bottom of a tart pan. Lifting the berries from the bowl with a slotted spoon so that most of the liquid drains off, spoon half of the mashed strawberries over the cake layer, then spread a thin layer of the whipped cream over the berries. Top with the middle cake layer, spoon on the rest of the strawberries, and spread another thin layer of cream over the berries. Center the top layer over the filling.

Working with a flexible metal icing spatula, frost the top and sides of the cake with whipped cream, leaving about ½ cup of the cream for decoration. Spoon the remaining whipped cream into a pastry bag fitted with a ¼-inch star tip and pipe 10 rosettes around the top of the cake, positioning the rosettes about an inch in from the edge and leaving an inch between each rosette.

Slice each berry in half from blossom to stem, leaving some of the hull on each half. Prop a berry half, cut side down, on top of each rosette and refrigerate the cake for at least an hour before serving.

Storing The cake can be refrigerated for several hours before serving. Keep it away from any foods in the refrigerator with strong odors, as cream picks up odors quickly. It would be ideal if you could store this cake in a box.

Contributing Baker **FLO BRAKER**

Raspberry Swirls

COLOR PHOTOGRAPH, PAGE 227

Makes 28 small cakes ■ Here, a génoise is brushed with red jam, then rolled and cut into inch-wide slices. Each slice is then given a cocoa glaze up to its midpoint, a dip in chopped nuts and coconut, and turned into a petit four. The small rounds, half raspberry swirl and half shiny chocolate dusted with pistachios and coconut, appear complicated and dressy, but are really quite easy to make. To get the cake into perfect shape, it is rolled, wrapped in parchment paper, and then supercompressed by pulling on the parchment and pushing the cake with the edge of a baking sheet. It's a turn-of-hand used by professional pastry chefs and one easily—and effectively—adapted to home use.

1 recipe Sheet Génoise batter (page 42)

½ cup seedless raspberry jam, pushed through a strainer

Position a rack in the lower third of the oven and preheat the oven to 450°F. Line a 12- by 15½-inch jelly-roll pan with aluminum foil, leaving a 2-inch overhang on the short ends. Grease and flour the foil.

Baking the Cake Gently pour the batter down the center of the pan, spreading it evenly with a long offset spatula or the back of a spoon. Bake until the cake is a light golden color and springs back when touched near its center, 5 to 8 minutes. Transfer the cake to a cooling rack.

Run a knife around the sides of the cake and cover the cake with a cotton towel and a baking sheet. Invert the cake onto the baking sheet, lift off the jelly-roll pan, and gently peel away the foil, using the overhang to get started; work slowly to avoid tearing the cake. Flip the foil over so that the sticky side is up and reposition the foil over the cake. Cover the cake with a large cooling rack (or the back of a jelly-roll pan) and invert it again so that the cake is right side up and resting on the foil. Let the cake cool for at least 30 minutes—an hour would be better—before cutting and decorating it.

Spreading the Filling Cut four rectangles of parchment paper, each 10 inches wide and 15 inches long, for rolling up the cake swirls and keep them close by.

Slide the cake off the cooling rack, but keep it on the foil. Spread the raspberry jam in a thin layer over the entire surface of the sheet cake. Using a long thin knife, cut the cake into quarters to make 4 rectangles, each 5 inches by 7½ inches.

Filling the Cake With a long edge facing you, tightly roll up one of the rectangles jelly-roll fashion. Set the cake on a piece of parchment, positioning it across the lower third of the paper. Pull the upper two thirds of the parchment around the cake, wrapping the cake loosely in the parchment and tucking about ½ inch of the upper portion of the paper under the cake, leaving about 2 inches of the upper portion free. Catch the edge of a rimless baking sheet or a thin board in the fold of the ½ inch of paper you tucked under the cake. With one hand, hold the baking sheet at a 45-degree angle between the cake and the work surface, and with the other, grasp the end of the bottom portion of parchment paper (making sure to grasp just the bottom sheet). Press the baking sheet against the cake, trapping the paper overhang, and push the sheet while simultaneously pulling the bottom portion of the paper toward you. This push-pull motion will compress the spongy cake. Wrap the excess parchment paper around the roll and slip one or two thin rubber bands over it. Repeat the procedure with the other rectangles.

Let the rolls stand for at least 30 minutes.

THE GLAZE

1 cup heavy cream

1 cup sugar

1 cup unsweetened cocoa powder

¼ stick (2 tablespoons) unsalted butter

1 tablespoon pure vanilla extract

1 cup finely chopped pistachios, for decoration

1 cup unsweetened shredded coconut for decoration (available at health food stores)

Pour the cream into a heavy-bottomed 1½-quart saucepan. Sift the sugar and cocoa powder together onto a sheet of waxed paper and stir this mixture into the cream, a little at a time, until blended. Add the butter, put the pan over very low heat, and, stirring constantly, heat until the butter melts and the glaze is smooth, about 5 minutes. The glaze needs to be warm, not hot. In fact, if you let it get too hot, it will separate.

Remove the pan from the heat and stir in the vanilla. At this point, the glaze will have the consistency of chocolate sauce; it thickens as it cools. (If the glaze thickens too much, set it over a pan of simmering water and stir until it reaches the correct consistency.)

Decorating the Cake Put the pistachios and coconut in bowls that are wide enough to dip the cake slices into and keep these and the glaze at hand.

Remove the parchment paper from the cake rolls and cut each roll into 1-inch-wide slices. Dip each slice up to its halfway point in the warm chocolate glaze, then dip the glazed portion into the pistachios, followed by the coconut. Lay the slices in a foil-lined cardboard container—a cake box is ideal—and cover the cut surfaces with a strip of plastic wrap.

Storing The cakes should be kept at cool room temperature and served the day they are made.

Contributing Baker **FLO BRAKER**.

Vanilla Chiffon Roll

COLOR PHOTOGRAPH, PAGE 216

Makes 6 servings ■ Here's a basic chiffon cake with a twist—a full vanilla flavor and a thin, flexible shape, ideal for rolling around the chocolate-laced walnut mousse. If you want, caramelize a few walnut halves (see page 453) to perch on the roll and mark off the portions.

THE CAKE

1½ **cups sugar**

1 **cup all-purpose flour**

1 **teaspoon baking powder**

1 **teaspoon baking soda**

¼ **teaspoon salt**

4 **large eggs, separated**

½ **cup vegetable or safflower oil**

½ **cup water**

2 **tablespoons pure vanilla extract**

2 **large egg whites**

Position a rack in the center of the oven and preheat the oven to 350°F. Coat a 17½- by 12½-inch jelly-roll pan with vegetable oil spray, line with parchment or waxed paper, and spray the paper lightly all over.

Sift together 1 cup of the sugar, the flour, baking powder, and baking soda onto a sheet of parchment or waxed paper; add the salt.

In a large bowl, whisk together the yolks, oil, water, and vanilla until blended. Add the dry ingredients gradually to the yolk mixture, whisking all the while; set aside.

Beat the 6 egg whites in the bowl of a mixer fitted with the whisk attachment or work with a hand-held mixer. At low speed, beat the whites until they're foamy and form very soft peaks. Increase the mixer speed to medium-high and gradually add the remaining ½ cup sugar, beating until the whites are thick and shiny and hold peaks. (If you run a finger through the whites, it should leave a smooth, even path.) Fold about one third of the whipped egg whites into the yolk mixture to lighten it, then turn the yolk mixture into the whites and fold it in gently but thoroughly.

Baking the Cake Pour and scrape the batter into the prepared pan, spreading it evenly with an offset spatula. Bake the cake for 10 to 12 minutes, until the edges of the cake just start to pull away from the sides of the pan. Transfer the pan to a rack and allow the cake to cool to room temperature.

continued

THE MOUSSE

1²/₃ cups walnuts, lightly toasted

2 tablespoons walnut or safflower oil

5 ounces bittersweet chocolate, melted

3 large egg yolks

¹/₃ cup sugar

¹/₄ cup water

1¹/₂ cups heavy cream

Put the walnuts and walnut oil in a food processor fitted with the metal blade and pulse, then process, scraping the bowl as needed, until the mixture forms a paste. Add the melted chocolate and process until thoroughly mixed. Set aside.

Put the yolks in the bowl of a heavy-duty mixer and whisk them lightly by hand; set the bowl aside close at hand. Bring an inch or two of water to the boil in a saucepan that can be used as a double boiler in conjunction with the bowl holding the yolks; reduce the heat and keep the water at the simmer while you proceed.

In a small saucepan, stir together the sugar and water and bring to the boil. Remove the pan from the heat and very gradually add the boiling syrup to the egg yolks, whisking the yolks steadily and without stop. Fit the bowl into the saucepan with the simmering water—your makeshift double boiler, or bain-marie—and continue to whisk until the mixture is foamy and hot to the touch.

Remove the bowl from the heat and fit it into the mixer. Working with the whisk attachment, beat the mixture on high speed until it is pale, holds a soft ribbon, and is cool to the touch. (If you have a water jacket for your mixer, you can speed the cooling process by filling it with ice cubes and cold water and beating the mixture over it.) Using a rubber spatula, fold in the reserved walnut paste.

Whip the heavy cream until it holds soft peaks. Fold it delicately but thoroughly into the walnut mixture. Refrigerate the mousse, tightly covered with plastic wrap, until needed. *You can make the mousse up to a day ahead and keep it well covered in the refrigerator; stir before using.*

TO FINISH THE CAKE

Confectioner's sugar

Unsweetened cocoa powder

Caramelized Walnuts (page 453; optional)

Sprigs of fresh mint (optional)

When you're ready to unmold the cake, sprinkle the top with a little confectioner's sugar and cover the cake with a piece of parchment or waxed paper. Place an inverted jelly-roll pan over the cake and turn the cake over, inverted pan and all. Remove the baking pan, peel off the paper the cake baked on, turn the paper over, and reposition it over the cake. Invert the baking pan, press it against the cake, and invert again so that the cake is right side up and resting on the inverted jelly-roll pan. With the cake on top of the pan, trim the edges of the cake with a long thin knife.

Keeping a 17-inch side of the cake in front of you, spread the chilled mousse evenly over the cake, leaving an inch of cake bare along the side closest to you. Starting at the side closest to you, roll the cake up into an even roll, using the paper to help you move it along. When you come to the end of the roll (it will have only rolled over on itself about one and a half times), the edges of the paper should meet. Grab the edges and use the paper to scoot the cake into the center of the jelly-roll pan.

Chilling the Cake Use a fork to tuck the ends of the paper under the cake and chill the cake, on the baking pan, for at least 2 hours. *Wrapped well, the cake can stay in the refrigerator overnight.*

At serving time, cut 5 strips of waxed paper and lay them across the cake at evenly spaced intervals. Dust the cake with cocoa powder and just a hint of confectioner's sugar; lift off the paper. If you've caramelized walnuts, place 1 walnut on each of the undusted areas. Using 2 spatulas, lift the cake onto a serving platter and, if desired, garnish with sprigs of fresh mint.

Storing The mousse-filled cake can be kept in the refrigerator overnight or wrapped airtight and frozen for 2 weeks. Thaw it in its wrapper in the refrigerator. It's best not to freeze the cake with the cocoa and walnut decorations—they'll become soggy.

Contributing Baker **MARY BERGIN**

Crème Brûléed Chocolate Bundt

Makes 10 to 12 servings ■ The foundation for this dessert is an airy chiffon cake as dark, fudgy, and deeply satisfying as devil's food. It may look like an old-fashioned Bundt cake with a cream poured into its center and drizzled down its ridges, but the cream is a crème brûlée, and hidden beneath it is a cache of fresh raspberries plumped with liqueur. When you pull out your blowtorch (page 5) to caramelize the crème brûlée, you can pull out the stops as well. Serve this with flourish and fanfare on fancy plates.

THE CRÈME BRÛLÉE

- ³/₄ cup heavy cream
- 1 vanilla bean
- 5 large egg yolks, at room temperature
- 3 tablespoons sugar

Pour the heavy cream into a medium saucepan. Split the vanilla bean and scrape the soft, pulpy seeds into the pan, toss in the pod, and stir to mix. Bring just to the boil over low heat.

Meanwhile, in a medium heatproof bowl, whisk the egg yolks and sugar together just to blend. Place the bowl over a pan of simmering water and whisk, continuously and energetically, until the mixture is very pale and hot to the touch. Remove the yolks from the heat. Gradually but steadily whisk the cream into the yolks, pod and all.

Put the bowl back over the hot water and let it sit there, with the heat turned off, whisking occasionally, for 5 to 10 minutes, until the cream thickens. Set the bowl into a larger bowl filled with ice cubes and cold water and allow the mixture to cool, whisking now and then. When the custard is cool to the touch, retrieve and discard the vanilla bean (or clean it and save it to flavor sugar) and push the mixture through a strainer into a clean bowl. Cover the bowl tightly and refrigerate for at least 2 hours. *The custard can be made the day before and kept covered and refrigerated until needed.*

THE CAKE

- 1¹/₂ cups sugar
- 1 cup all-purpose flour
- ³/₄ cup unsweetened cocoa powder
- 2 teaspoons baking powder
- 1 teaspoon baking soda
- ¹/₄ teaspoon salt
- 4 large eggs, separated
- ¹/₂ cup vegetable oil

½ cup water

1 teaspoon pure vanilla extract

2 large egg whites

1½ cups fresh raspberries

¼ cup Chambord or other raspberry liqueur

3 to 4 tablespoons sugar

Center a rack in the oven and preheat the oven to 350°F. Butter a 10-cup Bundt pan and dust the inside, including the center tube, with flour; tap out the excess.

Sift together 1 cup of the sugar, the flour, cocoa, baking powder, and baking soda onto a sheet of parchment or waxed paper; add the salt.

In a large bowl, whisk together the yolks, oil, water, and vanilla extract until blended. Whisk the dry ingredients gradually into the yolk mixture; set aside.

Beat the 6 egg whites in the bowl of a mixer fitted with the whisk attachment or work with a hand-held mixer. At low speed, beat the whites until they're foamy and form very soft peaks. Increase the mixer speed to medium-high and gradually add the remaining ½ cup sugar, beating until the whites are thick and shiny and hold peaks. (If you run a finger through the whites, it should leave a smooth, even path.) Fold about one third of the whipped egg whites into the yolk mixture to lighten it, then turn the yolk mixture into the whites and fold it in gently but thoroughly.

Baking the Cake Pour and scrape the batter into the pan. Place the pan on a jelly-roll pan and bake for 35 to 40 minutes, or until the cake is springy to the touch and starts to pull away from the sides of the pan. The top of the cake may show some cracks and a toothpick inserted in the center of the cake should come out clean. Remove the cake to a cooling rack and let it cool for at least 25 minutes before unmolding it onto a rack and allowing it to cool completely. *The cake can be made ahead, wrapped airtight, and frozen for up to a month; thaw, still wrapped, at room temperature.*

Finishing the Cake Place the cooled cake on a large serving plate. Toss the raspberries with the Chambord and spoon them, with their liqueur, into the center of the cake, filling the opening just to the top. Spoon the cold crème brûlée over the berries and drizzle it down the sides of the cake.

Sprinkle the crème brûlée on the top of the cake with a little of the sugar and, working with a blowtorch, close to the cake, caramelize the sugar. Continue sprinkling on sugar and caramelizing the top of the cake until it is evenly browned.

Storing The cake can be made up to 1 day ahead, covered, and kept at room temperature, or made a month ahead and frozen. The crème brûlée should be made several hours ahead, or it can be made the day before. However, once you assemble the cake and caramelize the crème brûlée, you must serve it immediately.

Contributing Baker **MARY BERGIN**

Mocha Brownie Cake

Makes 12 servings ■ Rich, luscious, and luxurious, this cake is supremely sophisticated yet guaranteed to please the kid in every chocolate-adoring adult. The cake has a brownie's density and power to delight, but it also has a connoisseur's blend of chocolates and the tang of sour cream. The filling and frosting are dark ganache mellowed with a measure of strong coffee. The cake has no decoration, just a smooth chocolate top (perfect for birthday candles).

THE CAKE

¾ cup all-purpose flour

¾ teaspoon baking powder

½ teaspoon salt

4½ ounces semisweet chocolate, coarsely chopped

2½ ounces unsweetened chocolate, coarsely chopped

¾ stick (3 ounces) unsalted butter

5 large eggs

1 cup sugar

1 teaspoon pure vanilla extract

3 tablespoons sour cream

Position a rack in the center of the oven and preheat the oven to 325°F. Butter a 9-inch round cake pan and dust with flour, tapping out the excess; set aside.

Whisk together the flour, baking powder, and salt in a small bowl and reserve.

Heat an inch of water in the bottom of a double boiler. Put the semisweet and unsweetened chocolates and the butter in the top of the double boiler, and heat, stirring occasionally, until the mixture is fully blended and smooth. Remove the pan from the heat.

Put the eggs, sugar, and vanilla in the bowl of a mixer fitted with the whisk attachment, or use a hand mixer, and whip on high speed for 4 to 5 minutes, or until the eggs are slightly thickened and doubled in volume. Add the melted chocolate and mix at medium speed for 15 seconds. Don't worry if the chocolate is not fully incorporated—it will blend in as you add the other ingredients. Remove the bowl from the mixer and, working with a rubber spatula, gently but thoroughly fold in the dry ingredients. Give the sour cream a vigorous turn or two with a whisk to loosen it, and fold it into the batter. The batter will be quite thick.

Baking, Cooling, and Chilling Pour the batter into the pan and, with a spatula, smooth and level the batter. Bake the cake for 45 to 50 minutes, until a toothpick inserted in the center comes out clean. Transfer the cake to a cooling rack and let cool in the pan for 20 minutes. Turn the cake out onto a cardboard cake round (or the round from a tart pan with a removable bottom) and refrigerate, uncovered, for 1 hour.

THE GANACHE

- **1¼ cups heavy cream**
- **3 tablespoons unsalted butter**
- **3 tablespoons sugar**
- **12 ounces semisweet chocolate, coarsely chopped**
- **¼ cup hot strong brewed coffee**

Heat the heavy cream, butter, and sugar in a medium saucepan over medium-high heat, stirring frequently, until the sugar is dissolved and the mixture reaches the boil. Put the chopped chocolate in a large bowl and pour in the boiling cream and the hot coffee. Set the mixture aside for 5 minutes, then stir until smooth. The ganache must cool thoroughly. You can leave it to cool at room temperature—which could take an hour or so—or you can refrigerate it. The ganache thickens as it cools. You want to use it when it just begins to thicken and can be poured rather than spread over the cake.

Assembling the Cake Remove the cake from the refrigerator and invert it onto a clean, dry work surface. Working with a long sharp knife, cut the cake into 3 even layers. Place the top layer of the cake, cut side down, in a 9-inch springform pan; check that the sides of the pan are closed. Pour 1 cup of the ganache over the layer, spreading it evenly to the edges with a rubber spatula; refrigerate, uncovered, until set, about 15 minutes. Top with the center layer, pressing it gently into place, and pour over another cup of ganache, again taking care to get the filling out to the edges; refrigerate until set. (If at any point the  ganache has thickened and is no longer pourable, heat it over the lowest heat, stirring constantly, until it returns to its proper consistency.) Place the last layer, cut side down, in the pan, and press down firmly but carefully to position it. Refrigerate the cake for at least 1 hour before applying the icing. Cover the remaining ganache with plastic wrap and keep it at room temperature.

Finishing the Cake To finish, run a knife around the inside edges of the cake pan; release the sides of the springform. Pour over the remaining ganache and use a long icing spatula to smooth the ganache over the top and around the sides. Allow the icing to set in the refrigerator or at room temperature.

To get a clean cut, heat the blade of a serrated knife under hot running water and wipe the blade dry before each cut. Place the slices on plates and, if cold, allow them to sit at room temperature for 15 to 20 minutes before serving.

Storing Once the ganache has set, the cake can be covered and kept in the refrigerator for up to 2 days.

Contributing Baker **MARCEL DESAULNIERS**

White Chocolate Patty Cake

Makes 10 servings ▪ This looks like a light, moist butter cake; in truth it's a substantial, very chocolaty, white chocolate cake. The whimsical name derives from the action of patting the edges of the cakes down to level and ready them for the crush, a mixture of berries and sugar. White chocolate, not really chocolate by definition because it doesn't contain chocolate liquor, is finicky. It can look pretty gloppy when you're melting it—and it burns easily—but its rich taste always rewards the extra care it demands. When buying white chocolate, make sure you choose a brand that contains cocoa butter.

THE CAKE

    12 ounces white chocolate, coarsely chopped

    ½ stick (2 ounces) unsalted butter

    2 tablespoons water

    6 large eggs, separated, at room temperature

    ¾ cup sugar

    4 large egg yolks, at room temperature

    ½ cup cake flour, sifted

    Melted butter, for greasing the pans

Position a rack in the center of the oven and preheat the oven to 325°F. Brush the bottom and sides of two 9-inch round cake pans with a light coating of melted butter, line with parchment paper rounds, and lightly butter the paper; set aside.

Heat an inch of water in the bottom of a double boiler. Put the chocolate, butter, and the 2 tablespoons water in the top of the double boiler and heat over low heat, whisking all the while, until the chocolate and butter are melted. The mixture may seem broken or curdled, but it will come together almost completely when it is whisked. (If it doesn't, the cake will still be fine.) Remove the pan from the heat and whisk vigorously to blend.

The ideal method for mixing this cake is to beat the yolks and ½ cup of the sugar together, then keep them mixing on low speed and, while they're mixing, beat the whites in another bowl. If you have both a standing and a hand-held mixer, you can do it this way. If not, follow these instructions for whites first: In a mixer fitted with the whisk attachment, whisk the egg whites until they form soft peaks, about 3 minutes. Still beating, add ¼ cup of the sugar, and continue mixing until the whites are stiff but still shiny, 2 to 3 minutes more. (See page 37 for information on making meringue.) Gently—very gently—transfer the meringue to another bowl and begin work on the yolks.

Working in the mixer (there's no need to wash the bowl), this time fitted with the paddle attachment, beat the 10 yolks and the remaining ½ cup sugar on high speed for 2 minutes; scrape down the bowl and continue to beat for 2 minutes more, or until the mixture is slightly thickened and pale yellow.

Add the melted chocolate to the yolks and increase the mixer speed to medium; beat for about 30 seconds to blend. Remove the bowl from the mixer and, working with a rubber spatula, gently fold in the sifted cake flour. Pile one third of the egg whites onto the mixture and stir them in with the spatula to lighten the batter. Gently fold in the remaining whites.

Baking the Cake Divide the batter between the two pans and smooth the tops. Bake for 26 to 28 minutes, or until a toothpick inserted in the center of the cakes comes out clean. Transfer the cakes to cooling racks and let them stand for 20 minutes. Invert the cakes onto cardboard cake rounds (or the rounds from tart pans with removable bottoms) and cool to room temperature, with the parchment rounds still in place. When the cakes are completely cool, remove the parchment paper, cover, and refrigerate until needed. *Covered well with plastic wrap and refrigerated, the cake layers can be made 2 to 3 days in advance; they can be frozen up to a month. Thaw, still wrapped, at room temperature.*

THE CRUSH

Two 8-ounce packages frozen whole raspberries in light syrup, thawed or still frosty

2 tablespoons sugar

1 teaspoon fresh lemon juice

½ pint fresh raspberries

Put the frozen raspberries, sugar, and lemon juice in the work bowl of a food processor fitted with the metal blade and whirl until smooth, 15 to 20 seconds. Push the mixture through a strainer: You should have about 1 cup. If you want, you can make more raspberry crush and use the extra as a sauce to decorate the plates.

Finishing the Cake To finish the cake, remove the layers from the refrigerator and press down on the edges with your fingers, patty-cake fashion. Spoon half of the raspberry crush onto one of the layers and spread to even. Top with the other layer, spoon on the remaining crush, spread it to smooth, and top with the fresh berries, placing them close together in a single layer. The cake should be refrigerated until just before serving time, or for up to 8 hours. Bring the cake back to a little cooler than room temperature before serving.

To serve, if you've made more crush, drizzle some in an abstract pattern on each dessert plate, and top with a slice of cake. To get a clean cut, heat the blade of a serrated knife under hot running water and wipe the blade dry before each cut.

Storing The assembled cake can be refrigerated for about 8 hours before serving. Bring the cake back to a little cooler than room temperature.

Contributing Baker **MARCEL DESAULNIERS**

Cardinal Slice

COLOR PHOTOGRAPH, PAGE 226

Makes 12 servings ■ Within the layers of this supremely elegant cake lies a lesson in the essentials of Austrian pastry. Each piece contains the trinity of Austrian pastry requisites: sleek, sophisticated looks, subtle, smooth flavors, and an appealing play of textures. Called a slice (or *schnitten*) because of the way in which it is served—it is a long rectangular cake that is presented in stand-up slices—the confection is a cross between pastry and cake. The layers are made by piping alternating strips of meringue and a cake batter similar to génoise. (After you have piped out the three layers, you'll have batter left over for nut-topped ladyfingers; see the Rothschilds, page 289.) When baked, the meringue crisps and the cake softens and takes on a light spring. The slice is built of three layers separated by a whipped cream intensely flavored with "espresso couleur," a syrupy extract of deeply caramelized sugar and freshly made espresso (guaranteed to become any coffee addict's favorite pantry staple). For a particularly posh presentation, decorate each plate with a berry-filled caramel basket (page 452).

THE COULEUR

1 cup sugar

½ cup hot brewed espresso

Place a wide straight-sided heavy sauté pan (a chicken fryer with high sides would be ideal) over medium heat. When the pan is hot, sprinkle a little sugar into the pan. As soon as some of the sugar melts, sprinkle more sugar over it. (You are going to caramelize the sugar spot by spot.) When half of the sugar has been added, start stirring the sugar with a wooden spoon and adding the remainder of the sugar about 1 tablespoon at a time. Again, you don't want to add more sugar than the caramel can absorb—you're still working spot by spot.

Keep cooking the caramel until it's darker than you ever thought caramel should be. The sugar will smoke—lots; be really, really, dark—really; and look foamy. When the sugar bubbles, remove the pan from the heat. Stand away from the pan and add a little of the hot espresso. Keep adding the espresso little by little and stirring it into the sugar. (If the espresso is too cold or you add it too quickly, the sugar will seize and you'll have lumps, a problem that's not irreparable—you can melt the lumps—but is avoidable.) When all of the espresso has been incorporated, turn up the heat and bring the mixture back to the boil.

Place a metal spoon in a heatproof canning jar, pour the extract into the jar, allow to cool, then cover. When it cools, its consistency will be syrupy. *You can make the couleur up to 2 months ahead and keep it in a cool place.*

THE MERINGUE

4 large egg whites, at room temperature

6 tablespoons granulated sugar

¾ cup confectioner's sugar

Position a rack in the center of the oven and preheat the oven to 300°F. Cut three pieces of parchment paper each 3 inches wide and the length of a jelly-roll pan. Butter the jelly-roll pan and lay the strips of paper on the pan, leaving a little space between each strip. Run your fingers along the paper to glue it to the pan; set aside.

Place the egg whites and granulated sugar in the bowl of a heavy-duty mixer (or work with a hand-held mixer). Holding the whisk attachment in your hand, mix the whites and sugar just enough to stir them up a bit. Fit the whisk attachment onto the mixer and beat the whites on medium speed for 2 minutes. Increase the speed to high and continue to beat for another 3 minutes, or until the meringue stands in stiff peaks when the whisk is lifted. Remove the bowl from the mixer and sift half of the confectioner's sugar over the meringue; fold it in using a large rubber spatula. Sift the rest of the sugar over the mixture and fold it in gently. The confectioner's sugar will thicken the meringue and dull its shine.

Piping the Meringue Spoon the meringue into a large pastry bag fitted with a ½-inch plain tip. Pipe three strips of meringue lengthwise down each piece of parchment, placing one strip along each side of the paper and one in the center; pipe the meringue by placing the tip down, applying pressure, and moving the tip along the length of the paper. When you reach the end, stop the pressure and pull the tip away. You'll have a fair amount of meringue left over; you'll use it to make the sponge batter.

Leave the jelly-roll pan on the counter.

Pipe three strips of meringue batter for each layer.

THE SPONGE BATTER

The remaining meringue batter (above)

4 large eggs

4 large egg yolks

¼ cup sugar

¾ cup all-purpose flour, sifted

Squeeze the leftover meringue batter into the mixer bowl. (A neat way to do this is to lay the pastry bag on the counter and draw a dough scraper against the bag, from tip to opening, to press the remaining batter out of the bag.) Add the eggs, yolks, and sugar to the bowl and, holding the whisk attachment in your hand, stir the mixture just to break up the eggs.

continued

Fit the whisk attachment onto the mixer (or use a hand-held mixer) and beat at medium speed for 2 minutes. Increase the speed to high and beat for another 2 minutes, then slow the machine down and continue to beat for a few minutes, until the batter forms a silky ribbon when some of it is lifted and allowed to fall back into the bowl. Once again, you'll have a batter with a slightly dull sheen.

This is a very fragile batter, more fragile than the meringue, so handle it gingerly. Remove the bowl from the mixer and sift half of the flour onto the batter; fold it in delicately with a large rubber spatula. Sift and fold in the remaining flour. Spoon the sponge batter into the pastry bag.

Pipe the sponge batter between the strips of meringue.

Piping the Batter Squeeze this batter into strips between the meringue so you have two strips of sponge on each sheet of parchment. You want to squeeze the batter with enough pressure to cause it to mound a little above the meringue. Cover the remaining batter; it can be used to make ladyfingers or Rothschilds (see page 289).

Baking the Cake Strips Place the jelly-roll pan in the oven and prop the oven door open a bit with the handle of a wooden spoon. Bake the layers for about 40 minutes, or until the meringue is dry and the sponge puffed. An exact baking time is not truly critical here—because the temperature is low and the oven door is open to allow steam to escape, you can even bake this for as long as 60 minutes without a problem. Transfer the pan to a cooling rack. *Once cooled, the cake strips can be kept overnight, lightly covered, at room temperature.*

THE CREAM

> **2 cups cold heavy cream**
>
> **2 tablespoons sugar**
>
> **2 tablespoons (approximately) espresso couleur (above)**

Whip the heavy cream and sugar together until the cream holds soft peaks. *You can whip the cream the night before, spoon it into a cheesecloth-lined strainer set over a bowl, cover, and keep refrigerated until needed. The cream will thicken and stabilize during this period.* Finish whisking the cream by hand—a precaution against overbeating—and fold in 2 tablespoons couleur. Taste the cream and add more espresso couleur if you'd like a stronger flavor.

TO FINISH THE CAKE

> **Confectioner's sugar**
>
> **Caramel Baskets (page 452; optional)**
>
> **Fresh berries or sliced fruit, such as peeled peaches, cherries, grapes, melon, apricots, or plums (optional)**

Cut a piece of heavy cardboard into a rectangle just a bit smaller than one of the cake strips; set aside. Carefully peel the parchment away from the cake strips. Give the strips a once-over and choose the prettiest strip for the top layer. Stack the strips one on top of the other, the prettiest on top. Using a long flat knife and a sawing motion, trim the sides and ends as necessary so that they form an even stack, reserving any crumbs. Then place the strip to be used as the bottom layer on the cardboard and sprinkle any crumbs from the trimming over it.

Spread the bottom layer with half of the whipped cream, smoothing it with a metal icing spatula. Place the middle cake strip over the cream and wiggle it around to settle it gently into the cream and align it properly. Top this layer with all but about ⅓ cup of the remaining cream. Position the last cake strip over the cream and settle it in. Use the rest of the cream to "spackle" the sides and ends of the cake with a very thin coat of cream.

Chilling the Cake Chill the cake for at least 1 hour.

Cutting the Cake To cut the cake, choose a long serrated knife and keep your dough scraper close at hand. Place the scraper flat against one long side of the cake with the metal bottom edge against the counter and cut through just the first layer of the cake, marking off 12 portions and dipping your knife into hot water and wiping it dry between cuts. Still using the scraper as a support (whipped cream cakes are slippery characters and can move around as you're slicing them), cut through the remaining layers. Sprinkle the top of the cake with confectioner's sugar, tapping the sugar through a strainer.

Place each piece of cake upright on a dessert plate and place a caramel basket in front of it, if you're using them. Fill the baskets with berries or tiny slices of fruit. Serve immediately.

Storing Although the components of the cake can be made ahead, the assembled cake can be refrigerated only for a maximum of 4 hours before it must be served.

Rothschilds

ROTHSCHILDS are chocolate-coated ladyfingers, so named because they are as rich as that famously wealthy family, and they can be made with the batter you have left over. Line a baking sheet with parchment paper and pipe the batter into ladyfingers (see page 333 for help on forming ladyfingers), making sure to leave room for spreading between them. Sprinkle the ladyfingers with a dusting of chopped almonds. Then, if you have the confidence, grab the sheet of parchment at the top and lift it up so that the excess nuts fall onto the counter—a real bravura move, and one that's effective too. Discard the excess nuts and bake the cookies in a preheated 300°F oven for about 30 minutes, or until they are puffed, golden, and set. Let the cookies cool on their parchment on a rack. When the ladyfingers are cool, peel away the parchment and spread their undersides with melted chocolate, the step that transforms them from ladyfingers to Rothschilds.

Contributing Baker **MARKUS FARBINGER**

Vanilla-Hazelnut Cheesecake

COLOR PHOTOGRAPH, PAGE 290

Makes 10 to 12 servings ■ The beautifully marbleized pattern of this cheesecake—a mixture of caramel and vanilla batters—makes this a cake worthy of serving at the end of your fanciest dinner parties. The fact that it has about half the fat of traditional cheesecakes makes it a good finish to even the richest meal. But there's no reason to mention its leanness—no one will ever know from its taste and super-creamy texture.

Plan ahead for this cake—the cottage cheese needs to drain for about an hour and the entire cake needs to chill for at least a day. And if you want to make your own (delicious, crunchy) Hazelnut Biscotti (see page 315) for the crust, you'll need a few more hours.

2 cups (1 pint) low-fat (2%) small-curd cottage cheese

1 cup plus 3 tablespoons sugar

1 tablespoon water

2 tablespoons toasted, skinned, and chopped hazelnuts (see page 315 for an easy way to skin hazelnuts)

8 ounces Neufchâtel cheese

1 vanilla bean, split, or 1 tablespoon pure vanilla extract

3 large eggs

¼ teaspoon salt

3 to 4 tablespoons crushed hazelnut biscotti or graham crackers

Draining the Cheese Set a strainer over a bowl and spoon the cottage cheese into it. Cover the set-up with plastic wrap and refrigerate for at least an hour, or until the excess moisture has drained out of the cheese.

Line a baking sheet with parchment paper and set aside.

Making the Hazelnut Paste While the cheese is draining, stir 3 tablespoons of the sugar and the water together in a small saucepan. Cover the pan, set it over medium heat, and bring to a simmer. Remove the cover, dip a pastry brush into cold water, and wash down any sugar crystals that may have formed on the sides of the pan. Keep the pan uncovered and continue to cook the sugar until it turns very pale yellow—drop a little on a white plate to test the color. Add the chopped hazelnuts to the pan and stir gently with a small wooden spoon or a chopstick just until the nuts are coated with syrup. Swirl the pan carefully and continue to cook until the syrup tests medium amber on a white plate. Immediately turn out the caramelized nuts onto the parchment-lined baking sheet. Set the caramel aside to cool and harden. Break the caramel into pieces and process to a paste in a food processor. Scrape the paste into a small bowl, cover, and set aside.

Position a rack in the lower third of the oven and preheat the oven to 350°F. Line a 2-inch-high 8-inch round cake pan with a parchment paper circle and coat the sides of the pan lightly with vegetable oil spray. Put a kettle of water on to boil and set aside a roasting pan that will hold the cake pan and about an inch of boiling water.

Making the Batter Spoon the drained cottage cheese into the work bowl of a food processor fitted with the metal blade and process for 2 to 3 minutes, scraping down the sides as needed. Don't try to cut the processing time short—you need this time to make the cottage cheese silken. Leave the cheese in the processor while you prepare the rest of the batter's ingredients.

Soften the Neufchâtel cheese by either warming it gently in the top of a double boiler or heating it in a microwave oven for about 30 seconds; stir until smooth. Put the Neufchâtel cheese into the work bowl along with the soft, pulpy seeds from the vanilla bean (just scrape them out of the pod with the point of a small knife) or the vanilla extract. Add the eggs, the remaining 1 cup sugar, and the salt and pulse just until the mixture is smooth, scraping down the sides of the bowl a couple times during the process. Don't overdo it, or you'll have a thin batter.

Measure out 1 cup batter and gradually add it to the hazelnut paste, mixing well. Pour the remaining batter into the prepared pan. Drop 10 spoonfuls of the hazelnut batter randomly over the vanilla batter. Dip a table knife into the pan and swirl the two batters to create a marbled pattern—take care not to overmix, or you'll end up blending, not marbleizing, the batters.

Baking the Cake Put the cake pan into the roasting pan, open the oven, slide out the lower rack, and place the pan on it. Pour boiling water into the roasting pan until it comes about 1 inch up the sides of the cake pan and then very carefully slide the oven rack back into position, taking care not to let any water slosh onto the cake. Bake for 40 to 45 minutes, until the cake has risen slightly and is just beginning to come away from the sides of the pan. Remove the cake from its water bath and put it on a rack to cool to room temperature.

Chilling the Cake When completely cool, cover and chill for at least 24 hours, or for as long as 2 days.

Unmolding the Cake To unmold the cake, run a thin metal spatula around the edges. Cover the pan tightly with plastic wrap, place a flat plate or a cardboard cake round against the plastic, and invert the cake and plate. Rap the pan lightly to release the cake—you'll feel it fall against the plate—then remove the pan and peel away the paper. Put a serving plate or cardboard cake circle on the cake and carefully turn the cake so that it is right side up on the circle. Remove the plastic wrap and press the crumbs around the sides of the cake. Cut the cake using a long sharp knife, dipping it into hot water and wiping it dry between cuts.

Storing The cake will keep for 2 days in the refrigerator, covered with plastic wrap.

Contributing Baker **ALICE MEDRICH**

A Glorious Wedding Cake

COMPOSED OF THREE DIAMOND-SHAPED tiers of dense almond cake and feather-light dacquoise, and perfectly finished with buttercream and marzipan fruits, this elegant wedding cake from Martha Stewart calls for a leisurely game plan. Although the cake, dacquoise, and buttercream can be made over a day or two, and the construction and final decorating can be done in an afternoon, the marzipan fruits will require several days. Fortunately, the fruits keep almost indefinitely, so you can start early and work at whatever pace you please.

With any baking project of this size, it's best to read through the recipe several times before going to work. And since, in all likelihood, you'll need some new equipment and supplies, it is also helpful to make lists. You'll probably be heading to the hardware store for dowels, sturdy wire clippers, and a hammer; to the bakers' and confectioners' supply houses for oversize cardboard rounds, powdered food colors, and candymakers' tools and brushes; and to the specialty housewares shop for the diamond-shaped pans. Clear a work space for the marzipan manufacturing and you're on your way.

Whether it is for your own wedding or a present for someone dear to you, your creation will be more than a culinary triumph; it will be a memory to be cherished.

Wedding Cake

COLOR PHOTOGRAPH, PAGE 232

Makes at least 50 servings, with the top layer left to freeze for the couple's first anniversary ■ This handsome and exquisitely detailed three-tier wedding cake couldn't be more romantic or elegant. The cake itself is a dense almond cake, almost a pound cake. Each diamond-shaped tier is cut in half, brushed with apricot jam, and layered with almond dacquoise (a nut meringue). The tiers are covered and beaded with rum-laced buttercream and decorated with winsome marzipan fruits.

Not unexpectedly, this project takes some time, but it's well within the range of an average home baker with above-average patience. Fortunately, everything can, and in fact should, be made ahead. The most demanding part is the marzipan fruit, and, if you'd rather not make the fruit, the cake can be beautifully decorated at the last minute with fresh flowers.

Wedding Cake Equipment

- 3 diamond-shaped baking pans, 16-, 8-, and 6-cup capacity
- oversize cardboard rounds, large enough to hold each layer
- 3 large baking sheets
- 16-inch pastry bag with plain ½-inch tip
- candy thermometer
- parchment paper, mat knife, and scissors
- marzipan tools (page 301)
- constructing and decorating tools (page 303)

Dense Almond Cake

In terms of technique, this is a basic cream-the-butter-and-sugar-together cake; in terms of texture, it is, as its name declares, a dense, tight-grained cake with a fine crumb and a firm structure; and in terms of taste, it is terrific, warmly flavored with almond paste and as accommodating as a cake that shares center stage with so many other sweets should be.

The three diamond-shaped tiers include: the base tier, made in a pan that measures 17¼ inches lengthwise from point to point and has a capacity of 16 cups; the middle tier, the pan for which is 13¾ inches long and holds 8 cups; and the top tier, needing a pan that measures

10 inches lengthwise from point to point and has a capacity of 6 cups. You will need one recipe of Dense Almond Cake for the top tier, two for the middle, and three for the base. If you have a heavy-duty mixer, you'll be able to make double the recipe. To prepare triple the amount of batter, you'll probably have to do it in two batches.

The pans are unusual, as are the oversize cardboard rounds you'll need to tote them around the kitchen and get them in and out of the refrigerator, but both are available in specialty and bakeware shops (see Sources, page 467). If you opt for a more traditional shape for your cake, a round, square, or rectangle, look for pans with similar capacities and run a test beforehand to get the baking times right.

Note To make the three layers, you will need to make 6 times the cake recipe.

> 9½ ounces (1 packed cup) almond paste, store-bought or special-ordered (see Sources, page 467)
>
> 2¼ sticks (9 ounces) unsalted butter, at room temperature
>
> 1 cup sugar
>
> 6 large eggs
>
> 1 cup cake flour, sifted

Position a rack in the center of the oven and preheat the oven to 325°F. Trace the outline of each baking pan onto a cardboard cake round and, using scissors or a mat knife, cut out the shapes. These will be the bases on which the finished cakes will rest and be decorated. Butter the baking pans, fit the bottom of each pan with a piece of parchment paper cut to size, dust the pans all over with flour, and tap out the excess. Set aside until needed.

Making the Top Tier Put the almond paste, butter, and sugar in the work bowl of a food processor fitted with the metal blade and process for a full minute, scraping down the sides of the bowl as needed. The mixture should look smooth, although it may still feel a bit grainy when you rub a bit between your fingers.

Scrape the almond mixture into the bowl of a mixer fitted with the paddle attachment and add the eggs. Beat at medium speed until the mixture is smooth and satiny, about 3 minutes, scraping down the sides of the bowl as needed. Turn the mixer up to high speed for the last 15 seconds of beating.

Remove the bowl from the mixer and sprinkle in the flour, about ¼ cup at a time, folding it in gently but thoroughly with a large rubber spatula. Turn the batter into the prepared pan and smooth the top with the spatula.

Bake the cake for 1½ to 1¾ hours, or until the top is golden, the cake starts to come away from the sides of the pan, and it feels springy to the touch. A long cake tester or a broom straw will come out clean when it's done.

Transfer the cake to a cooling rack. Allow the cake to cool in the pan for about 25 minutes before inverting it onto a cake rack. If the cake rose above the

sides of the pan, trim the cake with a long knife so that it is level with the pan. Then invert the cake. (The underside is now up and it will become the top of the cake.) Remove the parchment paper and let the cake cool to room temperature on the rack before lifting it onto its cut-to-size cardboard. Set the cake and its base on a large cardboard round, its transporter.

Making the Middle and Base Tiers Make a double recipe of almond cake for the middle layer and bake it for about 2 hours. Make a triple recipe for the base tier, and bake it for about 2 hours and 10 minutes. Turn each partially cooled layer out onto a cut-to-size cardboard. (When doubling or tripling the recipe, it is best to process the almond paste, butter, and sugar mixture one batch at a time to ensure that it is free of lumps.)

Storing Cooled cakes can be wrapped in plastic and kept at room temperature overnight, refrigerated for up to 2 days, or frozen for a month.

Almond Dacquoise

A dacquoise is a nut meringue disk; it is also the name of a finished dessert composed of two or three layers of this nut meringue spread with buttercream. Although it can be made with almost any nut, the classic dacquoise usually includes almonds or hazelnuts and, when made into the eponymous dessert, is layered with coffee or chocolate buttercream. In the wedding cake, the dacquoise rests between the layers of almond cake, providing snap and a textural tease in an otherwise soft and smooth confection.

This recipe makes enough for the three layers of dacquoise needed for the wedding cake. If your oven will not hold three baking sheets or if you do not have the availability of a second oven, make the recipe in two batches, the first time using half of the recipe to make the two smaller layers, the second time making another half recipe for the largest layer.

> 1⅓ cups sugar
>
> 1 cup (5½ ounces) blanched almonds
>
> 2 tablespoons cornstarch
>
> 8 large egg whites (reserve the yolks for the buttercream)
>
> ¼ teaspoon cream of tartar

Position the racks to divide the oven into thirds and preheat the oven to 200°F.

Cut three pieces of parchment paper to fit three baking sheets and, using a felt-tip marker or a dark pencil, trace the outline of each diamond baking pan on a piece of paper; turn the papers over and put one on each of the baking sheets. Fit a 16-inch pastry bag with a plain ½-inch tip and set aside until needed.

continued

Top and bottom: To pipe the dacquoise, start at one of the points and pipe a diamond shape. Continue piping diamonds until the space is filled, then smooth the dacquoise with an offset spatula.

Put 1 cup of the sugar and the almonds in the work bowl of a food processor fitted with the metal blade and pulse and process, scraping the sides of the bowl as needed, until the almonds are finely ground. Turn the almonds into a bowl, sift the cornstarch over them, and fold in the cornstarch with a rubber spatula; set aside for the moment.

Put the egg whites in the dry grease-free bowl of a mixer fitted with the whisk attachment, add the cream of tartar, and beat on high speed until the whites form soft peaks. With the mixer still on high, gradually add the remaining ⅓ cup sugar and whip until the whites are firm and glossy and hold a peak when the whisk is lifted. (See page 37 for further information on meringue.)

Remove the bowl from the mixer and, working with a large rubber spatula, gently fold in the ground almonds, adding a third at a time. Scoop the meringue into the pastry bag and twist the top to seal.

Secure the parchment paper to the pans by piping out small dabs of meringue in the corners of each baking sheet and pressing the paper into the "glue."

Piping the Meringue The easiest way to pipe the meringue into shape is to start with your tip directly over one of the points. Staying within the marked line, pipe along the edge to form a diamond. Aim for a line of meringue that is about ½ inch high. Continue piping diamonds, each one right next to the last, and staying within the marks, until the entire diamond is covered. Don't worry if you've missed a spot or two; you can fill in any holes with a dot of meringue. To finish, run an offset spatula very lightly across the top of the meringue to even it; you want to smooth, not flatten, it. Repeat to make the remaining diamonds.

Baking the Meringues Bake the meringues for 7 hours, until firm, dry, and lightly colored. When properly baked, the meringues should lift off the parchment without a problem. Transfer the meringues from the parchment to a cooling rack, running a large spatula under the meringues to separate them from the paper and help you with the transfer.

Storing The meringues can be made up to a few days ahead, wrapped in plastic, and kept in a cool, dry place.

Rum-Laced Buttercream

This is an extraordinarily elegant buttercream, based on a mixture of egg yolks and sugar beaten to the consistency of a marshmallowy meringue. Once the butter, rum, and vanilla are added, the texture becomes silky, the taste subtle. This buttercream is best suited to cool kitchens and climes. If you're going to decorate the cake for an outdoor wedding, keep the cake under refrigeration until it's time to serve it. (If this will be a problem, frost the cake with a meringue buttercream [see page 445], flavoring it, as this one is, with vanilla and rum.)

You will need two recipes of this buttercream to fill and frost the wedding cake. It is best to make one batch at a time and then combine the batches to get an even color.

8 sticks (2 pounds) unsalted butter, at room temperature

2 cups sugar

1½ cups cold water

16 large egg yolks

1 tablespoon dark rum

1½ teaspoons pure vanilla extract

For the butter to blend into the yolk mixture, it must be of a spreading consistency, soft and smooth but not oily or greasy. To achieve this consistency, put the butter in a mixer fitted with the paddle attachment and beat it briefly, just to soften it. Scrape it onto a sheet of plastic wrap, wrap it well, and keep it on the counter until needed. Wipe out the mixer bowl.

Stir the sugar and water together in a heavy-bottomed medium saucepan and place over high heat. Stir just until the sugar dissolves and then allow the mixture to bubble away on its own. Once the sugar has dissolved, brush down the sides of the pan with a pastry brush dipped in cold water; repeat as needed. The sugar needs to reach the soft-ball stage, which is 239°F measured on a candy thermometer, or the point at which a bit of syrup dropped into a glass of cold water can be formed into a soft, malleable ball if pressed between your fingertips. (It can take almost 30 minutes to reach this point.) Remove the pan from the heat.

Press the egg yolks through a fine strainer into the mixer bowl. Fit the mixer with the whisk attachment and set aside until needed. (Straining the yolks rids them of filaments that can spoil the smoothness of your buttercream and get stuck in the very fine piping tip used for the bead decoration.) Beat the yolks on low speed just to break them up and then increase the speed to high. Holding the pan with the sugar syrup close to the edge of the mixer bowl, add the sugar syrup slowly in a steady stream, keeping the stream between the bowl and the whisk so that the whisk doesn't throw syrup against the sides of the bowl. Scrape down the sides of the bowl as needed.

Once all of the syrup has been added, beat the yolks on high speed until they are creamy, pale, voluminous, and, most important, cool. (You can speed the cooling process by setting the mixer bowl in a larger bowl filled with ice cubes and cold water. If you have a water jacket for your mixer, just attach and fill it; if not, jury-rig a water bath by slipping a shallow bowl or pan under the mixing bowl and filling it with ice cubes. It's not elegant, but it does the job.)

continued

When the yolks are cool and tripled in volume, reduce the mixer speed to medium and add the softened butter about ¼ cup at a time. Keep mixing after the last addition until the buttercream is perfectly smooth. Add the rum and vanilla extract and beat to blend.

Remove the bowl from the mixer and run the whisk around it a few times so that you can judge the buttercream's consistency. If you are going to use the buttercream immediately, it must be of proper spreading consistency—too cold and stiff, and you'll be forcing it across the cake; too warm, and it may become oily and slip off the cake. If it's too warm, keep it (or set it) over ice to cool it; too cold, bring it to room temperature. In all likelihood, the buttercream will be perfect when it comes off the mixer, but it may need to be kept over ice to maintain its consistency as you're working, particularly if the weather is warm.

Storing The buttercream can be tightly covered and kept in the refrigerator for 2 or 3 days or in the freezer for a month. In either case, bring the buttercream to room temperature and beat it in a mixer fitted with the paddle attachment to bring back its smoothness before using. (Don't worry if the buttercream looks curdled as you're beating; keep beating and it will come together.)

Apricot Glaze

Heat about 4 pounds of best-quality apricot jam in a saucepan over low heat to liquefy it, then press it through a strainer to remove any large pieces of fruit. You can do this at any time up to a month before you need the glaze. Pour the glaze into a sealed container and keep it under refrigeration until needed. When you're ready to glaze the cake, reheat the jam.

Marzipan

Of course you can purchase marzipan, but, if you start with good-quality almond paste, you can make a superior marzipan in minutes at home. (See Sources, page 467, for mail-order almond paste.) Make two batches of this marzipan and you'll have enough to create an abundance of fruits and leaves. And because marzipan keeps for weeks at room temperature, you can make this at your convenience.

> **1 pound almond paste**
> **1 pound confectioner's sugar, sifted**
> **⅓ cup light corn syrup, plus additional for "glue"**

Put the almond paste and sugar in the work bowl of a food processor fitted with the metal blade. Pulse and process until the mixture is very fine—when you press bits of the mixture between your fingers, you should not be able to feel any pieces of almond paste. Add the corn syrup and pulse several times just to bring the mixture together—don't get carried away; you don't want to overmix it.

Remove the marzipan from the processor and finish blending it by hand, kneading it briefly on a work surface. Wrap the marzipan well in plastic or pack it into an airtight container and store in a dry place until needed.

Making the Marzipan Decorations This is the point at which art and craft meet and, depending upon your experience, enthusiasm, and sense of adventure, the moment at which you might weaken, throw up your hands, and head for the florist, ready to buy fresh flowers to decorate your cake. Hold on—these are doable and, once you get into the rhythm, enjoyable and wildly satisfying. As with so many crafts projects, having the right tools makes the difference. You can, of course, improvise, but if you equip yourself with a set of candymaker's tools (see Sources, page 467), you'll be assured of success.

Marzipan Tools

- candymaker's knife
- candymaker's arrow-tipped tool
- candymaker's burnisher
- box grater or wasabi grater
- raspberry leaf cutter
- veined leaf cutter
- latex pattern for veined leaves
- bubble wrap
- petal dust in the following colors: buttercup, spiced pumpkin, brown, moss green, and mango (see Sources, page 467)
- paintbrushes

Marzipan and tools for decorating.

It will take hours to make the raspberries and cherries and their stems and leaves, so start in advance and work whenever you have the time. If you can set aside a workplace for this project, you can start a week ahead, keep your equipment out, and work at your own pace.

It is hard to say how many pieces of fruit you'll need to decorate the wedding cake, but you'll want to be generous with the decorations. Work your way through the two batches of marzipan and then, using the empty baking tins as a template, lay out a rough version of what you'll want. If you think you'll need more, whip up another batch of marzipan and settle in to shaping fruit and leaves. The cake made in the photograph (page 232) was decorated with 75 raspberries, 48 cherries, 12 stems, and about 180 leaves, but there is no must-have number for any of the elements.

continued

As you work, you'll figure out the best work pattern for your own schedule and temperament. From an efficiency standpoint, it is probably best if you form at least a batch, if not all, of the fruits, leaves, and stems and then paint them, rather than paint each piece as it is formed. Of course, if you form and paint, you get instant gratification. The choice is yours.

TO MAKE THE CHERRIES, pinch off a small (cherry-size) piece of marzipan for each one and roll it between your fingers and palms to form a ball. Roll the blunt edge of the candymaker's knife along one side of the ball (going from top to bottom) to form the crease that's characteristic of cherries. Use the arrow-tipped tool to make a small hole at the top of the cherry.

TO MAKE THE CHERRY STEMS, for each one, roll a very skinny snake of marzipan, starting it in your palm and moving it to the work surface. If it gets too long, just cut it. When the stem is the length you want (keep it long; it'll make a pretty tendrillike decoration on the finished cake), taper one end.

TO MAKE THE RASPBERRIES, pinch off a piece of marzipan smaller than that which you used for the cherry and roll it into a ball. Roll the ball over the smallest holes of a box grater or over a wasabi grater to create the raspberry's little prickers.

Top and bottom: Form the crease for the cherry, then make a hole on the top for the leaves.

TO MAKE THE LEAVES, roll out some of the marzipan. Cut raspberry leaves with the special star-shaped leaf cutter. Use the arrow-tipped tool to make an indentation in the center. To form the veined cherry leaves, cut them with the special cutter. For the veins, press the leaves with the latex veined-leaf pattern.

The best way to store these pieces, painted or unpainted, is to nestle them in bubble wrap. Cut the bubble wrap to line plastic containers and rest the pieces in the wrap as they're finished; you can layer the bubble wrap. Store in a cool, dry place.

Painting the Decorations To paint the pieces, you use paints that are brushed on dry. Use the paints sparingly and with a light touch. The cherries are meant to be Queen Anne cherries; that is, they are a pale yellowish-ivory color and are blushed with a rosier peachy color. To get this effect, brush the cherries with buttercup and highlight with mango. The raspberries are golden raspberries, whose pale color is achieved by highlighting a buttercup base with pumpkin. The cherry stems are painted brown and moss green; the leaves are edged with moss green. To get a blended effect, you can either dip your brush into one color and then into another, or you can mix the colors on a piece of parchment paper the way an artist mixes colors on a palette.

If you want to attach raspberry leaves to berries or stems to cherries before you're ready to apply the decorations to the cake, you can do so. The "glue" for these decorations is corn syrup. For the berries, apply a tiny dab of corn syrup on top of each berry, lay on a star-shaped leaf, and press it into place with the burnisher. The cherry stems can be put into place with a touch of corn syrup as well; attach the tapered ends to the cherries.

Storing Keep the fruits in their bubble-wrap nests at room temperature until you're ready to decorate the cake.

Constructing and Decorating the Cake

Unless you're going to whisk the cake out to the party the instant it is finished, clear out your refrigerator so you'll have room to store it. Clear a large work area too, while you're at it.

Constructing and Decorating Tools

- cake decorator's turntable
- ruler
- toothpicks
- long serrated knife
- large cardboard cake rounds
- 12-inch pastry bag
- ¼-inch plain decorating tip
- pastry brush
- offset and straight metal icing spatulas
- serving platter
- 8 clear plastic drinking straws
- 8 wooden skewers, about ⅛ inch thick
- heavy-duty wire clippers
- ¼-inch-thick dowel, about 15 inches long, sharpened at one end
- hammer
- light corn syrup
- small paintbrush

Start with the bottom layer. Keeping it on its cardboard round, lift it onto the turntable. Measure the height of the cake and determine the midpoint. Mark the middle of the cake at 2-inch intervals by inserting toothpicks into the cake, leaving at least half of the pick exposed; these are your cutting guides. Hold the knife against the toothpicks and slowly rotate the turntable, allowing the knife to score a midpoint line around the cake. Insert the knife and cut

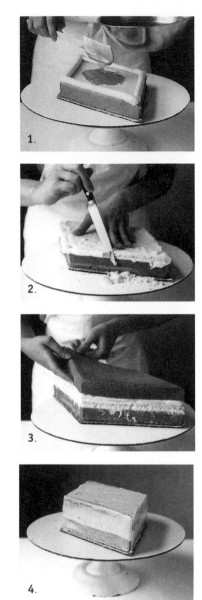

1. Pour warm apricot jam inside the buttercream dam.

2. Top with the dacquoise layer, trim to size, and follow with more buttercream and apricot jam.

3. Then add the other half of the cake layer.

4. Apply the crumb coat.

through the cake along the etched line with a sawing motion. Lift the top half of the layer off the cake and onto a cardboard round. Position the largest dacquoise on the cake and check that it is not larger than the cake. (If the dacquoise hangs over the edges of the layer, cut it to size with the serrated knife, using a sawing motion.) Remove the dacquoise and set it aside for the moment.

Fit a 12-inch pastry bag with a ¼-inch plain tip and fill it with buttercream. Pipe a strip of buttercream (a buttercream dam) along the edges of the cake. Pour some of the warm apricot jam onto the cake, keeping it within the dam; spread to level, if needed. Top with the dacquoise layer, gently pressing it into position. Pipe on another buttercream dam and pour on more jam. Top with the other half of the cake layer, cut side down.

Applying the Crumb Coat Use a pastry brush to clean the cake circle and rid the cake layer of any stray crumbs in preparation for applying the first layer of buttercream, called the crumb coat because it seals the cake, assuring that crumbs do not mar the finished creation. The crumb coat is like a primer, an important element but one that does not demand perfection.

Put four dollops of buttercream on top of the cake, positioning them close to the points. Using an offset icing spatula, spread the buttercream across the top to get a smooth finish, then draw some of the buttercream down from the top to the sides and coat the sides. Go all the way down to the cardboard, covering the cut-to-size cardboard as though it were part of the cake, and make sure to get the points covered—they're the hardest; they seem to resist frosting. If at any time while you're working the buttercream softens, stop work and chill it. Having to chill the buttercream now and then may be a nuisance, but it will save your cake; you've worked on it too long to get impatient now. Don't worry about small imperfections. Remember that the point of this round of frosting is to cover the crumbs and set the base for the next round.

When you've coated the entire base layer, transfer it to the refrigerator (don't cover it) and start work on the next layer. Chill that layer and tackle the last layer.

Applying the Smooth Coat This is the coat that counts, but because the cake and crumb coat have been chilled, you'll find that applying this second layer of buttercream is actually easier than applying the first one was. Work on the base tier first. Using two large spatulas, transfer the cake on its cardboard base to the serving platter. Center the cake on the platter and tuck strips of parchment or waxed paper under the cake, tucking them in just ¼ to ½ inch and leaving enough of the paper exposed to protect the platter.

The smooth coat is applied in the same manner as the crumb coat. Put four dollops of buttercream on top of the layer, smooth the top, and draw down buttercream from the top to coat the sides and the points. Work slowly and carefully and chill the buttercream and/or the cake at the first signs of trouble. A neat trick to keep in mind if you hit an area that won't smooth is to run your metal icing spatula under hot water, wipe it dry, and smooth the buttercream. The little bit of heat is usually all that's needed to give you an even coating. As soon as the smooth coat lives up to its name, refrigerate the layer and complete the other two layers, keeping the middle and top tiers on their cardboard rounds.

Apply the smooth coat.

Storing The layers can now be wrapped and frozen for up to a month. It's best to freeze the layers unwrapped until the buttercream is firm and then to wrap the layers airtight. Thaw, still wrapped, in the refrigerator.

Stacking the Layers This is one of the many moments of truth in the building of this cake. Take the bottom and middle tiers out of the refrigerator. Insert 4 straws into the bottom layer, spacing them so that each is about 3 inches in from the points of the cake. Clip the straws so that they protrude ½ inch above the cake and slip 4 wooden skewers into the straws. Using the wire clippers, clip the skewers so that they're even with the straws.

Now, take a deep breath and lift the middle layer, with its cardboard base, onto the bottom tier, centering it in relation to the bottom layer and resting it on the straws and skewers. Don't worry about the space between the layers—it will be filled with your lovely marzipan fruits.

Insert 4 straws and skewers into the middle layer, spacing them so that 2 straws are 3 inches in from the ends of the long diagonal and 2 are 2½ inches in from the points of the short diagonal. Clip the tips of the straws and skewers, and lift the top tier into place.

To secure the entire cake you need a centering skewer; that's the 15-inch dowel that's sharpened at one end. Find the center of the top tier and plunge the dowel, pointed end down, into the cake, stopping when you reach the first cardboard base. Take courage and the hammer and tap the skewer down through the cardboard. Continue tapping until the dowel has pierced the middle cake layer, its cardboard, and the bottom cake layer and is resting on the bottom cardboard base. The top of the dowel will need to be clipped, but you don't have to do it now. In fact, it's handy to have it sticking up—you can hold on to it when you're maneuvering the cake.

When the construction is completed, put the cake back in the refrigerator to chill for a while. At this point, the cake is very heavy, so get help if you need it or move it in stages if you're working far from the refrigerator.

Piping the Bead Trim Before starting this phase, make sure your buttercream is still in good shape: Chill it if it needs it, or warm it if that's what it needs. Spoon the buttercream into the 12-inch pastry bag fitted with the ¼-inch plain tip.

All three layers of the cake are to be edged with small beads of buttercream. To make the beads, squeeze a tiny dot of buttercream onto the edge of a cake tier and lift the tip away with a slight twist. If you make little points when you

Edge with small beads of buttercream.

lift, that's OK; just be consistent and make points all over. If you round off the beads, that's fine too—consistency is what matters here. Pipe little beads, each one touching its neighbor, along the edges and down the points of each of the layers. The design will be spare but sophisticated.

Once again, if the buttercream softens, either in the pastry bag or on the cake, head for the refrigerator. When all of the trim is in place, chill the cake until you're ready to add the marzipan fruit, a job that should be done the same day you're going to serve the cake.

Storing The cake can now be refrigerated for 1 day. It's best to put it into a refrigerator box (available at baking specialty shops and home-moving supply houses), but it will keep for a day uncovered. Make sure that you have nothing in the refrigerator with a strong odor, since buttercream picks up odors.

Finishing the Cake All that's left to do is arrange the marzipan fruit over the cake, and this should be done the day of the wedding. Keep some light corn syrup and a fine paintbrush at hand. Before you start, use the heavy-duty clippers to cut the centering dowel as close to the cake as possible. Don't worry about getting it level—you'll cover the dowel with the marzipan fruits, and, if needed, you can make a little mound.

This is the fun part and it's all yours—there is no set pattern in which these decorations should be arranged, but there are some hints that might be helpful. If you didn't attach the cherry stems earlier, do so now by dipping the end of each stem in the corn syrup and touching it to a cherry. As you place the cherries, twist the stems to trail off decoratively. If you have spaces you want to cover, use the veined leaves; they're particularly good at the base of the cake, where the cardboard meets the serving platter, but don't think you have to cover every little space—make the spaces part of the design. And keep in mind Martha's advice: "It's your cake, and it's finished when you say it's finished."

Contributing Baker **MARTHA STEWART**

Cookies
THE LITTLEST CAKES

WHETHER SAUCER-SIZED and grabbed right out of a cookie jar or dainty and served on fine silver, few treats delight more than cookies. Here you'll find all-American favorites like Rick Katz's thin, rich, and moist brownies and a pair of after-school drop cookies—Double Chocolate Cookies and Mocha Chocolate Chips—given adult status with the addition of coffee powder and chunks of dark chocolate. There are Italian cookies from ace baking teacher Nick Malgieri that run the gamut from crackly, super-crunchy biscotti to soft amaretti and fig-filled X cookies, and a couple of cookies from Eastern Europe. Try Lauren Groveman's Rugelach (plump roll-ups of fruit-, nut-, and jam-filled pastry) or Gale Gand's Hungarian

Shortbread layered with rhubarb jam when you're yearning for old-fashioned flavors. These are the cookies you serve on the spur of the moment or as a middle-of-the-afternoon treat.

But there are other cookies, fancier and finer—more like small pastries—and you'll find these here as well. There are delicate but devilish Chocolate-Mint Nightcaps, a sandwich of cocoa cookies and mint ganache from Marcel Desaulniers, and meringue cookies in beautiful shapes from New York pastry chef Charlotte Akoto. For crispness, try David Blom's curved, paper-thin tuiles, and for those who take tea, this treasury offers the ultimate tea cookies, madeleines, made from Flo Braker's génoise batter.

Chocolate-Mint Nightcaps

Makes 2 dozen sandwich cookies ■ These cookies are made as simple drop cookies with a batter that spreads and bakes to wafer thinness. When you're ready to serve, the delicate cookies are sandwiched with thick, unquestionably chocolaty, subtly minty ganache and topped with a ganache spiral, the eponymous "nightcap."

THE GANACHE

12 ounces semisweet chocolate, coarsely chopped

1½ cups heavy cream

1 tablespoon chopped fresh mint

Put the chocolate in a bowl and keep close at hand. Bring the cream and the mint to a boil in a saucepan over medium-high heat. As soon as the cream reaches the boil, pour it through a medium-gauge strainer onto the chocolate; discard the mint. Whisk the ganache until it is smooth and then pour it out onto a clean jelly-roll pan. Spread the chocolate to the edges of the pan with a rubber spatula and refrigerate for 30 minutes. (Spreading the chocolate in a thin layer hastens its chilling.) *The ganache can be made a few days ahead and stored, covered, in the refrigerator. If, when you're ready to use the ganache, it has chilled too much and is unworkable, just let it warm a bit at room temperature—it will be shiny and easily spreadable, the texture you want, in a few minutes.*

THE COOKIES

1½ cups cake flour

¼ cup unsweetened cocoa powder

¾ teaspoon baking powder

¼ teaspoon salt

2 sticks (8 ounces) unsalted butter, at room temperature

¾ cup sugar

4 large eggs

1 teaspoon pure vanilla extract

Set one oven rack in the center position and the other at the top and preheat the oven to 300°F. Line four baking sheets with parchment paper. (If you do not have four baking sheets, cut four pieces of parchment, drop the batter on the parchment as instructed, and bake in batches, transferring the batter-filled parchment to baking sheets as they become available—just remember to cool the baking sheets before using them again.)

Sift together the flour, cocoa, baking powder, and salt onto a sheet of waxed paper and reserve.

continued

Beat the butter and sugar for 2 minutes at medium speed in a mixer fitted with the paddle attachment or with a hand-held mixer; scrape down the bowl, increase the speed to high, and beat 1 minute more, until the mixture is pale and creamy. With the mixer at medium speed, add the eggs one at a time, beating until each egg is fully incorporated and scraping down the paddle and sides of the bowl as needed. Add the vanilla extract and beat for 30 seconds, then add the dry ingredients, mixing just 30 seconds more. Remove the bowl from the mixer and use a rubber spatula to finish mixing in the dry ingredients.

Baking the Cookies Drop a heaping teaspoonful of batter for each cookie onto the parchment-lined baking sheets, making 12 cookies per sheet and leaving room between each cookie for spreading. Bake the cookies, two sheets at a time, for 7 to 8 minutes, or until the cookies have just set, rotating the baking sheets top to bottom and front to back after 3 minutes. Cool on the baking sheets. Repeat with the remaining sheets of cookies. When completely cool, lift the cookies off the parchment and store in an airtight container until ready to assemble. The unfilled cookies can be kept in an airtight container at room temperature for 2 days or frozen for a month.

Assembling the Nightcaps To construct the nightcaps, spoon the ganache into a pastry bag fitted with a plain ¼-inch tip. Pipe about 1 tablespoon of ganache onto the tops of 24 of the cookies. Center 24 more cookies (domed side up) on the ganache and press them into place to make neat sandwiches. To form the "nightcap," decorate the top of each sandwich by piping about a teaspoonful of ganache in a small circle that spirals upward on itself (coil on top of coil) and ends in a curving point created by pulling away from the circle and letting a bit of the chocolate taper toward the edge of the cookie. Serve the cookies immediately.

Storing Both the ganache and the cookies can be made ahead. However, the nightcaps should be served soon after they are assembled.

Contributing Baker **MARCEL DESAULNIERS**

Meringue Cookies

COLOR PHOTOGRAPH, PAGE 218

Makes about 5 dozen cookies ■ Brittle, snap-crackly-and-crunchy cookies made from meringue can be simple or fanciful. Piping the cookies out with a plain tip in short sticks will give you a very basic cookie; fitting your decorating tube with a star tip and piping out shells, stars, and curlicues will produce whimsical cookies. Leave them plain and they'll be elegant little espresso go-alongs; sandwich them with bittersweet chocolate, luxurious buttercream, or berry-red jam and you've got the stuff of petits fours, perfect for Champagne.

1 recipe plain Meringue (page 37)

Position the racks to divide the oven into thirds and preheat the oven to between 175°F and 200°F. Cut parchment paper sheets to fit two large baking sheets or jelly-roll pans.

Gently spoon the meringue into a large grease-free pastry bag fitted with a star tip.

Lift each corner of the parchment paper and pipe out a little dab of meringue to glue the paper to the baking sheets. Pipe out rows of cookies in any variety of shapes that appeals to you. (See page 312 for piping instructions.) You can pipe the cookies close to one another, as these don't really spread. The number you get from a batch will depend on the size of the cookies you pipe, but you'll probably have about 5 dozen.

Baking the Cookies Bake the cookies for 45 minutes to 1 hour, keeping an eye on them. The finished meringues should be dry and crisp but still white—pull them from the oven the instant they take on any color (and turn your oven down slightly if they color quickly—it may be too hot). Slide the parchment paper off the baking sheets and onto cooling racks. When the cookies are cool, lift them off the paper—they should come off without a hitch. If you have a problem, run a spatula under the cookies. The cooled cookies are ready to serve or to frost, dip in chocolate, or spread with jam.

Storing Meringues will keep for a few days, if not weeks, if you store them in a cool, dry place. They must be kept airtight, because they turn chewy when the air around them is moist or humid. If you're not planning to do any more baking for a while, a turned-off oven is a great place to keep meringues—but don't forget they're in there.

continued

Top left: Stars.

Top right: Shells.

Bottom left: Logs.

Bottom right: S cookies.

Traditional Meringue Shapes

- **Rosettes or stars,** easily made by holding the tip directly above the baking sheet, applying a little pressure on the bag, and lifting the bag with a jerk to cut off the flow of meringue when the rosette is the size you want

- **Shells,** made by holding the tip at a 45-degree angle to the sheet and piping out a small mound of meringue, then lifting the bag a smidgen and pulling it toward you, piping about ½ inch of meringue as you go, and ending with the tip scraping against the sheet

- **Logs,** the simplest shape to make—just squeeze and stop when the log is as long as you want it; the firmer the squeeze, the plumper the log

- **S cookies,** created by holding the bag upright and, keeping the pressure steady, just drawing the letter S—these are prettiest when each cookie is piped into a tight, very plump S that resembles a figure eight

Contributing Baker **CHARLOTTE AKOTO**

Crispy Cocoa Cookies

Makes about 5½ dozen cookies ■ You can serve these as part of the chocolate extravaganza described on page 383, but these rolled-to-within-a-micrometer-of-their-life cookies are simple and lovely by themselves.

1¾ cups all-purpose flour

Pinch of salt

Pinch of baking powder

1½ sticks (6 ounces) unsalted butter, at room temperature

1 cup confectioner's sugar

2 tablespoons unsweetened cocoa powder

1 teaspoon pure vanilla extract

1 large egg yolk

1 tablespoon milk

Granulated sugar, for topping

Put the flour, salt, and baking powder on a piece of parchment or waxed paper; mix together lightly and set aside.

Put the butter into the bowl of a mixer fitted with the paddle attachment (or work with a hand-held mixer) and beat on medium speed just to cream. Add the confectioner's sugar, cocoa, and vanilla and turn the machine on and off a few times to get the dry ingredients incorporated without having them fly out of the bowl. Once the mixture comes together, beat on high speed for 1 minute. Decrease the mixer speed to low and add the yolk and milk. Mix on low to blend, then use a rubber spatula to scrape down the paddle and the sides of the bowl. Using the parchment paper as a funnel, add the flour mixture all at once, pulsing again so that the dry ingredients don't fly around, then, mixing on low, give the dough a few turns until it comes together again.

Turn the dough out onto a floured work surface and dust the dough lightly with flour. Working with a bit of dough at a time, smear the dough across the work surface with the heel of your hand. Gather the dough together, pat it into a rough rectangle, and cut it in half. Wrap each half in plastic and refrigerate until firm, at least 1 hour. *The dough can be made ahead to this point and refrigerated for up to 2 days or frozen for up to a month.*

Baking the Cookies Position the racks to divide the oven into thirds and preheat the oven to 350°F. Line two baking sheets with parchment paper.

Take one piece of dough out of the refrigerator and cut it in half. Work with one half at a time, keeping the other piece refrigerated. Tamp the dough down with a few presses of the rolling pin. Flour the work surface, flour the top of the dough, and roll out the dough, rolling all the way to, but not over, the edges of the dough, until it is as thin as you can possibly roll it, no thicker than 1/16 inch. Don't worry if the dough tears or cracks; you can cut out cookies around the cracks. Dip a 3-inch fluted round cookie or biscuit cutter into flour and cut out as many cookies as you can. Slide a metal spatula under the dough, then lift the cookies onto the baking sheets; sprinkle each cookie with a little granulated sugar. Bake for 10 to 12 minutes, or until the cookies are crisp and firm. Transfer the baking sheets to cooling racks and allow the cookies to cool on the pans. Repeat with the rest of the dough.

Storing The cookies can be stored at room temperature in airtight tins for up to 3 days or wrapped and frozen for up to a month. Thaw, still wrapped, at room temperature.

Contributing Baker **DAVID OGONOWSKI**

Cantuccini
COLOR PHOTOGRAPH, PAGE 223

Makes about 8 dozen biscotti ■ All Italian cookies are called *biscotti,* but these are what we think of as classic biscotti. Twice-baked cookies, they are first baked in a log shape, then sliced and baked again until they're dry and very crunchy. (Because they contain no butter or other fat, except that contained in the eggs, they can bake to a formidable state of crunchiness.) The techniques used to make these can't-stop-eating-them biscotti are, like the cookies themselves, classic; you'll find them somewhat different from those used for the Hazelnut Biscotti (page 315).

The traditional accompaniment is vin santo, but they're great with espresso or tea. No matter the libation, they're meant to be dipped.

2 cups all-purpose flour

¾ cup sugar

2 teaspoons baking powder

½ teaspoon cinnamon

¼ teaspoon salt

1½ cups unblanched whole almonds

3 large eggs

2 teaspoons pure vanilla extract

Position a rack in the center of the oven and preheat the oven to 350°F. Line a baking sheet with parchment and set aside.

Put the flour, sugar, baking powder, cinnamon, and salt in a large bowl and stir with a rubber spatula to mix. Stir in the almonds.

Whisk the eggs and vanilla together in a small bowl, then stir them into the flour mixture. The dough may seem dry at this point, but it will come together as it is kneaded.

Turn the dough out onto a lightly floured work surface and knead, folding it over onto itself until it is smooth, 1 to 2 minutes. Divide the dough in half and shape each half into a 12-inch-long log. Gently press down on the logs to flatten them until they are about 2 inches wide and 1 inch high. Transfer them to the prepared pan.

First Baking Bake the logs for about 30 minutes, or until they are slightly risen and firm to the touch. Slide the logs, parchment paper and all, off the baking sheet and onto a cooling rack. The logs must be completely cool before you can continue with the recipe. Since they will take about 30 minutes to cool, you can either turn the oven off or leave it on for the next step. *You can bake the biscotti up to this point several days ahead. Wrap the logs well in plastic and continue when it's convenient.*

Second Baking When the logs have cooled completely, preheat the oven to 350°F, if necessary. Line two baking sheets with parchment paper.

Working with a sharp serrated knife, cut the cooled logs diagonally into ¼-inch-thick slices. Place the sliced cookies cut side down on the pans and bake for 10 to 15 minutes, or until the biscotti are crisp and golden. Cool on the pans.

Storing These biscotti will keep for up to a month in an airtight tin or plastic container.

Contributing Baker **NICK MALGIERI**

Hazelnut Biscotti

COLOR PHOTOGRAPH, PAGE 221

Makes about 4 dozen biscotti ■ It's the baking soda in the dough that gives these biscotti their wonderful open, crunchy texture. Although they'll tenderize over the course of a few days (if they last that long), just-baked, they're exceptionally dry and crackly. It's also baking soda that makes easy work of the usually pesky job of peeling hazelnuts—they're boiled in a baking soda bath and emerge ready to shed their skins in a flash.

This recipe can be doubled and the choice of nuts varied. You can make the biscotti with almonds, pistachios, or even peanuts; you can add raisins, or try chocolate chips. And you can make the dough easily either by hand or in a mixer with a paddle. If you choose the mixer, whisk the dry ingredients together in a bowl, beat the liquid ingredients and sugar in the mixer, then add the dry ingredients to the liquid and continue with the recipe.

2 cups water
3 tablespoons baking soda
2/3 cup unblanched hazelnuts

1 2/3 cups all-purpose flour
1/2 teaspoon baking soda
1/4 teaspoon salt
2 large eggs
2 teaspoons hazelnut liqueur, such as Frangelico, or brandy
1 teaspoon pure vanilla extract
3/4 cup sugar

Center a rack in the oven and preheat the oven to 350°F.

Preparing the Nuts To skin the hazelnuts, bring the water to a boil in a medium saucepan, add the baking soda and the nuts, and boil for 3 to 5 minutes, until the water turns black. To test if the skins have loosened sufficiently, drop a nut into a bowl of cold water and rub lightly against the skin—if the skin just slides off, the nuts are ready to go. Turn the nuts into a colander and run cold water over them. Slip off the skins, toss the nuts onto a towel, pat dry, and transfer to a jelly-roll pan.

Place the pan in the oven and toast the nuts, stirring occasionally, for about 15 minutes, or until evenly browned. The best way to test for total toastiness is to bite into a nut—it should be brown to the center. Remove the nuts from the oven and cool. Lower the oven temperature to 300°F.

When the nuts are cool enough to handle, coarsely chop them and set them aside.

continued

Line a baking sheet with parchment paper and reserve until needed.

Making the Dough Put the flour, baking soda, and salt into a medium bowl and whisk just to blend.

In another bowl, whisk together the eggs, liqueur, vanilla, and sugar. Add the dry ingredients to the liquid and stir with a wooden spoon to mix. Add the nuts and continue to mix, just until well incorporated. (Since this dough is stiff, sticky, and hard to stir, you might find it easier just to reach in and mix it with your hands.)

Flour your hands and lift half of the dough onto one side of the parchment-lined baking sheet. Pat and squeeze the dough into a chubby log 12 to 13 inches long. Don't worry about being neat or smoothing the dough—it will even out as much as it needs to in the oven. Repeat with the other half of the dough, leaving about 3 inches between the logs.

First Baking Bake the logs for exactly 35 minutes. Transfer the pan to a cooling rack and let cool for at least 10 minutes. *At this point, the logs can remain on the pan overnight, if that's more convenient for you.*

Second Baking Using a serrated knife, cut the logs into ½-inch-thick slices, cutting straight across or diagonally. (You can make the biscotti thinner or thicker, as you wish, and adjust the baking time accordingly.) Lay the biscotti on their sides on a cooling rack—you may need to use a second rack—then place the cooling rack in the 300°F oven, directly on an oven rack. (Baking the biscotti like this allows the oven's heat to circulate around the cookies, so there's no need to turn them over.) The cookies may need to bake for as long as 15 minutes, but it's a good idea to start checking them after about 10 minutes. When the biscotti are golden brown, dry, and crisp, remove the cooling rack(s) from the oven. Let the cookies cool to room temperature before packing them for storage.

Storing The cookies will keep in an airtight container for about a month.

Contributing Baker **ALICE MEDRICH**

Cornmeal-Currant Biscotti
COLOR PHOTOGRAPH, PAGE 222

Makes 2½ to 3 dozen biscotti ■ Among pastry lovers, Venice is known for its cookies, and among the best known are these cornmeal-currant biscotti called *zaleti,* Venetian for "little yellow things." In northern Italy, cornmeal is a common ingredient in desserts, and in Venice, zaleti are as common as chocolate chip cookies are in the States. Traditionally made in diamond shapes, they also can be made like classic biscotti—i.e., sliced and twice-baked; see the box on page 318.

1 cup yellow cornmeal, preferably stone-ground

1 cup all-purpose flour

1/3 cup sugar

1 teaspoon baking powder

1/4 teaspoon salt

1 stick (4 ounces) cold unsalted butter, cut into 6 to 8 pieces

1 cup plump currants (or raisins)

1 large egg

1 large egg yolk

1 teaspoon grated lemon zest

1 teaspoon pure vanilla extract

Position a rack in the center of the oven and preheat the oven to 350°F. Line a baking sheet with parchment and set aside.

Put the cornmeal, flour, sugar, baking powder, and salt in a large bowl and stir with a rubber spatula to blend. Add the butter to the bowl and, working with your fingertips or a pastry blender, rub the pieces into the dry ingredients until the mixture resembles coarse meal. Don't worry if there are a few lumps; you'll work them out as you knead the dough later. Stir in the currants.

Whisk the egg, egg yolk, lemon zest, and vanilla together in a small bowl, then, with your fingers or a rubber spatula, stir them into the flour mixture. At this point, the dough won't come together in the bowl and it may seem a little dry, but if you pinch a bit between your fingers, it will hold together.

Clockwise from left:
X Cookies (page 318),
Cornmeal-Currant
Biscotti, and Cantuccini
(page 313).

Turn the dough out onto a lightly floured work surface and knead briefly, folding the dough over onto itself a few times, until smooth. Cut the dough into 4 pieces and shape each piece into a 12-inch-long log. Press down gently on the logs with your palms to flatten them slightly and then cut the logs on the diagonal every 1½ inches to make 7 or 8 diamonds from each log. Transfer the diamonds to the prepared pan. Since the ends of the logs will not form perfectly shaped diamonds, set the scraps aside, and then, after all the logs have been cut, gather them together and shape them into a mini-log. Flatten the log, angle each end by pressing it with the back of your knife, and cut into diamonds.

Baking the Cookies Bake the cookies for 12 to 15 minutes, or until they are a light golden color, firm to the touch, and just slightly puffed. Check after 5 minutes to see if the bottoms of the biscotti are browning too quickly; if so, slip a second baking sheet under the first one. Slide the cookies, parchment paper and all, off the baking sheet and onto a rack to cool. (To make classically shaped biscotti, see the box on page 318.)

Storing Diamond-shaped cookies will keep for up to a week in an airtight tin or plastic container; twice-baked biscotti will keep for about a month similarly stored.

continued

Classically Shaped Biscotti

After the dough has been kneaded, cut it in half and shape into 2 logs, each about 12 inches long. Flatten the logs slightly—they should be about ¾ inch high—and place on a parchment-lined baking sheet. Bake the logs in a preheated 350°F oven for 15 to 20 minutes, or until they are firm to the touch and just a little puffed. Let cool completely, then use a thin sharp serrated knife to carefully cut them into ⅓-inch-thick slices. Lay the cookies on parchment-lined baking sheets and bake for another 10 to 15 minutes, until they're lightly toasted. The biscotti may still be a bit soft, but they'll crisp as they cool. Cool the biscotti on the pans. (Makes 5 to 6 dozen.)

Contributing Baker **NICK MALGIERI**

X Cookies

COLOR PHOTOGRAPH, PAGES 222 TO 223

Makes about 5 dozen cookies ■ This interpretation of a Sicilian favorite is reminiscent of Fig Newtons, the classiest Fig Newtons in creation. Both the sumptuous filling, a mix of dried fruits, toasted almonds, sweet preserves, rum, and chocolate, and the sweet dough, a pasta frolla, are made quickly in the food processor. The dough is one you'll use repeatedly—it's the same dough that lines the Sweet Ricotta Pie (page 376) and even the savory Pizza Rustica (page 430). It's not only versatile, it's foolproof—you can knead and roll without a care since it's almost impossible to overwork.

THE DOUGH

    4 cups all-purpose flour

    ⅔ cup sugar

    1 teaspoon baking powder

    1 teaspoon salt

    2 sticks (8 ounces) cold unsalted butter or ½ pound cold lard,
      cut into 12 pieces

    4 large eggs

Put the flour, sugar, baking powder, and salt in the work bowl of a food processor fitted with the metal blade; pulse just to mix. Add the butter pieces to the bowl and pulse 15 to 20 times to cut the butter into the dry ingredients. Add the eggs and pulse until the dough forms a ball on the blade. Remove the dough from the processor and knead it briefly on a lightly floured work surface until it is smooth. Shape the dough into a log and wrap it in plastic; set aside while you make the filling. (You'll be using the food processor for the next step, so there's no need to wash it.)

THE FILLING

One 12-ounce package dried Calimyrna or Mission figs

¹/₂ cup unblanched almonds, toasted and coarsely chopped

¹/₃ cup apricot preserves

¹/₄ cup plump golden raisins

¹/₄ cup candied orange peel, diced

2 ounces semisweet chocolate, chopped

¹/₄ cup dark rum

¹/₂ teaspoon cinnamon

1 large egg beaten with a pinch of salt, for egg wash
Confectioner's sugar, for dusting

Remove the stems from the figs and cut the figs into medium-size dice. The figs should be soft and moist, the kind you'd like to eat out of hand. If they are hard, they won't improve during baking, so they need to be plumped: Cover them with boiling water and allow them to steep for 5 minutes, then drain well and carry on. Put the figs and the rest of the filling ingredients into the work bowl of the food processor and pulse with the metal blade until the mixture is finely chopped. Scrape the filling onto a lightly floured work surface. Knead the filling to blend it, and shape it into a rough log. Cut the log into 12 pieces.

Position the racks to divide the oven into thirds and preheat the oven to 350°F. Line two baking sheets with parchment paper and set aside.

Assembling the Cookies Divide the dough into 12 pieces. Working with one piece of dough at a time, on a lightly floured work surface, roll the dough under your hands to form a 12-inch rope. Use a rolling pin to roll the rope into a 3- by 12-inch rectangle. (Actually, because of the eggs, butter, and sugar, the dough is very soft and extremely easy to work, so easy that you can pat it out rather than roll it out with the pin if you prefer.) Run a blunt knife under the dough just to make certain it hasn't stuck to the work surface and brush the top of the dough with egg wash. Roll a piece of filling into a 12-inch rope and center it on the rolled-out dough. Pull the dough up around the filling, making a seam, and roll it into a cylinder, lengthening the dough a little as you roll so that the cylinder ends up about 15 inches long. Cut into 2¹/₂- to 3-inch lengths. (Once you've cut the first length, use it as a measuring guide for cutting the others.)

Place a cut piece of dough vertically in front of you, seam side down, and make two 1-inch-long cuts, one from the bottom, the other from the top, toward the center. Use your fingers to separate the slashes and create an X-shaped cookie. Transfer the cookies to the prepared baking pans and repeat with the remaining portions of dough and filling.

Top: Cutting the logs into cookie lengths.
Center: Slashing the dough.
Bottom: Separating the slashed dough to form the X.

continued

Baking the Cookies Bake the cookies for 15 to 20 minutes, or until they are a light golden color. Transfer to racks to cool. Just before serving, dust the cookies with confectioner's sugar.

Storing The cookies will keep for a week in a tightly sealed tin or plastic container.

Contributing Baker **NICK MALGIERI**

Amaretti

Makes about 3 dozen cookies ■ *Amaretti* means "little bitter things," from the practice, common in Italy, of using both sweet and bitter almonds in the dough. (Bitter almonds cannot be imported into the United States.) Here, these not-at-all-bitter macaroons are made with almond paste, the best of which is available in bulk at specialty markets or in cans at supermarkets. For cookies that have that characteristic thin, crisp outside and soft, chewy interior, avoid almond paste packaged in tubes—it has more sugar than the canned kind and won't produce a cookie with superior consistency.

> **One 8-ounce can almond paste**
> **¾ cup sugar**
> **2 large egg whites, beaten just to break up**
> **¼ pound (approximately) pine nuts (optional)**

Position a rack in the center of the oven and preheat the oven to 325°F. Line two baking sheets with parchment or brown paper and set aside.

Cut the almond paste into ½-inch cubes and toss into the bowl of a mixer fitted with the paddle attachment (or work with a hand-held mixer). Add half the sugar and mix on low speed until the paste is broken into small crumbs. Add the rest of the sugar and continue to mix until the crumbs are very fine, about 2 minutes. Add the egg whites in 3 to 4 additions, scraping down the bowl when the mixture starts to stick to the bottom and beating until the batter is free of lumps. You don't want to beat a lot of air into this mixture, because it will cause the amaretti to rise in the oven and then fall—what you're after is a nice, even puff that persists.

Piping the Cookies Fit a pastry bag with a ¾-inch plain tip and pipe the dough into mounds on the lined baking sheets, making each amaretti about 1¼ inches in diameter and ½ inch high; leave about 1½ inches between cookies. Alternatively, you can use a small scoop to form the amaretti, using about a tablespoon of batter for each cookie.

Just before baking, wet a cotton or linen kitchen towel (terry won't work) and gently squeeze the excess water from it; don't wring the towel out—you want it to be wet. Fold the towel into a strip 2 inches wide and, holding one end of the towel in each hand and letting the center droop, gently dab the tops of the cookies with the center of the wet cloth. Use an up-and-down motion to pat the cookies with the towel several times, until their tops are smooth, slightly flattened, and glistening. (Wetting the tops like this will remove the piping ridges and will help produce the crinkly top that is typical of these cookies.) If you're using the pine nuts, press them gently onto the amaretti.

Flatten and smooth the tops with a damp towel.

Baking the Cookies Bake the amaretti until they are well risen, lightly colored, and covered with fine cracks, 15 to 20 minutes. Transfer the cookies, parchment paper and all, to racks and cool completely.

Gently peel the amaretti off the paper. If any of the cookies stick, just lift the paper, brush the underside with a little hot water, and give it a few seconds to seep in, then peel off the cookie.

Storing Kept in an airtight tin or plastic container, amaretti will remain moist and chewy for a few days, then become dry and crisp.

Contributing Baker **NICK MALGIERI**

Tuiles

Makes about 3 dozen cookies ■ Fancy caramely cookies that are as easy to make as drop cookies. As soon as the cookies come off the baking sheet, they're pressed against a rolling pin so that they cool in a graceful curve, earning them their name, *tuile*, French for "tile" and a reference to the arched tile roofs of French country homes and châteaux. After the batter is mixed, it needs a long chilling in the refrigerator, so plan ahead.

½ **cup heavy cream**

½ **stick (2 ounces) unsalted butter, cut into 8 pieces**

⅛ **teaspoon pure vanilla extract**

¾ **cup coarsely ground blanched almonds**

⅔ **cup sugar**

2 **tablespoons all-purpose flour**

Grated zest of 1 orange

2 **ounces (approximately) semisweet chocolate, melted, for decoration (optional)**

continued

Put the heavy cream and butter in a small saucepan and heat over medium heat until the butter melts. Remove the pan from the heat and stir in the vanilla.

Put the almonds, sugar, flour, and zest in a medium bowl and stir with a rubber spatula. Add the warm cream mixture and stir with the spatula just until the batter is smooth.

Chilling the Batter Cover the batter with plastic wrap and refrigerate until thoroughly chilled and thickened, preferably overnight. *The batter can be made ahead, wrapped airtight, and kept refrigerated for up to 4 days.*

Baking the Cookies When you are ready to bake, position a rack in the center or lower third of the oven and preheat the oven to 325°F. Set aside two nonstick baking sheets and a rolling pin, wine bottle, or other cylinder on which you can mold the tuiles.

Stir the chilled batter briefly, just in case it has separated. Drop the batter onto the baking sheets, allowing 1 teaspoon of batter for each tuile and leaving about 2 inches between each one. There's no need to even out the batter; it's a self-spreader.

Bake the cookies for 5 to 8 minutes, just until they spread and turn a honey brown. Don't leave the kitchen—these go from almost done to overdone in a blink. Transfer the pans to cooling racks and let the cookies set for about 30 seconds.

Shaping the Cookies If you have baker's fingers (aka asbestos fingers), slide the cookies back and forth a bit on the baking sheet to release them, then pick them up, one by one, and lay them on the rolling pin. Alternatively, slide a wide metal spatula under the cookies and lift them onto the rolling pin. Either way, use your fingers to press the tuile lightly against the pin to get a nice curve. The cookies will mold and cool in a few seconds, so remove the shaped cookies as you need room on the rolling pin. If the cookies cool and are hard to remove from the baking sheets, just put the sheet back into the oven for a minute and then continue.

Repeat with the rest of the batter, making sure that the baking sheets cool between batches.

Decorating the Cookies To decorate the cookies, scrape the melted chocolate into a small parchment-paper piping cone or a zipper-lock plastic bag. Snip a tiny hole in the cone or bag and pipe very thin lines across the tuiles. If you're not up to piping, you can get a very attractive finish just by dipping the tines of a fork into the chocolate and waving it back and forth across the cookies; you're not aiming for symmetry here. Serve as soon as the chocolate sets.

Storing As delicate as these are, they can be kept if you take care. Stack tuiles between sheets of parchment or waxed paper in a tightly sealed container and store for up to 2 days.

Contributing Baker **DAVID BLOM**

Pizzelle

Makes about 2 dozen wafers ▪ These are the wafers you find fanned out atop a scoop of gelato or served alongside fresh sugared berries in Italy. They are among the simplest cookies to make—the batter is whisked together in under five minutes and the wafers are baked on fancifully imprinted pizzelle irons in less than half that time. Traditionally flavored with anisette, crispy pizzelle can take vanilla or almond extract or a few spoonfuls of freshly grated lemon zest. Whether you use a hand-held, over-the-burner iron or an electric iron, follow the manufacturer's directions when it comes to seasoning and greasing it.

1¼ cups all-purpose flour
1½ teaspoons baking powder
2 large eggs
Pinch of salt
½ cup sugar
1 tablespoon anisette or 1 teaspoon pure anise extract
¾ stick (3 ounces) unsalted butter, melted and cooled

Confectioner's sugar, for dusting

Preheat the pizzelle iron, and grease or spray it if suggested in the manufacturer's instructions. Set out a cooling rack for the baked cookies.

Put the flour and baking powder in a medium bowl and whisk to blend; set aside.

In another bowl, whisk together the eggs and salt until foamy, then gradually whisk in the sugar. When the mixture is smooth, whisk in the liqueur or extract, followed by the melted butter. Switch to a rubber spatula and fold in the reserved dry ingredients. You'll have a shiny, fairly thick batter that mounds easily on a spoon.

Baking the Pizzelle Using about 2 teaspoons of batter for each pizzelle, place the batter in the center of the iron, close the iron, and bake for about 2 minutes, or until golden and firm. Don't open the iron to peek until the steam stops. As soon as the pizzelle is baked, remove from the iron to the cooling rack and continue making pizzelle with the remaining batter. Should any of the pizzelle need coaxing to come off the iron, nudge them with a spatula or fork and then peel them off with your fingers. If you want to cut the pizzelle into quarters or roll them into cones, do so the instant they come off the iron, piping hot and still pliable. Dust with confectioner's sugar before serving.

Storing Stacked between sheets of waxed paper in an airtight container, pizzelle will keep at room temperature for at least 1 week.

Contributing Baker **NICK MALGIERI**

Gingersnaps

Makes about 2 dozen cookies ■ The dough for these dark, mildly spiced cookies is quickly made and can be rolled out into snaps. But if you double the
recipe, you'll have enough dough to turn out a large family of molasses-glazed
gingerpeople to be strung for Christmas decorations or nibbled with cider.

¼ **cup sugar**

3 **tablespoons unsulfured molasses**

2 **tablespoons unsalted butter, at room temperature**

⅛ **teaspoon ginger**

⅛ **teaspoon cinnamon**

⅛ **teaspoon baking soda**

⅛ **teaspoon salt**

1½ **tablespoons water**

¾ **cup all-purpose flour**

1 **tablespoon unsulfured molasses mixed with 1 tablespoon water,
  for glaze**

Put the sugar, molasses, butter, spices, baking soda, and salt in the bowl of
a mixer fitted with the paddle attachment (or work with a hand-held mixer).
Mix on medium-low speed just to cream the ingredients, about 2 minutes. Add
the water and flour and mix on low until the dough comes together, about 30
seconds.

Chilling the Dough Scrape the dough onto a piece of plastic wrap. Shape the
dough into a rough square or rectangle, wrap in the plastic, and refrigerate to
firm, about 2 hours. *You can make the dough ahead and refrigerate it for 2 or 3
days or freeze it for up to a month.*

Position the racks to divide the oven into thirds and preheat the oven to
325°F. Set aside two nonstick baking sheets or lightly grease two baking sheets.

Rolling and Cutting Place the chilled dough on a lightly floured work surface.
(Even after a long chill, the dough will be very soft and sticky, so you'll have to
flour the top of the dough and keep checking on the bottom, dusting the
counter with more flour as needed.) Use a rolling pin to roll the dough to a
thickness of between ⅛ and ¼ inch, taking care to roll up to but not over the
edges. Try to keep a square or rectangular shape—you'll be able to cut more
cookies than if you roll a circle.

Dip a small (about 2-inch) cookie cutter into flour and cut as many cookies
as you can. Place the cookies on the baking sheets, leaving just a bit of room
between each one—these barely spread. (Gather the scraps of dough together,
wrap them in plastic, and refrigerate until they are cool enough to roll again.)
Using a pastry brush, paint a light coating of the molasses glaze over each cookie.

Baking the Cookies Bake the cookies for 5 to 7 minutes, or until just slightly firm. Lift the cookies off the baking sheets and onto cooling racks with a wide metal spatula. The cookies will crisp as they cool.

Storing Gingersnaps will keep in a tightly sealed tin or plastic container for about 4 days.

Contributing Baker **DAVID BLOM**

Rugelach
COLOR PHOTOGRAPH, PAGE 228

Makes about 4 dozen cookies ■ These are probably the most abundantly stuffed, generously sized rugelach you'll ever come across—the most delicious too. The dough for these rolled-like-a-jelly-roll, filled-to-bursting cookies is a cream cheese dough, rich, sweet, flaky, and a pleasure to work with—made quickly, it rolls easily and can be used to line tartlet pans for both sweet and savory fillings or to make turnovers. And the filling—layer after layer of wonderful dried fruits and fruit butter. Don't skimp on the quality of the dried fruits you use for the filling, nor on the variety, for this is what makes the cookies so remarkable. The dough is spread with very thick prune or apricot butter (known as lekvar), either homemade or store-bought, sprinkled with cinnamon sugar, studded with nuts, and strewn with plump, moist pieces of dried fruit. Absolutely excessive, but exceedingly good.

THE CREAM CHEESE PASTRY

> 3 sticks (12 ounces) unsalted butter, at room temperature
>
> 12 ounces cream cheese, at room temperature
>
> ½ teaspoon salt
>
> ¼ cup sugar
>
> 3 cups unbleached all-purpose flour

Beat the butter, cream cheese, and salt together until smooth in a mixer fitted with the paddle attachment. Mixing on medium-low, gradually add the sugar and beat until light. Reduce the speed to low and add the flour, mixing only until the dough comes together. Turn the dough out onto a counter and work it gently into a ball. Divide the dough in half and press each half into a rough rectangle.

Chilling the Dough Wrap each half in plastic and refrigerate until firm, about 2 hours. *The dough can be wrapped well and stored in the refrigerator for up to 2 days. It can also be frozen for a month; thaw, still wrapped, in the refrigerator.*

continued

THE FILLING AND TOPPING

2 cups granulated sugar

½ cup (packed) light brown sugar

3½ tablespoons cinnamon

3½ cups coarsely chopped assorted toasted nuts (such as macadamias, pecans, walnuts, almonds, and/or hazelnuts)

2 cups (approximately) thick apricot or prune lekvar, homemade (pages 449 and 448) or store-bought

2 cups assorted dried fruits (such as Medjool dates, Calimyrna figs, Turkish apricots, raisins, and/or cherries), diced if large, plumped if dry (see page 10)

1 large egg beaten with 1 tablespoon cream or milk, for egg wash

Whisk together ½ cup of the granulated sugar, the brown sugar, and 1 tablespoon of the cinnamon in a small bowl and set aside.

Put the remaining 1½ cups granulated sugar, 2½ tablespoons cinnamon, and 1½ cups of the assorted nuts into the work bowl of a food processor and pulse until the nuts are finely chopped. Turn into a bowl and reserve for topping the rugelach.

Line a baking sheet with waxed paper.

Rolling and Filling Working with one piece of the chilled dough at a time, place it on a lightly floured work surface or pastry cloth and let it soften for a few minutes. Flour your rolling pin and roll the dough into a rectangle 14 inches by 10 inches and ¼ inch thick. Don't be tempted to roll the dough thinner—you need a sturdy wrapper for all the chunky filling ingredients. Trim the edges of the dough and, using a long knife or a pizza cutter, cut the dough in half lengthwise, to make two 14- by 5-inch rectangles; leave the halves in place.

Spread each half generously with one quarter of the prune or apricot lekvar. Sprinkle with one quarter of the brown sugar–cinnamon mixture, pressing it lightly with your fingers to spread it evenly if necessary, then finish by strewing ½ cup of the remaining chopped nuts and ½ cup of the dried fruit over each dough half. Starting with a long edge of dough, roll up each rectangle jelly-roll fashion, tucking in any fruit or nuts that fall out along the way.

Chilling the Dough Transfer the rolls to the paper-lined baking sheet and roll and fill the remaining dough. Cover the rolls with plastic wrap and refrigerate until firm, at least 4 hours or preferably overnight.

Position the oven racks so that they divide the oven into thirds and preheat the oven to 375°F. Line two baking sheets with parchment paper. If possible, double up the baking sheets, a precaution against burning the sugar on the bottom of the rugelach. Push the egg wash through a sieve and reserve.

Slicing and Baking Although you can bake two rolls' worth at a time, you will probably have to bake these in batches, so work with one roll of dough at a time. Brush the roll all over with the egg wash. Using a serrated knife and a sawing motion, slice the roll into pieces that are 1 to 1½ inches wide. Toss each slice in the cinnamon-sugar-nut mixture to coat generously (you may need to press the topping onto the rugelach with your fingers). Transfer the rugelach to the prepared baking sheets, cut sides down, leaving an inch between each pastry. Bake for 25 to 30 minutes, rotating the pans top to bottom and front to back halfway through the baking period. The rugelach are done when the tops are golden and the bottoms are caramelized. Cool the pastries on the pans for 5 to 10 minutes, then release them from the parchment by running a thin spatula under them. Cool to room temperature on a rack. Repeat with the remaining rolls of dough.

Storing The rugelach will keep for a week in airtight containers; sealed in plastic bags, they can be frozen for up to a month. Thaw, still wrapped, at room temperature.

Contributing Baker **LAUREN GROVEMAN**

Hungarian Shortbread

COLOR PHOTOGRAPH, PAGE 231

Makes 12 to 24 bars ■ For the taster, the hallmark of great shortbread is its buttery flavor and sandy texture; for the shortbread baker, the hallmark is the dough's stick-to-your-fingers stubbornness—it can be tough to work with. But you won't have a problem with this recipe. The dough is mixed quickly, shaped into balls, and frozen until firmish. Then you grate it into a cake pan, spread it with a layer of homemade rhubarb jam (or store-brought preserves), and grate another layer of dough over it. There's little that's simpler. These bars deliver a full measure of shortbread goodness with no fuss and mess.

THE JAM

>   **1 pound rhubarb, trimmed and cut into 1-inch pieces**
>   **½ cup sugar**
>   **½ cup water**
>   **½ vanilla bean**

Place the rhubarb, sugar, and water in a medium saucepan. Split the vanilla bean, scrape the soft, pulpy seeds into the pan, and toss in the pod. Bring to a simmer over low heat, and cook, stirring often, until the rhubarb softens and almost seems to melt. The cooking time will depend on the rhubarb, but it probably won't be more than 10 minutes. Remove the pan from the heat, retrieve the vanilla bean (discard or save, see page 25), and cool the jam to room temperature. *The jam can be made up to a week ahead and stored, tightly covered, in the refrigerator. Bring the jam to room temperature if necessary before using.* (If you do not want to make rhubarb jam, substitute about 1 cup of your favorite jam or preserves.)

THE SHORTBREAD

4 cups all-purpose flour

2 teaspoons baking powder

¼ teaspoon salt

4 sticks (1 pound) unsalted butter, at room temperature

4 large egg yolks

2 cups granulated sugar

Confectioner's sugar, for dusting

Whisk the flour, baking powder, and salt together in a bowl and set aside.

In a mixer fitted with the paddle attachment (or using a hand-held mixer), beat the butter on high speed until it is pale and fluffy. Add the egg yolks and sugar and beat until the sugar is dissolved and the mixture is light. Reduce the mixer speed to low and add the dry ingredients, mixing only until the ingredients are incorporated.

Chilling the Dough Turn the dough out onto a work surface and cut in half. Shape each half into a ball and wrap each ball in plastic. Freeze the dough for about 30 minutes, until firm. *You can freeze the dough, tightly wrapped, for up to a month at this point. Thaw overnight, still wrapped, in the refrigerator.*

Assembling and Baking Center a rack in the oven and preheat the oven to 350°F.

Remove one ball of dough from the freezer and, using the side of a box grater with the largest holes, grate the dough into a 9- by 12-inch baking pan. Pat the dough gently just to get it into the corners (you don't want to press it down) and spread with the rhubarb jam. Grate the remaining dough over the jam and press it lightly to distribute it evenly. Bake the shortbread for about 40 minutes, or until golden brown.

As soon as you remove the pan from the oven, dust the top of the shortbread heavily with confectioner's sugar. Cool to room temperature on a rack.

Cut the shortbread into bars when it is cool. You can cut whatever size bars please you, although, as a rough guide, 3-inch squares or rectangles 1½ inches by 3 inches make nice servings.

Storing Covered at room temperature, the shortbread will keep for about 2 days. It can be wrapped airtight and frozen for up to a month. Thaw, still wrapped, at room temperature.

Contributing Baker **GALE GAND**

Double Chocolate Cookies

Makes about 2 dozen large cookies ■ Cookies to put a grin on anyone's face—they're great. They use a pound of chocolate, mostly bittersweet and mostly melted, except for some coarsely chopped chunks that have a way of being soft in some places and crunchy in others. The dough is unusual, not at all similar to a Toll House dough. When finally mixed, it looks almost like a cake batter and a lot like a chocolaty marshmallow. It bakes up into a confection that seems half cookie, half brownie.

- ½ **cup all-purpose flour**
- ½ **teaspoon baking powder**
- ½ **teaspoon salt**
- 12 **ounces bittersweet chocolate, cut into larger-than-chip-size chunks**
- 1 **stick (4 ounces) unsalted butter**
- 4 **ounces unsweetened chocolate, coarsely chopped**
- 4 **large eggs, at room temperature**
- 1½ **cups sugar**
- 1½ **tablespoons instant coffee powder**
- 2 **teaspoons pure vanilla extract**

Whisk together the flour, baking powder, and salt in a medium bowl and set aside until needed. Divide the bittersweet chocolate in half and set half aside.

Place the butter, the remaining bittersweet chocolate, and the unsweetened chocolate in the top of a double boiler over, but not touching, simmering water. (Alternatively, you can use a heatproof bowl positioned over a saucepan of simmering water.) Heat the mixture, stirring occasionally, until the butter and chocolates are melted and smooth. Remove from the heat.

Meanwhile, put the eggs, sugar, coffee, and vanilla in the bowl of a mixer fitted with the whisk attachment and beat at high speed for about 10 minutes, until the mixture is very thick and forms a slowly dissolving ribbon when the whisk is lifted and the mixture is allowed to drizzle back into the bowl.

With the mixer on low speed, very gradually add the warm butter-chocolate mixture. Scape down the sides of the bowl and work your rubber spatula around the bottom of the bowl, then continue to mix just until the chocolate is thoroughly incorporated. Add the dry ingredients and the remaining bittersweet chocolate chunks and mix thoroughly. (You might find it more efficient to finish the mixing by gently folding the ingredients in with the rubber spatula.) The mixture will look like a thick, marshmallowy cake batter.

Chilling the Dough Cover the bowl with plastic and chill for several hours, or overnight. *The dough can be made ahead and kept refrigerated for up to 4 days.*

continued

Baking the Cookies When you are ready to bake, position the racks to divide the oven into thirds and preheat the oven to 350°F. Line two large baking sheets with parchment paper.

Using a heaping tablespoon of dough for each cookie, drop the dough onto the lined sheets, leaving at least 2 inches of space between each mound of dough—these are spreaders. Bake the cookies for 10 to 12 minutes, rotating the pans front to back and top to bottom halfway through the baking period. The cookies will puff, then sink and crinkle and wrinkle around the edges. These cookies are better underdone than overbaked, so if you have any doubts, pull them out of the oven earlier rather than later. These shouldn't appear dry and they won't be crisp. Use a wide metal spatula to transfer the cookies to cooling racks to cool to room temperature. Repeat with the remaining dough.

Storing The cookies can be wrapped in plastic and kept at room temperature for 2 days or frozen for up to a month. Thaw, still wrapped, at room temperature.

Contributing Baker **RICK KATZ**

Mocha Chocolate Chips

Makes about 4 dozen cookies ■ Here is the thinking person's chocolate chip cookie: Its flavors are expertly balanced, its texture is pleasurably soft and chewy, and its looks have a genteel homeliness. There's a pound of chocolate in these cookies, chopped up as chips. You can use all bittersweet or go with a half pound of bittersweet, a quarter pound of milk, and a quarter pound of white. Whatever you decide, use the best chocolate you can—it makes all the difference in the world.

> 2 cups unbleached all-purpose flour
>
> 2 to 3 tablespoons instant coffee powder (according to your taste)
>
> 1 teaspoon baking soda
>
> 1 teaspoon salt
>
> 2 sticks (8 ounces) unsalted butter, cut into chunks
>
> ¾ cup granulated sugar
>
> ¾ cup (packed) dark brown sugar
>
> 2 large eggs
>
> 1 teaspoon pure vanilla extract
>
> 1 pound chocolate (bittersweet, milk, or white, or a combination), cut into larger-than-chocolate-chip-size chunks
>
> ½ pound plump, moist apricots, coarsely chopped (optional)

Whisk the flour, coffee powder, baking soda, and salt together in a medium bowl to blend; set aside.

Put the butter in the bowl of a mixer fitted with the paddle attachment (or work with a hand-held mixer) and beat on medium speed until the butter lightens in color. Add the granulated sugar and beat for about 30 seconds, just to blend. Add the brown sugar and beat for another 30 seconds. Add the eggs one at a time, beating for a minute after each addition. The mixture should be light and fluffy; if necessary, beat 1 more minute. Add the vanilla and beat until blended.

Turn the mixer speed down to low and add the dry ingredients, mixing only until they are incorporated. Remove the bowl from the mixer and clean the paddle and the sides of the bowl with a rubber spatula. Add the chocolate chunks and the apricots, if you're using them, and stir them with the spatula to distribute equally.

Chilling the Dough Wrap the dough in plastic and chill for several hours, or overnight, to firm.

Baking the Cookies When you are ready to bake, position the racks to divide the oven into thirds and preheat the oven to 350°F. Line two heavy-duty baking sheets with parchment paper. (If you do not have very heavy baking sheets, double up the pans—these cookies need heavy sheets so that their bottoms don't burn.)

Using a heaping tablespoon of dough for each cookie, drop the dough onto the lined sheets, leaving at least 2 inches of space between each mound of dough so that the cookies have room to spread. Bake for 10 to 12 minutes, rotating the pans front to back and top to bottom halfway through the baking period, until the center is just baked—they'll still be soft to the touch. Use a wide metal spatula to transfer the cookies to cooling racks to cool to room temperature. Repeat with the remaining dough.

Storing Wrapped in plastic bags or in tins, the cookies will keep at room temperature for 2 days. They can be frozen for up to a month and should be thawed at room temperature.

Contributing Baker **RICK KATZ**

Best-Ever Brownies

Makes 18 brownies ■ Those who are passionate about brownies argue in defense of their favorite type, cakey or fudgey. If you're a cakey fan, go on to another recipe. These are the epitome of soft, dark, baked-just-until-barely-set brownies. Their creamy texture makes them seem wildly luxurious and very much a treat to be meted out in small servings (just small enough for a scoop of ice cream and some chocolate sauce). The mixing method is unorthodox for a brownie. Half of an egg-sugar mixture is stirred into the melted chocolate and butter, while the other half is whipped until it thickens and doubles in volume. The lightened eggs are folded into the chocolate with a delicate touch, as are the dry ingredients—tricks that enhance the brownies' lovely texture.

continued

1¼ cups sifted all-purpose flour

1 teaspoon salt

2 sticks (8 ounces) unsalted butter

4 ounces unsweetened chocolate, coarsely chopped

2 ounces bittersweet chocolate, coarsely chopped

2 cups sugar

1 teaspoon pure vanilla extract

4 large eggs

Center a rack in the oven and preheat the oven to 350°F.

Sift the flour and salt together and set aside.

Melt the butter and chocolate together in a medium saucepan over low heat, stirring frequently and keeping a watchful eye on the pot to make certain the chocolate doesn't scorch. (Alternatively, you can melt the ingredients in the top of a double boiler over, not touching, simmering water.) Add 1 cup of the sugar to the mixture and stir for half a minute, then remove the pan from the heat and stir in the vanilla. Pour the mixture into a large bowl.

Put the remaining 1 cup sugar and the eggs into the bowl of a mixer (or a mixing bowl if you're using a hand-held mixer) and whisk by hand just to combine. Little by little, pour half of the sugar and eggs into the chocolate mixture, stirring gently but constantly with a rubber spatula so that the eggs don't set from the heat. Fit the whisk attachment to the mixer and whip the remaining sugar and eggs until they are thick, pale, and doubled in volume, about 3 minutes. Using the rubber spatula, delicately fold the whipped eggs into the chocolate mixture. When the eggs are almost completely incorporated, gently fold in the dry ingredients.

Baking the Brownies Pour and scrape the batter into an unbuttered 9-inch square pan—a heavy ceramic or glass pan is ideal. Bake the brownies for 25 to 28 minutes, during which time they will rise a little and the top will turn dark and dry. Cut into the center at about the 23-minute mark to see how the brownies are progressing: They'll be perfect if they're just barely set and still pretty gooey. They're still awfully good on the other side of set, so don't worry if you miss the moment on your first try. Cool the brownies in the pan on a rack. Cut into 1½- by 3-inch bars to serve.

Storing The brownies will keep, covered, for 2 to 3 days at room temperature and can be frozen for up to a month. Thaw, still wrapped, at room temperature. These never freeze solid, so you might want to think about using them as a mix-in for ice cream.

Contributing Baker **RICK KATZ**

Ladyfingers and Madeleines

Makes 6 dozen 3-inch ladyfingers or 24 large madeleines ■ Although dainty ladyfingers and plump madeleines (those shell-shaped tea cakes that caused Proust to remember things past) are not often thought of as cookie cousins, they can both be made from the same batter, in this case a pipeable génoise.

The ladyfingers are piped onto parchment paper that has been ruled and penciled so you finish with perfectly proportioned pastries. The madeleines get their shape from madeleine pans, which come in regular and miniature sizes and can be purchased with a nonstick finish. For another type of ladyfinger, turn to Rothschilds (page 289).

LADYFINGERS

1 recipe Ladyfinger Génoise batter (page 41)
1 cup (approximately) confectioner's sugar

Position the oven racks to divide the oven into thirds and preheat the oven to 400°F.

Line two 12- by 15½-inch baking sheets with parchment paper and, using a ruler and a pencil, draw pairs of parallel lines 3 inches apart across the baking sheets, the short way, spacing them ½ to 1 inch apart. Marked this way, each sheet will give you room to pipe 3 dozen ladyfingers. Fit a 16-inch-long pastry bag with a ½-inch plain decorating tip and scoop all of the batter into the pastry bag. Using the marked lines on the baking sheets, pipe out ladyfingers that are ½ inch wide and 3 inches long, keeping them about ½ to ¾ inch apart so they'll have room to expand.

Piping ladyfingers between the guidelines.

Turn the confectioner's sugar into a sieve and, tapping the sieve with the side of your hand, coat each ladyfinger heavily with sugar.

Baking the Cookies Bake for 5 to 6 minutes, or until the ladyfingers are firm but feel spongy when you press them lightly with your finger. You want just a light, thin crust to develop on the delicate cakes. These should barely color, so take care not to overbake them.

Transfer the ladyfingers, parchment paper and all, to cooling racks. When the ladyfingers are cool, slide a broad spatula (a pancake turner is good) under a long side of each ladyfinger and lift the cakes off the paper. If the ladyfingers have puffed and baked together, as they often do, separate them by running a pizza cutter between them.

continued

MADELEINES

1 recipe Ladyfinger Génoise batter (page 41)

1 cup (approximately) confectioner's sugar

Position the oven racks to divide the oven into thirds and preheat the oven to 400°F.

Butter and flour two madeleine plaques.

Baking the Cookies Using a spoon or a pastry bag without a tip, fill the molds with the batter. Bake for about 10 minutes, until the madeleines are puffed, spring back when prodded gently, and start to come away from the sides of the molds. Let the madeleines cool for a minute or two before turning them out onto a rack to cool.

Storing Both ladyfingers and madeleines are best the day they are made, although slightly stale madeleines are wonderful dipped in tea, à la Proust. You can keep the cookies in an airtight tin for a day or two or freeze them for up to 10 days in a plastic container with waxed paper between the layers. Thaw, still packed, at room temperature.

Contributing Baker **FLO BRAKER**

PASTRIES

Phylloccine Ice Cream Sandwiches PAGE 405

Tropical Napoleon   PAGE 393

Raspberry–Fig Crostata PAGE 374

Nectarines and plums for the cobbler

Johnnycake Cobbler PAGE 389

Caramel-poached fruits for the Brioche Tart

Brioche Tart with White Secret Sauce **P A G E 386**

Espresso Profiteroles **PAGE 411**

Chocolate crusts PAGE 372

Chocolate Truffle Tartlets PAGE 382

343

Berry Galette PAGE 377

Blueberries and raspberries in the unbaked galette PAGE 377

Rolling Pie Dough

1.

2.

1. On a well-floured surface, roll the chilled dough from the center out, slightly rotating the disk every few rolls to keep the dough round.

2. It's best to roll on one side and in one direction.

3. Lift and turn the dough frequently to keep it round and to keep it from sticking.

4. When the dough is the right size (about an inch larger than the pie pan), fold it in quarters, center it over the pan, and unfold it.

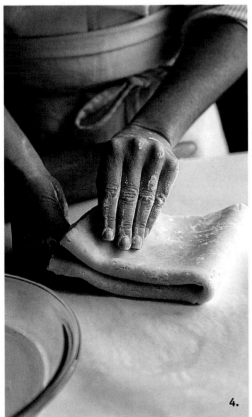

4.

3.

Single-Crust Pie Shell

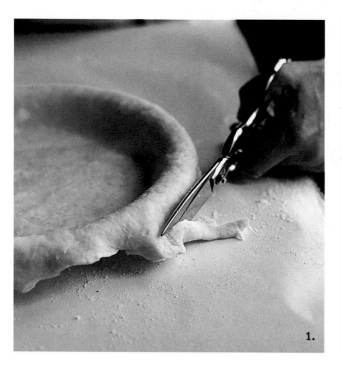

1. Trim the overhanging dough to one-half inch.

2. Fold the overhanging dough under to build an even rim around the pan.

3. To create scallops, push the index finger or knuckle of one hand against the thumb and index finger of the other.

4. By varying the crimp, you can create a multitude of decorative effects.

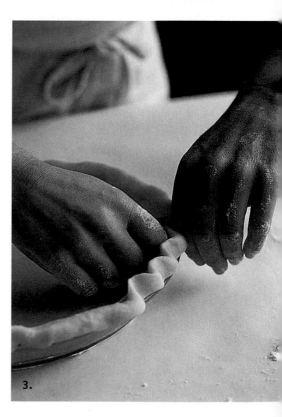

Double-Crust Pie Shell

1.

2.

3.

1. Unfold the bottom crust in the pan and add the filling. Brush the rim with egg wash to create a seal.

2. Center the top crust over the filled pie and unfold.

3. Trim the overhanging dough of both crusts and fold both under to create a thick rim around the edge of the pan.

4. To create scallops around the rim, push the thumb of one hand against the thumb and index finger of the other hand.

5. For a glistening golden crust, glaze the top with egg wash and sprinkle turbinado sugar over it.

6. Cut steam vents in the top dough in a decorative pattern.

6.

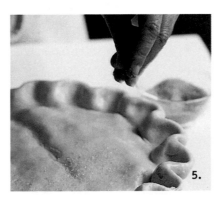

5.

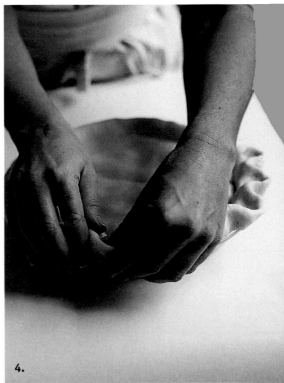

4.

Blueberry-Nectarine Pie   PAGE 384

Blueberry and nectarine filling for the pie

A slice of Blueberry-Nectarine Pie

Lining a Tart Pan

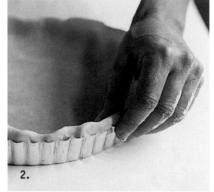

2.

1.

1. Center the rolled dough and unfold it in the tart pan.

2. Press the dough into the bottom and sides of the pan, raising the excess dough above the rim.

3. Roll the pin along the top of the pan to remove the excess dough.

4. Gently press the sides again to create a rim slightly higher than the top of the pan.

5. Decorate the edge by scoring diagonally with a straightedge.

6. When baking an empty tart shell ("blind baking"), line it with parchment paper and fill with weights to keep it from puffing.

3.

6.

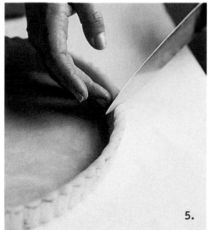

5.

4.

A slice of French Apple Tart PAGE 379

French Apple Tart PAGE 379

Three Lattices

WOVEN LATTICE

1. With strips cut from the rolled-out top crust, lay half the strips in one direction across the pie.

2. One at a time, place the remaining strips at right angles, weaving them through the first set.

3. Weave top strips over and under bottom strips to create a woven effect.

OVERLAID LATTICE

4. Place one strip vertically across one edge of the pie, the next horizontally, the third vertically, and so on, overlaying all the strips set in the other direction.

CRISSCROSS LATTICE

5. Lay half the strips across the pie at even intervals, then crisscross the remaining strips diagonally over the first set of strips.

Poached pears for Chocolate Napoleons

Chocolate Napoleon PAGE 400

Savarin PAGE 416

Baba PAGE 413

Tourte Milanese PAGE 423

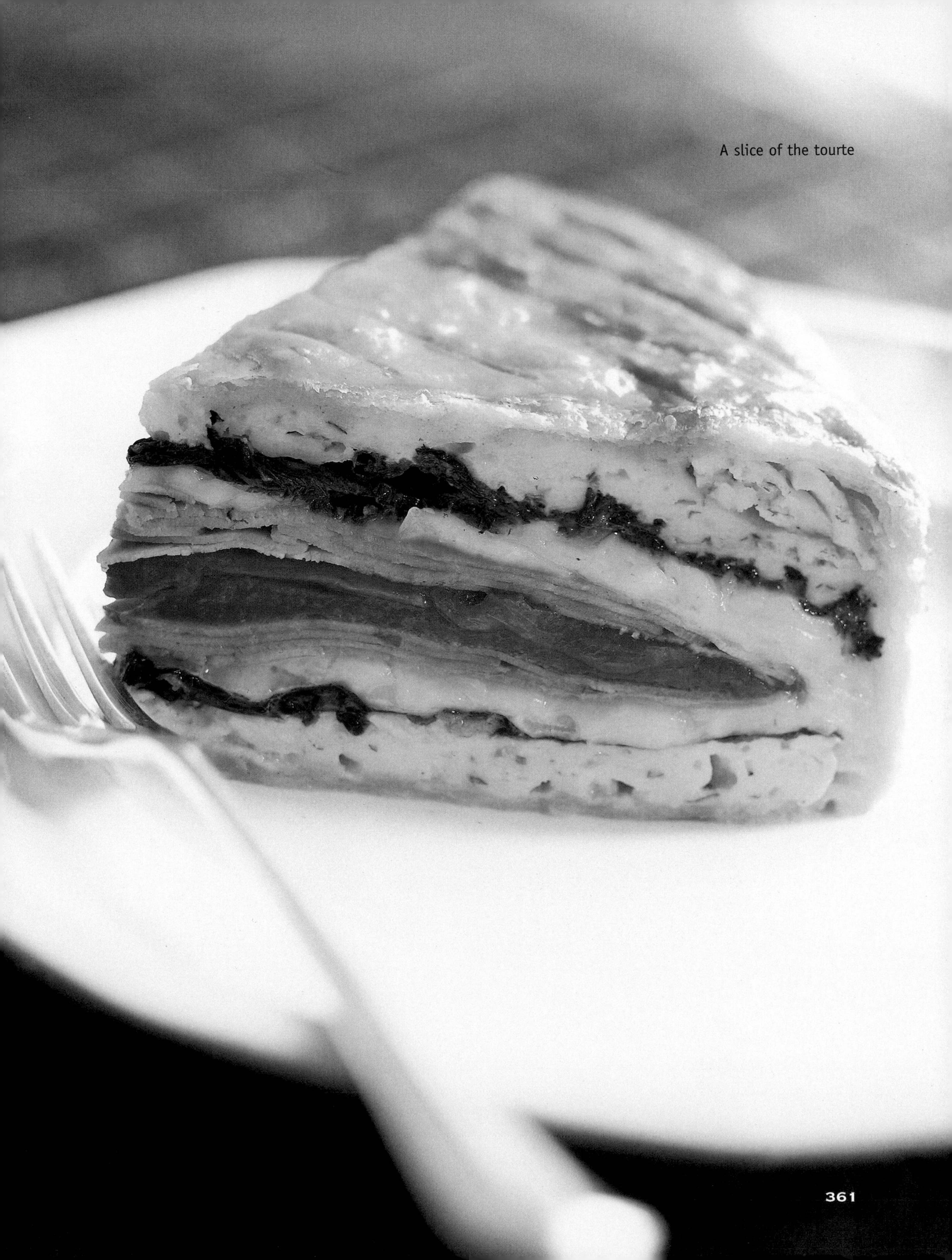

A slice of the tourte

Scallop and Pesto Purses PAGE 435

Pizza Rustica PAGE 430

Savory Brioche Pocket   PAGE 421

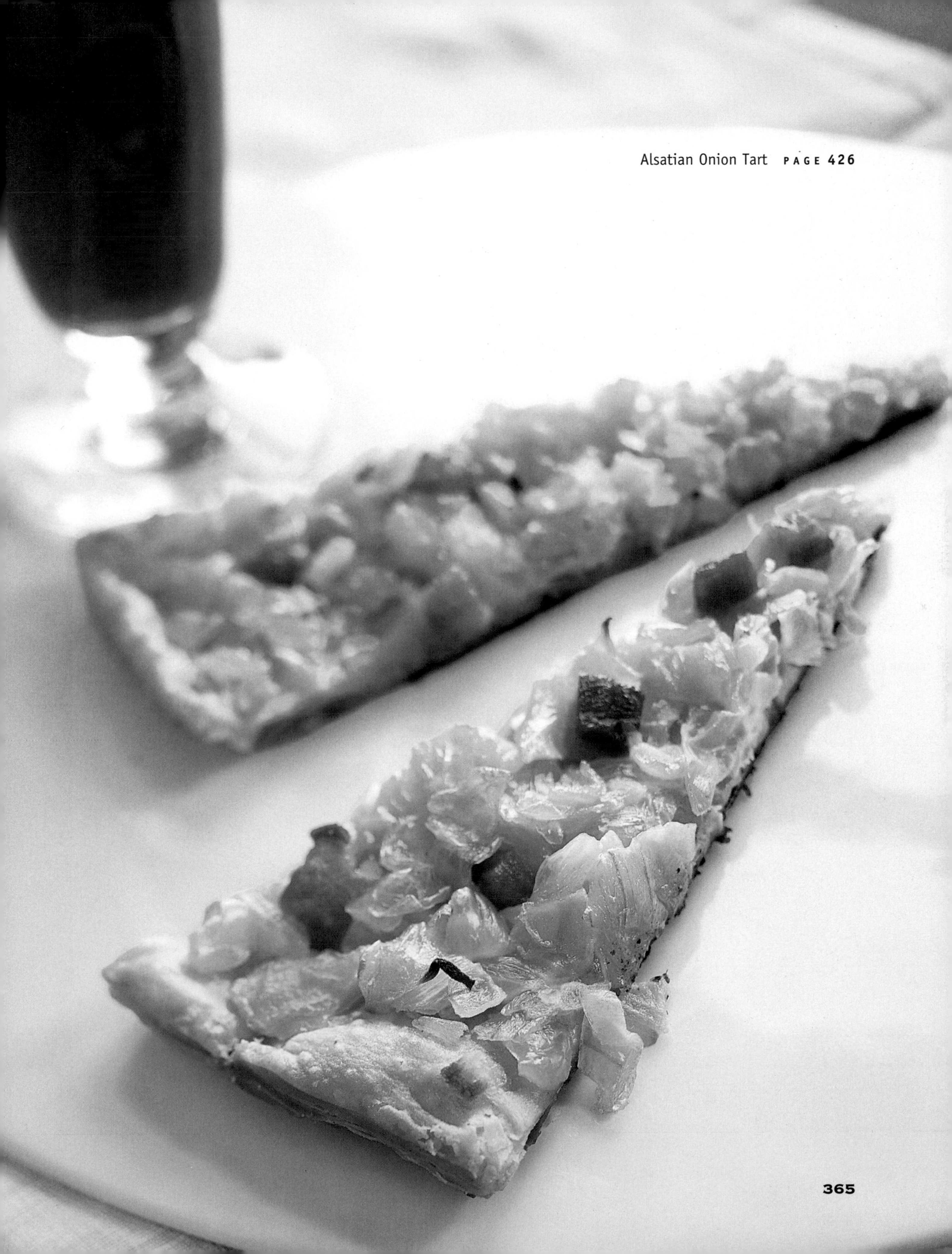

Alsatian Onion Tart PAGE 426

Cheese and Tomato Galette PAGE 429

Homey Pies and Tarts

FEW KITCHEN FEATS provide as extraordinary a sense of accomplishment as making a pie. It's all in the crust, confide the experts, and the crusts in this chapter beckon to all: Each is an inspiration for old hands, and few are too tough for beginners to tackle.

If you're uncertain about your crust capabilities, read through the pointers on pages 33 to 34 and then head for veteran baking teacher Nick Malgieri's Pasta Frolla. A great recipe for first-timers, this sweet Italian pie dough is made in the food processor and guaranteed to withstand mishandling. Master that and you can move on to Seattle baker Leslie Mackie's Flaky Pie Dough (it will become your "house" dough) and her fragile cinnamon-scented Sesame-Almond Dough. Then try Boston baker David Ogonowski's Chocolate Dough—dark, delicious, and demanding, it's a challenge you'll welcome once you've worked your way up to it.

Conquer the crusts and you're ready for fillings, both fruity and creamy. When soft fruits and berries are fragrant and bountiful, make the lattice-topped Raspberry-Fig Crostata or Blueberry-Nectarine Pie. Then, when winter comes and the choices for fillings narrow, make these desserts with apples, bananas, mangoes, or gently poached dried fruits. Think of crusts and fillings as a jumping-off point for limitless improvisations: Fill truffle tartlets with chocolate one day and fruit and whipped cream the next, or bake Flo Braker's galette, a rustic, free-form tart, with berries in the summer and thin slices of pear or pineapple in the winter—they'll always be great.

Sesame-Almond Dough

Makes enough for a 9-inch lattice-topped tart ■ This shortbreadlike crust is buttery, crumbly, cookieish, and subtly flavored with cinnamon, vanilla, and lemon zest. The flavor is reminiscent of a linzer tart, and in fact, the crust behaves like a linzer crust—it may break as you're rolling it, but it will come together perfectly with just a press of the finger. Use this versatile crust as the base for a fruit tart (try the Raspberry-Fig Crostata, page 374) or experiment—it's terrific with a chocolate ganache filling (see the truffle tart filling on page 382, for example) or rolled out and cut into small cookies to be served with espresso.

2 large eggs

1 teaspoon pure vanilla extract

3/4 cup unblanched almonds, lightly toasted and cooled

1/2 cup sesame seeds, lightly toasted and cooled

1/2 cup sugar

2 cups all-purpose flour

1/4 teaspoon cinnamon

1/4 teaspoon salt

1/8 teaspoon finely chopped lemon zest

2 sticks (8 ounces) cold unsalted butter, cut into 1/2-inch cubes

Whisk the eggs together with the vanilla extract until blended; set aside until needed.

Put the almonds, sesame seeds, and 1 tablespoon of the sugar in the work bowl of a food processor fitted with the metal blade. Pulse until the almonds are very finely chopped, but not oily or pasty. Turn the mixture into the bowl of a mixer fitted with the paddle attachment and add the remaining sugar, the flour, cinnamon, salt, and zest. Mix on low speed for a few seconds, just to combine the ingredients.

Keeping the mixer on low, add the butter and mix until the mixture resembles fine crumbs. Don't worry if a few large pieces of butter remain; you can work these out later. Add the egg mixture, mixing only until the dough is uniformly moistened and forms curds, about 15 seconds. Turn the mixture out onto a smooth work surface.

Kneading the Dough Knead the dough gently a couple of times just to fully blend the ingredients.

TO MAKE A LATTICE-TOPPED TART, gather the dough into a ball and cut it into lopsided halves. Shape both pieces into disks (the smaller "half" will be used for the lattice).

continued

TO MAKE 2 SMALLER TARTS, make the pieces even; or use the whole batch for a larger tart. Wrap each piece of dough in plastic and refrigerate for at least 1 hour.

Storing The dough can be made ahead and refrigerated, wrapped in plastic, for up to 2 days before using or wrapped airtight and frozen for a month. Thaw, still wrapped, in the refrigerator.

Contributing Baker **LESLIE MACKIE**

Pasta Frolla

Makes enough for a 9-inch lattice-topped pie ■ Pasta frolla—*pasta* means "paste" or "dough" and *frolla* means "tender"—is a sweet Italian pie dough. It is indeed tender, light and crumbly too, and a crust as commendable with savory fillings as with sweet (see page 430 for a savory pie). If you are new to crusts, this is a good starter dough. It's a made-in-the-food-processor dough that's almost indestructible. And because of the relatively large amount of sugar, you don't have to worry about overworking it, nor do you need to be concerned if it cracks as it goes into the pie plate—everything is fixable.

2 cups all-purpose flour

$\frac{1}{3}$ cup sugar

$\frac{1}{2}$ teaspoon baking powder

$\frac{1}{4}$ teaspoon salt

1 stick (4 ounces) cold unsalted butter or 4 ounces cold lard, cut into 8 pieces

2 large eggs, lightly beaten

Put the flour, sugar, baking powder, and salt into the work bowl of a food processor fitted with the metal blade; pulse a few times just to mix the ingredients. Add the butter and pulse 15 to 20 times, or until the mixture resembles fine cornmeal. With the machine running, add the eggs and process until the dough forms a ball on the blade, about a minute or so. Remove the dough from the processor and knead it, folding it over on itself, until it is smooth, 1 to 2 minutes. Wrap the dough in plastic and set aside for up to 30 minutes, or chill until needed.

Storing The dough can be made up to 3 days ahead, wrapped well, and refrigerated, or frozen, tightly wrapped, for up to a month. Thaw, still wrapped, in the refrigerator.

Contributing Baker **NICK MALGIERI**

Galette Dough

Makes enough for two 8-inch galettes ▪ The cornmeal in this wonderfully buttery dough not only gives it a bit of crunch, it makes it crisp enough to stand up to soft and syrupy fillings and sturdy enough to be rolled to extreme thinness. You can use this dough to line a tart pan, but it is particularly well suited to rustic tarts called galettes—flat, open-face, free-form tarts whose edges are folded over the filling like the ruffled top of a drawstring purse.

The dough is made quickly either by hand or in a food processor and produces enough for two galettes. Since it is equally good with sweet and savory fillings, you might make the Cheese and Tomato Galette (page 429) to start a meal and the Berry Galette (page 377) to finish one.

> 3 tablespoons sour cream (or yogurt or buttermilk)
> ⅓ cup (approximately) ice water
> 1 cup all-purpose flour
> ¼ cup yellow cornmeal
> 1 teaspoon sugar
> ½ teaspoon salt
> 7 tablespoons cold unsalted butter, cut into 6 to 8 pieces

TO MAKE THE DOUGH BY HAND, stir the sour cream and ⅓ cup ice water together in a small bowl and set aside. Put the flour, cornmeal, sugar, and salt in a large bowl and stir with a fork to mix. Drop the butter pieces into the bowl, tossing them once or twice just to coat them with flour. With a pastry blender, work the butter into the flour, aiming for pieces of butter that range in size from bread crumbs to small peas. The smaller pieces will make the dough tender, the larger ones will make it flaky.

Sprinkle the cold sour cream mixture over the dough, 1 tablespoon at a time, tossing with a fork to evenly distribute it. After you've added all of the sour cream, the dough should be moist enough to stick together when pressed; if it's not, add additional cold water, 1 teaspoon at a time. With your hands, gather the curds of dough together. (You'll have a soft, malleable dough, the kind you might want to overwork.)

Chilling the Dough Turn the dough out of the bowl and divide it in half. Press each piece of dough into a disk, wrap in plastic, and refrigerate for at least 2 hours.

Top: Use a pastry blender to work in the butter.
Bottom: Gather up the finished dough and chill it.

TO MAKE THE DOUGH IN A FOOD PROCESSOR, stir the sour cream and ⅓ cup ice water together in a small bowl; set aside. Put the flour, cornmeal, sugar, and salt in the work bowl of a processor fitted with the metal blade; pulse to combine. Drop the butter pieces into the bowl and pulse 8 to 10 times, or until the mixture is speckled with pieces of butter that vary in size from bread crumbs to peas. With the machine running, add the sour cream mixture and process just until the dough forms soft, moist curds.

Chilling the Dough Remove the dough from the processor, divide it in half, and press each half into a disk. Wrap in plastic and chill for at least 2 hours.

Storing The dough can be kept in the refrigerator for a day or two, or it can be wrapped airtight and frozen for a month. Thaw, still wrapped, in the refrigerator. It is convenient to roll the dough into rounds, place parchment between each round, and freeze them wrapped in plastic; this way, you'll need only about 20 minutes to defrost a round of dough at room temperature before it can be filled, folded into a galette, and baked.

Contributing Baker **FLO BRAKER**

Chocolate Dough

Makes enough for six 5-inch tartlets or one 10-inch tart ■ Imagine the best tart crust you can—buttery, flaky, and just a little sweet—and now imagine that it's chocolate through and through. This crust is made the way a classic French tart shell is made: The butter is worked into the dry ingredients, the mixture is then moistened with egg yolk and water, and the dough is given a *fraisage*—the French term for a good working under the heel of your hand—to bring it all together. (In fact, following these directions, but substituting an equal amount of flour for the cocoa, you'd produce a delectable traditional pâte sucrée.) The difference is, of course, the full, fabulous flavor of chocolate. Use this crust to make the extravagantly rich Chocolate Truffle Tartlets (page 382), to fill with pastry cream or crème fraîche and top with fruits, or to create a grown-up ice cream pie, filled with superior ice cream and drizzled with Bittersweet Chocolate Sauce (page 446).

   1¼ **cups all-purpose flour**
   ¼ **cup unsweetened cocoa powder, preferably Dutch-processed**
   ¼ **cup sugar**
   ¼ **teaspoon salt**
   1 **stick (4 ounces) cold unsalted butter, cut into small pieces**
   1 **large egg yolk**
   1 **tablespoon ice water**

TO MAKE THE CRUST BY HAND, put the flour, cocoa, sugar, and salt on a smooth work surface, preferably a cool surface such as marble. Toss the ingredients together lightly with your fingertips, then scatter the butter pieces across the dry ingredients. Use your fingertips to work the butter into the flour mixture until it forms pieces the size of small peas. Then use a combination of techniques to work the butter further into the flour: Break it up with your fingertips, rub it lightly between your palms, and chop it with the flat edge of a plastic or metal dough scraper.

Gather the mixture into a mound, make a volcanolike well in the center, and pour in the yolk and ice water. Use your fingers to break up the yolk and start moistening the dry ingredients, then, just as you did with the flour and butter, toss the ingredients with your fingers and use the dough scraper to chop and blend it. The dough will be crumbly and not really cohesive. Bring it together by smearing small portions of it across the work surface with the heel of your hand.

Chilling the Dough Gather the dough together and shape it into a rough square. Pat it down to compress it slightly, and wrap it in plastic. Chill until firm, at least 30 minutes.

TO MAKE THE DOUGH IN A FOOD PROCESSOR FITTED WITH THE METAL BLADE, put the flour, cocoa, sugar, and salt in the work bowl and pulse just to blend. Add the butter and pulse 8 to 10 times, until the pieces are about the size of small peas. With the machine running, add the yolk and ice water and process, in bursts, just until crumbly—don't overwork it. Turn it out onto the work surface and, working with small portions, smear the dough across the surface with the heel of your hand.

Chilling the Dough Gather the dough together and shape it into a rough square. Pat it down to compress it slightly, and wrap it in plastic. Chill until firm, at least 30 minutes.

Storing The dough can remain in the refrigerator for 3 days, or it can be wrapped airtight and frozen for a month. Thaw the dough, still wrapped, overnight in the refrigerator before rolling it out.

Contributing Baker **DAVID OGONOWSKI**

Raspberry-Fig Crostata
COLOR PHOTOGRAPH, PAGE 338

Makes 8 to 10 servings ■ This lattice-topped tart, or *crostata* (Italian for "tart"), is made with a Sesame-Almond crust and filled with a raspberry-fig combination that is both luxurious and luscious, a lovely counterpoint to the crust's bit of cinnamon and lemon. But the crostata can be made with other fruits as well, and is best when there are least two kinds of fruit, one firm and the other juicy. Think of raspberries and rhubarb, or nectarines and blueberries when they're available, or mix apples and raisins, pears and almonds, or cranberries and nuts when winter pickings are slim.

¾ **pound fresh figs, quartered**

¾ **pound fresh raspberries**

½ **cup granulated sugar**

¼ **cup (packed) light brown sugar**

1½ **tablespoons all-purpose flour**

½ **teaspoon grated lemon zest**

1 **tablespoon unsalted butter**

Fresh lemon juice to taste

1 **recipe Sesame-Almond Dough (page 369), divided into 2 uneven "halves" and chilled**

1 **large egg beaten with 1 tablespoon cold water, for egg wash**

Coarse or turbinado sugar

Put half the fruit in a medium saucepan, keeping the remaining fruit close at hand. Add the granulated sugar, brown sugar, flour, lemon zest, and butter and stir to mix. Bring the mixture to a soft boil over medium heat, stirring constantly. The fruits will release their juices and the liquid will thicken. Turn the mixture into a bowl and stir in the uncooked fruit. Taste a spoonful, paying particular attention to the saucy liquid, and add lemon juice as needed. Cool the filling to room temperature.

Remove the smaller piece of dough from the refrigerator and give it a few bashes with the end of your rolling pin to soften it enough to get it rolling. Working on a floured sheet of parchment paper, roll the dough into a 10-inch circle. Using a ruffle-edged pastry wheel or a thin sharp knife, cut the circle into ½-inch-wide strips. Slip the parchment onto a baking sheet, cover the strips with waxed paper, and chill the dough while you roll out the bottom crust.

Lining the Tart Pan Working on a floured surface, roll the bottom crust into an 11-inch circle. Carefully center the dough over a 9-inch fluted tart pan with a

removable bottom and gently work it into the pan, pressing it evenly into the bottom and up the sides. Don't worry if the dough breaks (as it inevitably will); it is easily patchable. In fact, the dough, when soft, is similar to a press-in crust—just press a piece of dough into any hole and it will stick. (If the crust is really soft and unworkable at this stage, refrigerate it again before proceeding.) Trim, leaving a bit of dough as an overhang, about ⅛ inch, and use it to build up a slight ledge around the edge of the tart.

Filling the Tart Pan Pour the cooled filling into the tart shell and brush the edges of the shell with the egg wash.

Forming the Lattice Remove the lattice strips from the refrigerator and count the number of strips you cut. Plan on using half for the vertical strips, half for the horizontal, and figure out the spacing between each strip accordingly. Lift one strip of dough from the parchment paper with the help of a long icing spatula and place it vertically across the left side of the tart. Brush with a little egg wash and trim the ends even with the edge of the tart. Now place a strip horizontally across the top of the tart, crossing the first strip; brush and trim. Continue in this way, alternating vertical and horizontal strips, until the top is covered.

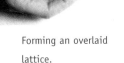

Chilling the Tart Chill the tart for about 30 minutes before baking. *It can be kept in the refrigerator for a couple of hours if necessary; cover with plastic.* Cover the remaining egg wash with plastic wrap and refrigerate.

Forming an overlaid lattice.

Baking the Tart Position a rack in the center of the oven and preheat the oven to 350°F.

Remove the tart from the refrigerator and brush once more with egg wash. Sprinkle the top with coarse sugar. Place the tart on a parchment-lined jelly-roll pan to catch any drips and bake for about 45 minutes, until the pastry is a rich golden brown and the filling is bubbling. Transfer to a cooling rack. After about 10 minutes, remove the sides of the tart pan and slide the tart off the base onto a platter. Serve the tart at room temperature.

Storing This is best the day it is made, but leftovers can be covered and stored in the refrigerator for 1 day. Bring to room temperature before serving.

Contributing Baker **LESLIE MACKIE**

Sweet Ricotta Pie

Makes 8 to 10 servings ■ This is a dessert version of the savory Pizza Rustica (page 430). Its lattice-topped crust is made from pasta frolla and its made-in-a-minute filling is based on sweetened ricotta. Anisette, licorice-flavored liqueur, is the traditional flavoring for this type of cheesecake, but you can use anise extract or alter the flavor completely by substituting vanilla or almond extract, using brandy, or mixing in a little fruit-flavored liqueur, such as Grand Marnier.

1 pound whole milk ricotta

⅓ cup sugar

1 tablespoon anisette

3 large eggs, beaten

½ teaspoon cinnamon

1 recipe Pasta Frolla (page 370)

Stir the ricotta, sugar, anisette, and eggs together in a bowl until smooth; set aside.

Position a rack in the lower third of the oven and preheat the oven to 350°F. Butter a 9-inch glass pie plate. (If you don't have a glass pie plate, use metal, but increase the oven temperature to 375°F.)

Working with two thirds of the dough, knead it into a disk and roll it on a lightly floured work surface into a 12-inch circle. Transfer the dough to the pie plate and press it gently against the bottom and up the sides of the plate. Don't worry if the dough tears—just press it back together. Use the dull side of a knife to trim the excess dough even with the rim. Scrape the filling into the pie shell, smooth the top, and dust with cinnamon.

Forming the Lattice Knead and shape the remaining piece of dough into a block and roll it on a lightly floured surface into a 9-inch square. Using a pizza or pastry cutter (a ruffle-edged pastry wheel is nice) or a thin sharp knife, cut the dough into 12 even strips. To form the lattice top, lay 6 of the strips across the pie at 1¼-inch intervals, then crisscross with the remaining strips, placing them diagonally across the first strips. Trim the ends of the lattice even with the edge of the pan.

Baking the Pie Bake for 35 to 40 minutes, or until the crust is golden and the filling is firm and slightly puffed. Transfer the pie to a rack and cool completely before serving.

Storing Leftovers can be kept, well covered in the refrigerator, for up to 3 days. Serve slightly chilled or at room temperature.

Contributing Baker **NICK MALGIERI**

Berry Galette

COLOR PHOTOGRAPH, PAGE 344

Makes 4 to 6 servings ■ This, as heirloom cookbooks used to say, is a keeper. It is so simple and inviting and so enjoyable to construct that you'll find yourself turning to it frequently. It's called a galette because it's flat, open-faced and free-form—the crust is rolled into a circle, the filling is piled in the center, and the edges of the crust are turned in and ruffled. The filling can be mixed berries, as suggested here (if you include strawberries, don't include many, as they're too watery), peeled soft fruits, like peaches or apricots, or, in fall and winter, tart apples or sweet pears.

½ **recipe Galette Dough (page 371), chilled**

1½ **cups mixed fresh berries (or cut-up peeled fruit)**
1 **tablespoon plus 1 teaspoon sugar**
1 **tablespoon honey (optional)**
1 **tablespoon cold unsalted butter**

Position a rack in the lower third of the oven and preheat the oven to 400°F. Line a baking sheet with parchment paper.

Put the dough on a lightly floured work surface and roll it into an 11-inch circle that's about ⅛ inch thick. Since the dough is soft, you'll need to lift it now and then and toss some more flour under it and over the top. Roll up the dough around your rolling pin and transfer it to the prepared baking sheet.

Spread the berries over the dough, leaving a 2- to 3-inch border. Sprinkle 1 tablespoon of the sugar over the fruit and drizzle on the honey, if you're using it. Cut the butter into slivers and scatter it on top of the fruit. Fold the uncovered border of dough up over the filling, allowing the dough to pleat as you lift it up and work your way around the galette. (Because you're folding a wide edge of dough onto a smaller part of the circle, it will pleat naturally —just go with it.) Dip a pastry brush in water, give the edge of the crust a light coating, and then sprinkle the crust with the remaining teaspoon of sugar.

Baking the Galette Bake the galette for 35 to 40 minutes, or until the pastry is golden and crisp. Transfer the baking sheet to a cooling rack and let the galette rest on the sheet for 10 minutes. Slip a wide spatula or a small baking sheet under the galette and slide it onto the cooling rack. Serve warm or at room temperature, cutting the tart with a pizza wheel or a sharp knife.

Storing The galette is best eaten the day it is made.

Contributing Baker **FLO BRAKER**

Baked Yogurt Tart

Makes 8 servings ∎ The simplicity of this tart's primary ingredients, nonfat yogurt, lots of vanilla, and fresh fruit, belies the appeal of its flavor—rounded, soothing, and full of sweetness and warmth—and texture—creamy like a firm custard or a baked cheesecake. The recipe calls for mixed berries, but you can use any fruit that's available. In summer, when there are so many soft, colorful fruits, the choices are almost limitless; in fall, Italian plums are a treat; and in winter, the apple-and-pear season, try topping the tart with these or with poached dried fruits. You can even bake the tart untopped and serve it with a sauce—raspberry (page 450) is a natural, and bittersweet chocolate (page 446) a pleaser.

¼ **recipe Flaky Pie Dough (page 31), well chilled**

3 **large eggs**

¾ **cup sugar**

2 **cups plain nonfat yogurt**

2 **tablespoons pure vanilla extract**

¾ **cup all-purpose flour**

1½ **cups (approximately) fresh blackberries, blueberries, and/or raspberries (you can also use sliced plums, peaches, or nectarines)**

⅓ **cup coarsely chopped toasted almonds**

Confectioner's sugar, for dusting

Working on a lightly floured surface, roll the dough into a 12-inch circle that's between ⅛ and ¼ inch thick. Fit the dough into a 9-inch round cake pan or a 9-inch springform. (The sides of the pan should be about 1½ inches high.) Press the dough against the bottom and up the sides of the pan and cut the overhang to an even ½ inch all around. Fold the overhang under itself and press and pinch the edge to crimp in a zigzag pattern.

Chilling the Crust Chill the pan for about 30 minutes.

Baking the Crust Center a rack in the oven and preheat the oven to 400°F.

Fit a piece of parchment paper or aluminum foil into the pan and fill with rice, dried beans, or pie weights. Bake for 20 to 25 minutes, until the crust is set and lightly browned. Remove the paper and weights and cool the shell to room temperature on a rack. Turn the oven temperature down to 325°F.

Beat the eggs and sugar together with a hand-held mixer (or a mixer fitted with the paddle attachment) on medium speed until they thicken slightly and turn pale, 2 to 3 minutes; they needn't form a ribbon. Switch to a rubber spatula, add the yogurt and vanilla extract, and mix just until blended. Gradually add the flour through a sifter, folding it in gently with the spatula.

Pour the yogurt filling into the cooled tart shell, smoothing the top with the spatula. The filling will come only about two thirds of the way up the pan—that's fine. Scatter the fruit over the top of the tart; it will probably push the filling up to the top of the crust. Sprinkle the chopped nuts around the edge of the tart.

Baking the Tart Place the tart on a jelly-roll pan to catch any drips and bake for 35 to 40 minutes, or until the top is golden brown. Transfer to a cooling rack and cool to room temperature.

To unmold the tart, if you used a cake pan, cover the top of the tart with plastic wrap and a cardboard cake circle or the removable metal bottom of a tart pan. Invert the tart, remove the pan, and invert again onto a cardboard cake circle or a serving platter so that the tart is right side up; remove the plastic wrap. Or remove the sides of the springform (you can leave the base in place). The tart can be served at room temperature or it can be chilled if desired. Dust with confectioner's sugar at serving time.

Storing Serve the tart the day it is made if possible, although it can be kept, covered, in the refrigerator for a day if necessary.

Contributing Baker **LESLIE MACKIE**

French Apple Tart

COLOR PHOTOGRAPH, PAGE 354

Makes 8 to 10 servings ■ This open-faced tart is beautiful. The top is a blossoming rosette of dark-edged, paper-thin apple slices, a pattern considered classic among French pâtissiers and one that's easier to reproduce at home than you'd think at first glance. Beneath the gossamer blossom is what the French call a *compote*, a sweet, thick purée of oven-roasted Granny Smith apples. Each forkful delivers the butter and crackle of the crust, the sweetness and smoothness of the purée, and the pure apple flavor of the topping. All this, and the pride of presenting a polished tart any professional baker would be happy to claim.

¼ recipe Flaky Pie Dough (page 31), well chilled

6 Granny Smith apples

¾ cup sugar

1 tablespoon all-purpose flour

Pinch of cinnamon

½ cup fresh, fluffy bread crumbs

2 teaspoons (approximately) fresh lemon juice

continued

Decorate the edge by pressing a knife at ¹/₂-inch intervals.

On a lightly floured surface, roll the dough into a circle about ⅛ inch thick and fit it into a 9-inch fluted tart pan with a removable bottom. Press a little of the overhang against the edge of the pan so that it produces a small ledge protruding over the inside of the pan. The best way to do this is to press the index finger of one hand against the dough running up the side of the pan and use the thumb of the other hand to form the inner ledge by pressing the overhanging dough against the rim of the pan and the top of your inside finger. The ledge will be about ½ inch wide. Press it against the edge of the pan to cut off the excess dough. Now, working with your thumb perpendicular to the bottom of the pan, press against the ledge you've created so that some of the ledge's dough is pressed down against the side of the pan and the rest of it is lifted up above the rim of the pan. Use the back of a knife to decorate the edge by pressing it diagonally at each flute or at ½-inch intervals around the tart.

Chilling the Crust Chill the crust for at least 30 minutes.

Baking the Crust Center a rack in the oven and preheat the oven to 400°F.

Fit a piece of parchment paper or foil into the tart shell and fill with pie weights, rice, or dried beans. Bake for 20 to 25 minutes, until golden brown. Transfer the crust, with the paper and weights, to a cooling rack and let cool while you make the filling. Lower the oven temperature to 375°F.

Making the Filling Peel and core the apples, cut each one in half, and cut each half into 12 pieces. Put the apples in a large bowl and toss with the sugar, flour, cinnamon, and bread crumbs. Add just a squeeze of lemon juice to start—you'll be able to adjust the flavor later. Spread the apples on a jelly-roll pan and bake

for 15 to 20 minutes, or until the apples give up their juices, start to form a sauce, and are soft enough to mash. Scrape the apples into a bowl and mash with a potato masher or a heavy spoon. Don't be overzealous—a few small lumps and bumps will add interest to the filling. Taste and add more lemon juice if you think it needs it, then cool the filling for about 15 minutes.

Filling the Shell Spoon the purée into the cooled tart shell and smooth the top with an offset spatula. The filling should come to just below the rim you've created. (If you have too much, you can serve the extra as a simple dessert topped with whipped cream.)

THE TOPPING

2 to 3 Granny Smith apples

1 tablespoon fresh lemon juice (or more to taste)

2 tablespoons unsalted butter, melted

1½ teaspoons granulated sugar

Confectioner's sugar, for dusting

If you have turned off the oven, reset it to 375°F.

Peel, core, and quarter the apples (cutting from end to end), then cut them into slices that are between ⅛ and ¼ inch thick. As you work, toss the slices with the lemon juice to prevent discoloration. Save the smaller pieces from the ends of the apples—they'll make good packing and "even-outers."

Working slowly and carefully and starting at the edge, arrange the apples in a circle on the purée. The slices should overlap and the points should just touch the shell. Since these will shrink, make a well-packed circle. Lay on another circle overlapping the first by just about ⅛ inch, tucking a few small pieces under the circle to level it and trimming the slices as necessary so that they fit. You'll probably have enough room for two circles and a center rosette. For the rosette, choose a large, thin slice of apple, cut it into a round, and place it, propped up slightly, in the center of the tart. Or, if your apples were small and the opening in the center is too large to be covered by one slice of apple, arrange as many slices as needed to create an attractive rosette.

With a light hand, evenly brush the apple slices with the melted butter (use a feather brush if you have one) and sprinkle with the granulated sugar.

Baking the Tart Put the tart on a parchment- or foil-lined jelly-roll pan and bake for 25 to 30 minutes, or until the top is beautifully glazed and the apple slices are edged in black, a stunning effect. Check that the apples are baked through by piercing a couple with the tip of a sharp knife. If the apples aren't baked but the tart is very brown, cover the tart with a foil tent and bake a few minutes longer. Transfer the tart to a cooling rack. Just before serving, remove the tart from the pan and dust its edges with confectioner's sugar.

Storing This tart is at its prime ever so slightly warm or at room temperature. You can cover any leftover tart tightly with plastic wrap and refrigerate it, but don't expect it to retain its just-baked grace.

Contributing Baker **LESLIE MACKIE**

Chocolate Truffle Tartlets

COLOR PHOTOGRAPH, PAGE 343

Makes 6 individual tartlets ■ Intensely, unmistakably, and irresistibly chocolaty. The chocolate pastry shell is a cross between a cookie crust and a buttery, flaky pie dough, and the filling is a creamy bittersweet chocolate truffle concoction given crunch with cubes of milk chocolate, white chocolate, and crackly biscotti. The tartlet (the name seems too small to contain its excitement) is very sophisticated, very elegant, and totally over the top.

1 recipe Chocolate Dough (page 372), well chilled

5 tablespoons unsalted butter, cut into 10 pieces

6 ounces bittersweet chocolate, finely chopped

8 large egg yolks

1 teaspoon pure vanilla extract

¼ cup sugar

2 ounces white chocolate, cut into small dice

2 ounces milk chocolate, cut into small dice

4 biscotti, homemade or store-bought (you can use amaretti di Saronno), chopped

Line a jelly-roll pan with parchment paper and keep at hand. Remove the bottoms from six 4½-inch fluted tartlet pans (or use pans with permanent bottoms and just plan to pop the tartlets out once they're filled, baked, and cooled); spray the pans with vegetable oil spray or brush with melted butter.

Cut the dough into 6 even pieces. Working with one piece at a time, shape the dough into a rough circle, then tamp it down with a rolling pin. Flour the work surface and the top of the dough and roll it into a circle ⅛ to ¼ inch thick. As you roll, lift the dough with the help of a dough scraper to keep it from sticking. If the dough breaks (as it sometimes does even when pros are rolling it), press it back together and keep going—it will be fine once it's baked. Fit the dough into a tartlet ring, pressing it into the fluted edges and cutting the top level with the edges of the pan. Again, patch as you go. Use a pastry brush to dust off any excess flour and place the lined tartlet ring on the prepared baking pan.

Chilling the Crusts When all of the shells are rolled out, chill them for at least 20 minutes.

Baking the Crusts Center a rack in the oven and preheat the oven to 350°F.

Prick the bottoms of the crusts all over with the tines of a fork and bake for 12 to 15 minutes, rotating the pan halfway through the baking time, until the crusts are dry, blistery, and firm. Transfer the baking pan to a rack so that the crusts can cool while you make the filling. Reduce the oven temperature to 300°F.

Making the Filling Bring an inch of water to the simmer in a saucepan. Put the butter and bittersweet chocolate in a large metal bowl and place the bowl over the saucepan—don't let the bottom of the bowl touch the water. Allow the chocolate and butter to melt slowly, stirring from time to time, as you work on the rest of the filling. Remove the chocolate from the heat when it is melted and allow it to cool until it is just slightly warmer than room temperature.

Put the yolks and vanilla extract in the bowl of a mixer fitted with the whisk attachment or in a large mixing bowl. Using the whisk or a hand-held mixer, start beating the yolks at medium speed and then, when they are broken up, reduce the speed to low and gradually add the sugar. Increase the speed to medium-high and beat the yolks and sugar until the yolks thicken and form a slowly dissolving ribbon when the beater is lifted.

Spoon about one third of the yolks onto the cooled chocolate mixture and fold them in with a rubber spatula. Don't worry about being too thorough. Pour the chocolate into the beaten yolks and gently fold the two mixtures together until they are almost completely blended. Add the cubed chocolates and biscotti, folding to incorporate the chunky pieces.

Baking the Tartlets Using an ice cream scoop or ¼-cup measure, divide the filling evenly among the cooled shells. Smooth the filling with a small offset spatula, working it into the nooks and crannies as you circle the tops of the tarts. Bake the tarts for 10 to 12 minutes, until the tops look dry and the filling is just set. Remove to a rack to cool for about 20 minutes before serving.

Storing Best the day they're made, these are still terrific after they've been refrigerated—they lose their textural finesse, but the taste is still very much there. For longer keeping, wrap the tartlets airtight and freeze them for up to a month. Thaw, still wrapped, at room temperature.

A Baker's Extravaganza

On a sky's-the-limit evening, place each tartlet in the center of a dessert plate. Put a Crispy Cocoa Cookie (page 312) off to one side and top the cookie with a small scoop (or quenelle) of richer-than-ice-cream Espresso Parfait (page 447). Finish the extravaganza by decorating each plate with Chocolate Waves (page 450), undulating shards of tricolor chocolate.

Contributing Baker **DAVID OGONOWSKI**

Blueberry-Nectarine Pie

COLOR PHOTOGRAPH, PAGE 350

Makes 6 to 8 servings ■ A picture-perfect double-crusted pie, its rim crimped and decorated with the back of a fork, its top golden brown, its starburst-patterned slits stained around the edges, and its bubbling filling sending out puffs of steam scented with the aroma of warm fruits. Here, as with the crostata (page 374) and the cobblers (page 389), the filling is cooked briefly on top of the range so that you can adjust the flavors before the pie goes into the oven—a good idea and a guarantee of success from pie to pie, no matter the sweetness, or lack thereof, of a particular batch of fruit. As with all pies and tarts, you can play around with the filling. Don't make this a summer-only recipe; use the crust and the filling proportions to create a winter pie with fruit combinations and spices à la maison. And, when you're feeling ambitious, double or triple the recipe and bake for the freezer: These pies can be filled, frozen, and baked without thawing.

THE FILLING

   3 cups fresh blueberries (about 1½ pints)

   2 cups sliced nectarines (about 3 large nectarines)

   ¾ cup sugar

   1½ tablespoons all-purpose flour

   Large pinch of grated lemon zest

   2 teaspoons (approximately) fresh lemon juice

Put half of the fruit in a medium saucepan, keeping the remaining fruit close at hand. Add the sugar, flour, and lemon zest and stir to mix. Bring the mixture to a soft boil over medium heat, stirring constantly. The fruits will release their juices and the liquid will thicken. Turn the mixture into a bowl and stir in the uncooked fruit. Taste a spoonful, paying particular attention to the saucy liquid, and add lemon juice as needed. Cool the filling to room temperature.

THE CRUST

   ½ recipe Flaky Pie Dough (page 31), chilled

   1 tablespoon unsalted butter, cut into bits

   1 large egg beaten with 1 tablespoon cold water, for egg wash

   Crystal or turbinado sugar, for sprinkling

Lining the Pie Pan Cut the dough in half and roll one half out on a lightly floured work surface into a circle about 11 inches across. Fit the crust into a 9-inch cake pan with 1-inch-high sides. (Alternatively, you can use an 8-inch cake pan with 1½-inch-high sides.) Allow the excess dough to hang over the sides for the moment.

Roll the remaining piece of dough into a circle about 10 inches across. Place the pie pan in the center of the dough and, using the pan as a template, cut the bottom round of dough so that it is about ½ inch larger all around than the pan.

Filling the Pie Pan Spoon the cooled filling into the pie shell and dot the top with the butter.

Top Crust Trim the overhanging dough to about ½ inch. Lift the rolled-out circle of dough onto the pie (this is easily done by folding the dough into quarters, transferring it to the top of the pie, and then unfolding it), aligning the edges of the top crust with the bottom crust. If necessary, use a kitchen knife or scissors to trim any ragged edges.

Crimping the dough.

Fold both layers of overhanging dough under to create a thick edge around the rim of the pan. Crimp the edges by pushing the thumb of one hand against the thumb and index finger of your other hand, creating scallops every 1 or 2 inches around the rim. Press the tines of a fork against the flat scallops to decorate. Paint the crust with the egg wash and sprinkle with a little crystal or turbinado sugar.

Chilling the Pie Using the point of a thin knife, cut 4 to 6 slits in the crust and chill for about 20 minutes. *At this point, the pie can be frozen. Place it on a baking sheet and freeze until firm, then wrap airtight and freeze for up to a month. There's no need to thaw the pie before baking, but you should apply another coat of egg wash and will have to bake the pie about 10 minutes longer.*

Baking the Pie Position a rack in the center of the oven and preheat the oven to 375°F.

Place the pie on a parchment- or foil-lined jelly-roll pan and bake for 40 to 50 minutes, until the crust is golden and the fruit bubbling. Let cool for at least 30 minutes before you cut it so that the crusts, top and bottom, have a chance to set.

Storing Pies are at their peak the day they're made, but you can cover and chill leftovers for a day.

Contributing Baker **LESLIE MACKIE**

Brioche Tart with White Secret Sauce

COLOR PHOTOGRAPH, PAGE 341

Makes 8 to 10 servings ▪ A simple but completely satisfying creation. The brioche dough is fitted into a flan ring, its edge beautifully crimped. It is allowed to rise and then spread with a crème fraîche custard mix. When baked, the brioche is golden, the custard bubbling, and the whole, a perfect blend. It can be served plain as morning fare, a luxurious breakfast treat to be sure, or offered as a sumptuous dessert topped with White Secret Sauce, an outstanding chilled sabayon made with caramelized sugar, and garnished with caramel-poached fruit, fresh or dried.

½ **recipe (about 1 pound 2 ounces) Brioche dough (page 43), chilled**

1 cup crème fraîche, homemade (page 447) or store-bought, or sour cream

1 large egg

⅓ **to** ½ **cup sugar**

1 large egg white, beaten
Crystal sugar, for sprinkling

Line a baking sheet with parchment paper and butter a 1¼-inch-high 10-inch flan ring or the ring of a 10-inch springform pan.

Gently work the dough into a ball, flatten it into a 5-inch disk, and roll it out on a lightly floured surface into a circle that's at least 1 to 1½ inches larger than the flan ring. If your circle is ragged, trim it to an even round.

Using a flan ring to mark the dough.

Center the flan ring on the dough and press down on the ring gently so that, when lifted, it leaves a clear impression. This impression will be your crimping guide. Keeping the fingers of your left hand (right, if you're left-handed) against the guideline, lift a little of the dough from the edge with your right hand and fold it over so that it falls about ¼ inch past the guideline. In this position, you should be able to pinch the dough between the index fingers of both hands and crimp it. Twist your fingers slightly and the dough will have an attractive diagonal crimp. Work your way around the tart and don't be concerned about getting it just so—as luxurious as this custard-filled brioche will be, it is still a simple, rustic tart.

Place the flan ring on the parchment-lined baking sheet and lift the dough up and into the ring. Work your fingers around the crimped edge, pressing your fingers into the dough so that you lift up the thick, crimped edge a bit and firmly press down the base of the dough.

Rise Let the dough rise, uncovered, at room temperature until it doubles in size, 45 minutes to 1 hour.

Center a rack in the oven and preheat the oven to 275°F.

Filling the Tart Whisk the crème fraîche and egg together in a small bowl and keep close at hand.

Press your fingertips into the dough, covering all of the tart, except for the crimped edge, with abundant and deep dimples—don't be afraid to press your fingers down almost to the bottom of the pan. Spread the crème fraîche mixture evenly over the bottom of the tart, going right up to where the crimping begins. Sprinkle ⅓ to ½ cup sugar over the custard. You'll know how much sugar to use because the custard will tell you—it will only absorb a certain amount. Stop when it appears that the custard won't take any more.

Baking the Tart Brush the crimped edge of the dough with the beaten egg white and sprinkle it with crystal sugar. Bake the tart for 30 to 40 minutes, or until the crust is golden brown and the custard is just about set. The custard should be a little loose; it should jiggle slightly when you shake the pan gently. Remove to a cooling rack. A few minutes after the tart comes from the oven, slide a cardboard cake round under the tart and lift off the ring. Serve the tart slightly warm or at room temperature, with or without the sauce and fruit garnish.

THE SAUCE

1½ **cups sugar**

2 **vanilla beans, preferably Tahitian**

⅓ **cup water**

2¼ **cups dry white wine**

4 **large egg yolks**

1 **cup heavy cream, whipped to soft peaks**

Top: Crimping the dough around the guideline.
Center: Using your fingertips to press the base of the dough down while lifting the crimped edge.
Bottom: The just-baked tart.

To make the caramel syrup for the sauce, put the sugar into a heavy-bottomed medium skillet with high sides or a saucepan. Split the vanilla beans, scrape the soft, pulpy seeds into the pan, and toss in the pods. Pour in the water—it should be just enough to cover the sugar—but don't stir. Turn the heat to high and bring the mixture to the boil. Now you can either cover the pan for a couple of seconds to wash down any sugar that has crystallized on the sides of the pan or you can wash them down with a pastry brush dipped in cold water.

As the caramel continues to cook, you'll notice that the bubbles will get bigger and shortly after that you'll see the first sign of color—there's always a hot spot. As soon as the caramel starts to color, begin to swirl the skillet gently over the heat. Keep cooking and swirling frequently until the caramel is a deep gold color—test the color by putting a drop of the caramel on a white plate. It probably will take 7 to 10 minutes to get the right color.

continued

When you've got the color you want, immediately remove the pan from the heat and add the white wine. Stand back as you pour in the wine because the caramel will bubble and sizzle—it will also seize and harden. Return the pan to the heat and bring the syrup to the boil again to melt the caramel. Pour 1½ cups of the syrup through a strainer into a heatproof measuring cup. Reserve the remaining syrup in the pan; you'll use it to cook the fruit garnish.

Put the yolks into the bowl of a heavy-duty mixer (or use a heatproof bowl) and, whisking constantly, drizzle in the hot caramel. Put the bowl over a saucepan of boiling water—the water should not touch the bottom of the bowl—and whisk without stop until the yolks are voluminous and almost too hot for you to stand when you dip your finger into the mixture: This should take at least 5 minutes, but the yolks may need as long as 8 minutes of heat and constant stirring. (If the eggs start to cook, a bad sign, or are heating unevenly, lift the bowl out of the pan, whisk for a few seconds off the heat, and then return the bowl to the heat and continue to whisk.)

Attach the bowl to the mixer, fit the mixer with the whisk attachment (or use a hand-held mixer), and beat the yolk mixture at medium-low speed for 10 to 15 minutes, or until the mixture is cool to the touch, pale in color, and about tripled in volume. The bottom of the bowl should feel cold and the mixture should have the look of whipped mayonnaise. Gently fold in the whipped cream. *The sauce can be kept covered in the refrigerator for about 24 hours.*

THE GARNISH

Assorted ripe but firm fruits, such as apricots, peaches, nectarines, and/or plums, or assorted dried fruits, such as raisins, prunes, apricots, and/or peaches

The remaining caramel-wine syrup (above)

Chopped toasted blanched almonds

Confectioner's sugar

If you are using fresh fruits, slice them. If you are using a selection of dried fruits, dice the fruits, soak them in hot water to plump them, and then drain them. Pat them dry before using.

Bring the caramel-wine syrup to a boil in the skillet in which it was made. Add the fruit and swirl the pan. Cook the fruit, swirling the pan and stirring the fruit as needed, until the fruit is softened.

To serve, place a slice of the tart on each plate (this would be nice on largish plates). Spoon on some of the sauce and the caramel-poached fruit, lifting the fruit from the skillet with a slotted spoon, and decorate the plate with a shower of toasted nuts and a dusting of confectioner's sugar.

Storing Although the sauce can be made ahead, and the dough must be made in advance, the tart must be served the day it is made.

Contributing Baker **NANCY SILVERTON**

Johnnycake Cobblers

COLOR PHOTOGRAPH, PAGE 339

Makes 4 to 6 servings ■ The cobbler and its cousins, the pandowdy, the slump, and the grunt, are members of a family of old-fashioned, down-home American desserts that mix sweetened fruits with biscuits of varying kinds. Here, sliced nectarines and purple plums are spooned into individual soufflé cups and topped with a sweet cream and johnnycake meal biscuit. Johnnycake meal is what Rhode Islanders call white cornmeal, used here to give this bursting-with-fruit cobbler an extra measure of flavor and structure and just a tad of added crunch. You can order johnnycake meal by mail (see Sources, page 467), or use yellow cornmeal and delight in the tinge of gold it will give the cobbler's craggy top. And while you're improvising, feel free to use different combinations of fruit, sprinkle in a little spice, or spoon the rich biscuit topping over a family-size cobbler.

THE FRUIT

3 tablespoons unsalted butter

¼ cup sugar, or more to taste

6 cups sliced nectarines and purple plums (9 to 12 pieces of fruit)

Melt the butter in a large skillet over medium heat. Add the sugar, stirring to dissolve, then toss in the fruit. Stir the fruit around to coat each piece and then cook, stirring now and then, until the fruit is soft and gives up some of its liquid. Increase the heat to high and cook for a few minutes more, to boil down the juices a bit. Spoon the fruit into 4 to 6 individual soufflé molds, ramekins, or ovenproof bowls (they should hold 6 to 8 ounces) and set aside while you make the cobbler biscuit.

THE BISCUIT

1½ cups unbleached all-purpose flour

½ cup stone-ground white cornmeal (you can use yellow)

3 tablespoons sugar

1 tablespoon baking powder

½ teaspoon baking soda

1 teaspoon kosher or fine sea salt

1 teaspoon minced ginger (optional)

½ stick (2 ounces) cold unsalted butter, cut into 12 pieces

1¼ to 1½ cups heavy cream

Heavy cream or ice cream, for serving (optional)

continued

Position a rack in the center of the oven and preheat the oven to 425°F.

Put the flour, cornmeal, sugar, baking powder, baking soda, salt, and the ginger, if you're using it, in the work bowl of a food processor fitted with the metal blade. Pulse 5 or 6 times, just to mix the ingredients.

Add the pieces of cold butter. Being extremely careful not to cut your fingers, reach in and toss the butter around to coat each piece with flour. (This will help cut the butter evenly into the flour—it's an optional step; if you'd rather skip it, you'll still have a great cobbler.) Pulse the machine 18 to 20 times, or until there are no lumps and the mixture resembles coarse meal.

Transfer the mixture to a large bowl. Make a well in the center of the ingredients and pour in 1¼ cups heavy cream, stirring with a fork to draw in the dry ingredients from the sides of the bowl and form a dough. If the mixture is too dry and does not hold together, add more cream, as much as ¼ cup more. You want a soft, moist dough that forms curds as you stir it.

Baking the Cobblers Spoon the dough onto the top of the fruit, dividing it evenly among the cobbler pans. Don't worry if the fruit isn't completely covered or if it's covered unevenly—this is a homey dessert and part of its charm is its rough, craggy top. If the fruit bubbles up and over the top, so much the better.

Place the cobblers on a foil- or parchment-lined jelly-roll pan and bake for 12 to 14 minutes, or until the tops are nicely browned. (The golden biscuit is the key; you don't have to worry about the fruit, as it was cooked before it went into the oven.) Transfer the cobblers to a rack and let them cool for 5 to 10 minutes—they're best served warm. If you must make them ahead of time, keep them at room temperature—do not reheat.

If you're serving the cobblers with a pitcher of heavy cream, encourage people to crack the tops and create a little opening for the cream to be poured in; ice cream can be scooped right onto the cobbler tops, cracked or not.

Storing The cobblers are meant to be served minutes out of the oven. If necessary, they can be made a few hours ahead and kept, uncovered, at room temperature.

Large Cobbler

This amount of fruit and biscuit is perfect for making a cobbler in a 10-inch deep-dish pie pan (with a capacity of 1½ quarts). Turn the cooked fruit into the pan and spoon on the biscuit topping—there's enough topping to cover all of the fruit. Bake for 14 to 16 minutes, until the biscuit is golden and the fruit bubbling.

Contributing Baker **JOHANNE KILLEEN**

Grand Pastries

THE "GRAND" IN THE TITLE has nothing to do with the size of these pastries and everything to do with their impact. These pastries are show-stopping replicas of individually plated restaurant desserts, detailed so that you can make them at home. Contained within the recipes for each of these sumptuous sweets is a lesson in modular baking: You'll learn to make everything you need ahead of time in order to construct your desserts at the last minute, just the way restaurant pastry chefs do. And what desserts they'll be.

From Chicago's most talked about restaurant pastry chef, Gale Gand, you'll learn to turn phyllo into fantastic pastries. You'll make caramelized phyllo pillows for her Inside-out Upside-down Tirami Sù, chocolate phyllo shards for ganache-layered

Chocolate Napoleons, sugary triangles for featherweight Not-Your-Usual Lemon Meringue Pie, and crunchy nests for Phylloccine Ice Cream Sandwiches topped with a fruit skewer. You'll make the fillings, toppings, and decorations ahead and then, with a mini assembly line set up in your kitchen, you'll combine the components for a polished presentation.

Whether it's David Blom's yeast-raised babas and savarins soaked in exotic liqueur syrups, elegant meringues piped as nests or layered with tropical fruit from Charlotte Akoto, or Norman Love's wondrously light and elegant beignets and profiteroles, these pastries promise—and deliver—make-ahead practicality and guaranteed dinner-table delight.

Tropical Napoleons
COLOR PHOTOGRAPH, PAGE 337

Makes 6 to 8 servings ■ The napoleon, a tall dessert named for a short general, was made traditionally with puff pastry and is now made regularly with phyllo (see page 400 for a wonderful rendition). Here it is given the lightest treatment yet, wafer-thin rounds of meringue. The meringue is a plain one, beaten a little softer than the norm, and then stabilized and taste-boosted with flaked coconut and a sprinkling of sesame seeds. The technique for achieving paper-thinness with the meringue is interesting and easily done: The meringue is spread across a homemade template the way you might skim-coat a wall with plaster. Once the wafers are cool, they're stacked between layers of rummy whipped cream, berries, and slices of soft, colorful tropical fruits. Depending on how thin you spread the meringue, you may end up with extra wafers—they're great with coffee.

THE WAFERS

3 large egg whites, at room temperature

Pinch of salt

½ cup sugar

1 cup sweetened flaked coconut

¼ cup sesame seeds

Position the oven racks to divide the oven into thirds and preheat the oven to 325°F. You'll probably have to bake the meringues in two batches, so butter and flour three baking sheets or jelly-roll pans and line a fourth sheet or a tray with parchment paper; it will be the holding tray for the baked meringues.

Prepare a template by cutting a ring out of the plastic top from a large container of yogurt, cottage cheese, ice cream, or the like: Cut away the rim so that the top lies flat. Draw a 4-inch circle in the center and cut that away. (If you can make only a 3½-inch ring, it will be fine.)

Cutting the plastic template.

Put the egg whites and salt in the bowl of a mixer fitted with the whisk attachment, or use a hand-held mixer. Beat the whites at high speed for about 3 minutes, until they hold medium-soft peaks. With the mixer running, gradually add three quarters of the sugar and continue to beat until the peaks are shiny and firm, about 4 minutes. Add the remaining sugar and beat for another 2 minutes. Remove the bowl from the mixer and gently but thoroughly fold in ½ cup of the coconut with a rubber spatula.

Forming the Meringues Place the template flat against a buttered and floured baking sheet, and spoon a heaping tablespoon of meringue into the center of the ring. Using a short, flexible metal spatula, preferably an offset one, spread the meringue to the edge of the template to form a thin circle of batter. Lift

Top: After spreading meringue to the template's edges, lift the template and continue to make more disks.

Bottom: A stack of baked wafers.

the template and continue making circles, spacing them fairly close together, since the meringue won't spread during baking; you should be able to get 6 to 8 wafers on each sheet. Sprinkle the circles with the remaining coconut and the sesame seeds.

Baking the Meringues Bake the meringues for 5 to 7 minutes, checking them at the 4-minute mark and then every minute thereafter—these bake (and then burn) quickly—and removing them from the baking sheets as they just start to color. The easiest way to get the wafers off the sheet is to put the baking sheet on the opened oven door (the heat from the door will keep the circles supple) and slip a wide metal spatula or pancake turner under each wafer, pushing the spatula against the baking sheet, not the wafer, so that the meringue remains flat. Transfer the wafers to the parchment-lined baking sheet to cool. Because the meringues are so thin, they cool quickly, and you can stack them on the baking sheet between layers of parchment. *The wafers can be made ahead, wrapped airtight—take care, they're extremely fragile—and kept at room temperature for a day or two.*

THE CREAM

1 cup cold heavy cream

1 tablespoon dark rum

1/4 teaspoon pure vanilla extract

3 tablespoons sifted confectioner's sugar

1 1/2 cups (approximately) assorted fresh berries and small slices of tropical fruit, such as mango, papaya, or kiwi, for layering

Confectioner's sugar, for dusting

Working in a chilled bowl with a chilled whisk or beaters, whip the cream until it holds soft peaks. Add the rum and vanilla extract and beat until the peaks are firm. Switch to a rubber spatula and fold in the confectioner's sugar. Keep the cream covered and chilled until needed.

Finishing the Napoleons Spoon the whipped cream into a pastry bag fitted with a small (1/8-inch) star tip; or, if you want, you can just use a small spoon to spread the cream over the wafers. Pipe or drop a dot of whipped cream in the center of each of six to eight dessert plates to act as glue for the napoleons. Construct each napoleon by wiggling a wafer into the cream to settle it, piping or spooning on a puff of whipped cream, arranging a few berries and fruit slices over the cream, and topping with another wafer, more cream, more fruit, and a final wafer. Dust each dessert with a little confectioner's sugar and serve immediately.

Storing The wafers can be made ahead of time, but the assembled dessert should be served as soon as it's ready.

Contributing Baker **CHARLOTTE AKOTO**

Cocoa Nests with Caramel Mousse

Makes 8 to 10 servings ■ This is a fancy restaurant-style dinner-party dessert, which means your guests will be bowled over and you, having done everything in advance the way it's done in restaurants, will be free to sit at the dinner table with your guests until the last minute. The dessert has three components: crisp cocoa meringue nests, based on the recipe for meringue, which can be made a week or more in advance (turn to page 37 if you need a refresher course on meringue); pecan praline, made up to a week ahead and kept on hand to add crunch to this and other sweets; and caramel mousse, a classic, not-too-sweet, incredibly creamy mousse that can be made the day before the party. Each component takes a little fussing, but none is hard. When the dessert is assembled, it is a marvel of textural contrasts and a splendid blend of tastes.

THE NESTS

> 4 large egg whites, at room temperature
>
> Pinch of salt
>
> ½ cup granulated sugar
>
> ¼ cup sifted confectioner's sugar
>
> 2 tablespoons unsweetened cocoa powder

Position the oven racks to divide the oven into thirds and preheat the oven to 200°F. Cut two pieces of parchment paper to line baking sheets or jelly-roll pans. Using a dark pencil or felt-tip marker, draw four 4-inch ovals on each piece of parchment; these are your templates. Put a template, marked side down, on each of two baking sheets. The markings should be visible—if not, make them darker. Set the pans aside.

Put the egg whites and salt in the bowl of a mixer fitted with the whisk attachment, or use a hand-held mixer. Starting on the highest speed, beat the whites for 1 to 3 minutes, until they increase in volume and form medium-soft peaks that hold their shape. With the machine still running, gradually add ⅓ cup of the granulated sugar and continue to beat for 3 to 5 minutes, or until the peaks are stiff. Add the remaining sugar and beat 2 to 3 minutes more, until the sugar is dissolved and the peaks are shiny.

Sift the confectioner's sugar and cocoa together onto a sheet of parchment or waxed paper. When the peaks are firm and shiny, use a rubber spatula to fold the confectioner's sugar and cocoa into the meringue one third at a time. As you fold, the sugar-cocoa mixture will make the meringue less airy—don't panic, just keep folding and working in the rest of the sugar and cocoa. Be patient; it can take a while to get everything incorporated.

Spoon the cocoa meringue into a large pastry bag fitted with a small (about ⅛- to ¼-inch) star tip. Pipe a dab of meringue into each corner of the baking sheets to serve as glue for the sheet of parchment.

continued

Top: Pipe cocoa meringue ovals by starting at the center and spiraling out.
Bottom: Top the ovals with a ring of rosettes.

Piping the Meringues To pipe the ovals, start at the center of each template and, holding the pastry bag at a very slight angle, work your way around the oval in a tight spiral. Keep the piping tip close to the paper and try not to leave any space between the coils. (Tight spirals are the ideal, and you'll get them with practice, but relax—if there are spaces, you can fill them by running a spatula over the surface.) To make the "lip" that will turn the ovals into cups or nests, pipe small rosettes, one touching the other, atop the outer coil of each oval.

Baking the Meringue Bake the nests for 2 to 2½ hours, or until dry and crisp. Let the meringues cool on the parchment and then lift them off or, if necessary, run a spatula under them. *Cooled meringues can be stored, wrapped airtight, in a cool, dry place for at least a week.*

THE PRALINE

1 cup sugar
1 cup pecan halves or pieces

Brush a baking sheet with oil and set aside.

Put the sugar in a very heavy saucepan over high heat and stir it with a wooden spoon. Don't be discouraged when the sugar forms lumps, as it will—just keep stirring, and the lumps will dissolve as the sugar melts. When the melted sugar starts to take on color, lower the heat slightly and continue to cook, stirring, until the sugar turns a light caramel color. (Test it by dropping a little on a white plate.) As soon as the caramel is the right color, add the nuts all at once and stir with the spoon to make certain they're all coated with caramel; boil and stir for 30 seconds, or until the nuts are separated (they may have clumped), then turn the caramelized nuts out onto the oiled baking sheet. Set them aside to cool and harden.

When the praline is hard, break it into pieces and transfer it to the work bowl of a food processor fitted with the metal blade; process until chopped fine. *The praline can be made up to a week in advance and kept in an airtight container at room temperature.*

THE MOUSSE

1 teaspoon unflavored gelatin
6 tablespoons cold water
2 tablespoons dark rum
¾ cup sugar
6 large egg yolks
2 cups heavy cream

Cocoa powder, for sprinkling
Confectioner's sugar, for sprinkling

Dissolve the gelatin in ¼ cup of the cold water: Sprinkle it over the water, add the dark rum, and stir. Set aside.

Put the sugar in a very heavy saucepan over high heat and cook, stirring with a spoon, as you did for the praline—but this time cook until the sugar turns a deep, dark caramel color (as tested on a white plate). The sugar may color quickly, so keep an eye on it. At the first sign of color, lower the heat and continue to cook and stir with a long-handled spoon.

As soon as the caramel is the right color, remove it from the heat. Stand back and stir in the remaining 2 tablespoons cold water to stop the cooking and set the color. The water will cause the caramel to bubble, sizzle, and seize—just keep stirring to dissolve the lumps. When there are no longer any bubbles, add the gelatin. The caramel will bubble again, but once again, if you just keep stirring, it will settle down; set it aside for the moment.

Put the egg yolks in a mixer fitted with the whisk attachment (or work with a hand-held mixer) and beat on high speed until the yolks thicken and turn pale yellow. Reduce the speed to low and slowly pour in the caramel-gelatin mixture, then increase the speed to high and beat until the mousse is cool to the touch. It will take between 5 and 10 minutes of beating to cool the mousse. (To speed the cooling process, you can place the mixer bowl in a larger bowl filled with a mixture of ice cubes and cold water and beat the mousse over it.)

Whip the heavy cream in a large bowl until it holds soft peaks. Using a rubber spatula, fold half of the whipped cream into the mousse; fold the mousse into the remaining cream and cover the bowl tightly with plastic wrap. Chill the mousse for at least an hour before filling the nests. *The mousse can be made up to 1 day ahead and kept covered in the refrigerator until needed.*

Finishing the Dessert Place each nest on a dessert plate. Sprinkle one half of each nest with cocoa powder and the other half with confectioner's sugar. Sprinkle praline over the bottom and pipe (you can use a plain ¼-inch pastry tip) or spoon in the caramel mousse. Top with a shower of praline.

Storing Each part of this dessert can be made ahead, but once you combine them, it's best to serve the pastry quickly.

Contributing Baker **CHARLOTTE AKOTO**

Inside-out Upside-down Tirami Sù

Makes 4 servings ■ This praiseworthy dessert rethinks all the elements of a traditional tirami sù. Instead of a soft cake soaked in a warm espresso syrup, this dessert is all crunch and chill. It is based on a disk of phyllo, a single scrunched-up sheet brushed with butter and sprinkled with ginger and sugar so that it bakes to a shiny, caramelized little cake. Here it is layered with cappuccino granita and mascarpone sabayon, but you'll find yourself using it also as a foundation for warm sautéed fruits, the best-ever bottom to a hot-fudge sundae, or the sandwichers for a mousse-filled "flying saucer." As with other phyllo desserts, this is a sweet of parts, and each part can be made ahead.

THE GRANITA

    1¼ **cups cold brewed espresso**
    ¼ **cup skim milk**
    ¼ **cup simple syrup (see page 23), cooled**

Pour all of the ingredients into a 9-inch square metal pan and stir to combine. Unlike other granitas, this one requires no more stirring. Place the pan, uncovered, in the freezer and freeze until solid. If you are not going to use the frozen granita within an hour or two, cover it well with plastic wrap or foil. When you are ready to serve, use the edge of a metal spoon or the tines of a fork to scrape the granita, allowing it to mound in the pan. You are looking for a texture like grainy shaved ice. Once scraped, the granita can remain frozen for an hour or so, but it is really best used as soon after scraping as possible.

THE SABAYON

    3 **large egg yolks**
    ¼ **cup sugar**
    ¼ **cup milk (2% milk is fine)**
    ⅛ **teaspoon cinnamon**
    ⅓ **cup heavy cream**
    ⅔ **cup mascarpone**

Bring an inch or two of water to a simmer in the bottom of a double boiler or in a saucepan over which you can place a metal bowl. Half-fill a large bowl with ice cubes; set aside.

Combine the egg yolks, sugar, milk, and cinnamon in the top of the double boiler or a metal bowl and set it in place over, but not touching, the hot water. Keeping the water at a simmer, whisk the ingredients until they are slightly thickened and foamy, about 8 minutes. The tracks of your whisk should remain for an instant before dissolving and the consistency of the sauce should remind you of a custard sauce or a thin pastry cream. Remove the top of the double boiler or the bowl and place it in the bowl of ice cubes. Whisk constantly until the sauce is cool, about 3 minutes. *You can make the sabayon to this point and refrigerate it for up to a day.*

Beat the heavy cream until it holds soft peaks; set aside for a moment. Soften and lighten the mascarpone by stirring it with a rubber spatula. With the spatula, fold the mascarpone and whipped cream into the chilled sabayon. Keep the sauce covered in the refrigerator until needed. *Chilled, the sauce will keep for about 4 hours.*

THE PHYLLO

¼ **cup sugar**

¼ **teaspoon ginger**

4 **sheets phyllo dough**

3 **tablespoons clarified unsalted butter (see page 5)**

Milk chocolate curls or finely chopped milk chocolate, for garnish

Confectioner's sugar, for sprinkling

Preheat the oven to 350°F. Butter the bottom and sides of eight 4-inch round baking pans (see Sources, page 467) and dust them with sugar, tapping out the excess. (The butter and sugar for the pans are in addition to the amounts called for in the ingredients list.)

Whisk the sugar and ginger together in a small bowl; set aside.

Lay the phyllo sheets out on your work surface. Cut the sheets in half crosswise and work with a half sheet at a time, keeping the remaining sheets covered with a kitchen towel. Brush the phyllo with some of the butter and sprinkle with some of the ginger-sugar. Peel the dough off the counter (you will have buttered it down, no doubt) and scrunch it into a disk, trying to keep the buttered side out. Don't worry if the phyllo tears in places, it will still make a fine pillow. Place the disk in a prepared pan, press down lightly, and continue working through the batch.

Baking the Phyllo Place the pans on a baking sheet and bake for 8 to 10 minutes, or until the sugar has caramelized and the phyllo is golden brown. Turn the disks out onto a rack and cool to room temperature.

Finishing the Pastries For each serving, place 1 phyllo pillow in a bowl and top with some granita, a big spoonful of mascarpone sabayon, and another pillow. Scatter chocolate curls over the top, sprinkle with confectioner's sugar, and serve immediately.

Storing Each element of this dessert can be made ahead, but the assembled tirami sù must be served at once—granita has a short lifespan.

Contributing Baker **GALE GAND**

Chocolate Napoleons

Makes 4 servings ■ Here's a triple-decker napoleon made with shards of chocolate phyllo—an inspired idea. Each sheet of phyllo is brushed with a blend of butter and cocoa, sprinkled with sugar, and baked until it is transformed into a delicate shatter-at-a-touch pastry with deep chocolate flavor. It's the perfect companion to mocha ganache, poached pears, whipped cream beaten with ginger and brown sugar, and orange-spiked cranberry compote, the remaining players in this extravaganza. Save this for the finish to a grand dinner—it makes a dazzling presentation—and don't be put off by the number of components. Nothing takes long to do and everything can be made in advance.

THE PHYLLO

1 stick (4 ounces) unsalted butter, clarified (see page 5)

¼ cup unsweetened cocoa powder, preferably Dutch-processed

3 sheets phyllo dough

6 tablespoons to ¾ cup sugar

Center a rack in the oven and preheat the oven to 350°F. Line a baking sheet with parchment paper and have two more sheets of parchment and another baking sheet at hand.

Stir the clarified butter and cocoa together in a bowl; set it aside for the moment.

Brushing the phyllo with butter and cocoa.

Stack the phyllo sheets on your work surface and cut the pastry in half crosswise. You'll be working with one piece of phyllo at a time and should keep the remainder covered with a kitchen towel. Place a piece of phyllo on the parchment-lined baking sheet, brush it with some of the cocoa-butter, and sprinkle it with 1 to 2 tablespoons of the sugar. Cover with another sheet of phyllo, brush with cocoa-butter, and sprinkle with sugar. Repeat with one more phyllo sheet. Cover the stack with a piece of parchment paper and repeat the stacking, brushing, and sprinkling with the remaining 3 sheets of phyllo. Cover the sheets with a piece of parchment paper and top with a baking sheet, which will weight the phyllo and keep it from puffing.

Baking the Phyllo Bake the phyllo for 8 to 10 minutes, until the sheets are golden and crispy. (Even though the phyllo is dark from the cocoa, when you lift the parchment, you'll be able to see that the edges of the pastry are tinged with gold.) Transfer the baking sheet to a wire rack, remove the top baking sheet, and allow the phyllo to cool to room temperature.

When the phyllo is cool, remove the parchment liners and separate the two stacks of pastry, each of which should now be fused and feel like one flaky sheet. Break or cut each sheet into pieces about 4 inches long and 3 inches wide. Don't worry about getting smooth edges or pieces that are all the same size—the irregular forms are part of this dessert's appeal. However, you should try to get a total of 12 pieces, since you will need 3 phyllo shards for each napoleon. Keep at room temperature until needed. *You can make the phyllo shards up to 1 day ahead and keep them at room temperature, covered with plastic wrap. If they need it, crisp them in a 350°F oven for a couple of minutes and let them cool before assembling the dessert.*

A stack of crispy phyllo shards.

THE PEARS

4 cups water

2 cups sugar

1 cup white wine

2 cinnamon sticks

Grated zest and juice of 1 orange

1 vanilla bean, partially split lengthwise

2 ripe pears, peeled, halved, and cored

Combine all of the ingredients except the pears in a medium saucepan and bring to the boil. Lower the heat to a simmer and add the pears. Press a circle of waxed paper against the pears and cook the fruit at the simmer until tender enough to be pierced easily with the tip of a knife. Lift the pears onto a plate with a slotted spoon (keep the syrup in the refrigerator for another round of poaching); cover with plastic wrap and cool to room temperature before chilling. *The pears can be made a day or two ahead and kept well covered in the refrigerator.*

THE COMPOTE

1 cup fresh or frozen (not thawed) cranberries

1 cup fresh orange juice

¼ cup sugar

Put all of the ingredients in a medium saucepan and bring to the boil, stirring to dissolve the sugar. Boil, stirring occasionally, until most of the berries have popped. The compote will seem thin, but it will thicken as it cools. Remove the pan from the heat and cool to room temperature. *The cranberry compote can be made up to 4 days ahead and kept covered in the refrigerator.*

THE GANACHE

10 ounces bittersweet chocolate, coarsely chopped

½ cup whole milk

½ cup heavy cream

⅓ cup sugar

1 to 3 tablespoons ground coffee (depending on your taste for coffee)

continued

Place the chocolate in a large heatproof bowl and set aside.

Place the remaining ingredients in a medium saucepan and bring to the boil. Pour the hot liquid through a fine sieve into the bowl of chocolate and whisk the mixture gently until smooth, taking care not beat air into it. Press a piece of plastic wrap against the surface of the ganache and refrigerate until set, about 15 minutes. While the ganache will set up, or thicken, in the refrigerator, it should be used at room temperature, or just a tad above. If you've chilled it (*and it can be chilled for up to 2 days*), either allow it to sit at room temperature until it returns to its smooth, mousselike consistency, or warm it over the lowest possible heat.

THE CREAM

> **1 cup cold heavy cream**
> **2 tablespoons brown sugar (make certain it's free of lumps)**
> **¼ teaspoon grated ginger**
>
> **Confectioner's sugar, for dusting**
> **Mint sprigs, for garnish**

Working either in a mixer fitted with the whisk attachment or a bowl with a hand-held mixer, whip the cream, brown sugar, and ginger together until the cream holds firm peaks. *The cream can be whipped, covered with plastic, and kept in the refrigerator for about 4 hours. Give it a turn or two with a whisk to bring it back to shape before using.*

Finishing the Napoleon Remove the pears from the refrigerator and drain them on paper towels, blotting well to take up the excess moisture. Place the pears on a baking sheet and slice each pear half in half again. Working with one piece at a time, cut each pear quarter from blossom to stem end into thin slices, stopping about ½ inch from the top so that the slices remain connected. Fan the pieces of pear.

To assemble each napoleon, place a dab of ganache in the center of each of four dessert plates. Rest a shard of cocoa phyllo on the dab and press it down gently to settle it into place. Top with a spoonful of ganache, a fanned pear, and a bit of ginger cream, then repeat—phyllo, ganache, pear, and cream—and top with a third piece of phyllo. Spoon some cranberry compote around the plates, dust one edge of each napoleon with confectioner's sugar, and garnish with mint sprigs.

Storing Once assembled, the dessert must be served immediately.

Contributing Baker **GALE GAND**

Not-Your-Usual
Lemon Meringue Pie

Makes 6 servings ■ Lemon meringue pie for the individual and the individualist. This is a pie-per-person dessert that breaks with tradition. All of the elements you expect are here; they've just been shaken up in this playful rendition. Because the customary sturdy crust has been replaced by feather-light phyllo triangles, the lemon flavor seems to come through with more punch and the meringue with more subtlety. Take note of the lemon curd—it, too, is not-your-usual. Because it is made with whole eggs rather than yolks and uses less butter than the norm, the result is an extremely light, almost custardy curd, perfect in this pie and nice to have on hand for spreading over biscuits and scones.

THE CURD

4 large eggs

1 cup sugar

2/3 cup fresh lemon juice

Grated zest of 1 lemon

**1/2 stick (2 ounces) unsalted butter, at room temperature,
cut into 8 pieces**

Choose a saucepan that will hold the bowl from your mixer (or a heatproof mixing bowl) in a double-boiler arrangement. Fill the pan with 2 to 3 inches of water and bring to the simmer.

Put the eggs and sugar in the mixer fitted with the whisk attachment and whip at high speed until very light and fluffy. (Or put in the mixing bowl and use a hand-held mixer.) Still whisking, add the lemon juice and grated zest. Set the bowl in the saucepan, making sure that the bottom of the bowl does not touch the simmering water, and cook the mixture, whisking constantly by hand, until it is smooth, thick, and custardlike. Be patient; this can take a while. Transfer the bowl to the counter and whisk in the butter piece by piece. Scrape the curd into another bowl (so your mixer is free), press plastic wrap against the top, and refrigerate until thoroughly chilled and set; or whisk the curd over ice until chilled. *The curd can be made up to a week in advance and kept in an airtight container in the refrigerator.* Once the curd is set, it should not be stirred again.

THE PHYLLO

3 sheets phyllo, cut crosswise in half

1/2 cup clarified unsalted butter (see page 5)

6 tablespoons to 3/4 cup sugar

continued

Center a rack in the oven and preheat the oven to 350°F. Line a baking sheet with parchment paper and have two more sheets of parchment and another baking sheet at hand.

Phyllo cut into triangles and ready to bake.

Stack the phyllo sheets on your work surface. You'll be working with one piece of phyllo at a time and should keep the remainder covered with a kitchen towel. Place a piece of phyllo on the parchment-lined baking sheet, brush it with some of the butter, and sprinkle it with 1 to 2 tablespoons sugar. Cover with another sheet of phyllo, brush with butter, and sprinkle with sugar; repeat with one more phyllo sheet. Using a long sharp knife and a ruler, cut the phyllo crosswise into 3 equal strips, cutting through all the layers of phyllo but keeping the pieces intact. Cut 3 equal triangles in each of the thirds; you'll be left with a long thin triangle on each end—they'll make good nibbles for the cook after they're baked.

Working on another piece of parchment paper, repeat the stacking, brushing, and sprinkling with the remaining 3 sheets of phyllo. Cut this stack of phyllo in the triangle pattern and place it on the baking sheet (on top of the first stack). Cover the phyllo layers with a piece of parchment paper and top with another baking sheet, which will weight the phyllo and keep it from puffing.

Baking the Phyllo Bake the phyllo for 8 to 10 minutes, until the sheets are golden and crispy. Transfer the baking sheet to a wire rack, remove the top baking sheet, and allow the phyllo to cool to room temperature. *The phyllo triangles can be made up to a day ahead, covered with plastic wrap, and kept at room temperature.*

THE MERINGUE

8 large egg whites, at room temperature
¾ cup (packed) light brown sugar, pressed through a sieve

Confectioner's sugar, for dusting
Mint sprigs, for garnish

Piping meringue over
the lemon curd.

Prepare the meringue just before you're ready to serve. Put the whites in the clean, dry, grease-free bowl of a mixer fitted with the whisk attachment (or use a hand-held mixer) and beat on high speed until they form soft peaks. Keeping the mixer on high speed, gradually add the brown sugar and beat until the meringue forms firm, glossy peaks.

Assembling the "Pies" Spoon the meringue into a pastry bag fitted with a ¼-inch plain tip. Pipe a dab of meringue in the center of each dessert plate and "glue" a phyllo triangle onto the plate. Place 2 spoonfuls of curd on the phyllo and pipe over a layer of meringue, zigzagging it so that the lines of meringue touch one another and cover the top of the curd. Brown the meringue with a small blowtorch and top with a phyllo triangle. (A blowtorch is the only tool that will caramelize the meringue without melting the curd. If you don't have a blowtorch, cover the curd completely with meringue and run the meringue under the broiler, keeping a watchful eye on the dessert and pulling it out the instant the meringue is browned. Working this way, it will probably be easiest to do just one layer.) Spoon another layer of curd onto each dessert, pipe and caramelize another zigzag of meringue, and finish each one with a phyllo triangle. Dust the top of the "pies" with confectioner's sugar, garnish the plates with sprigs of mint, and serve.

Piping the second layer of meringue over the caramelized layer.

Storing Once put together, the "pies" must be served immediately.

Contributing Baker **GALE GAND**

Phylloccine Ice Cream Sandwiches
COLOR PHOTOGRAPH, PAGE 336

Makes 8 servings ■ Think of this as a classy and sweet club sandwich: The phyllo fettuccine is the bread, the raspberry purée the condiment, the vanilla ice cream the filling, and the fruit-laced skewer the replacement for the frilly toothpick that holds it all together. It's more than a clever idea—it's a wonderful play of flavors and textures. And the technique for making phyllo fettuccine, or "phylloccine," is as whimsical as the finished pastry is delightful. The phyllo is kept rolled up as it is in the box, sliced, and then tossed like a bowl of pasta before it is baked in little nests.

THE PHYLLO
1 box phyllo dough, thawed if frozen
½ cup clarified unsalted butter (see page 5)
2 tablespoons sugar, for sprinkling

Position the racks to divide the oven into thirds and preheat the oven to 350°F. Line two baking sheets with parchment paper and keep them close at hand.

Remove the phyllo from the box and bag. Unroll the phyllo and remove and discard the waxy paper, then reroll the sheets into their original shape. Put the phyllo on a cutting board and, using a long serrated knife, cut the roll into ½-inch thick slices. Toss the phyllo between your fingertips to separate the strands, creating a mound of what will look like phyllo fettuccine. Divide the strands into 16 little piles and place on the parchment-lined baking sheets. Splatter each nest with clarified butter and sprinkle with the sugar.

continued

Baking the Phyllo Bake the nests for 8 to 10 minutes, or until just golden. Allow the phyllo to cool on the pans while you make the rest of the dessert. *The phyllo can be baked a day ahead, left on the pans, covered with plastic wrap, and kept at room temperature until needed.*

THE SALAD

2¼ cups (about 1½ pints) fresh raspberries
Sugar to taste
2 mint leaves, julienned

Purée ¼ to ½ cup of the raspberries in a blender or food processor; strain if you prefer seedless purée. Transfer to a bowl and toss with the remaining whole berries, as much sugar as you like, and the cut mint; keep close at hand.

THE FRUIT SKEWERS

8 blueberries
8 raspberries
8 blackberries
8 strawberries with hulls

(or any other combination of small or cut-up fruits)

Thread 1 of each type of fruit onto each of 8 bamboo skewers and set aside.

THE CREAM

1 cup cold heavy cream
1 teaspoon brown sugar

2 pints (approximately) vanilla ice cream, for serving
Confectioner's sugar, for dusting

Whip the heavy cream and brown sugar together until the cream forms soft peaks. Keep chilled until needed. *The cream can be kept covered in the refrigerator for about 2 hours.*

Assembling the Sandwiches Put a dab of whipped cream in the center of each of eight dessert plates to act as "glue." Put a phyllo nest on the cream, press down gently to set, spoon on some of the raspberry salad, and add a scoop of vanilla ice cream. Top with another phyllo nest and pierce the package with a fruit skewer. Dust the sandwiches lightly with confectioner's sugar, spoon some of the softly whipped cream onto the plates, and serve immediately.

Storing Although you can make each of the dessert's components ahead, once assembled, the dessert has to be served—and eaten—posthaste.

Contributing Baker **GALE GAND**

Chocolate-Cinnamon Beignets

Makes 10 to 12 servings ■ This is, in fact, a beignet and it is, in fact, a pastry made of choux paste, but it resembles neither, really. Most beignets are like fritters, puffs of fried dough sprinkled with confectioner's sugar or holding together kernels of corn, and most choux paste pastries are piped and baked. This beignet is cinnamon-sparked chocolate, it's filled with vanilla pastry cream and caramelized bananas, and it's made from chilled pâte à choux that's been thickened to rolling consistency with some extra flour. It's a highly innovative way to treat pâte à choux.

Unlike traditional pâte à choux, this dough should be made ahead to give it time to chill; ditto the pastry cream and bananas. You can do all the preparations at your own pace, but once you've fried the beignets, head for the dining room—pronto.

THE BEIGNETS

1/2 **cup whole milk**

1/2 **cup water**

3/4 **stick (3 ounces) unsalted butter**

2 **tablespoons sugar**

1 1/2 **tablespoons unsweetened cocoa powder**

1 **teaspoon cinnamon**

1/4 **teaspoon salt**

1 1/2 **cups all-purpose flour**

5 to 6 **large eggs, at room temperature**

2/3 **cup (approximately) all-purpose flour, for kneading**

Put the milk, water, butter, sugar, cocoa, cinnamon, and salt into a 2-quart saucepan and bring to a full boil over medium heat, stirring frequently with a wooden spoon until the butter melts. Still stirring, add the flour all at once. Stir energetically and without stop until the flour is thoroughly incorporated, then continue to cook and stir for another 30 to 45 seconds, or until the dough forms a ball and a light crust is visible on the bottom of the pan.

Remove the pan from the heat and scrape the paste into a medium bowl. Immediately, while the dough is still hot, beat in the eggs one at a time, stirring vigorously with a wooden spoon or spatula to incorporate each one before adding the next. The first couple of eggs are the hardest to mix in, but as the mixture loosens it softens, smoothes, and becomes easier to blend. (If you want, you can beat the eggs in with a mixer—hand-held, or standing with the paddle attachment—just keep the speed low and take care not to beat too much air into the dough.)

continued

After you've incorporated 5 eggs, take a good look at the mixture—it might not need the last egg. You'll know the dough is perfect when, as you lift the wooden spoon, the spoon pulls up some of the dough that then detaches and forms a slowly bending peak. If the dough's too thick and doesn't yet peak, add the last egg.

Chilling the Dough Wrap the dough in plastic and refrigerate until thoroughly chilled, about 2 hours. *The dough can be kept refrigerated for up to 2 days.*

Divide the cold dough in half and keep one half in the refrigerator while you work with the other. Turn the dough out onto a lightly floured work surface and slowly knead in enough flour to produce a dough that can be rolled easily, about ⅓ cup flour. The dough will be very soft and sticky at first and is most easily worked with a metal spatula or a bench scraper. Keep adding the flour a few tablespoons at a time, until you can actually knead the dough. Don't expect it to be like a firm pie dough—it will always remain somewhat sticky—but you will have a dough that is pliable and rollable. Wrap and chill the dough before rolling it out. Repeat with the remaining dough.

Line 2 baking sheets with parchment paper.

To make decorations, cut triangles of dough and use decorating tips to cut out a line of holes.

Cutting the Choux Circles On a floured work surface, roll the dough out to a thickness of ¹⁄₁₆ to ⅛ inch, taking care not to press down too firmly on the pin. Using a 4-inch round cutter, cut as many circles as you can from the dough; gather and reroll the scraps and cut out more circles. You should end up with about 18 circles. Lift the circles onto the baking sheets, cover lightly with plastic, and refrigerate for at least 1 hour. If you want, cut fewer circles and use some of the dough to make decorations, such as large triangles dotted with a line of holes (use the decorating tips from a pastry bag to make the holes) or half-moons with cutouts. Repeat with the remaining piece of dough.

THE PASTRY CREAM

1 cup whole milk

½ vanilla bean or 1½ teaspoons pure vanilla extract

3 large egg yolks

⅓ cup sugar

2 tablespoons cornstarch

Butter, for glossing

Put the milk in a medium saucepan. Split the vanilla bean lengthwise, scrape the soft, pulpy seeds into the saucepan, and toss in the pod. (If you're using vanilla extract, don't add it yet.) Put the saucepan over medium heat and bring to the boil.

While the milk is heating, whisk together the yolks and sugar in a medium bowl until blended. Add the cornstarch and whisk until smooth.

When the milk is at a full boil, remove the vanilla pod (to save, see page 25) and pour half of the boiling milk into the yolk mixture in a slow, steady stream, taking care to whisk without stop. Pour the yolk mixture back into the saucepan with the boiling milk and whisk vigorously, again without stop, until bubbling and thickened, about 1 minute. When the cream is thick, turn it into a clean bowl (now's the time to add the vanilla extract if you're using it). Rub the top of the cream with the end of a stick of butter (this glossing will prevent the cream from forming a skin), and cover the bowl with plastic wrap. Refrigerate the pastry cream until it is thoroughly chilled. *It can be refrigerated for up to 2 days.*

THE BANANAS

2 large bananas

¼ cup sugar

1 tablespoon unsalted butter

3 tablespoons heavy cream

1 large egg beaten with 1 teaspoon cold water, for egg wash

Slice each banana in half lengthwise and then cut each half into 3 pieces to make a total of a dozen chunks; set aside.

Put a heavy medium sauté pan (nonstick would be good) over medium heat and, when warm, sprinkle in half of the sugar. Cook the sugar, stirring with a wooden spoon, until it just starts to take on color, then sprinkle in the remaining sugar. Continue to cook and stir until the sugar is a medium-dark amber. (Test the color by dropping a little on a white plate.) Stir in the butter (which will stop the caramelization) and then add the bananas, giving them a few turns to coat them with the caramel. Add the cream and continue to stir and cook until the bananas can be pierced easily with the tip of a knife. Transfer the bananas and caramel to a large flat plate and set aside to cool. The bananas must be completely cool before they can be used.

Remove the pastry cream from the refrigerator and stir in the cooled caramelized bananas. Mash the bananas until they are broken into small pieces and distributed throughout the cream.

Shaping and Filling the Beignets Take one tray of the choux circles from the refrigerator and dust the tops of the circles very lightly with flour. Place one circle in a potsticker press. Spoon a scant tablespoon of banana filling onto one half of the circle, brush the borders with a little egg wash, and close the press. Remove the sealed beignet from the press and return it to the parchment-lined baking sheet. Continue with the remaining circles. (To shape the beignets by hand, place a circle of dough on a work surface and add the filling. Brush the edges with egg wash, fold the dough over turnover-style, and press the edges to seal. To make certain that the filling is well contained, center one half of a round biscuit cutter, dull side down, over the filling; press the cutter against the dough to mark it lightly.)

Shaping a beignet by hand.

continued

Freezing the Beignets Freeze the beignets for 3 to 4 hours to firm them. *Or wrap and store them in the freezer for up to 1 week.*

THE SAUCE

2 cups heavy cream

1 stick (4 ounces) unsalted butter, cut into pieces

½ cup sugar

½ cup toasted walnuts, finely ground (this can be done in a food processor)

1 tablespoon walnut oil (optional)

Pinch of salt

Put all of the ingredients into a heavy medium saucepan and bring to the boil over medium heat. Allow the sauce to simmer slowly and steadily until it is reduced by half, about 20 minutes. Remove the pan from the heat and set it aside to cool; it should be served only slightly warm or at room temperature. *You can make the sauce up to 2 days ahead and keep it covered in the refrigerator; heat it in a small saucepan to warm and thin it before serving.*

TO FRY AND SERVE

Canola or vegetable oil, for frying

Confectioner's sugar

Melted semisweet chocolate (optional)

Fresh berries (optional)

If necessary, warm the walnut sauce over gentle heat.

To cook the beignets, heat a few inches of canola oil to 375°F to 400°F (as measured on a deep-frying thermometer) in a deep saucepan or casserole. Drop the beignets, two or three at a time, into the hot oil and fry, turning them frequently, until browned, about 2 minutes. Lift the beignets out of the oil with a slotted spoon and onto a double thickness of paper towels to drain. If you've made decorative shapes, fry them in the same manner.

To serve, arrange 3 beignets in the center of each plate and add a decorative shape if you've made one; dust them all lightly with confectioner's sugar. If you'd like, pour some melted chocolate into a small piping cone and pipe a design on one side of each plate. Spoon a bit of the walnut sauce near the beignets, garnish with berries, if desired, and serve warm.

Storing The components must be made ahead and the finished dessert served immediately.

Contributing Baker **NORMAN LOVE**

Espresso Profiteroles

COLOR PHOTOGRAPH, PAGE 342

Makes 12 to 16 servings ■ A classic combination—espresso, cinnamon and chocolate—in an almost-classic concoction. In these profiteroles—small ice cream–filled puffs of pâte à choux—the water that is normally part of the pâte à choux's liquid is replaced by strong coffee punched up with a tablespoon of ground espresso. Pack them with homemade cinnamon ice cream (or a good-quality store-bought ice cream), drizzle with homemade chocolate sauce, and don't ever expect to have leftovers.

THE ICE CREAM

- **1 cup whole milk**
- **½ cup heavy cream**
- **1 teaspoon cinnamon**
- **½ vanilla bean**
- **3 large egg yolks**
- **3 tablespoons sugar**

Half-fill a large bowl with ice cubes and water; set aside.

Put the milk, cream, and cinnamon into a medium saucepan. Split the vanilla bean, scrape the soft, pulpy seeds into the liquid, toss in the pod, and bring the mixture to the boil. Meanwhile, whisk the yolks and sugar together in a medium bowl until they thicken enough to form a thin, quickly dissolving ribbon when you lift the whisk.

Continuing to whisk, gradually add the boiling milk mixture to the yolks. When everything is well blended, return the mixture to the saucepan and, still whisking, cook over medium heat until thickened, taking care not to allow it to boil. Remove the pan from the heat, pour the custard through a fine strainer into a clean bowl, and cool quickly by placing the bowl in the ice-cube filled bowl. When cool, freeze according to the directions for your ice cream maker. *The ice cream can be made a week or two in advance and stored, tightly covered, in the freezer.*

THE PROFITEROLES

- **½ cup whole milk**
- **½ cup brewed coffee**
- **¾ stick (3 ounces) unsalted butter**
- **2 tablespoons sugar**
- **1 tablespoon finely ground espresso beans**
- **1½ cups all-purpose flour**
- **5 to 6 large eggs**
- **1 large egg beaten with 1 teaspoon cold water, for egg wash**

continued

Position the racks to divide the oven into thirds and preheat the oven to 400°F.

Put the milk, coffee, butter, sugar, and espresso into a 2-quart saucepan and bring to a full boil over medium heat, stirring frequently with a wooden spoon until the butter melts. Still stirring, add the flour all at once. Stir energetically and without stop until the flour is thoroughly incorporated, then continue to cook and stir for another 30 to 45 seconds, or until the dough forms a ball and a light crust is visible on the bottom of the pan.

Remove the pan from the heat and scrape the paste into a medium bowl. Immediately, while the dough is still hot, beat in the eggs one at a time, stirring vigorously with a wooden spoon or spatula to incorporate each one before adding the next. The first couple of eggs are the hardest to mix in, but as the mixture loosens it softens, smoothes, and becomes easier to blend. (If you want, you can beat the eggs in with a mixer—hand-held, or standing with the paddle attachment—just keep the speed low and take care not to beat too much air into the dough.)

After you've incorporated 5 eggs, take a good look at the mixture   it might not need the remaining egg. You'll know the dough is perfect when, as you lift the spoon, it pulls up some of the dough that then detaches and forms a slowly bending peak. If the dough is too thick and doesn't yet peak, add the last egg.

Piping the Choux Paste To make the profiteroles, you must use the pâte à choux while it is warm. Spoon the choux paste into a pastry bag fitted with a ½-inch plain tip and pipe quarter-sized puffs onto parchment-lined baking sheets, leaving about 1 inch between puffs. Finish piping each puff with a quick twist, as if you were writing the letter C, so that a tail or point isn't formed. (Don't worry if your puffs end up with tails—you can poke them down and adjust small imperfections with a moistened fingertip.) Brush each of the pastries with a little egg wash.

Baking the Puffs Bake for 20 minutes; lower the temperature to 350°F and bake 5 to 7 minutes longer, or until the pastries are golden brown and feel hollow. Halfway through the baking period, rotate the baking sheets top to bottom and front to back. Transfer the sheets to cooling racks and allow the puffs to cool to room temperature before cutting and filling.

THE SAUCE

> **11 ounces bittersweet chocolate, finely chopped**
>
> **1¼ cups whole milk**
>
> **6 tablespoons light corn syrup**
>
> **2 tablespoons unsalted butter, at room temperature**
>
> **2 tablespoons Grand Marnier or other orange liqueur**

Put the chopped chocolate in a medium bowl and set close by. Put the milk and corn syrup in a medium saucepan and bring to the boil. Slowly pour the boiling liquid over the chopped chocolate and stir with a rubber spatula until the chocolate is melted. Add the butter and continue to stir until the butter is melted and thoroughly incorporated into the sauce. Stir in the liqueur, and serve while still warm. *The sauce can be made up to 1 week in advance and stored in a covered container in the refrigerator. To serve, warm the sauce in a double boiler or a microwave oven.*

Assembling the Profiteroles To serve, cut each puff in half crosswise and fill with cinnamon ice cream. Serve a generous three to a person, arranging the profiteroles on dessert plates and drizzling some warm chocolate sauce over each puff.

Storing All of the elements can be made ahead, but the assembled profiteroles must be served immediately.

Contributing Baker **NORMAN LOVE**

Babas

COLOR PHOTOGRAPH, PAGE 359

Makes 8 servings ■ The classic baba looks like a miniature chef's toque: It rises up tall and straight, then puffs into a crown that may, on occasion, tip to one side. The yeast dough, studded with raisins and enriched with butter and eggs, bakes to a soft, open sponge, just the right texture to sop up the pastry's traditional sugar syrup and dark rum bath (hence, baba au rhum). In this version, pastry cream is tucked into each baba and the topknots are studded with glacéed fruit.

The name "baba" pays homage to Ali Baba, the hero of *The 1001 Arabian Nights*, a favored story of the baba's inventor, the Polish king Stanislas Leszczynski. The king was exiled in France's Lorraine and, dissatisfied with the region's cake—too dry for his taste—he added rum.

If you don't have baba molds, mold these in anything you've got: custard cups or muffin tins; dariole tins or brioche molds are great.

THE DOUGH

6 tablespoons lukewarm water (about 100°F)

1½ teaspoons active dry yeast

1 teaspoon sugar

1 large egg, at room temperature

¾ cup all-purpose flour

2 tablespoons unsalted butter, cut into 4 pieces, at room temperature

continued

Pour the warm water into a medium bowl and sprinkle over the yeast and sugar. Add the egg and stir briefly with a rubber spatula just to mix.

Put the flour in a mixer fitted with the paddle attachment and add the yeast mixture. Mix on low speed for a minute or two, just until the ingredients are blended, then increase the speed to medium-low and beat for about 8 minutes, until the mixture is smooth. Add the butter and beat on low only until the butter is absorbed, 1 to 3 minutes.

First Rise Remove the bowl from the mixer and cover with plastic wrap. Let the dough rise in a warm place (85°F to 90°F) for about 15 minutes, just until slightly risen; it will not double. (If your room or rising place is cool, the rising time will be longer. You're looking for a noticeable increase in volume and a lightness.)

THE FRUIT

¼ cup raisins or currants

⅓ cup (approximately) dark rum

Clarified unsalted butter (see page 5), for brushing the molds

While the dough is proofing, put the raisins or currants in a small bowl and pour over just enough dark rum to cover.

Brush the 8 molds (see above) that you'll be using for the babas with clarified butter; place on a jelly-roll pan and set aside.

Shaping and Second Rise When the dough has risen, drain the raisins, reserving the rum, and stir them into the dough with a rubber spatula. Using your hands, a spoon, or a pastry bag, fill the baba molds to the halfway point. (Pastry chefs often grab some of the dough in one hand, flip it around as though they were tossing a small ball attached to a rubber string, and cut off the amount needed to fill a mold with a swipe of the other hand's index finger—a neat trick that takes practice.) Let the dough rest in a warm place (85°F to 90°F) until it fills the molds, about 30 minutes.

Baking the Babas Position a rack in the upper third of the oven and preheat the oven to 350°F.

Bake the risen babas for about 20 minutes, or until they are golden, have shrunk slightly from the sides of the molds, and can be removed easily from them. Unmold the pastries onto a cooling rack and cool before soaking and filling. *The babas can be made ahead to this point, wrapped airtight, and frozen for about 3 weeks. Bring to room temperature before soaking in the sugar syrup.*

THE PASTRY CREAM

1 cup milk

1 vanilla bean, split

4 large egg yolks

¼ cup sugar

2 tablespoons cornstarch

1 tablespoon unsalted butter, at room temperature

⅓ cup heavy cream, lightly whipped

Put the milk in a medium saucepan and use the point of a small knife to scrape the soft, pulpy seeds of the vanilla bean into the pan. Toss in the pod and bring the milk to the boil.

While the milk is heating, whisk the yolks and sugar together in a medium bowl until well blended. Add the cornstarch and continue to whisk until thoroughly incorporated. As soon as the milk comes to the boil, pour a little of it into the yolks, whisking without stop. Still whisking wildly, pour the yolks into the saucepan and continue to cook and whisk until the pastry cream thickens enough for the whisk to leave lingering tracks on the bottom of the pan. This happens in about a minute, so stay alert.

Remove the pan from the heat, retrieve the vanilla bean pod (which can be saved, see page 25), and whisk in the butter. Scrape the pastry cream into a bowl, press a piece of plastic wrap against the surface to make an airtight seal, and cool as quickly as you can—it's a good idea to put the bowl over ice or put ice over the plastic. Refrigerate to chill. *The pastry cream can be made up to 3 days ahead and kept covered and refrigerated.*

When you are ready to fill the babas, fold the whipped cream into the chilled pastry cream.

THE SYRUP

2 cups water

1 cup sugar

Reserved dark rum, or more to taste, for garnish

Glacéed or sliced fresh fruits or berries, for garnish

Put the water and sugar in a medium saucepan and bring to the boil. Boil for 30 seconds and then turn off the heat.

Line a jelly-roll pan with waxed paper and set a cooling rack on top of it. Drop the babas, one or two at a time, into the syrup and let them soak, turning them once, for about a minute. Using a slotted spoon, lift the pastries out of the syrup and onto the cooling rack. Allow the babas to cool before dousing with rum and filling with cream.

continued

Finishing the Babas Sprinkle, splash, or spoon some dark rum—just how much is your call—over the cooled babas (use the rum you reserved from macerating the raisins). To fill, either make a cut about ½ inch deep across the top of each baba and, using a small pastry bag fitted with a ⅛-inch star tip, pipe in some whipped cream–lightened pastry cream, or turn the baba over and use the decorating tip to punch a little hole about ½ inch deep into the pastry; squeeze some of the pastry cream into the hole and pipe a tiny rosette on the top of the baba—a hint of what's within. Top each baba with glacéed or sliced fresh fruits or an assortment of berries. If you wish to follow tradition, put each baba in a fluted paper cup to serve.

Storing Unsoaked, unfilled babas can be well wrapped and kept at room temperature for a day or two or frozen for a month. Thaw, still wrapped, at room temperature.

Contributing Baker **DAVID BLOM**

Savarin

COLOR PHOTOGRAPH, PAGE 358

Makes about 6 servings ■ Named for one of France's most celebrated gastronomes, Brillat-Savarin, and first baked in the mid-nineteenth century, well after the baba was invented, the savarin is baba dough minus the raisins and baked in a ring mold, the kind often associated with crème caramel. If you don't have a ring mold, spoon the dough into the bottom of a Bundt pan or use a gelatin mold with a center tube.

A savarin can be served with just a dollop of whipped cream, sauced (try puréed mango with sugar and lemon juice, poured into a plastic squeeze bottle and squiggled over the plate), decorated with fresh fruits, or piled to the hilt with one of everything. Here's a recipe for an elaborate savarin, soaked in poire (pear-flavored) eau-de-vie and dressed with a warm berry sauce.

THE DOUGH

   1 recipe Baba dough (page 413), made without raisins and allowed
      to rise once

   Clarified unsalted butter (see page 5), for brushing the mold

Brush a ring mold (see above) with clarified butter and fill with the dough. Cover the mold and let rise in a very warm place (85°F to 90°F) for about 30 minutes, or until the dough fills the mold.

Position a rack in the upper third of the oven and preheat the oven to 350°F.

Put the savarin on a parchment-lined jelly-roll pan and bake for about 20 minutes, or until it is golden and starts to shrink from the sides of the mold. Unmold onto a cooling rack and cool completely before soaking.

FOR SOAKING AND ASSEMBLING

1 recipe soaking syrup (page 415)

A few tablespoons Raspberry Purée (page 450)

About 1 cup assorted fresh berries, such as blueberries, blackberries, and sliced strawberries

Sugar to taste

1 cup raspberries (optional)

About 3 tablespoons poire (pear) eau-de-vie

Whipped cream

Bring the soaking syrup to the boil and turn off the heat. Place the cooling rack over a parchment- or waxed paper–lined jelly-roll pan. Spoon the hot syrup over the savarin, a few tablespoons at a time, continuing to soak the pastry until it is plump and cannot hold any more liquid. Leave the savarin on the rack until it is cool.

Put about 2 teaspoons of water into a sauté pan, preferably nonstick, and add the raspberry purée (exact amounts are not vital here). Warm the sauce and then add ½ to 1 cup of the assorted berries. Sugar the berries to taste and bring the mixture to the boil. Add the raspberries, if you're using them, and stir just to mix. You want to warm, not cook, the berries. Remove the skillet from the heat and let the mixture cool for a minute.

Transfer the savarin to a serving plate and drizzle with the pear eau-de-vie.

Fill the center of the savarin with whipped cream and top with the warmed, saucy berries. Spoon some whipped cream into a pastry bag fitted with a small ¼-inch star tip, and pipe a ring of rosettes around the base of the savarin. Serve immediately.

Storing Unsoaked savarin can be well wrapped and kept at room temperature for a day or two or frozen for a month. Thaw, still wrapped, at room temperature.

Contributing Baker **DAVID BLOM**

Savory Pastries

GALETTES, PIZZETTES, TOURTES, AND TARTS

A QUICK GLANCE at this chapter reveals that the doughs you've mastered in the dessert kitchen also are the foundation of a world of savory and sophisticated hors d'oeuvre and main dishes.

Playful and pleasing, many of these pastries proffer tucked-away treasures. Only the baker knows that Gale Gand's artfully shaped purse of phyllo protects a plump pesto-topped scallop, or that a golden pillow of Nancy Silverton's brioche, flagged with a sage leaf, encloses a savory mound of potatoes and caramelized onions. It is Norman Love's secret that a cream puff hides a dollop of smoked salmon mousse, and Michel Richard's delight that his Tourte Milanese, a tall, spectacularly beautiful, two-crusted puff pastry pie, contains pleasure upon pleasure—herbed scrambled eggs, roasted peppers, melted cheese, and tasty spinach.

Of course, some of the recipes, like Parmesan Puffs, conceal little but the ease of making them, and the ruffled galette and bite-size puffed pizzettes proudly flaunt their delectable fillings.

If you are accustomed to making the last—and most lasting—impression with desserts, here, with these starters and main courses, you'll find yourself setting the stage for all that follows.

Savory Brioche Pockets

COLOR PHOTOGRAPH, PAGE 364

Makes 12 to 15 pockets ■ In the tradition of coulibiac (brioche-wrapped salmon) or tête de brioche encasing silken foie gras, these savory pockets pair brioche with a flavorful filling, in this instance a blend of potatoes, goat cheese, caramelized onions, and tender asparagus tips. There isn't a time when these wouldn't be welcome—at a brunch buffet, passed at a cocktail party, or served as a starter for a sit-down dinner. Any number of fillings would make an interesting variation. After you've played around with the potato filling, give some thought to grilled eggplant, roasted peppers (well-drained), a piquant fish mix, or maybe a jumbo Armagnac-soaked prune stuffed with liver pâté, a rich option that would give you a pocket within a pocket. And while you're experimenting, you can vary the pastry's size, too—consider a large pocket to be sliced at the table. Because you don't need much filling, a large pocket can make a lavish container for leftovers.

THE FILLING

　　4 small red potatoes, peeled

　　½ cup crumbled goat cheese

　　Salt and freshly ground black pepper to taste

　　3 tablespoons chopped fresh chives

　　1 onion, chopped

　　2 tablespoons unsalted butter

　　24 to 30 asparagus tips, 2 to 3 inches long

Steam the potatoes until they can be pierced easily with the point of a knife. Drain the potatoes well, put them in a large bowl, and mash with a fork. Add the goat cheese, stir to mix, and taste for seasoning, adding salt and pepper as needed. Set the mixture aside to cool to room temperature, or cover and chill it for a few hours. When the mixture is cool—everything must be cool before going into the pockets—stir in the chopped chives.

Cook the chopped onions in the butter, in a small skillet over low heat for about 20 minutes, until the onions turn a caramel color. Set aside to cool.

Drop the asparagus tips into a large pot of boiling salted water and cook until tender, or until a knife point meets just a little resistance when piercing the asparagus. Drain and then plunge the asparagus into ice water. Drain again and dry before tucking into the pockets.

continued

THE POCKETS

1 recipe Brioche dough (page 43), chilled

2 large egg yolks, beaten

¼ cup poppy seeds

12 to 15 fresh sage leaves

Top: The pocket filling—caramelized onions, goat cheese, and asparagus. *Center:* Sealing the filling in place with the back of a biscuit cutter. *Bottom:* A shaped pocket ready to glaze.

Divide the brioche in half; keep one half covered in the refrigerator while you work with the other. Working on a lightly floured cool surface, roll the brioche out to a thickness of ⅛ inch—don't worry about the shape of the dough; you'll be cutting rounds from it. Place the rolled-out dough on a parchment-lined baking sheet, cover lightly with plastic wrap, and chill while you roll out the other half of the dough.

Again, work with half of the dough at time. Using a 4- or 4½-inch round biscuit or cookie cutter, cut out as many circles of dough as you can from the brioche. You should be able to get a total of 24 to 30 circles from the entire batch of dough. Scraps of dough can be chilled and, once firm, rerolled and cut. If the circles are very soft, chill them again before filling.

Place 1 tablespoon of the caramelized onions on each of half of the circles. Top with 2 tablespoons of the potato mixture and finish with 2 asparagus tips. One at a time, take an unfilled circle and dimple it with your fingertips to stretch it a little. Place the circle, dimpled side down, over a circle with the filling, using your fingertips to press the dough down around the mounded filling; or seal the mound of filling by pressing the back of a biscuit cutter against the dough, positioning it so that it encircles the mound of filling and delineates it. Pick up the edges of both layers of dough and roll them in toward the mound of filling, folding them over so that they form a rim around the filling; press the rim down gently to seal. *At this point the filled pockets can be wrapped airtight and frozen for up to a month. Thaw overnight, still wrapped, in the refrigerator before proceeding.* Place the pockets on two parchment-lined baking sheets and brush with the beaten egg yolks.

Rise Set the pockets aside to rise, uncovered, at room temperature until puffy and spongy to the touch, about 20 minutes.

Baking the Pockets Position the racks to divide the oven into thirds and preheat the oven to 350°F. Give the pockets another coat of egg wash, sprinkle some poppy seeds on each one, and top with a sage leaf. Bake for 15 to 20 minutes, or until they are beautifully browned, rotating the baking sheets top to bottom and front to back halfway through the baking period. Serve warm or at room temperature.

Storing Once baked, the pockets should be enjoyed the day they are made.

Contributing Baker **NANCY SILVERTON**

Tourte Milanese

COLOR PHOTOGRAPH, PAGE 360

Makes 6 to 8 servings ■ Big, bold, and beautiful. Neat, colorful layers of ham, cheese, vegetables, and eggs are stacked in a puff pastry crust and topped with a puff pastry crown that shatters into its characteristic thousand leaves when cut. This versatile dish can be toted to a picnic or served with an elegant red wine at a dressy dinner. The instructions are long because the tourte has several components, but many of the components, including the sautéed spinach, roasted peppers, scrambled eggs, and the puff pastry itself, can be prepared in advance, at your convenience, and the savory tourte can be constructed *à la minute*.

1 pound puff pastry, homemade (page 46) or store-bought, chilled

10 large eggs
1 tablespoon chopped fresh chives
1 tablespoon chopped fresh flat-leaf parsley
2 teaspoons snipped fresh tarragon
Salt and freshly ground black pepper to taste
3 tablespoons unsalted butter

Preparing the Pastry Generously butter an 8½-inch springform pan. (The thick layer of butter will help the dough stick to the sides of the pan.) Cut off one quarter of the pastry, cover, and set it aside. Working on a lightly floured work surface (cool marble is ideal), roll out the remaining puff pastry to a round that is ¼ inch thick. Carefully fit the pastry into the pan, pressing against the pan to get a smooth fit—don't worry about perfection, but do leave a 1-inch (or slightly more) overhang.

Roll out the smaller piece of pastry until it is ¼ inch thick. Cut out an 8-inch circle of dough for the top of the tourte and lift it onto a plate or baking sheet. Cover both the crust and the lid with plastic wrap and keep them both refrigerated while you prepare the filling. (Save the scraps of puff pastry for other uses. Stack them, wrap in plastic, and refrigerate or freeze until needed.)

Making the Eggs You need to make a batch of seasoned scrambled eggs to seal the tourte: Whisk the eggs, herbs, and salt and pepper together in a medium bowl. Melt the butter in a large skillet over low heat and, when the bubbles subside, pour in the eggs. Gently but constantly stir the eggs around in the pan, pulling the eggs that set into the center of the pan and tilting the pan so that the liquid eggs run to the sides and cook—the eggs should be cooked slowly and scrambled loosely, as they will cook again in the tourte. Slide the eggs onto a plate, without mounding them, and cover immediately with plastic wrap. The eggs must cool before they can be used in the tourte. If you want to cool them very quickly, set a layer of ice cubes over the plastic wrap; remove when the eggs are cold.

THE FILLING

6 large red bell peppers

Salt and freshly ground black pepper to taste

1½ pounds spinach, trimmed and washed

1 tablespoon olive oil

1 tablespoon unsalted butter

2 cloves garlic, peeled and minced

¼ teaspoon grated nutmeg

3 tablespoons (approximately) heavy cream (optional)

8 ounces Swiss cheese, thinly sliced

8 ounces smoked ham, thinly sliced

1 large egg beaten with 1 tablespoon water and a pinch of salt, for egg wash

To roast the peppers, place the peppers, whole and untrimmed, directly over the flame of a gas burner or under the broiler (if you're using the broiler, put the peppers on a baking sheet). As soon as one portion of a pepper's skin is charred, turn the pepper to char another section. When the peppers are black and blistered all over, drop them into a bowl of cool water. While the peppers are submerged, use your fingers to rub off the blackened skin. Rinse each pepper under running water and dry well. Cut each pepper once from top to bottom, cut away the stem, open up the peppers, and lay them flat. Trim away the inside veins and discard the seeds; season the peppers with salt and pepper and set them aside, covered, until needed.

Cook the spinach in a large quantity of boiling salted water for 1 minute, just to blanch it. Drain the spinach in a colander, rinse with cold water, and, when it's cool enough to handle, press it between your palms to extract all of the excess moisture.

Heat the oil, butter, and garlic in a large skillet over medium heat. Add the blanched spinach (if you ended up with a tight little ball of spinach after squeezing it dry, pull it apart with your fingers so that you have several pieces) and sauté for 2 to 3 minutes. Season with salt and pepper and the nutmeg, and if you want, add a little heavy cream. Bring the cream quickly to the boil and stir so that it mixes with the spinach. Remove the spinach from the skillet with a slotted spoon or spatula and set aside.

Position a rack in the lower third of the oven and preheat the oven to 350°F.

Assembling the Tourte Remove the pastry-lined springform pan from the refrigerator and layer the filling ingredients in the following order: half the eggs (discard any liquid that may have accumulated on the plate), half the spinach, half the cheese, half the ham, and all the roasted red peppers, laid out flat, then continue layering in reverse order—the remaining ham, cheese, spinach, and eggs. With each layer, make certain that the ingredients are spread to the edge of the pan.

If you haven't already done so, trim the bottom crust overhang to 1 inch. Fold the excess in over the filling, and brush the rim of crust you've created with the egg wash. Center the rolled-out top crust over the tourte and gently push the edge of the top crust down into the pan, pressing and sealing the top and bottom crusts along the sides. Use your palm to pat the top of the tourte down and level the crust. Brush the top with the egg wash (reserve the remainder in the refrigerator—you'll need it later) and cut a vent in the center of the crust, using a small sharp knife. Use the point of the knife to etch a design in the top crust, taking care to cut only halfway into the dough. A classic way to decorate the top crust is to cut lines that radiate like spokes from the center vent and delineate portions, making cutting the tourte easier later. You can embellish the design by etching a series of diagonal lines within each portion, alternating the slant of the lines from wedge to wedge.

Chilling the Tourte Chill the fully loaded tourte for 30 minutes to 1 hour before baking.

Baking the Tourte Place the tourte on a jelly-roll pan, give it another coat of egg wash, and bake it for 1 hour and 10 minutes to 1 hour and 15 minutes, or until wonderfully puffed and deeply golden. Remove from the oven and let the tourte rest on a rack until it is only just warm, or until it reaches room temperature. (The cooler the tourte, the easier it is to cut it neatly.) *If it fits into your schedule, you can make the tourte a day ahead, refrigerate it, and serve it cool or at room temperature.* Run a blunt knife around the edges of the pan and release the sides.

Storing The cooled tourte can be kept for several hours at room temperature or wrapped in plastic and refrigerated overnight.

Contributing Baker **MICHEL RICHARD**

Alsatian Onion Tart

COLOR PHOTOGRAPH, PAGE 365

Makes 4 servings ■ The classic Alsatian onion tart—a flat, pizzalike galette covered to its very edge with meltingly tender soubise, a mix of onions and bacon—was once typical Sunday fare in Alsace. On their way to church, the locals would drop their tarts off at the village oven to have them baked while they prayed (for redemption, not dinner, one assumes). Those crusts were always rolled very thin so that they would bake quickly, but this can be made in any size, and the recipe can be multiplied without care.

About ¹/₂ pound puff pastry scraps, chilled

4 very large onions, peeled and diced

1 cup chicken broth (homemade or canned low-sodium)

3 tablespoons heavy cream

Salt and freshly ground black pepper to taste

¹/₄ pound slab bacon

Preparing the Pastry Roll out the puff pastry on a lightly floured work surface until it is very thin, ¹/₈ to ¹/₄ inch thick. Using the lid of a pot as a guide, cut the pastry with a very sharp knife into a circle 10 to 12 inches across. Transfer the rolled-out pastry to an ungreased baking sheet and prick the dough all over, using either a docker or the tines of a fork. Go overboard with this—try arming yourself with a fork in each hand and playing out a lively tattoo on the dough—the docking, or pricking, will keep the pastry from puffing, just what you want for this tart. Cover the pastry with plastic wrap and refrigerate until needed. *You can prepare the pastry up to 1 day ahead.*

Making the Topping Put the diced onions and the chicken broth in a medium saucepan over low heat and cook, stirring occasionally, until the onions are very soft, about 30 minutes. Drain, discarding any liquid, and let the onions cool. When the onions have cooled, stir in the heavy cream and season with salt and pepper. (Keep tasting—you may want to go easy on the salt because of the bacon.)

Remove the rind from the bacon and cut the bacon into ¹/₄-inch cubes. Drop the cubes into a large pot of boiling water and boil for 1 minute, just to blanch them. Drain and rinse under cold water, then pat dry with paper towels.

Heat a medium skillet over moderately high heat, toss in the bacon pieces, and cook, stirring, for just a minute or two—you don't want to overcook these, or they'll turn tough; season with pepper. Remove the bacon from the pan and drain well on paper towels. *At this point, the topping can be covered and refrigerated for 1 day.*

Assembling and Baking Position a rack in the lower third of the oven and preheat the oven to 350°F.

Remove the pastry round from the refrigerator and top with the cooled onions, spreading the onions all the way to the edge of the pastry. Scatter the bacon pieces over the onions, pushing them down into the onions just a little (this will not only protect the bacon from burning, it will flavor the onions). Bake the tart for about 30 minutes, or until golden brown. Serve immediately.

Storing Both the pastry and the topping can be made ahead, but the tart is at its best just baked.

Contributing Baker **MICHEL RICHARD**

Parmesan Puffs

This is a great-tasting, quick-to-make way of using leftover puff pastry. The leftover pieces of puff are deep-fried to a golden crisp and sprinkled with Parmesan cheese—that's all, and that's a lot in the taste department. Deep-fried puff pastry is not something you come across every day, but it is, in fact, a classic preparation.

The puffs can be served as nibbles with drinks, floated in soups, or tossed into a Caesar salad to make the best-ever croutons. This method of frying scraps can also be used to make a sweet snack. Instead of dusting the just-fried puffs with Parmesan, use confectioner's sugar and cinnamon.

Chilled puff pastry scraps
Peanut oil, for deep-frying
Freshly grated Parmesan cheese

Working on a lightly floured surface, roll out the scraps to a thickness of ⅛ inch. Transfer the dough to a parchment-lined baking sheet, cover with plastic wrap, and refrigerate for at least 30 minutes. (The brief refrigeration will give you greater puff, but you can omit this step and still make tasty, plump puffs.)

Line a baking sheet with a triple thickness of paper towels; set aside. Pour about 2 inches of peanut oil into a deep saucepan and heat to 325°F.

Frying the Puffs Using a large chef's knife, cut the chilled dough into diamonds 1½ to 2 inches on a side. Fry the diamonds in batches of 10, stirring constantly, until they are crisp, puffed, and golden, about 5 minutes. With a slotted spoon transfer the diamonds to the towel-lined baking sheet. Drain briefly, then, while they are still hot, sprinkle them with Parmesan cheese. Serve hot, warm, or at room temperature.

Storing Eat these the day they are made. If you must hold them for a few hours, keep them uncovered at room temperature. If they need a crisping, pop them into a 350°F oven for about 5 minutes.

Contributing Baker **MICHEL RICHARD**

Puff Pastry Pizzettes

Not a single scrap of puff pastry should ever go to waste, since even the smallest nubbin can make a tasty tidbit. One of the easiest—and most delicious—ways to use puff pastry trimmings is to make tiny tartlets or pizzettes. They can be either sweet or savory, either round or square, and need be only just large enough for the topping to sit in the center so that when the bite-or-two pizzette is baked, you get a morsel of topping and a mouthful of crust.

Puff pastry scraps, chilled
Cherry tomatoes, cut in half
Soft goat cheese
Freshly ground black pepper, to taste
Olive oil, for brushing
Fresh basil leaves, for garnish (optional)

Position a rack in the lower third of the oven and preheat the oven to 350°F.
On a lightly floured surface, roll out the puff pastry until it is ⅛ to ¼ inch thick. Cut out pastry circles with a small (about 2-inch) cookie or biscuit cutter and place the rounds on a parchment-lined baking sheet.
Top each round with a cherry tomato half, cut side up. Gently push the tomato into the pastry so it doesn't slide off in the oven, and top with a spoonful of goat cheese. Give each pizzette a grind or two of black pepper.

Baking the Pizzettes Bake the pizzettes for 12 to 15 minutes, until golden. As soon as the pizzettes come from the oven, give them a shine with a brushing of olive oil and garnish each with a fresh basil leaf, if desired. Serve warm.

Storing These are meant to be eaten, not saved. You can make them a few hours ahead and keep them at room temperature if necessary.

Sweet Pizzettes

The pastry rounds can be topped with a slice or two of almost any kind of fruit, a few berries, a cherry cut in half, or even a spoonful of a fruit compote. When the sweet pizzettes come from the oven, brush them with a little apricot jam that has been heated with a few drops of water and strained.

Contributing Baker **MICHEL RICHARD**

Cheese and Tomato Galette

COLOR PHOTOGRAPH, PAGE 366

Makes 2 to 4 servings ■ This rustic tart has the look of a Mediterranean pizza. The crust is a wonderful cornmeal-crunchy dough, rolled into a thin circle and drawn up in pleats and ruffles over the filling, a blend of cheeses topped with sliced garden tomatoes, red and juicy. Because of the cornmeal in the dough, the crust will stay crisp enough for this galette to be served either warm or at room temperature. It will even travel, so think of it when you're headed off on a picnic or want to bring friends a lovely something to have with drinks.

½ **recipe Galette Dough (page 371), chilled**

2 ounces Monterey Jack cheese, shredded
2 ounces mozzarella, preferably fresh, shredded
¼ **cup fresh basil leaves, cut into chiffonade or torn**
2 to 3 firm but ripe plum tomatoes, cut into ¼**-inch-thick slices**

Fresh basil leaves, for garnish

Position a rack in the lower third of the oven and preheat the oven to 400°F. Line a baking sheet with parchment paper.

Put the dough on a lightly floured work surface and roll it into an 11-inch circle that's about ⅛ inch thick. Since the dough is soft, you'll need to lift it now and then and toss some flour under it and over the top. Roll the dough up around your rolling pin and unroll onto the prepared baking sheet.

Making the Filling Toss the cheeses and basil together in a small bowl, then scatter them over the rolled-out dough, leaving a 2- to 3-inch border. Place the tomatoes in concentric circles, one slice slightly overlapping the last, on top of the cheese. Fold the uncovered border of dough up over the filling, allowing the dough to pleat as you lift it up and work your way around the galette. (Because you're folding a wide edge of dough onto a smaller part of the circle, it will pleat naturally—just go with it.)

Baking the Galette Bake the galette for 35 to 40 minutes, or until the pastry is golden and crisp and the cheese is bubbly. Transfer the baking sheet to a cooling rack and let the galette rest on the sheet for 10 minutes. Slip a wide spatula or a small rimless baking sheet under the galette and slide it onto the cooling rack. Serve warm or at room temperature, garnished with fresh basil leaves.

Storing The galette can be kept at room temperature for several hours, but it is best served the day it is made.

Contributing Baker **FLO BRAKER**

Pizza Rustica

COLOR PHOTOGRAPH, PAGE 363

Makes 8 to 10 servings ■ Pizza Rustica is a savory pie with a sweet crust, a combination that sounds unlikely but tastes terrific. The crust, a pasta frolla like the one used to make X Cookies (page 318), is a nice contrast to the salty prosciutto and Pecorino Romano cheese, its crunch a good foil for the smooth ricotta and mozzarella. Although the pie, with its crisscross lattice top, looks like special-occasion fare, it is considered casual finger food in Italy, where it is traditionally served as a starter, although it would be grand as a luncheon dish or a supper with salad.

THE DOUGH

2 cups all-purpose flour

⅓ cup sugar

½ teaspoon baking powder

¼ teaspoon salt

1 stick (4 ounces) cold unsalted butter or 4 ounces cold lard, cut into 8 pieces

2 large eggs, lightly beaten

Put the flour, sugar, baking powder, and salt into the work bowl of a food processor fitted with the metal blade; pulse a few times just to mix the ingredients. Add the butter and pulse 15 to 20 times, or until the mixture resembles fine cornmeal. With the machine running, add the eggs and process until the dough forms a ball on the blade, about a minute or so. Remove the dough from the processor and knead it, folding it over on itself, until it is smooth, 1 to 2 minutes. Wrap the dough in plastic and set aside until needed. *If you're not going to make the pizza now, wrap the dough well and refrigerate for up to 3 days.*

THE FILLING

1 pound whole milk ricotta

3 large eggs

¼ cup freshly grated Pecorino Romano cheese

¼ pound mozzarella cheese, grated

¼ pound thinly sliced prosciutto, shredded

2 tablespoons chopped fresh parsley

¼ teaspoon freshly ground black pepper

Scoop the ricotta into a medium bowl and stir until smooth with a rubber spatula. Add the rest of the filling ingredients one at a time, stirring until each addition is incorporated and the mixture is well blended.

Position a rack in the lower third of the oven and preheat the oven to 350°F. Butter a 9-inch glass pie plate. (If you don't have a glass pie plate, use metal, but increase the oven temperature to 375°F.)

Rolling the Dough Divide the dough into two pieces, one twice as large as the other. Working with the larger piece, knead it into a disk and roll it out on a lightly floured work surface into a 12-inch circle.

Lining the Pie Plate Transfer the dough to the pie plate and press it gently against the bottom and up the sides of the plate. Don't worry if the dough tears—just press it back together. Use the dull side of a knife to trim the excess dough even with the rim.

Filling the Pie Scrape the filling into the pie shell and smooth the top.

Forming the Lattice Knead and shape the remaining piece of dough into a block and roll it into a 9-inch square. Using a pizza or pastry cutter (a ruffle-edged pastry wheel is nice) or a thin sharp knife, cut the dough into 12 even strips. To form the lattice top, lay 6 of the strips across the pie at 1¼-inch intervals, then crisscross the strips, placing the remaining strips diagonally across the first. Trim the ends of the strips even with the edge of the pan and pinch to seal.

A crisscross lattice ready to be trimmed.

Baking the Pie Bake for 35 to 40 minutes, or until the crust is golden and the filling is firm and slightly puffed. Transfer the pie to a rack and cool completely before serving.

Storing Leftovers can be kept well covered in the refrigerator for up to 4 days.

Contributing Baker **NICK MALGIERI**

Savory Puffs

Makes about 5 dozen puffs and éclairs ■ These savory puffs and éclairs are made with a pâte à choux base (see page 35 for choux paste basics), that has the sharp, distinctive flavor of cucumber and red onion juices. (The juice is most easily obtained using a juice extractor, but you could use a food processor and press the purée through a strainer to extract the juice.) The éclairs are filled with a mix of vegetables and mascarpone and the puffs with a sumptuous smoked salmon mousse, both easily made and both just starting points—fill these with any of your favorite fillings, or try them with Smoked Trout Spread (page 458), Vegetable Cream Cheese (page 456), or even Chopped Chicken Liver (page 457). These are wonderful as part of a luncheon or cocktail party.

THE PUFFS

½ cup cucumber juice (extracted from 1 peeled small cucumber)

1½ tablespoons red onion juice (extracted from ¼ onion)

½ cup milk

7 tablespoons unsalted butter

Pinch of salt

1 cup all-purpose flour

5 to 6 large eggs

2 teaspoons chopped fresh dill

1 large egg beaten with 1 teaspoon cold water, for egg wash

Position the racks to divide the oven into thirds and preheat the oven to 400°F. Line two baking sheets with parchment paper.

Making the Choux Paste Put the cucumber and onion juices, milk, butter, and salt into a 2-quart saucepan and bring to a full boil over medium heat, stirring frequently with a wooden spoon until the butter melts. Still stirring, add the flour all at once and stir energetically and without stop until the flour is thoroughly incorporated. Then continue to cook and stir for another 30 to 45 seconds, or until the dough forms a ball and a light crust is visible on the bottom of the pan.

Scrape the paste into a medium bowl. Immediately, while the dough is still hot, beat in the eggs one at a time, stirring vigorously with a wooden spoon or spatula to incorporate each one before adding the next. The first couple of eggs are the hardest to mix in, but as the mixture loosens it softens, smoothes, and becomes easier to blend. (If you want, you can beat in the eggs with a mixer—hand-held, or standing with the paddle attachment—just keep the speed low and take care not to beat too much air into the dough.)

After you've incorporated 5 eggs, take a good look at the mixture—it might not need the remaining egg. You'll know the dough is perfect when, as you lift the spoon, it pulls up some of the dough that then detaches and forms a slowly bending peak. If the dough is too thick and doesn't yet peak, add the last egg. Fold in the chopped dill.

Piping the Pastries To make the puffs and éclairs, you must use the pâte à choux while it is warm. Spoon the choux paste into a pastry bag fitted with a ½-inch plain tip and pipe out puffs on one baking sheet, making each puff about 2 inches across; finish piping each one with a quick twist, as if you were writing the letter C so that a tail or point isn't formed. (Don't worry if your puffs end up with tails—you can poke them down and adjust small imperfections with a moistened fingertip.) Pipe the second pan with éclairs, piping thin logs of dough about 5 inches long.

Brush each of the pastries with a little egg wash and run the back of the tines of a fork along the length of each éclair. (This will not only be decorative, it will help the éclairs to puff evenly during baking.)

Baking the Pastries Brush the éclairs and puffs with egg wash again and bake at 400°F for 15 minutes; lower the temperature to 350°F and bake for 10 to 15 minutes longer, or until the pastries are golden brown and feel hollow. Halfway through the baking period, rotate the baking sheets top to bottom and front to back. Transfer the sheets to cooling racks and allow the puffs and éclairs to cool to room temperature before cutting and filling. *The pastries can be wrapped airtight and frozen for a week or two. Bring to room temperature and fill, or, if desired, warm for 5 minutes in a 350°F oven before cutting and filling.*

THE MOUSSE

½ **pound smoked salmon, cut into pieces**

4 **ounces cream cheese**

1 **teaspoon Pernod, or more to taste**

Cracked black pepper to taste

Sprigs of fresh dill, for garnish

Put the smoked salmon and cream cheese into the work bowl of a food processor fitted with the metal blade and process until satiny, scraping down the sides of the bowl as needed. Add the Pernod and pepper and pulse to blend. Taste the mousse and correct the seasonings if necessary. *The mousse can be covered and refrigerated for up to 3 days.*

continued

THE MASCARPONE-VEGETABLE MEDLEY

1/4 **cup finely diced carrot**

1/4 **cup finely diced celery**

1/4 **cup finely diced summer squash**

1/4 **cup finely diced onion**

1/4 **cup finely diced peeled and seeded tomato**

1/4 **cup finely diced red bell pepper**

1/4 **cup finely diced peeled cucumber**

1/4 **cup finely diced mango**

1/2 **cup mascarpone, at room temperature**

1 **tablespoon balsamic vinegar**

Salt and freshly ground black pepper to taste

Gently fold all of the ingredients together in a medium bowl. *This can be made up to a day ahead and kept covered in the refrigerator.*

Filling the Pastries Just before serving, spoon the salmon mousse into a pastry bag fitted with a 1/2-inch plain tip. To pipe the mousse into the puffs, turn the puffs upside down, punch a small hole in the bottom of each puff, and squeeze in the mousse. Finish with a small rosette of mousse on the top and garnish with a sprig of fresh dill.

To fill the éclairs, use a sharp serrated knife to cut them open along one long side, taking care not to cut all the way through. Working with one éclair at a time, hold it between your thumb and index finger—this will gently squeeze it open—and spoon vegetable-mascarpone filling into the opening, being generous with the filling so that a little of it peeks out when the éclair is closed.

Serve the filled pastries immediately. They'll hold for a while on a buffet, but they're at their best (and least soggy) when eaten as soon after filling as possible.

Storing The components can be made ahead, but the finished pastries are made for *à la minute* eating.

Contributing Baker **NORMAN LOVE**

Scallop and Pesto Purses

COLOR PHOTOGRAPH, PAGE 362

Makes 12 appetizer servings ■ This savory starter is edible proof of the adage "good things come in small packages." The package is a draw-string-style purse made of phyllo dough and the good thing is a succulent sea scallop seasoned with a dollop of pungent pesto, the basil paste. The phyllo, which crisps beautifully on the outside and around the ruffled top of the purse, serves as a steam chamber for the scallop, allowing the mollusk to cook in its own juices and soak up the flavors of the pesto. When you break into the package, you're treated to an aromatic puff of steam, an appetite whetter for what's to come. If you'd like, drizzle a little basil oil, homemade or best-quality bottled, around the purses.

 4 **sheets phyllo**

 ⅓ **cup clarified unsalted butter (see page 5)**

 ⅓ **cup freshly grated Parmesan cheese**

 12 **sea scallops**

 2 **scallions, thinly sliced**

 3 **tablespoons pesto (homemade or store-bought)**

Center a rack in the oven and preheat the oven to 375°F. Line a jelly-roll pan with parchment paper and keep it close at hand. Cut 12 pieces of string into 6-inch lengths and butter the strings.

Stack the sheets of phyllo on a work surface. Working with one sheet of phyllo at a time and keeping the others covered with a kitchen towel, brush a sheet with butter and sprinkle it with Parmesan cheese. Cover with a second piece of phyllo and give it a coating of butter and a sprinkling of cheese. Using a long sharp knife and a ruler as a guide, cut the sheets lengthwise in half and crosswise in thirds. Place 1 scallop in the center of each of the 6 rectangles, top with a little sliced scallion, and add a dab of pesto. Gather up the corners of the rectangles, tie the purses with the buttered strings, and place them on the jelly-roll pan. Repeat with the remaining phyllo and scallops.

Baking the Purses Bake the purses for about 12 minutes, or until golden brown. Snip off the strings and serve immediately.

Storing You can assemble the purses early in the day and keep them covered in the refrigerator until you are ready to bake them, at which point they may need an extra 2 or 3 minutes of baking time. Once baked, the purses should be served quickly.

Contributing Baker **GALE GAND**

Summer Vegetable Tart

Makes 6 to 8 servings ■ Here, endlessly versatile phyllo puts in an appearance as a tart crust. Nothing could be simpler. Sheets of phyllo are pressed into a tart ring, their edges are left to zigzag like fluttering handkerchiefs, and the crust is baked until it is honey brown and flaky. Once cooled, it's filled with a warm savory mix of sautéed vegetables and crumbled goat cheese. For this vegetable tart, the phyllo is spread with butter and cracked pepper; if you want to make a sweet tart shell for a different filling, keep the technique, omit the pepper, and dust the phyllo with granulated sugar.

4 sheets phyllo
½ cup clarified unsalted butter (see page 5)
Freshly ground black pepper, to taste

3 tablespoons olive oil
1 medium onion, sliced
2 cloves garlic, minced
½ pound mushrooms, sliced
2 red bell peppers, cored, seeded, deveined, and sliced
½ teaspoon fresh thyme leaves
Salt and freshly ground black pepper, to taste
1 cup crumbled goat cheese

Position a rack in the center of the oven and preheat the oven to 375°F. Butter a 9-inch fluted tart pan with a removable bottom or a pie pan and place it on a parchment paper–lined baking sheet; set aside until needed.

Stack the phyllo sheets on a work surface, cut them in half crosswise (so that each piece yields 2 rectangles about 8½ by 13 inches), and cover the stack with a kitchen towel. Working with one piece of phyllo at a time, brush the sheet with clarified butter and season with a little freshly ground black pepper. Lay the phyllo in the pan, pressing the pastry against the bottom and up the sides and allowing the edges to hang over the rim. Continue with the rest of the phyllo, spreading each sheet with butter and dusting with pepper, and laying each one in the pan at an angle to the last so that the overhang forms a pattern of jagged triangles.

Baking the Tart Shell Keeping the tart on the baking sheet, bake the shell until it is golden and crispy, 7 to 10 minutes. Take a look at it while it's baking: If the center puffs, press it down gently with a fork or spatula. Place the tart, on its baking sheet, on a rack while you make the filling. *The shell can be made a few hours ahead and kept at room temperature.*

Filling and Assembling the Tart Heat the olive oil in a large sauté pan over medium-high heat. Add the onion and garlic and cook, stirring often, until they're soft and translucent. Add the remaining vegetables and sauté until tender. Season with the thyme and salt and pepper and toss in the goat cheese, stirring and just letting it heat ever so slightly—you don't want it to melt. Spoon the vegetables and cheese into the tart shell and serve warm.

Storing This tart is meant to be served as soon as it is made, but no one will complain if you serve it at room temperature—its flavor and texture will hold up for a few hours.

Contributing Baker GALE GAND

Brie in Brioche

Makes 16 to 20 servings ■ A large, showy dish that could easily take center stage at a party for a crowd. The dough, a buttery brioche made in the bread machine, is fitted into a springform pan and wrapped around a perfectly ripe Brie. The Brie is topped with onion halves, caramelized in a slow cooker, finished with another round of brioche and a handsome brioche braid, and baked to a burnished golden brown. Plan ahead, because both the onions and the brioche need to be made twenty-four hours in advance.

THE ONIONS

6 to 8 very large mild onions (about 3 pounds), preferably Spanish or Vidalia

1 stick (4 ounces) unsalted butter, cut into 4 pieces

Start to cook the onions at least 1 day in advance: Cut off both the root and stem ends of each onion, peel, and leave whole. Put the onions and butter in a slow cooker, set the pot to high (or just turn it on if your pot doesn't have heat settings), and cook the onions for 24 hours, or until they are a deep golden brown. To get a really rich color, you may want to cook the onions even longer. (If you do not have a slow cooker, you can place the onions and butter in a roasting pan and bake in a 275°F oven, stirring occasionally, until they are deeply browned and caramelized.)

Turn off the pot, remove the cover, and allow the onions to cool in the liquid. Lift the onions out of the pot with a slotted spoon, transfer them to a colander set over a bowl, top with a plate, and weight the onions down—a can will do the trick here—to extract as much liquid as possible. Your goal is to drain the onions, not mash them, so take care. Let the onions drain for at least 1 hour, then remove them to a cutting board and, with a very sharp thin knife, cut them in half horizontally. Save the liquid for flavoring soups or stews. *The onions can be prepared up to a week ahead and kept covered in the refrigerator. They can also be wrapped airtight and frozen for 3 months.*

THE BRIOCHE

1 tablespoon active dry yeast, preferably SAF Instant (*not* rapid-rise)

3 tablespoons nonfat dry milk

3 tablespoons sugar

1½ teaspoons salt

3¼ cups unbleached all-purpose flour (or more as needed)

2 sticks (8 ounces) unsalted butter, melted and cooled slightly

3 large eggs

⅓ cup water

1 large egg beaten with ½ cup heavy cream, for egg wash

One 9-inch wheel ripe Brie

Start the brioche at least 24 or up to 36 hours ahead. Put all the ingredients for the dough in the bread machine, program the machine for "dough" or "manual," and press Start. Expect the dough to be sticky at the start but to become less sticky during kneading. If the dough, which will be very soft, does not form a ball after the first few minutes of kneading, add 1 tablespoon more flour—no more. Some of the dough will stick to the bottom of the pan and all of the dough will seem very loose—this is just as it's supposed to be. The dough will become firmer when it is chilled.

Chilling the Dough After the final knead, remove the dough from the machine and put it into a plastic bag; refrigerate for at least 24 or up to 36 hours.

At least 4 hours before you want to serve the Brie in Brioche, butter a 9-inch springform pan.

Assembling the Pastry Turn the cold brioche dough out onto a lightly floured work surface. Cut off one third of the dough and roll it into a 12-inch circle about ¹⁄₁₆ inch thick. Fit the dough into the bottom of the prepared pan, push-ing the dough out from the center so that it covers the bottom and goes up the sides of the pan a little. Brush the sides of the dough with a little of the egg wash.

Cover the Brie with caramelized onions.

Center the Brie on the dough. Arrange the onions, cut side down, on the Brie. If you have some onions left over, you can either reserve them for another use or make a second layer of onions over the Brie.

Cut off one third of the remaining dough and roll it into a 14-inch circle. Center the dough over the onion-covered Brie and work your way around the dough, tucking the sides in to meet the bottom piece of dough. The top and sides will probably be bumpy—don't worry about them; they'll even out as the dough rises.

Roll the remaining piece of dough into a strip about 30 inches long and 4 to 6 inches wide. Make 3 cuts the long way, leaving the lengths attached at the top. Starting at the attached end, braid the strips together, then position the braid around the edge of the brioche, like a wreath.

Rise Brush the dough with the egg wash and place the pan, uncovered, to rise at room temperature until doubled in volume, about 40 minutes.

While the dough is rising, position a rack in the lower third of the oven and preheat the oven to 425°F.

Baking the Pastry Bake the brioche for 15 minutes, then lower the oven temperature to 375°F and bake for 30 minutes more. If, as sometimes happens with very buttery breads, the top starts to turn very brown before the baking time is completed, cover it loosely with a foil tent.

Top: Tucking in the pastry around the sides of the Brie.
Bottom: Positioning the braid around the edge of the pastry.

Cool the brioche for at least 30 minutes before serving, or cool it to room temperature and serve.

Storing The dish is best served the day it is made. Leftovers can be covered and stored overnight in the refrigerator and brought to room temperature before serving.

Contributing Baker **LORA BRODY**

Salsa Quitza

Makes 8 servings ■ Not quite a quiche, not quite a pizza. The dough for this hybrid is made in a bread machine and then baked, fully loaded, in a conventional oven. One look at the ingredients for the crust and you'll see that there's nothing conventional about it—it's a spicy, Southwestern-inspired mix based on refried beans and it can stand up to the topping of cheeses and chunky salsa. (It can also be baked in the bread machine or the oven as a loaf and served alongside dinner.) One quitza, one big salad, a few frosty beers, and a game on TV, and you've got the fixings for a great Sunday afternoon.

THE DOUGH

1 tablespoon active dry yeast, preferably SAF Instant (*not* rapid-rise)

$1/2$ cup yellow cornmeal

3 tablespoons nonfat dry milk

3 cups unbleached all-purpose flour

$1^{1}/_{2}$ teaspoons salt

2 teaspoons chili powder

1 cup canned vegetarian refried beans

$1/4$ cup chile-infused olive oil or vegetable oil

1 large egg

1 tablespoon honey

$2/3$ cup (approximately) water

Put all the dough ingredients into the bread machine and program for "dough" or "manual." Start the machine. This is a moist dough, but it should form a ball; if it doesn't, add up to $1/3$ cup more water a little at a time. At the end of the last cycle, deflate the dough, remove it from the machine, and let it rest on a lightly floured work surface for 5 minutes. (If you want to make a loaf from this dough, either allow it to finish the rising and baking cycles in the machine or shape the dough into a loaf, fit it into a pan, and place it in a conventional oven preheated to 375°F. Bake for 35 to 45 minutes, or until an instant-read thermometer plunged into its center reads 200°F.)

The quitza can be made in a $12^{1}/_{2}$-inch slope-sided springform pan or a traditional 12-inch springform. Lightly spray the pan with vegetable oil spray. (You can also make this as a flat pizza, in which case it should be baked on a preheated baking or pizza stone.)

Lining the Pan Working on a lightly floured surface, roll the dough into a 16-inch circle. Fit the dough into the pan, stretching and pressing it so that it covers the bottom of the pan and comes up the sides.

THE TOPPING

12 ounces cream cheese, at room temperature

2 cups chunky salsa (homemade or store-bought)

1 cup shredded Cheddar or Monterey Jack cheese

Carefully spread the softened cream cheese over the bottom of the dough. Check the salsa—if it's watery, spoon it into a strainer and shake out the excess liquid. Spoon the salsa over the cream cheese and top it with the shredded cheese.

Rise Let the quitza rise, uncovered, at room temperature for about 30 minutes, or until the dough is puffy and doubled in bulk.

While the dough is rising, center a rack in the oven and preheat the oven to 475°F.

Baking the Quitza Bake the quitza for 20 to 25 minutes, or until the crust is deep brown and the cheese is bubbling. Serve hot or at room temperature.

Storing The quitza is best served the day it is made.

Contributing Baker **LORA BRODY**

Sweet Fillings and Savory Spreads

IT'S THE SMALL THINGS IN BAKING that count, that add a touch of style and an extra dollop of flavor to freshly baked cakes and tarts, pastries and breads. Whether you're looking for a recipe for a lush raspberry purée to drizzle over pound cake or a minty yogurt dip to scoop up with crusty bread, it's here. Also included in this eclectic collection is a handful of basic must-haves such as crème fraîche and chocolate sauce, a selection of frills and fancies such as caramel baskets and chocolate cups, and little savory dishes—such as chopped chicken liver and lentil salad—that perk up any meal. Turn to these when you're in the mood to improvise, trying the apricot lekvar, traditional with rugelach and Danish pastries, in the recipe for rolled-up scones, or set a bountiful brunch table with an assortment of savories. What could be more appealing than home-made bagels and bialys served with a trio of spreads: rosy salmon, smoked trout, and colorful vegetable cream cheese?

Sweet Fillings

Chocolate Meringue Buttercream

Makes 1 quart ■ Buttercream made with a base of cooked meringue has a silky quality. The whites and sugar are first whipped over heat until they are blended, then beaten until cool and light before being smoothed with a generous amount of sweet butter. The finished buttercream has a lovely feel on the tongue and is particularly easy to use—it will stand up to just about any reworking, can be piped perfectly, and holds up in humid weather, making it the best choice for summer desserts and party cakes. Once you get the hang of this recipe, you can vary the flavorings as you wish. The basic buttercream is great made with a nut paste or flavored with espresso couleur (page 286). In fact, a spoonful or two of couleur added to this chocolate recipe gives you a heady mocha buttercream that is an appealing alternate filling for Chocolate-Mint Nightcaps (page 309) or a fine frosting for a Perfect Génoise (page 39).

4 large egg whites

1 cup sugar

3 sticks (12 ounces) unsalted butter, at room temperature

5 ounces semisweet chocolate, melted and cooled to room temperature

Using a whisk and working in a large heatproof bowl (the bowl of a heavy-duty mixer would be fine), whisk together the egg whites and sugar. Place the bowl directly over medium-low heat and whisk constantly until the sugar dissolves, a layer of foam forms over the liquid portion of the eggs, and the mixture is hot (really hot) to the touch, about 2 minutes.

Transfer the whites to the bowl of a mixer fitted with the whisk attachment, or fit the mixer bowl, if you've used it, into the stand, and whip on high speed until the meringue forms glossy peaks. Unlike ordinary meringue, this meringue will not double in volume; it will, however, firm up.

When the peaks have formed and the meringue is still ever-so-slightly warm, reduce the mixer speed to medium and start adding the butter 2 tablespoons at a time, waiting until the last of the butter is incorporated each time before adding the next batch. When all the butter has been added, stop the mixer, remove the bowl, pour in the chocolate, and use a hand whisk to incorporate it completely. At this point, the buttercream needs to firm a little before it can be used—cover the bowl and put it in the refrigerator until it reaches a spreadable consistency. Give the buttercream a few turns with the whisk to smooth it before use.

continued

Storing You can chill the buttercream for up to 3 days, but it will have to be warmed before it can be used. Put chilled buttercream over direct heat for a minute or so to soften it and then beat until smooth.

Contributing Baker **CHARLOTTE AKOTO**

Bittersweet Chocolate Sauce

Makes about 3 cups ■ A grown-up, not-too-sweet sauce with shine and a wonderful fill-your-mouth viscosity, this sauce is perfect over Oven-Roasted Plum Cakes (page 255), made for pound cake, and just the right touch drizzled over Hazelnut Baby Loaves (page 249).

4 ounces semisweet chocolate, coarsely chopped
4 ounces unsweetened chocolate, coarsely chopped
2 cups heavy cream
½ cup sugar
¼ cup unsweetened cocoa powder, sifted
2 tablespoons dark crème de cacao
1 teaspoon pure vanilla extract

Place the semisweet and unsweetened chocolate in a medium bowl. Heat the cream and sugar in a medium saucepan over medium-high heat, stirring to dissolve the sugar. When the sugar is dissolved, bring the mixture to the boil. Remove the saucepan from the heat and whisk in the cocoa, whisking energetically until smooth; stir in the crème de cacao and vanilla. Pour the hot mixture over the chopped chocolate and let it sit for 5 minutes, then whisk to smooth the sauce. Serve the sauce warm or at room temperature.

Storing The sauce can be kept in a tightly covered jar in the refrigerator for a week and warmed in a double boiler or a microwave oven before serving.

Contributing Baker **MARCEL DESAULNIERS**

Crème Fraîche

Makes about 1 cup

1 cup heavy cream
1 tablespoon buttermilk

Put the heavy cream and buttermilk in a jar or container with a tight-fitting lid and shake it a couple of times to blend the two liquids. Let the jar sit at room temperature for 12 to 24 hours, or until it thickens. (Keep an eye on it: Crème fraîche will thicken faster in a warm room than a cool one.) Once thickened, chill the crème fraîche for at least 1 day before using.

Storing Refrigerated, the crème fraîche will keep for 2 weeks and become tangier.

Espresso Parfait

Makes about 2½ cups ▪ Creamy, rich, and almost instantaneous in its melt-down, a parfait—frozen, not churned—is like ice cream but even richer than any of the super-premium brands. It has an elegant texture that doesn't quit—even straight from the freezer a parfait is soft and scoopable. A French classic not often seen nowadays, the parfait is worth considering as a change from your usual toppings or garnishes for cakes and tarts.

1 cup cold heavy cream
⅓ cup sugar
2 tablespoons water
5 large egg yolks
2 teaspoons instant espresso powder

Whip the heavy cream to very soft peaks and set aside over a bowl of ice water or covered in the refrigerator.

Put the sugar and water in a small heavy-bottomed saucepan and bring to the boil over medium-high heat, using a pastry brush dipped in cold water to wash down any sugar crystals that may form. Cook until the syrup reaches the soft-ball stage, or 238°F on a candy thermometer. As soon as the sugar comes up to temperature, plunge the bottom of the pan into cold water for a couple of seconds to stop the cooking.

While the sugar is cooking, beat the egg yolks and espresso powder on high speed with a hand-held mixer in a medium bowl (or a mixer fitted with the whisk attachment) until the yolks thicken and form a ribbon when the beater is lifted; scrape down the sides of the bowl as needed.

continued

Decrease the mixer speed to low and gradually pour in the hot sugar syrup. When it is blended, increase the mixer speed to high and beat until the mixture is cool, not cold, and thickened, about 2 minutes. You can hasten the cooling by setting the mixing bowl into a larger bowl filled with ice cubes and cold water.

Using a large rubber spatula, fold about one third of the whipped cream into the yolks. Don't worry about getting it folded in perfectly; this portion is primarily to lighten the mixture. Fold in the rest of the cream. The parfait will look a little soupy, but that's just fine.

Freezing the Parfait Spoon the parfait into a shallow freezer container. Press a piece of plastic wrap against the surface to make an airtight seal and cover the container tightly. Freeze the parfait for at least 6 hours.

Storing The parfait can remain frozen for as long as 3 weeks.

Contributing Baker **DAVID OGONOWSKI**

Prune Lekvar

Makes about 1 cup ■ A sweet prune butter or, as it is known by Hungarian bakers, lekvar, to be used to fill Rugelach (page 325) or any of the Danish pastry shapes (pages 200 to 206), or enjoyed on toast.

> **3 cups (packed) pitted prunes**
> **1 tablespoon fresh lemon juice**
> **⅓ cup sugar**
> **¼ cup very finely chopped walnuts**

Put the prunes in a medium saucepan, cover with water, and bring to the boil. Lower the heat and simmer, uncovered, until the prunes are very soft, about 10 minutes; drain, reserving 1 tablespoon of the liquid. Place the prunes and liquid, lemon juice, and sugar in the work bowl of a food processor fitted with the metal blade and process until puréed. Scrape the prune butter into a bowl and stir in the walnuts.

Storing Packed in a tightly sealed jar, the prune butter will keep in the refrigerator for at least 2 weeks.

Contributing Baker **LAUREN GROVEMAN**

Apricot Lekvar

Makes about ¾ cup ■ Sunny-gold, sweet, and extra-apricoty—the addition of amaretto and toasted almonds brings out the apricots' deepest flavor—this was created to fill Rugelach (page 325) but is luscious spread on Croissants (page 185), Brioche (page 188), or a slice of toasted whole wheat bread (page 83).

2 cups whole dried apricots
¼ cup (packed) light brown sugar
1½ tablespoons amaretto liqueur or fresh lemon juice
¼ cup finely chopped toasted blanched almonds

Place the apricots in a medium saucepan, cover with water, and simmer until the fruit is soft, 10 to 15 minutes. Drain the apricots, reserving about 1 tablespoon of the liquid, and put the fruit in the work bowl of a food processor fitted with the metal blade. Purée the apricots with the brown sugar and amaretto, adding a bit of the reserved poaching liquid if the mixture seems too stiff to be spreadable. Scrape the butter into a bowl and stir in the almonds.

Storing Packed in a tightly sealed jar, the apricot butter will keep in the refrigerator for at least 2 weeks.

Contributing Baker **LAUREN GROVEMAN**

Raspberry Purée

Makes about 1 cup ■ This is an all-purpose raspberry purée, or coulis. A drizzle or two over the simplest dessert provides a polished, professional look—and an extra shot of great taste.

Two 8-ounce packages frozen raspberries in light syrup, thawed or still frosty
2 tablespoons sugar
1 teaspoon fresh lemon juice

Put the ingredients in the work bowl of a food processor fitted with the metal blade or in a blender and whirl until smooth, 15 to 20 seconds. Push the mixture through a strainer. Use immediately or keep covered in the refrigerator.

Storing The purée can be kept refrigerated for up to 2 days.

Contributing Baker **MARCEL DESAULNIERS**

Chocolate Waves

Makes enough to decorate 8 to 12 dessert plates ■ Whimsical waves of tricolor chocolate make the mundane magnificent. Part Jackson Pollock, part pastry-chef panache, these waves are made by spattering white and milk chocolates across a sheet of parchment and then spreading the sheet with a thin layer of tempered bittersweet chocolate. (Don't stop here because of the tempering—it's done easily in this recipe.) While everything is still warm and malleable, the parchment is draped over any assemblage of kitchen cups and utensils you can amass so that the chocolate sets in a truly undulating wave. When you're ready to dress a plate, just break off a wafer of wave in any size from tiny to tidal.

There are no exact measurements given for the chocolates. Although you won't need much for the spatters and only slightly more for spreading, you'll find it easiest to work with at least half a pound of bittersweet chocolate, even better with a pound. There won't be any waste—leftovers can be remelted and used in other recipes.

White chocolate

Milk chocolate

Bittersweet chocolate (at least ½ pound)

To get ready, cut a long sheet of parchment paper lengthwise in half. (The size is not important here because the shapes are so free-form.) Make an arrangement of kitchen objects tall and short to give yourself an uneven landscape over which to drape the paper: for example, a coffee mug, a lemon, and a strainer, or a can of tomatoes, a couple of wineglasses, and an orange.

Melt the white and milk chocolates separately over hot water. Lay one piece of the parchment in front of you, dip the fingers of one hand into the white chocolate, and let the chocolate drip with abandon over the paper as you swing your hand around to create a random design. Give your hand a quick wash and dry (make sure your fingers are thoroughly dried), then dip your fingers into the milk chocolate and spatter that over and around the white chocolate. Quickly rinse your hand and lay the second sheet of parchment over the wet chocolate; press your hands against the surface of the top piece to smooth it over the bottom. Peel it away and you'll have two sheets of spattered parchment. Put each piece of parchment, spatter side up, on a baking sheet and chill for 5 to 10 minutes. (Do not freeze the chocolate.)

Tempering the Chocolate Meanwhile, put all but a large chunk (about one quarter the weight of your original piece) of the bittersweet chocolate into the top of a double boiler over simmering water and heat it, stirring occasionally, until it measures 120°F on an instant-read thermometer. Remove the chocolate from the water and heat, add the reserved chunk of chocolate, and, stirring the chocolate constantly, let it cool to 90°F. Pull one sheet of parchment out of the refrigerator and pour some—not much—of the bittersweet chocolate over the crazy pattern. Spread the bittersweet chocolate over the entire sheet and smooth with an offset spatula—you want a thin covering layer of dark chocolate—then drape the paper over your assemblage. Repeat with the other sheet of chocolate-spattered parchment. Allow the chocolate to set at room temperature.

When the chocolate is set, peel off the paper and give the waves a karate chop to break them into shards to use as decoration.

Storing The chocolate waves will keep for a few hours on their parchment at cool room temperature.

Contributing Baker **DAVID OGONOWSKI**

Chocolate Balloon Cups

A playful addition to any dessert plate—molded chocolate cups to be filled with whipped cream and berries, mousses or parfaits, ice cream, or candies. The real fun is in the construction: Heavy-duty balloons are dipped into melted chocolate, rocked around a bit to give them a tulip edge, and chilled. Once the chocolate is set, pop the balloons and fill the cups.

Heavy-duty balloons (any size you like)
1 pound semisweet chocolate, coarsely chopped

Blow up the balloons, making certain to knot each one securely. Line baking sheets with parchment and set aside.

Heat an inch of water in the bottom of a double boiler. Put the chocolate in the top of the double boiler and heat, stirring constantly, until melted, 4 to 5 minutes.

Transfer the chocolate to a metal bowl (choose a bowl that's just a little larger than a blown-up balloon) and stir until the temperature of the chocolate drops to 90°F, measured with an instant-read thermometer, about 5 minutes.

One at a time, dip the balloons into the melted chocolate and rock them back and forth, coating the bottom of the balloons and causing the chocolate to come up the sides unevenly—you'll get a tulip edge. Lift the balloons and let the excess chocolate drip back into the bowl before placing them, knots up, on the paper-lined baking sheets. (Save the leftover chocolate for another use; it can be remelted.) Refrigerate for 30 minutes to set and harden the chocolate.

continued

Remove the balloons from the refrigerator and pop each one with the tip of a sharp knife. Gently lift the deflated balloons from the cups and discard. Fill the balloon cups immediately, or keep them refrigerated, covered with plastic wrap.

Storing The unfilled cups can be kept in the refrigerator for up to 3 days.

Contributing Baker **MARCEL DESAULNIERS**

Caramel Baskets

Makes at least 12 baskets ■ These charming baskets are a delightful—and dressy—addition to any dessert. They can be made in any size, from about three inches across, just right for cradling a couple of berries, to about six inches in diameter, nice for fruit and whipped cream or, turned upside down, to top a scoop of mousse or ice cream. Shaped like medieval maidens' headdresses, the pointy little baskets are easier to make than appearances would have you believe.

1 cup sugar (use more if you want to make more than a dozen small baskets)
Vegetable oil

Cut as many squares of parchment paper as you want baskets—a cup of sugar will yield at least a dozen baskets. If you cut a 3-inch square, you'll get a basket with an opening that's about 3 inches across, so figure the size of your baskets from this model.

Fold one square into quarters, putting pressure on each fold so that you make a definite crease. Open the square and bring the edges of one quarter together—you should now have a pyramid, or a small pointy-topped cap with the fold on the inside. Staple the folded quarter closed and continue making pyramids from the remaining parchment squares. Lightly brush each pyramid with a little vegetable oil.

Put some ice cubes and water in a roasting pan and keep it close to your stovetop.

Place a heavy-bottomed sauté pan or skillet over medium heat. You're going to be caramelizing the sugar spot by spot, so the larger your pan, the faster things will go. When the pan is hot, sprinkle in a little of the sugar—about 1 tablespoon should do it. As soon as some of the sugar melts, sprinkle a little more sugar over it. When you've added about half the sugar, start stirring the sugar with a wooden spoon. Continue stirring as you add the remaining sugar 1 tablespoon at a time.

When the sugar turns a medium amber, tested by dropping some on a white plate, remove the skillet from the heat and dip the bottom of the pan into the ice water for a second—don't keep it there. The cold will stop the cooking and leave the caramel liquid but thickened—a spoon should leave tracks in it now. Immediately start to make the baskets by dribbling the caramel from a wooden spoon onto the parchment pyramids. Go heavier on the top of each pyramid and aim for a spare and lacy effect on the body of the basket.

When you have completed the batch, peel away the parchment from each basket.

Storing The baskets will be fine for a couple of days in an airtight tin in a cool, dry environment.

Contributing Baker **MARKUS FARBINGER**

Caramelized Walnuts

Makes 12 candied nuts ■ Caramelized walnuts—or pecans, almonds, or any other nuts—make a nice trim for a cake or a nibblette with espresso. This recipe is written for a dozen nuts—just enough to decorate a cake roll or round—but it can be multiplied easily.

¹⁄₂ cup sugar
12 shelled walnuts or other nuts

Line a baking sheet with parchment paper and keep it close at hand.

Put the sugar in a small saucepan and heat over medium heat, stirring constantly. Once the sugar starts to color, check the color often by dropping a bit of the caramel onto a white plate—you're aiming for a golden caramel.

When you've got the color you want, add the nuts 2 at a time, dropping them into the caramel, turning them around with a fork to coat them, and then lifting them out and onto the parchment to cool and harden.

To make fast work of cleaning the sugar pot, fill the pot with hot tap water and bring it to the boil. Pour out the water and the sticky, hardened-onto-the-bottom-and-sides-of-the-pan caramel will follow.

Storing The caramelized nuts can be kept in an airtight container in a cool, dry place for a couple of days.

Contributing Baker **MARY BERGIN**

Savory Spreads

Lebanese Chickpea Salad

Makes 4 servings ■ Chickpeas, also called garbanzos, are really more bean than pea. Here they're the main player in a type of salad popular throughout the Middle East. This version features sumac, a classic ingredient in Lebanese cooking. Purchased dried at specialty stores, sumac looks like chili powder but has a bright, acidic, lemony flavor. In fact, if you can't find sumac, you can add another tablespoon of lemon juice to the dressing. Serve this salad, accompanied by Pita Breads (page 154) or Oasis Naan (page 149), as part of a mezze platter or as a snack.

> 2 cups cooked chickpeas or drained canned chickpeas
> 1 teaspoon ground sumac (see Sources, page 467)
> 1 small garlic clove, peeled and crushed
> 2 tablespoons dried spearmint
> 2 tablespoons fresh lemon juice, or more to taste
> 1 tablespoon red wine vinegar
> 3 tablespoons olive oil
> Salt to taste

Put the chickpeas in a serving bowl. Mix the remaining ingredients together either by whisking them in a bowl or measuring them into a jar, sealing the jar, and shaking it vigorously. Toss the chickpeas with the dressing and taste for salt and other seasonings. Allow the salad to sit for 30 minutes so that the flavors have a chance to blend.

Storing The salad can be made up to 4 hours ahead and kept refrigerated until serving time. Bring to room temperature before serving.

Contributing Bakers **JEFFREY ALFORD AND NAOMI DUGUID**

Mediterranean Lentil Salad

Makes 8 to 10 appetizer servings ■ A fresh-tasting salad that's an ideal go-along with flatbreads like Pita Breads (page 154) and Persian Naan (page147) or slices of Eastern European Rye (page 98). You can make the salad with either fast-cooking green lentils (Le Puy lentils from France) or softer brown lentils. They can be cooked ahead, but the peppers and vinaigrette should be added right before you're ready to serve.

1 cup brown or green lentils, picked over and washed

2 garlic cloves, peeled and halved

1 red bell pepper, cored, seeded, deveined, and diced

2 tablespoons extra-virgin olive oil

$\frac{1}{2}$ teaspoon coriander seeds, toasted and finely ground

$\frac{1}{2}$ teaspoon salt

$\frac{1}{2}$ teaspoon freshly ground black pepper

3 tablespoons fresh lemon juice

$\frac{1}{4}$ cup (packed) fresh coriander (cilantro) leaves, finely chopped

Put the lentils, 3 cups water, and the garlic in a 2-quart saucepan, bring to the boil over medium-high heat, and reduce the heat so that the liquid just simmers. Partially cover the pan and cook until the lentils are tender but not mushy, 30 to 45 minutes for brown lentils, 20 to 30 minutes for green. Drain the lentils and discard the garlic. *You can make the lentils up to 2 days ahead and keep them refrigerated in a tightly sealed container.*

Spoon the lentils into a shallow serving bowl and add the bell peppers.

Making the Vinaigrette Whisk the olive oil with the ground coriander, salt, pepper, and lemon juice to blend. Stir in the coriander leaves. Gently toss the lentils and peppers with the dressing, and serve.

Storing The lentils and the vinaigrette can be made up to 2 days ahead, and refrigerated, but the salad should not be tossed until serving time.

Contributing Bakers **JEFFREY ALFORD AND NAOMI DUGUID**

Mint-Yogurt Dip

Makes about 2 cups ■ A refreshing dip that is found throughout the Middle East and parts of Central Asia. Always a component of a mezze or appetizer buffet, this dip is a natural with flatbreads.

1$\frac{1}{2}$ cups plain yogurt (you can use low-fat)

1 cup (packed) fresh mint leaves, finely chopped

3 to 4 cloves garlic, peeled and finely minced

$\frac{1}{2}$ teaspoon salt

$\frac{1}{2}$ teaspoon freshly ground black pepper

Mix all of the ingredients together in a bowl and refrigerate until well chilled.

Storing You can make the dip up to 6 hours ahead; cover and chill until needed.

Contributing Bakers **JEFFREY ALFORD AND NAOMI DUGUID**

Yogurt Cheese

Makes about ½ pound ■ Made from either cow's or goat's milk yogurt, these cheese balls are a treat to have on hand for nibbling with flatbreads and serving with drinks. Called labneh, the cheese is made by draining fresh yogurt and shaping it into balls. They are lovely served fresh and delightful bathed in olive oil and sprinkled with fresh herbs.

> **2 cups plain yogurt (you can use low-fat)**
> **1 teaspoon salt (optional)**
> **Olive oil, for storing (optional)**
> **Chopped fresh herbs (optional)**

Line a colander or a large sieve with cheesecloth and place over a bowl. Stir the yogurt and salt together and pour it into the colander. Draw up the edges of the cheesecloth and tie the topknot with a string or a rubber band. Suspend the package over the colander and allow it to drain for 24 hours in a cool spot.

Once drained, the yogurt will have turned creamy. Use a tablespoon to scoop up walnut-size mounds of the yogurt cheese and shape them into balls between your moistened palms. *The cheese is ready to serve now, or it can be kept in a covered bowl in the refrigerator for 3 to 4 days.*

Drying the Labneh If you want to store the labneh for a longer time, lay the balls on a plate, allowing a bit of space between each one, and cover the plate loosely with cheesecloth. Refrigerate the cheese for a day or two, during which time the balls will become firmer and drier. Pack them into a sterilized jar and add olive oil to cover. Seal the jar well and store in a cool, dark place. To serve, roll the labneh in freshly chopped herbs.

Storing The cheese can be kept in the refrigerator for 3 to 4 days or, when packed into sterilized jars, stored in a cool, dark place for up to a month.

Contributing Bakers **JEFFREY ALFORD AND NAOMI DUGUID**

Vegetable Cream Cheese

Makes about 3 cups ■ Here's a popular bagel topper that can be served with bialys, pumpernickel, and crackers too. It's chock-full of vegetables, chunky, fresh-tasting, and easy to make. This is more an idea than a formal recipe—use whatever vegetables you favor and toss in the seasonings you like best.

12 ounces whipped cream cheese, at room temperature

½ to 1 cup chopped unpeeled seedless cucumbers, squeezed dry

⅓ cup minced radishes (about 6 radishes)

⅓ cup minced scallions (the white part and about 2 inches of the green)

½ cup minced carrots

Freshly ground black pepper, to taste

Put all of the ingredients in a medium bowl and mix with a rubber spatula until blended. Cover and chill until needed.

Storing The spread can be refrigerated, covered, for up to 2 days.

Contributing Baker **LAUREN GROVEMAN**

Chopped Chicken Liver

Makes about 1 quart ■ Good chicken livers are naturally sweet, but this pâté is given an extra-sweet note with the addition of golden, caramelized onions—a nice touch with the garlic and hard-cooked eggs. (If you want to garnish the livers with a ring of caramelized onions, caramelize extra onions when you're cooking the onions to be incorporated into the pâté, then just spoon them out and keep them in reserve.) After the livers and onions are sautéed, they're tossed into the food processor, which makes fast work of turning the mix into a perfect pâté. For an unbeatable combination, make this the day you're making Eastern European Rye (page 98) or Pumpernickel Loaves (page 95).

2 tablespoons rendered chicken fat (or butter or margarine)

2 large onions, peeled and thinly sliced

2 cloves garlic, peeled and minced

Pinch of sugar

2 tablespoons butter or margarine

1 pound chicken livers, connective tissue removed, rinsed,
   and patted dry

3 large eggs, hard-cooked and peeled

1 teaspoon coarse salt (or more to taste)

Freshly ground black pepper to taste

Minced onion and minced fresh parsley (optional)

Melt the chicken fat in a large skillet over medium heat. Stir in the onions and cook until softened, 5 to 10 minutes. Stir in the garlic and sugar and cook, stirring occasionally, until the onions are deeply golden and evenly caramelized, about 25 minutes.

continued

Clear a spot in the center of the skillet by pushing the onions to the sides, and add the 2 tablespoons butter. When the butter is bubbling, add the chicken livers and cook over high heat, stirring, until brown on all sides, about 6 minutes. Stir to combine the onions and livers and cover the skillet. Reduce the heat to very low and continue to cook until the livers are cooked through and pink only in the center, 2 to 5 minutes. Uncover, raise the heat to medium, scrape up any bits of caramelized onion or liver, and cook for another 2 minutes.

Scrape the onions and livers into the work bowl of a food processor fitted with the metal blade. Add the eggs and season generously with coarse salt and pepper. Pulse until the ingredients are finely chopped but not puréed—an uneven texture will make the pâté even more interesting. Taste and adjust the seasonings.

Chilling the Chopped Liver Turn the mixture into a container, cover with a paper towel, and let cool. When the chopped liver is cool, cover with plastic wrap and refrigerate for at least 4 hours, or preferably overnight.

Let the chilled chopped liver sit at room temperature for 1 hour before serving. At serving time, you can garnish the liver with coarse salt and freshly ground pepper, and minced onion and parsley if you like.

Storing Packed into a well-sealed container, the chopped chicken liver can be kept in the refrigerator for about 3 days.

Contributing Baker **LAUREN GROVEMAN**

Smoked Trout Spread

Makes about 2 cups ■ Depending on what you spread it on, this trout pâté can be either rough and rustic or suave and elegant. It's as at home piled on a bagel to be downed with cups of steaming coffee as it is on pumpernickel points or crackers that will accompany Champagne. A nice spread to have on hand for cocktails.

> 2 cups (packed) skinned and flaked smoked trout (about 1 pound fillets)
> ³/₄ cup mayonnaise
> ¹/₂ cup (packed) minced scallions (the white part and about 2 inches of the green)
> 3 tablespoons chopped fresh flat-leaf parsley
> 2 cloves garlic, peeled and minced
> 1 teaspoon fresh lemon juice
> 1 teaspoon freshly ground white pepper
> Freshly ground black pepper, to taste

Place all of the ingredients in the work bowl of a food processor fitted with the metal blade. Pulse until the ingredients are finely chopped but not puréed. Take care not to overprocess the spread—it should not be like a mousse.

Chilling the Spread Spoon into a container, cover with plastic wrap, and chill for at least 4 hours, or preferably overnight. Remove the spread from the refrigerator 15 minutes before serving.

Storing Well covered, the spread will keep in the refrigerator for 2 to 3 days.

Contributing Baker **LAUREN GROVEMAN**

Salmon Spread

Makes about 2 cups ■ Everything you want on a bagel—cream cheese, smoked salmon, and onion—rolled into one. Smoked salmon is wildly expensive and an extravagance you might not want to mince and mix for this spread. Fortunately, this spread can be made with scraps, the trimmings many delicatessens offer at a greatly reduced price (if they're not saving them to make this kind of spread for their shops). If you don't see a sign saying trimmings are available, ask.

> **12 ounces whipped cream cheese**
> **2½ tablespoons sour cream**
> **½ pound smoked salmon, minced**
> **½ cup (packed) minced scallions (the white part and about 2 inches of the green)**
> **½ teaspoon freshly ground white pepper**
> **½ teaspoon freshly ground black pepper**

Stir the cream cheese and sour cream together in a medium bowl until blended. Add the remaining ingredients and fold in with a rubber spatula. Spoon the mixture into a serving bowl or storage container and chill until ready to serve.

Storing The spread can remain in the refrigerator, covered, for up to 4 days.

Contributing Baker **LAUREN GROVEMAN**

About the Bakers

Charlotte Akoto, born in Ghana, West Africa, originally learned to cook from her grandmother. After a culinary education and apprenticeship in England, she moved to New York in 1984 and landed a pastry position at the Drake Swissotel. Charlotte worked at the Algonquin, where she quickly became adept at elaborate pastry preparation, and later became the head pastry chef at the Pierre Hotel. Currently, Charlotte is the head of pastry production at the Old Williamsburg Company.

Mary Bergin, head pastry chef of Spago in Las Vegas, began her work with Wolfgang Puck at the Los Angeles–based Spago more than ten years ago. She is responsible for training the pastry chefs at both restaurants, and her innovative desserts have been enjoyed by celebrities, world leaders, and fellow chefs alike. Mary is the author of the well-received *Spago Desserts* and has contributed to several other cookbooks.

David Blom is a third-generation baker who learned his craft in his parents' small German bakery in Philadelphia. After graduating from the Culinary Institute of America, David worked in several of New York's best restaurants, and was for many years the pastry chef at the famous Montrachet restaurant. Recently, David moved to North Miami to become the pastry chef at Chef Allen's.

Flo Braker, born and raised in Evansville, Indiana, received her formal culinary education at the École Lenôtre in France and the Richemont Professional School in Switzerland. Flo specializes in cakes and pastries prepared in the European tradition, and is the author of two best-selling books, *Sweet Miniatures* and *The Simple Art of Perfect Pastry*. Now residing in Palo Alto, California, she is a food columnist for the *San Francisco Chronicle*, the president of the International Association of Culinary Professionals, and an active member of the American Institute of Wine & Food.

Lora Brody has been an influential force in the American kitchen for nearly two decades. Well known for popularizing the bread machine, she is the author of fourteen cookbooks, including *Growing Up on the Chocolate Diet* and *Bread Machine Baking: Perfect Every Time*. Lora, a frequent contributor to major magazines and newspapers, is an active spokesperson, lecturer, and cooking instructor. In 1978, Lora founded the Women's Culinary Guild, a prototype for dozens of sister organizations across the country.

Marion Cunningham spent the early part of her culinary career assisting James Beard in his nationwide cooking classes. A columnist for the *San Francisco Chronicle* and the *Los Angeles Times*, Marion also writes for *Bon Appétit*, *Gourmet*, *Food & Wine*, and *Saveur*. In 1993, Marion received the Grand Dame Award from Les Dames d'Escoffier, and in 1994 was named scholar-in-residence by the International Association of Culinary Professionals. Best known for her work on the *Fannie Farmer Cookbook,* Marion has written several best-selling cookbooks. Her most recent book is *Cooking with Children.*

Marcel Desaulniers is the executive chef and co-owner of the Trellis Restaurant in Williamsburg, Virginia. A graduate of the Culinary Institute of America, Marcel was named Best Chef Mid-Atlantic States by the James Beard Foundation. He has written four cookbooks, including the award-winning *Desserts to Die For* and *Death by Chocolate,* which is based on his popular television series. He is currently writing a cookbook for children.

Naomi Duguid and Jeffrey Alford are culinary adventurers who traveled extensively to research their award-winning *Flatbreads and Flavors* cookbook. As freelance food and travel writers and photographers, this wife-husband team writes often for magazines such as *Food & Wine, Bon Appétit,* and *Eating Well.* Naomi and Jeffrey live in Toronto but spend much of their time eating, writing, and photographing their way through the lesser traveled byways of the gastronomic world.

Markus Farbinger is currently the team leader for the baking and pastry arts curriculum at the Culinary Institute of America. A graduate of Salzburg's School for Economic Development, Markus honed his baking and pastry skills in his native Austria. Markus, former pastry chef at the world famous Le Cirque restaurant in New York City, was honored recently with the grand prize at the Domaine Carneros wedding cake competition.

Danielle Forestier, a resident of Oakland, California, travels extensively throughout Europe, Asia, and the United States, giving seminars and addressing culinary associations. Prior to becoming a baking consultant, Danielle studied under Professor Raymond Calvel in France and apprenticed in several bakeries in Paris. She operated the successful French Bakery in Santa Barbara, California, and was the first American woman to attain the title of *maître boulanger* from the Chambre de Commerce in Paris.

Gale Gand began her career as a silver- and goldsmith and soon discovered that her skills translated well to cuisine and started her own catering company. Gale attended pastry classes at La Varenne in Paris, and then worked in several New York restaurants. After winning raves in England, Gale and her husband, Rick Tramonto, moved to Chicago, where they were partners in the innovative and popular Trio Restaurant. They have since opened Brasserie T, an instant success.

Lauren Groveman a former actress, studied classical cooking before founding Lauren Groveman's Kitchen Company, which keeps her busy teaching classes in cooking and baking from her home and at cooking schools throughout the Northeast. She wrote her first cookbook, *Lauren Groveman's Kitchen,* based on these classes. Lauren appears often on television and serves on the board of directors of the New York Association of Cooking Teachers.

Johanne Killeen, named one of the top twenty women chefs in the country, was educated at Rhode Island School of Design as a photographer. Now, the kitchen is her studio, the food her canvas, and desserts her passion. Along with husband George Germon, Johanne is chef and co-owner of Al Forno, an extremely popular restaurant in Providence, Rhode Island. Together they wrote *Cucina Simpatica.* Recently, Johanne was inducted into the Johnson and Wales University Culinary Hall of Fame.

Craig Kominiak began his cooking career in the U.S. Navy, preparing meals for two hundred sailors daily. When his tour of duty ended, he enrolled in the Culinary Institute of America to polish his technique. In 1990, Craig took on the position of pastry chef for the Arizona 206 restaurant in New York. Today, Craig is executive chef for New York's renowned Ecce Panis Bakeries, supplying breads to many restaurants, New York–area Starbucks, and locals, who line up outside the shops at all hours.

Norman Love, the Naples, Florida–based pastry chef known for his artistic, sculptural pastry creations, is corporate pastry chef of The Ritz-Carlton Hotel Company. A native of Philadelphia, Norman served as executive pastry chef for the Beverly Hills Hotel for several years before joining The Ritz-Carlton Company in 1990. Intrigued by the tropical flavors and ethnic influences of South Florida, Norman features exotic fruits and Caribbean spices in much of his work.

Leslie Mackie, a graduate of the California Culinary Academy, started her culinary career in Boston with Biba's Lydia Shire and Susan Regis, then traveled extensively through the Italian countryside, where she was influenced by the tastes, textures, and techniques of village bakers. After her return to the United States, Leslie was head baker at the acclaimed Grand Central Bakery and then opened Macrina Bakery and Café, both in Seattle, Washington.

Nick Malgieri, former executive pastry chef of New York's famous Windows on the World, graduated from the Culinary Institute of America. Nick has taught and guest-lectured extensively, and in 1996, was named to the James Beard Foundation's Who's Who and honored with a Beard Award for his book *How to Bake.* Nick is an active member of several culinary associations and currently serves as the vice president and director of baking programs at Peter Kump's New York Cooking School.

Esther McManus is well known throughout the Philadelphia area for her buttery croissants and pastries at Le Bus Restaurant and Bakery. Born in Marrakech, Esther traveled and studied in many countries including France, Israel, and Italy. In the United States, Esther has held positions as chef, baker, instructor, and consultant to establishments from Vermont to Philadelphia. In addition to her work at Le Bus, Esther serves as board chef for the Campbell Soup Company.

Alice Medrich is the only two-time recipient of the James Beard Cookbook of the Year Award, having won for *Cocolat* and *Chocolate and the Art of Low-Fat Baking*. Well known as the founder of San Francisco's chocolate and dessert company, Cocolat, Alice created the large-sized American chocolate truffle, and the world has been a happier place ever since. An active member of the American Institute of Wine & Food, and the International Association of Culinary Professionals, Alice continues to write, teach, and lecture across the country.

David Ogonowski has been a pastry chef and baker for the past ten years. He started out in San Francisco, then moved to Boston, where he garnered the prestigious Best of Boston Best Desserts award while serving as pastry chef at Olives Restaurant in Charlestown, Massachusetts. David is currently working on plans to open his own bakery and café.

Beatrice Ojakangas approaches baking under the influence of her 100 percent Finnish heritage. A lifelong resident of Duluth, Minnesota, and a home economics graduate of the University of Minnesota, Beatrice went on to open a restaurant, teach cooking courses, and host a local television show. She has written more than a dozen cookbooks, including *The Great Holiday Baking Book, Quick Breads,* and *A Finnish Cookbook*. Beatrice also serves as a consultant to the Pillsbury Corporation and other major food companies.

Joe Ortiz is the co-owner of Gayle's Bakery & Rosticceria in Capitola, California. His breads have received critical acclaim from the International Bread Competition, as well as from culinary publications like *Cook's Magazine, Food & Wine,* and *Bon Appétit*. Joe shares his skills and knowledge through frequent lectures and demonstrations across the country. His book, *The Village Baker,* is the recipient of the International Association of Culinary Professional's Julia Child Cookbook Award.

Michel Richard, author of *Michel Richard's Home Cooking with a French Accent,* began his culinary apprenticeship at the age of thirteen in France. Pastry became Michel's passion and, for a number of years, his profession, as he worked with the world famous *pâtissier* Gaston Lenôtre. In 1974, Michel moved to New York to open Lenôtre's first American shop. Soon after, Michel opened his own pastry shops and, later, his much heralded flagship restaurant, Citrus, in Los Angeles. Michel has been honored with the James Beard Foundation's Best Chef of California award, and was a featured chef in the Julia Child–hosted series *Cooking with Master Chefs*.

Nancy Silverton, one of America's best bread bakers, worked with Wolfgang Puck at his Los Angeles Spago prior to opening her extremely successful Campanile Restaurant and La Brea Bakery in Los Angeles with her chef-husband, Mark Peel. Nancy demonstrated her bread making to millions of enthusiastic followers of Julia Child's *Cooking with Master Chefs* series, and her most recent book, *Nancy Silverton's Breads from the La Brea Bakery,* has been well received. A graduate of the Cordon Bleu and Lenôtre Pastry School, Nancy is considered a mentor to young bakers.

Martha Stewart is the author of sixteen best-selling books about food, entertaining, gardening, and home renovations. She is the editor-in-chief of *Martha Stewart Living* magazine, and serves as host of the Emmy Award–winning weekly television show by the same name. Having trained at the famous Cordon Bleu, Martha was a caterer for many years. She is credited with transforming the way Americans receive guests into their homes and is an authority on the rituals of entertaining and style.

Steve Sullivan began his culinary career in 1975, when he moved to Berkeley, California, and took a job as a busboy at Alice Waters's now legendary Chez Panisse restaurant. Steve began to make bread as a hobby. He quickly perfected his skills and, in short order, began baking outside of Chez Panisse. Soon he established his own bakery, the Acme Bread Company, where his sourdough and levain breads were a huge success—no small feat in San Francisco, the sourdough capital of America. Acme's breads are distributed throughout the Bay Area and have earned Steve a devoted following among chefs, restaurateurs, and residents.

Sources

The following sources offer a wide range of bakeware and equipment.
Many also supply harder-to-find ingredients and tools.

AMERICAN STONECRAFTERS INC.
378 North Cherry Extension
Wallingford, CT 06492
800-US-STONE
*quarry tiles, marble and
granite*

BETHANY HOUSEWARES
423 2nd Avenue SW
Cresco, IA 52136
319-547-5873
lefse griddles and sticks

BORGEAT
20 Fernwood Road
Boston, MA 02132
800-469-0188

BRIDGE KITCHENWARE
214 East 52nd Street
New York, NY 10022
212-688-4220
candymaker's tools

CHEF'S CATALOGUE
3215 Commercial Avenue
Northbrook, IL 60062
800-338-3232

CHOCOLATES EL REY
P.O. Box 853
Fredericksburg, TX 78624
800-ELREY-99
bittersweet chocolate sticks

CUISINARTS
1 Cummings Point Road
Stamford, CT 06904
800-726-0190

DAIRYLAND USA
311 Manida Street
Bronx, New York 10474
718-842-8700
*chocolates, including a wide selec-
tion of Valrhona, Tahitian vanilla
beans, and other specialty pastry
ingredients*

ELK CANDY CO. INC.
240 East 86th Street
New York, NY 10028
212-650-1177
almond paste, marzipan

FARBERWARE MILLENNIUM
1500 Bassett Avenue
Bronx, NY 10461
718-863-8000

FLAVORBANK
4710 Eisenhower Boulevard
#E-8
Tampa, Fl 33614
800-825-7603
*poppy seeds and other seeds, sumac
and other spices*

GRAY'S GRIST MILL
P.O. Box 422
Adamsville, RI 02801
508-636-6075
jonnycake meal

JACOBS
5250 Highway 71NE
Willmar, MN 56201
612-235-7594
*canvas-covered pastry boards,
dough stamps/dockers, hardtack
rolling pins, lefse rolling pins and
sticks*

J. B. PRINCE
29 West 38th Street
New York, New York 10018
212-302-8611

KING ARTHUR FLOUR COMPANY
The Baker's Catalogue
P.O. Box 876
Norwich, VT 05055
800-827-6836
*bread and cake baking supplies
including flour, rolling pins, baking
stones, and bannetons*

KITCHENAID/WHIRLPOOL
950 Sater Street
Greenville, OH 45331
800-253-1301
heavy-duty mixers and attachments

KITCHEN ARTS
161 Newbury Street
Boston, MA 02116
617-320-3666

KITCHEN ETC.
550 Providence Highway Rt. 1
Dedham, MA 02026
617-320-3666

LA CUISINE
323 Cameron Street
Alexandria, Virginia 22314
*Valrhona chocolate and specialty
pastry equipment*

LAMALLE KITCHENWARE
36 West 25th Street (6th floor)
New York, NY 10010
800-660-0750
*wedding cake pans and cardboard
rounds*

NEW YORK CAKE AND BAKING
DISTRIBUTORS
56 West 22nd Street
New York, NY 10010
212-675-CAKE
candymaker's tools, petal dust,
poppy seeds, wedding cake pans
and cardboard rounds

SAHADI
187-189 Atlantic Avenue
Brooklyn, NY 11201
800-SAHADI-1
poppy seeds and other seeds, sumac
and other spices

SUR LA TABLE
Catalogue Division
410 Terry Avenue North
Seattle, WA 98109
800-243-0852
grooved and hardtack rolling
pins, wedding cake pans
and cardboard
rounds

WILLIAMS-SONOMA
Mail Order Department
P.O. Box 7456
San Francisco, CA 94120-7456
800-541-2233

WILTON INDUSTRIES/ROWOCO
2240 West 75th Street
Woodridge, IL 60517
800-794-5866
cake decorating tools,
wedding cake pans
and cardboard
rounds

Additional Credits

The photographs of the bakers on pages xx to xxiii are copyright © 1996 by Bill O'Connell, James Scherer, and A La Carte Communications, Inc., with the exception of the following: Marion Cunningham, by Leslie Flores; Nancy Silverton, by Brian Leatart; and Beatrice Ojakangas, by Ken Moran. We have tried to trace copyright holders of all photographs and apologize for any unintended omission. We would be pleased to insert appropriate acknowledgment in subsequent editions.

WE WOULD LIKE TO THANK THE FOLLOWING INDIVIDUALS
FOR THEIR CONTRIBUTIONS TO THIS BOOK:

Copyediting by Deborah Weiss Geline and Judith Sutton
Production by Karen Lumley
Publicity and promotion by Kim Yorio
Design by Vertigo Design, New York
Composition by Westchester Book Composition
Separations by Black Dot Group
Printing and binding by Quebecor Printing Hawkins

INDEX

flour (*continued*)

Pillsbury, 12

semolina, 102

sifting of, 13

storing of, 12

weighing of, measuring of flour vs., 13

White Lily, 12

flouring pans, 5–6

focaccia, *63,* 143–145

dough, leaf-shaped fougasse from, 146–147

fruit, *176,* 196–198

herb–olive oil topping for, 145

sandwich, grilled vegetable, *63,* 145

folding, 13–14

of light into heavy mixtures, 13–14

rubber spatula for, 13–14, 23

food processors, 14

chocolate dough in, 373

flaky pie dough in, 32

galette dough in, 371–372

johnnycake cobbler topping in, 389–390

making bread in, 14–15

making pastry in, 14

metal blade of, for pastry, 14

pasta frolla in, 370

savory wheat crackers in, 163–164

semolina bread in, 102

Forestier, Danielle, *xx,* 112, 462

classic French bread, 123–127

fougasse:

leaf-shaped, *59,* 146–147

sweet berry, *170,* 194–195

framboise syrup, for chocolate ruffle cake, 266

freezer burn, preventing, 15

freezing:

of baked goods, 15

of dough, 15

see also specific recipes

French:

apple tart, *353, 354,* 379–381

bread, classic, 123–127

(cooked) meringue, 38

rolling pin, 21

strawberry cake, 273–274

fresh:

berry jam filling, 204

rhubarb upside-down baby cakes, 244–246

fresh (compressed) yeast, 26

proofing of, 26

storing of, 26

frostings and fillings:

almond, 202

apricot, 203

chocolate meringue buttercream, 445–446

chocolate-mint ganache, 309

confectioner's cream, 204

crème fraîche, for chocolate ruffle cake, 266

espresso whipped cream, 288

fig-almond, for X cookies, 319

fresh berry jam, 204

ginger cream, 402

mocha ganache, for chocolate napoleons, 401–402

mocha ganache, for mocha brownie cake, 283

pastry cream, 408–409, 415

prune, 203

rum-laced buttercream, 298–300

spatulas for spreading, 23

streusel, for nectarine upside-down chiffon cake, 242

see also glaze

fruit:

in baked yogurt tart, 378–379

berry galette, *344–345,* 377

blueberry muffins, *168,* 208–209

blueberry-nectarine pie, *350, 351,* 384–385

caramel-poached, for brioche tart, 388

dried, 10

dried, in buttermilk scones, 210

focaccia, *176,* 196–198

French apple tart, *353, 354,* 379–381

fresh rhubarb upside-down baby cakes, 244–246

in johnnycake cobblers, *339,* 389–390

marzipan, for a glorious wedding cake, *233, 236,* 300–303

nectarine johnnycake cobbler, *339,* 389–390

nectarine upside-down chiffon cake, *238,* 241–243

oven-roasted plum cakes, *229,* 255–256

poached apricots, for poppy seed torte, 258–259

poached apricots, for sunny-side-up pastries, 192

poached pears, for chocolate napoleons, *356,* 401

raspberry-fig crostata, *338,* 374–375

in savarin, *358,* 416–417

skewers, for phylloccine ice cream sandwiches, 406

sweet berry fougasse, *170,* 194–195

in tropical napoleons, *337,* 393–394

see also specific fruits

galette:

berry, *344–345,* 377

cheese and tomato, 429

dough, 371–372

ganache:

chocolate-mint, 309

mocha, 283

mocha, for chocolate napoleons, 401–402

white chocolate, for petits fours, 269–270

Gand, Gale, *xxi,* 307, 391, 419, 462

chocolate napoleons, 400–402

Hungarian shortbread, 327–328

inside-out upside-down tirami sù, 398–399

not-your-usual lemon meringue pie, 403–405

phylloccine ice cream sandwiches, *336,* 405–406

scallop and pesto purses, *362,* 435

summer vegetable tart, 436–437

génoise:

batter, "ribbon" stage of, 21, *39*

in chocolate ruffle cake, *225,* 263–268

clarified butter in, 8, 40

in French strawbery cake, 273–274

in glazed mini-rounds, *227,* 271–272

ladyfinger, 41

madeleines from, 41–42, 333–334

in miniature Florentine squares, *227,* 268–270

perfect, 39–40

petits fours from, 39

sheet, 42

as sponge cake, 23

whys and hows of, 40

gingerbread:

baby cake, *217,* 247–248

cake, large, 248

ginger cream, for chocolate napoleons, 402

gingersnaps, 324–325

glaze:

apricot, 300

cocoa, for raspberry swirls, 276

white chocolate, for petits fours, 269–270

see also fillings and frostings